THE UNITED METHODIST MUSIC AND WORSHIP PLANNER

2013–2014

David L. Bone
and
Mary J. Scifres

Abingdon Press
Nashville

THE UNITED METHODIST MUSIC AND WORSHIP PLANNER 2013–2014

Copyright © 2013 by David L. Bone and Mary J. Scifres

All rights reserved.
Worksheets in this book may be reproduced by local congregations, provided the following credit line and copyright notice appear on all copies: "From *The United Methodist Music and Worship Planner.* Copyright © 2013 by Abingdon Press. Used by permission." No other part of this work may be reproduced or transmitted in any form or by any means, electronic or mechanical, including photocopying and recording, or by any information storage or retrieval system, except as may be expressly permitted by the 1976 Copyright Act or in writing from the publisher. Requests for permission should be addressed to Abingdon Press, P.O. Box 801, 201 Eighth Avenue South, Nashville, TN 37202-0801 or e-mailed to permissions@abingdonpress.com.

This book is printed on acid-free, recycled paper.

ISBN 978-1-4267-5824-9

All scripture quotations are from the New Revised Standard Version of the Bible,
copyright 1989, Division of Christian Education of the National Council of the Churches of Christ in the United States of America. Used by permission. All rights reserved.

13 14 15 16 17 18 19 20 21 22—10 9 8 7 6 5 4 3 2 1

MANUFACTURED IN THE UNITED STATES OF AMERICA

Do you have the book you need?

We want you to have the best planner, designed to meet your specific needs. How do you know if you have the right resource? Simply complete this one-question quiz:

Do you lead worship in a United Methodist congregation?

Yes.

Use *The United Methodist Music and Worship Planner, 2013–2014*
(ISBN: 9781426758249)

No.

Use *Prepare! An Ecumenical Music and Worship Planner, 2013–2014*
(ISBN: 9781426758188)

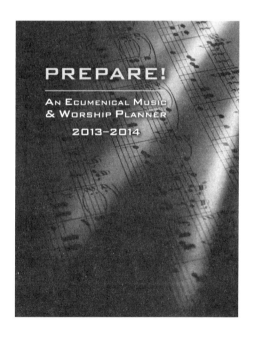

To order these resources, call Cokesbury Music Service toll-free at 1-877-877-8674, or shop online at www.cokesbury.com. Do you find yourself rushing at the last minute to order your new planner? Subscribe today and receive your new *United Methodist Music and Worship Planner* or *Prepare!* automatically next year and every year. Call toll-free 1-800-672-1789 to request subscription.

USING THIS PLANNER

How We Organize the Resource Lists

This *United Methodist Music and Worship Planner (UM Planner)* is designed to give you as many ideas as possible about a given worship service. Use it alongside a worship plan notebook that you create, and copies of *The United Methodist Hymnal, The United Methodist Book of Worship, The Faith We Sing,* and *Worship & Song.* Features of the *UM Planner* include:

- Each week **Primary Hymns and Songs for the Day** are suggested first. These suggestions include various helps for singing the hymns. These hymns and songs have the closest relationship to the scriptures and are widely known. The lengthier lists of **Additional Hymn Suggestions** and **Additional Contemporary Suggestions** will add variety to your musical selections.
- The musical suggestions are chosen to suggest a wide variety of styles, using *The United Methodist Hymnal, The Faith We Sing,* and *Worship & Song* to their fullest.
- Each item is referenced to scripture or occasion.
- **Opening (O) and Closing (C) hymns** are suggested for each worship service.
- At least one **Communion hymn** is recommended for the first Sunday of each month and liturgical season. When appropriate, communion hymns related to the scriptures are noted on other days as well.
- The *UM Planner* also includes **Contemporary Suggestions** for use in contemporary, blended, or informal worship services. Under **Contemporary Suggestions**, you will find not only praise choruses but also global and ethnic music, folk music, and meditative music from traditions such as Taizé. Several resources are referenced in this section. Information about these resources can be found on page 7.
- **Vocal Solos** and **Anthems** provide ideas for vocal music "performance" offerings, but may also inspire ideas for additional congregational selections.
- The **Vocal Solos** are taken from a group of eleven collections that range from contemporary settings of hymn texts and praise choruses to spirituals to well-known classics (see p. 7). Augment these suggestions from your own library.
- The **Anthem Suggestions** include new works as well as generally known works that are already in many church choral libraries. Your study of the Scripture and hymn texts will lead you to anthems in your church library that are appropriate.

- **ONE WORD OF ADVICE:** Be sure to consult all the music suggestions regardless of the type of service you are planning. Many songs that are used in contemporary services are listed under the **Hymn Suggestions** and many songs for traditional services can be found under **Contemporary Suggestions**. Don't let the designation here deter you from using any item that will enhance your worship service. Planners should consult both lists when choosing congregational music.
- Suggestions for **"Visuals"** are offered for each service. See the article "Visuals in Worship" (page 4) for discussion on these suggestions. Visual ideas are found in the **Other Suggestions** lists. They have been compiled by Ashley M. Calhoun of Knoxville, Tennessee, and supplemented by our authors. Ashley is known for his inventive use of "found" items in creating visual worship settings. Worship committees, visual artists, dancers, and altar guilds can use these ideas to create their own unique worship centers, altar pieces, banners, and dance images. Screen visual artists can use these themes to select appropriate background and theme screens for worship.
- **Other Suggestions** also includes words for worship, primarily from *The United Methodist Book of Worship* and *Worship and Song* (Worship Resources edition); suggestions for choral introits ("Call to Worship") and sung benedictions; and ideas for musical responses related to the spoken liturgy.
- In response to your requests, we have added a two-year, at-a-glance **2013–2014 Calendar** following the **Worship Planning Sheets** (see page 143). It includes a note on the lectionary years covered in this edition of *The UM Music and Worship Planner.* We hope you find this new feature helpful, and we look forward to your feedback on its addition.

Planning Worship with These Resources

When planning any worship service, it is always best to start with the scripture and let it guide your thoughts and plans. If your church is not using the Revised Common Lectionary, but you do know what the scripture text will be for a service, look up that text in the **Scriptural Index** on page 136.

NEW THIS YEAR! While the lectionary verses found on facing pages of this year's *Planner* are from the New Revised Standard Version of the Bible, lectionary verses from the brand new Common English Bible (CEB) are available online at http://www.commonenglishbible.com/ceb/planner, accessible using the password acBwCW9K.

As you read and study the scripture passages, read all of the suggested hymn texts. The hymns may remind you of anthems, solos, or keyboard selections. It is wise to mark your hymnal with the dates individual hymns are sung to avoid singing some too frequently. The **Hymn Resources** (see p. 7) can enhance congregational singing, but should be used sparingly.

Use a three-ring binder to organize your plans. For each service of worship, include a copy of one of the **Worship Planning Sheets** found on pages 140–42 (or design your own!) along with blank paper for listing further ideas. Do not simply "fill in the blanks" for each service, but use the Planning Sheet to guide your work.

Use the suggestions in the *UM Planner* along with your own page of ideas to begin making decisions about worship. Will the choir sing a "Call to Worship"? Can a hymn verse serve as a prayer response? Can a particular anthem or vocal solo give direction to the sermon? What prayers will be used?

Once your decisions are made, complete the **Worship Planning Sheet**. Make a separate list of tasks related to that service. Planning worship is an awesome responsibility, but one that can be accomplished with an organized effort along with spiritual guidance.

VISUALS IN WORSHIP
Ashley M. Calhoun

The suggestions for visuals in this planner are meant to help worship leaders use objects and images to increase the impact of the gospel on a people who are increasingly visually oriented. These suggestions can be incorporated into many visual elements: hanging and processional banners, worship settings (whether on the altar or in the chancel or narthex), worship folder covers, and bulletin boards. The ideas can also be used to suggest ways to use classical and contemporary works of art, sculpture, needlework, and photography in worship services.

With more churches incorporating screens and video walls into their worship spaces, there is tremendous potential for the use of still or moving imagery. Also, interpretive movement and drama can be very strong in visual impact. The visual suggestions in the planner have several characteristics:

- The suggestions are meant not to give detailed plans, but to spark your imagination and creativity.
- Some are drawn literally from the lessons; others are thematic.
- The suggestions are organized by reference to the lectionary passages:

O	Old Testament or Acts reading
P	Psalm reading or Canticle
E	Epistle or New Testament reading
G	Gospel reading

- Chapter and verse numbers are sometimes given to indicate actual phrases in the scripture passage that can serve as visual elements.
- Themes such as "forgiveness," "love," or "rejoicing" are offered to encourage creative use of video and photographic images of people engaged in demonstrating those themes.

So much about worship is visual and intended to strengthen the proclamation of the gospel. The worship space is filled with visual elements that send a message. The church year is a treasure trove of color, texture, symbolism, and visual imagery. Special Sundays and special days in the cultural and denominational calendars also offer opportunities for visual expression. Evaluate the visual aspects of your worship services and find ways to enhance the worship experience with thoughtful, intentional use of visual elements and images.

THE LECTIONARY AS LIBERATOR
A Practical Basis for Utilizing
the "Revised Common Lectionary" in Worship Planning

Mary J. Scifres

The question arises for worship leaders and ordained ministers, "How does one prepare worship services that allow the flexibility necessary for the work of the Holy Spirit while also ordering the life of prayer and meditation to encourage disciplined growth?" The Revised Common Lectionary can be one of the liberating and organizing aspects of worship. Although my writing partner David Bone and I recognize that there are objections to lectionary use, we see the lectionary as a helpful tool on which to base inspired worship planning to encourage growth in the life of the church.

Attempting to coordinate the message of the musical selections, the visual images, and the words of worship with the message of the pulpit is a time-consuming and important task for church staff and worship leaders. Church musicians, artists, laypersons, worship coordinators, and pastors give many hours each week to plan worship services that proclaim the Word, strengthen and challenge the community, and deepen the participants' faith. Ordained and diaconal ministers face the challenge of writing and choosing texts, prayers, and sermons for worship each week; musicians select, plan, and rehearse a variety of vocal and instrumental music to enhance and facilitate the worship experience of the churches they serve; and church artists and lay worship leaders pursue means of leading worship, preparing the sanctuary for worship, designing additional creative elements, and devising other aspects of the worshiping experience.

The preacher can ease this task significantly by utilizing the Revised Common Lectionary and communicating on a regular basis with other church worship leaders regarding worship service needs. A church can find both freedom and unity when the pastoral leadership uses the lectionary as the basis for planning worship and its individual aspects (sermon, hymns, anthems, prayers) without exalting it to a level of sole importance. First, lectionary use prevents the abusive appeal to a limited number of scriptures and topics, toward which some preachers are tempted. Regarding the concern for local needs, the lectionary need not be used to ignore specific spiritual, emotional, or physical needs of a congregation. Rather, the lectionary can provide a means for integrating such needs into the worship service by relating scriptural messages to the current needs and situation of the community. While interpreting the lections for worship, both planners and preachers can find ways of exploring the historical meanings of the texts and bringing such historical understandings into the present.

Second, the pedagogical advantage of using the lectionary to acquaint Christians with the broad tradition of which we are a part can deepen worship and learning experiences of the community of faith. As pastors in the twenty-first century face growing concern regarding the types of burn out that result from remaining static in a setting that has become routine instead of a challenge, following the lectionary cycle can open up opportunities for growth and support in a number of ways. Being forced to grapple with difficult texts in addition to familiar passages enlivens the mind and encourages the preacher to look to new exegetical resources and homiletic aids. Support can also come from an ecumenical community of pastors in one's city or county who are studying the same text during the cycle. Study groups within the local church can wrestle with the lectionary scriptures, growing their biblical and theological knowledge in the process.

Likewise, church musicians who wade through piles of contemporary and classical music every season to choose the anthems, organ selections, hymns, responsive psalms, and other musical contributions to the worship service can find a common guide to that selection when the lectionary is used. In the local church, the musician finds the opportunity to be a minister of music and Word when the lections provide the core of the worship service. In a time when the shortage of church musicians affects many churches, a church musician may be able to serve several churches and utilize the same musical selections in each setting. If a church musician, called to full-time ministry of music, can be employed by two or three local congregations who agree to use the same anthems and hymns each week and to schedule worship services at different times, both musician and congregation can benefit from this new approach to music ministry, which supports full-time service and receives music of high quality. The possibilities for providing equitable salaries for ministers of music as well as nurturing several local church communities through spirit-filled, well-performed music are enhanced when the unifying elements of ecumenical cooperation and common lections are available.

In terms of teaching, the lectionary can provide a helpful method of coordinating church school, weekly Bible study groups, prayer and devotional groups, music rehearsals, singing and praise gatherings, and other small groups in the life of the church with the community worship experience of Sunday morning. Small groups, which sometimes seem to go off in their own direction, away from the Sunday morning community, would more easily feel a part of the fold with the integrative element of the lectionary. And the educational system of the church, which so often leaves teachers and students feeling excluded and separated from the worshiping body, can find inclusion in the integrative element of the lectionary. How much more easily a child would sit through a sermon and find meaning in mysterious hymns when the basic scriptural text has been heard and discussed in church school prior to worship or explored in church school after worship!

Overall, lectionary use can benefit the entire life of the church, when used in its various dimensions through curriculum, worship resources, music selections, and local cooperative church events. Where proclamation of the Word is central, that Word can and should be the integrative element of a holistic worship service. In churches that seek to reach people with a message that is unified

thematically, lectionary use provides a scriptural base that all planners know well in advance and can utilize when choosing and developing the themes or topics for the Sundays of any given season. When the lectionary is used in this way, choirs or music teams have adequate time to rehearse appropriate music, liturgists or worship facilitators have sufficient time to write or find liturgy and prayers for the service, and other church artists (actors, dancers, composers, visual artists, banner makers, arts guilds, and screen programmers) may plan and prepare their contributions to the service and the season.

With this book, we invite your congregation and its worship leaders to begin the process of integrating various aspects of worship planning by means of the Revised Common Lectionary. As thematic ideas begin to emerge in each week's worship service and as the various scriptures provide diverse bases for worship planning, we hope that you will find worship becoming an increasingly growth-filled and exciting aspect of your congregation's life.

RESOURCE KEY

UM	Young, Carlton R., ed. *The United Methodist Hymnal.* Nashville. The United Methodist Publishing House, 1989. ISBN #9780687431328.
2000 or S2000	Hickman, Hoyt L., ed. *The Faith We Sing.* Nashville: Abingdon Press, 2000. Cokesbury Order #090547 (Pew Edition). NOTE: All hymn numbers 2000 to 2284 are from this hymnal.
3000 or WS3000	Smith, Gary Alan, ed. *Worship & Song.* Nashville: Abingdon Press, 2011. Accompaniment, singer, guitar, and planning editions available. ISBN #9781426709937 (Pew Edition). NOTE: All hymn numbers 3000 and higher are from this hymnal.
WSL	Smith, Gary Alan, ed. *Worship & Song Worship Leader Edition.* Nashville: Abingdon Press, 2011. ISBN #9781426709944. *These resources WSL1– WSL222 refer to the written words for worship (prayers, litanies, benedictions) available in worship resource editions of* Worship and Song.
BOW	Langford, Andy, ed. *The United Methodist Book of Worship.* Nashville: Abingdon Press, 1992. Leader and accompaniment editions available. ISBN #978068735724.

HYMN RESOURCES

S-1	Smith, Gary Alan, ed. *The United Methodist Hymnal: Music Supplement.* Nashville: Abingdon Press, 1991. Cokesbury Order #431476.
S-2	Bennett, Robert C., ed. *The United Methodist Hymnal: Music Supplement II.* Nashville: Abingdon Press, 1993. Cokesbury Order #430135.
H-3	Hopson, Hal H. *The Creative Church Musician Series.* Carol Stream, IL: Hope Publishing Co. **Hbl** Vol. 1 *The Creative Use of Handbells in Worship.* 1997. Cokesbury Order #921992. **Chr** Vol. 2 *The Creative Use of Choirs in Worship.* 1999. Cokesbury Order #732807. **Desc** Vol. 3 *The Creative Use of Descants in Worship.* 1999. Cokesbury Order #732864. **Org** Vol. 4 *The Creative Use of the Organ in Worship.* 1997. Cokesbury Order #323904.

VOCAL SUGGESTION RESOURCES

V-1	Kimbrough, Steven, ed. *Sweet Singer.* Chapel Hill, NC: Hinshaw Music, 1987. Catalogue #CV-1. Cokesbury Order #811712.
V-2	Handel, George Frederick. *Messiah.* Various editions available.
V-3	Hayes, Mark. *7 Praise and Worship Songs for Solo Voice.* Alfred Music Publishing, 2010. Catalogue #23656. Cokesbury Order #525648.
V-4	Scott, K. Lee. *Sing a Song of Joy.* Minneapolis, MN: Augsburg Fortress, 1989. Catalogue #0800647882 (*Medium High Voice.* ISBN #9780800647889 or 0800652827; *Medium Low Voice.* ISBN #9780800652821).
V-5	Various Editors. *With All My Heart: Contemporary Vocal Solos.* Augsburg Fortress, 2004. *Volume 1: Autumn and Winter* (ISBN #9780800676841). *Volume 2: Spring and Summer* (ISBN #9780800676858).

	Volume 3: Baptisms, Weddings, and Funerals (ISBN #9780800679460).
V-6	Walters, Richard, arr. *Hymn Classics: Concert Arrangements of Traditional Hymns for Voice and Piano.* Hal Leonard Publishing, 1993. (*High Voice.* ISBN #9780793560080; *Low Voice.* ISBN #9780793560073).
V-7	Johnson, Hall, arr. *Thirty (30) Spirituals.* G. Schirmer, Inc., 1949. Catalogue #HL50328310.
V-8	Wilson, John F., Don Doig, and Jack Schrader, eds. *Everything for the Church Soloist.* Carol Stream, IL: Hope Publishing Company, 1980. Catalogue #804; Cokesbury Order #810103.
V-9	Scott, K. Lee. *Rejoice Now My Spirit: Vocal Solos for the Church Year.* Augsburg Fortress, 1992. ISBN #9780800651084.
V-10	Hayes, Mark et al. *From the Manger to the Cross, Seasonal Solos for Medium Voice.* Dayton, OH: The Lorenz Corporation, 2006. Catalogue #30/2157L; Cokesbury Order #526369.
V-11	Pote, Allen. *A Song of Joy.* Carol Stream, IL: Hope Publishing, 2003. Catalogue #8135; Cokesbury Order #515068.

CONTEMPORARY RESOURCES

SP	Various. *Songs for Praise and Worship: Singalong Edition.* Waco, TX: Word Music, 1992. Catalogue #080689-006395; ISBN #9783010203494.
M1-M55	Barker, Ken, ed. *More Songs for Praise and Worship: Choir/Worship Team Edition.* Waco, TX: Word Music, 2000. Cokesbury Order #509802 (Keyboard Edition: Catalogue #0-80689-39087-6; Cokesbury Order #509776. Piano/Guitar/Vocal Edition: Catalogue #0-80689-31018-8; Cokesbury Order #509764).
M56-M115	Barker, Ken, ed. *More Songs for Praise and Worship 2: Choir/Worship Team Edition.* Waco, TX: Word Music, 2002. Catalogue #0-80689-35117-4; Cokesbury Order #512053 (Keyboard Edition: Catalogue #0-80689-41187-8; Cokesbury Order #512075. Piano/Guitar/Vocal Edition: #0-80689-31418-6; Cokesbury Order #080689314186).
M116-M168	Barker, Ken, ed. *More Songs for Praise and Worship 3: Choir/Worship Team Edition.* Waco, TX: Word Music, 2005. Catalogue #0-80689-36917-5; Cokesbury Order #523357 (Keyboard Edition: Catalogue #0-80689-45187-4; Cokesbury Order # 523418. Piano/Guitar/Vocal Edition: #0-80689-31818-4; Cokesbury Order #523369).
M169-M219	Barker, Ken, ed. *More Songs for Praise and Worship 4: Choir/Worship Team Edition.* Waco, TX: Word Music, 2006. Catalogue #0-80689-41217-2; Cokesbury Order # 529198 (Keyboard Edition: Catalogue #0-80689-47287-9; Cokesbury Order #529244. Piano/Guitar/Vocal Edition: #0-80689-32018-7; ISBN #9785557996822).
M220-M279	McClure, Mark and Sarah G. Huffman, eds. *More Songs for Praise and Worship 5.* Waco, TX: Word Music, 2011. (Piano/Guitar/Vocal Edition #0-80689-32118-4. Choir/Worship Team Edition #0-80689-44417-3. Keyboard/SATB Edition Catalogue #0-80689-50087-9.)

See also Vocal Solo suggestions from V-3.

SEPTEMBER 1, 2013

Jeremiah 2:4-13

⁴Hear the word of the LORD, O house of Jacob, and all the families of the house of Israel. ⁵Thus says the LORD:

What wrong did your ancestors find in me
  that they went far from me,
and went after worthless things, and became worthless
  themselves?
⁶ They did not say, "Where is the LORD
  who brought us up from the land of Egypt,
who led us in the wilderness,
  in a land of deserts and pits,
in a land of drought and deep darkness,
  in a land that no one passes through,
  where no one lives?"
⁷ I brought you into a plentiful land
  to eat its fruits and its good things.
But when you entered you defiled my land,
  and made my heritage an abomination.
⁸ The priests did not say, "Where is the LORD?"
  Those who handle the law did not know me;
the rulers transgressed against me;
  the prophets prophesied by Baal,
  and went after things that do not profit.
⁹ Therefore once more I accuse you,
                              says the LORD,
  and I accuse your children's children.
¹⁰ Cross to the coasts of Cyprus and look,
  send to Kedar and examine with care;
  see if there has ever been such a thing.
¹¹ Has a nation changed its gods,
  even though they are no gods?
But my people have changed their glory
  for something that does not profit.
¹² Be appalled, O heavens, at this,
  be shocked, be utterly desolate,
                              says the LORD,
¹³ for my people have committed two evils:
  they have forsaken me,
  the fountain of living water,
  and dug out cisterns for themselves,
cracked cisterns
  that can hold no water.

Psalm 81:1, 10-16

¹ Sing aloud to God our strength;
  shout for joy to the God of Jacob.
. . . .
¹⁰ I am the LORD your God,
  who brought you up out of the land of Egypt.
  Open your mouth wide and I will fill it.
¹¹ "But my people did not listen to my voice;
  Israel would not submit to me.
¹² So I gave them over to their stubborn hearts,
  to follow their own counsels.
¹³ O that my people would listen to me,
  that Israel would walk in my ways!
¹⁴ Then I would quickly subdue their enemies,
  and turn my hand against their foes.
¹⁵ Those who hate the LORD would cringe before him,
  and their doom would last forever.

¹⁶ I would feed you with the finest of the wheat,
  and with honey from the rock I would satisfy you."

Hebrews 13:1-8, 15-16

¹Let mutual love continue. ²Do not neglect to show hospitality to strangers, for by doing that some have entertained angels without knowing it. ³Remember those who are in prison, as though you were in prison with them; those who are being tortured, as though you yourselves were being tortured. ⁴Let marriage be held in honor by all, and let the marriage bed be kept undefiled; for God will judge fornicators and adulterers. ⁵Keep your lives free from the love of money, and be content with what you have; for he has said, "I will never leave you or forsake you." ⁶So we can say with confidence,

"The Lord is my helper;
  I will not be afraid.
What can anyone do to me?"

⁷Remember your leaders, those who spoke the word of God to you; consider the outcome of their way of life, and imitate their faith. ⁸Jesus Christ is the same yesterday and today and forever. . . . ¹⁵Through him, then, let us continually offer a sacrifice of praise to God, that is, the fruit of lips that confess his name. ¹⁶Do not neglect to do good and to share what you have, for such sacrifices are pleasing to God.

Luke 14:1, 7-14

¹On one occasion when Jesus was going to the house of a leader of the Pharisees to eat a meal on the sabbath, they were watching him closely. . . . ⁷When he noticed how the guests chose the places of honor, he told them a parable. ⁸"When you are invited by someone to a wedding banquet, do not sit down at the place of honor, in case someone more distinguished than you has been invited by your host; ⁹and the host who invited both of you may come and say to you, 'Give this person your place,' and then in disgrace you would start to take the lowest place. ¹⁰But when you are invited, go and sit down at the lowest place, so that when your host comes, he may say to you, 'Friend, move up higher'; then you will be honored in the presence of all who sit at the table with you. ¹¹For all who exalt themselves will be humbled, and those who humble themselves will be exalted." ¹²He said also to the one who had invited him, "When you give a luncheon or a dinner, do not invite your friends or your brothers or your relatives or rich neighbors, in case they may invite you in return, and you would be repaid. ¹³But when you give a banquet, invite the poor, the crippled, the lame, and the blind. ¹⁴And you will be blessed, because they cannot repay you, for you will be repaid at the resurrection of the righteous."

COLOR: GREEN **15th SUNDAY AFTER PENTECOST**

Primary Hymns and Songs for the Day
2236 "Gather Us In" (Luke, Communion) (O)
2031 "We Bring the Sacrifice of Praise" (Heb.) (O)
   SP1
432 "Jesu, Jesu" (Heb., Luke)
   H-3 Chr-114; Org-19
   S-1 #63. Vocal part
616 "Come, Sinners, to the Gospel Feast" (Luke,
   Communion)
   S-1 #164-166. Various treatments
629 "You Satisfy the Hungry Heart" (Ps., Communion)
   S-1 #144. Four-part setting of refrain
557 "Blest Be the Tie That Binds" (Heb.) (C)
   H-3 Hbl-49; Chr-14; Desc-27; Org-25

Additional Hymn Suggestions
151 "God Created Heaven and Earth" (Jer.)
439 "We Utter Our Cry" (Jer.)
649 "How Shall They Hear the Word of God" (Jer.)
443 "O God Who Shaped Creation" (Jer., Ps.)
450 "Creator of the Earth and Skies" (Jer., Ps.)
2048 "God Weeps" (Jer., Ps.)
2172 "We Are Called" (Jer., Ps.)
2279 " The Trees of the Field " (Ps.)
96 "Praise the Lord Who Reigns Above" (Ps.)
57 "O For a Thousand Tongues to Sing" (Ps., Luke)
   (O)
523 "Saranam, Saranam" (Heb.)
529 "How Firm a Foundation" (Heb.) (O)
579 "Lord God, Your Love Has Called Us Here" (Heb.,
   Luke)
2009 "O God Beyond All Praising" (Heb.)
2094 "Carol of the Epiphany" (Heb.)
2130 "The Summons" (Heb.)
2178 "Here Am I" (Heb.)
2181 "We Need a Faith" (Heb.)
3033 "God of Great and God of Small" (Heb.)
3147 "Built on a Rock" (Heb.)
3152 "Welcome" (Heb.)
2175 "Together We Serve" (Heb., Luke)
2254 "In Remembrance of Me" (Heb., Luke,
   Communion)
2268 "As We Gather at Your Table" (Heb., Luke,
   Communion)
2269 "Come, Share the Lord" (Heb., Communion)
166 "All Praise to Thee, for Thou, O King Divine"
   (Luke)
194 "Morning Glory, Starlit Sky" (Luke)
339 "Come, Sinners, to the Gospel Feast" (Luke)
340 "Come, Ye Sinners, Poor and Needy" (Luke)
568 "Christ for the World We Sing" (Luke)
2155 "Blest Are They" (Luke)
2197 "Lord of All Hopefulness" (Luke)
2263 "Broken for Me" (Luke, Communion)
2265 "Time Now to Gather" (Luke, Communion)
581 "Lord, Whose Love Through Humble Service"
   (Luke) (C)

Contemporary Song Suggestions
S2132 "You Who Are Thirsty" (Jer., Ps.)
   SP219
S2006 "Lord God Almighty" (Ps.)

S2074 "Shout to the Lord" (Ps.)
   M16
S2144 "Someone Asked the Question" (Ps.)
WS3108 "Trading My Sorrows" (Ps.)
   M75
M123 "Made Me Glad" (Ps.)
WS3001 "O For a Thousand Tongues to Sing (Ps., Luke)
S2179 "Live in Charity" ("Ubi Caritas") (Heb.)
WS3117 "Rule of Life" (Heb.)
WS3151 "The Jesus in Me" (Heb.)
M24 "Jesus, We Crown You with Praise" (Heb.)
M79 "I Stand Amazed" (Heb.)
M211 "I Will Not Forget You" (Heb.)
S2176 "Make Me a Servant" (Heb., Luke)
   SP193
S2131 "Humble Thyself in the Sight of the Lord" (Heb.,
   Luke)
   SP223
S2222 "The Servant Song" (Luke)
   SP193

Vocal Solos
"Praise the Lord, He Never Changes" (Heb.)
   V-8   p. 62
"The Heart of Worship" (Heb.)
   M71
"Author of Life Divine" (Luke, Communion)
   V-1   p. 39

Anthems
"Song of Gentleness" (Heb., Luke)
Douglas Wagner; Beckenhorst Press BP1192
Unison with keyboard or handbells

"O Bread of Life from Heaven" (Luke)
David Ashley White; Augsburg 0800650913
Two-part mixed, organ

Other Suggestions
Visuals:
   O   Exodus, abundance, fountain, broken cistern
   P   Singing, Exodus, hard hearts, wheat, honey/rock
   E   Welcome, prison ministry, marriage certificate,
       money, Heb. 13:6 or 8, Jesus
   G   Meal, marriage feast, table, poor, maimed, lame,
       blind
Litany: WSL49 (Ps., Luke)
Opening Prayer: BOW465 or WSL54 (Heb.)
Canticle: UM646. "Canticle of Love" (Heb.)
Prayers of Confession: UM893 (Jer., Ps., Heb.)
Prayer of Confession: BOW489 (Heb., Luke)
Prayer: WSL205. Loving God, we spend so much time (Luke)
Prayer: BOW511. For God's Reign (Luke)
Prayers: WSL90, WSL191, BOW443, BOW465, UM409
   (Labor Day)
Blessing: WSL169. As you have been fed (Luke,
   Communion)

SEPTEMBER 8, 2013

Jeremiah 18:1-11

[1]The word that came to Jeremiah from the LORD: [2]"Come, go down to the potter's house, and there I will let you hear my words." [3]So I went down to the potter's house, and there he was working at his wheel. [4]The vessel he was making of clay was spoiled in the potter's hand, and he reworked it into another vessel, as seemed good to him.

[5]Then the word of the LORD came to me: [6]Can I not do with you, O house of Israel, just as this potter has done? says the LORD. Just like the clay in the potter's hand, so are you in my hand, O house of Israel. [7]At one moment I may declare concerning a nation or a kingdom, that I will pluck up and break down and destroy it, [8]but if that nation, concerning which I have spoken, turns from its evil, I will change my mind about the disaster that I intended to bring on it. [9]And at another moment I may declare concerning a nation or a kingdom that I will build and plant it, [10]but if it does evil in my sight, not listening to my voice, then I will change my mind about the good that I had intended to do to it. [11]Now, therefore, say to the people of Judah and the inhabitants of Jerusalem: Thus says the LORD: Look, I am a potter shaping evil against you and devising a plan against you. Turn now, all of you from your evil way, and amend your ways and your doings.

Psalm 139:1-6, 13-18

[1] O LORD, you have searched me and known me.
[2] You know when I sit down and when I rise up;
        you discern my thoughts from far away.
[3] You search out my path and my lying down,
        and are acquainted with all my ways.
[4] Even before a word is on my tongue,
        O LORD, you know it completely.
[5] You hem me in, behind and before,
        and lay your hand upon me.
[6] Such knowledge is too wonderful for me;
        it is so high that I cannot attain it.
. . . .
[13] For it was you who formed my inward parts;
        you knit me together in my mother's womb.
[14] I praise you, for I am fearfully and wonderfully made.
        Wonderful are your works;
        that I know very well.
        [15]My frame was not hidden from you,
        when I was being made in secret,
        intricately woven in the depths of the earth.
[16] Your eyes beheld my unformed substance.
        In your book were written
        all the days that were formed for me,
        when none of them as yet existed.
[17] How weighty to me are your thoughts, O God!
        How vast is the sum of them!
[18] I try to count them—they are more than the sand;
        I come to the end—I am still with you.

Philemon 1-21

[1]Paul, a prisoner of Christ Jesus, and Timothy our brother, To Philemon our dear friend and co-worker, [2]to Apphia our sister, to Archippus our fellow soldier, and to the church in your house: [3]Grace to you and peace from God our Father and the Lord Jesus Christ.

[4]When I remember you in my prayers, I always thank my God [5]because I hear of your love for all the saints and your faith toward the Lord Jesus. [6]I pray that the sharing of your faith may become effective when you perceive all the good that we may do for Christ. [7]I have indeed received much joy and encouragement from your love, because the hearts of the saints have been refreshed through you, my brother.

[8]For this reason, though I am bold enough in Christ to command you to do your duty, [9]yet I would rather appeal to you on the basis of love— and I, Paul, do this as an old man, and now also as a prisoner of Christ Jesus. [10]I am appealing to you for my child, Onesimus, whose father I have become during my imprisonment. [11]Formerly he was useless to you, but now he is indeed useful both to you and to me. [12]I am sending him, that is, my own heart, back to you. [13]I wanted to keep him with me, so that he might be of service to me in your place during my imprisonment for the gospel; [14]but I preferred to do nothing without your consent, in order that your good deed might be voluntary and not something forced. [15]Perhaps this is the reason he was separated from you for a while, so that you might have him back forever, [16]no longer as a slave but more than a slave, a beloved brother— especially to me but how much more to you, both in the flesh and in the Lord.

[17]So if you consider me your partner, welcome him as you would welcome me. [18]If he has wronged you in any way, or owes you anything, charge that to my account. [19]I, Paul, am writing this with my own hand: I will repay it. I say nothing about your owing me even your own self. [20]Yes, brother, let me have this benefit from you in the Lord! Refresh my heart in Christ. [21]Confident of your obedience, I am writing to you, knowing that you will do even more than I say.

Luke 14:25-33

[25]Now large crowds were traveling with him; and he turned and said to them, [26]"Whoever comes to me and does not hate father and mother, wife and children, brothers and sisters, yes, and even life itself, cannot be my disciple. [27]Whoever does not carry the cross and follow me cannot be my disciple. [28]For which of you, intending to build a tower, does not first sit down and estimate the cost, to see whether he has enough to complete it? [29]Otherwise, when he has laid a foundation and is not able to finish, all who see it will begin to ridicule him, [30]saying, 'This fellow began to build and was not able to finish.' [31]Or what king, going out to wage war against another king, will not sit down first and consider whether he is able with ten thousand to oppose the one who comes against him with twenty thousand? [32]If he cannot, then, while the other is still far away, he sends a delegation and asks for the terms of peace. [33]So therefore, none of you can become my disciple if you do not give up all your possessions."

COLOR: GREEN   **16th SUNDAY AFTER PENTECOST**

Primary Hymns and Songs for the Day
553 "And Are We Yet Alive" (Luke) (O)
382 "Have Thine Own Way, Lord" (Jer.)
　　　S-2 #2. Instrumental descant
2152 "Change My Heart, O God" (Jer.)
　　　SP195
2051 "I Was There to Hear Your Borning Cry" (Ps.,
　　　Baptism)
3011 "All My Days" (Ps.)
2129 "I Have Decided to Follow Jesus" (Luke)
415 "Take Up Thy Cross" (Luke) (C)
　　　H-3 Chr-178, 180; Org-44
　　　S-1 #141-143 Various treatments

Additional Hymn Suggestions
393 "Spirit of the Living God" (Jer.)
719 "My Lord, What a Morning" (Jer.)
2237 "As a Fire Is Meant for Burning" (Jer.)
2060 "God the Sculptor of the Mountains" (Jer., Ps.)
2117 "Spirit of God" (Jer., Ps.)
60 "I'll Praise My Maker While I've Breath" (Ps.)
98 "How Great Thou Art" (Ps.)
103 "Immortal, Invisible, God Only Wise" (Ps.)
109 "Creating God, Your Fingers Trace" (Ps.)
139 "Praise to the Lord, the Almighty" (Ps.)
411 "Dear Lord, Lead Me Day by Day" (Ps.)
414 "Thou Hidden Love of God" (Ps.)
2123 "Loving Spirit" (Ps.)
2046 "Womb of Life" (Ps., Communion)
2050 "Mothering God, You Gave Me Birth" (Ps.)
2052 "The Lone, Wild Bird" (Ps.)
2214 "Lead Me, Guide Me" (Ps.)
3019 "Bidden, Unbidden" (Ps.)
548 "In Christ There Is No East or West" (Philem.)
560 "Help Us Accept Each Other" (Philem.)
2140 "Since Jesus Came Into My Heart" (Philem.)
2175 "Together We Serve" (Philem.)
2260 "Let Us Be Bread" (Philem., Luke, Communion)
338 "Where He Leads Me" (Luke)
424 "Must Jesus Bear the Cross Alone" (Luke)
453 "More Love to Thee, O Christ" (Luke)
　　　(see especially stanza 2)
585 "This Little Light of Mine" (Luke)
615 "For the Bread Which You Have Broken" (Luke)
2102 "Swiftly Pass the Clouds of Glory" (Luke)
2137 "Would I Have Answered When You Called" (Luke)
2149 "Living for Jesus" (Luke)

Additional Contemporary Suggestions
M112 "Jesus, Lover of My Soul" (Jer.)
M85 "The Potter's Hand" (Jer., Stewardship)
S2003 "Praise You" (Jer., Stewardship)
　　　M84
S2253 "Water, River, Spirit, Grace" (Jer., Baptism)
S2139 "Oh, I Know the Lord's Laid His Hands on Me"
　　　(Ps.)
WS3015 "How Great You Are" (Ps.)
M38 "In the Secret" ("I Want to Know You") (Ps.)
M109 "He Knows My Name" (Ps.)
M101 "These Hands" (Ps., Stewardship)
S2218 "You Are Mine" (Ps., Luke)
M87 "Let the Peace of God Reign" (Philem.)

S2165 "Cry of My Heart" (Luke)
　　　M39
M53 "Let It Be Said of Us" (Luke)
M122 "Every Move I Make" (Luke)
M150 "Everyday" (Luke)
WS3160 "We Will Follow" ("Somlandela") (Luke)

Vocal Solos
"Have Thine Own Way, Lord!" (Jer.)
　　　V-8　　　p. 191
"Here I Am" (Jer., Luke)
　　　V-9　　　p. 19
"Borning Cry" (Ps., Baptism)
　　　V-5(1)　　　p. 10
"Sing a Song of Joy" (Ps.)
　　　V-4　　　p. 2
"Christ Living Within You" (Luke)
　　　V-8　　　p. 177
"Lead Me to Calvary" (Luke)
　　　V-8　　　p. 226

Anthems
"Psalm 139" (Ps.)
Allen Pote; Choristers Guild CGA-610
SATB, keyboard

"Follow Jesus" (Luke)
Anne Organ; Augsburg 0800677420
Two-part, organ

Other Suggestions
Visuals:
　　O　Potter's wheel/clay, hands/clay, building, planting
　　P　Sitting/standing, open mouth, hand on shoulder
　　E　Letter, old man writing, manacles, heart
　　G　Carrying crosses, tower, calculator, document, dove
Greeting: BOW343 (Luke)
Sung Response: UM98 and WS3015. "How Great" (Ps.)
Create a choral medley or praise band song set, using the
　　traditional "How Great Thou Art" and the new "How
　　Great You Are."
Opening Prayer: BOW469 (Jer., Ps.) or BOW466 (Philem.)
Prayer of Confession: BOW479 (Jer.) or BOW492 (Philem.)
Prayer: BOW508 (Luke)
Prayer: BOW519 or 526 (Philem.)
Blessing: WSL158. Here in this sanctuary (Philem., Luke)
See also *The Abingdon Worship Annual 2013.*

SEPTEMBER 15, 2013

Jeremiah 4:11-12, 22-28

[11]At that time it will be said to this people and to Jerusalem: A hot wind comes from me out of the bare heights in the desert toward my poor people, not to winnow or cleanse—[12]a wind too strong for that. Now it is I who speak in judgment against them. . . .

[22] "For my people are foolish,
   they do not know me;
 they are stupid children,
   they have no understanding.
 They are skilled in doing evil,
   but do not know how to do good."

[23] I looked on the earth, and lo, it was waste and void;
   and to the heavens, and they had no light.

[24] I looked on the mountains, and lo, they were quaking,
   and all the hills moved to and fro.

[25] I looked, and lo, there was no one at all,
   and all the birds of the air had fled.

[26] I looked, and lo, the fruitful land was a desert,
   and all its cities were laid in ruins
 before the LORD, before his fierce anger.

[27] For thus says the LORD: The whole land shall be a
   desolation; yet I will not make a full end.

[28] Because of this the earth shall mourn,
   and the heavens above grow black;
 for I have spoken, I have purposed;
   I have not relented nor will I turn back.

Psalm 14:1-7

[1] Fools say in their hearts, "There is no God."
   They are corrupt, they do abominable deeds;
   there is no one who does good.

[2] The LORD looks down from heaven on humankind
   to see if there are any who are wise,
   who seek after God.

[3] They have all gone astray, they are all alike perverse;
   there is no one who does good,
   no, not one.

[4] Have they no knowledge, all the evildoers
   who eat up my people as they eat bread,
   and do not call upon the LORD?

[5] There they shall be in great terror,
   for God is with the company of the righteous.

[6] You would confound the plans of the poor,
   but the LORD is their refuge.

[7] O that deliverance for Israel would come from Zion!
   When the LORD restores the fortunes of his people,
   Jacob will rejoice; Israel will be glad.

1 Timothy 1:12-17

[12]I am grateful to Christ Jesus our Lord, who has strengthened me, because he judged me faithful and appointed me to his service, [13]even though I was formerly a blasphemer, a persecutor, and a man of violence. But I received mercy because I had acted ignorantly in unbelief, [14]and the grace of our Lord overflowed for me with the faith and love that are in Christ Jesus. [15]The saying is sure and worthy of full acceptance, that Christ Jesus came into the world to save sinners—of whom I am the foremost. [16]But for that very reason I received mercy, so that in me, as the foremost, Jesus Christ might display the utmost patience, making me an example to those who would come to believe in him for eternal life. [17]To the King of the ages, immortal, invisible, the only God, be honor and glory forever and ever. Amen.

Luke 15:1-10

[1]Now all the tax collectors and sinners were coming near to listen to him. [2]And the Pharisees and the scribes were grumbling and saying, "This fellow welcomes sinners and eats with them." [3]So he told them this parable: [4]"Which one of you, having a hundred sheep and losing one of them, does not leave the ninety-nine in the wilderness and go after the one that is lost until he finds it? [5]When he has found it, he lays it on his shoulders and rejoices. [6]And when he comes home, he calls together his friends and neighbors, saying to them, 'Rejoice with me, for I have found my sheep that was lost.' [7]Just so, I tell you, there will be more joy in heaven over one sinner who repents than over ninety-nine righteous persons who need no repentance.

[8]"Or what woman having ten silver coins, if she loses one of them, does not light a lamp, sweep the house, and search carefully until she finds it? [9]When she has found it, she calls together her friends and neighbors, saying, 'Rejoice with me, for I have found the coin that I had lost.' [10]Just so, I tell you, there is joy in the presence of the angels of God over one sinner who repents."

COLOR: GREEN   **17th SUNDAY AFTER PENTECOST**

Primary Hymns and Songs for the Day

339 "Come, Sinners, to the Gospel Feast" (Luke) (O)
         S-1 #164-166. Various treatments
719 "My Lord, What a Morning" (Jer., Ps., Luke)
378 "Amazing Grace" (1 Tim.)
         H-3 Hbl-14, 46; Chr-27; Desc-14; Org-4
         S-2 #5-7. Various treatments
2162 "Grace Alone" (1 Tim.)
         M100
103 "Immortal, Invisible, God Only Wise" (1 Tim.) (C)
         H-3 Hbl-15, 71; Chr-65; Desc-93; Org-135
         S-1 #300. Harmonization

Additional Hymn Suggestions

107 "La Palabra Del Señor Es Recta" ("Righteous and
        Just Is the Word of the Lord") (Jer.)
450 "Creator of the Earth and Skies" (Jer., Ps.)
704 "Steal Away to Jesus" (Jer., Ps., Luke)
730 "O Day of God, Draw Nigh" (Jer., Ps.)
2048 "God Weeps" (Jer., Ps.)
523 "Saranam, Saranam" ("Refuge") (Ps.)
700 "Abide With Me" (Ps.)
2053 "If It Had Not Been for the Lord" (Ps., 1 Tim.)
294 "Alas! And Did My Savior Bleed" (1 Tim.)
355 "Depth of Mercy" (1 Tim.)
3097 "Depth of Mercy" (1 Tim.)
365 "Grace Greater Than Our Sin" (1 Tim.)
371 "I Stand Amazed in the Presence" (1 Tim.)
3110 "By Grace We Have Been Saved" (1 Tim.)
2147 "There Are Some Things I May Not Know" (1 Tim.)
2211 "Faith Is Patience in the Night" (1 Tim.)
2255 "In the Singing" (1 Tim., Communion)
2030 "The First Song of Isaiah" (1 Tim., Luke)
400 "Come, Thou Fount of Every Blessing" (1 Tim.,
        Luke)
113 "Source and Sovereign, Rock and Cloud" (Luke)
115 "How Like a Gentle Spirit" (Luke)
187 "Rise, Shine, You People" (Luke)
341 "I Sought the Lord" (Luke)
381 "Savior, Like a Shepherd Lead Us" (Luke)
436 "The Voice of God Is Calling" (Luke)
443 "O God Who Shaped Creation" (Luke)
732 "Come, We That Love the Lord" (Luke)
733 "Marching to Zion" (Luke)
2047 "Bring Many Names" (Luke)
2151 "I'm So Glad Jesus Lifted Me" (Luke)
2197 "Lord of All Hopefulness" (Luke)
3101 "Love Lifted Me" (Luke)

Additional Contemporary Suggestions

SP185 "The Steadfast Love of the Lord" (Jer., Luke)
S2118 "Holy Spirit, Come to Us" (Ps.)
UM394 "Something Beautiful" (1 Tim.)
S2141 "There's a Song" (1 Tim.)
M44 "Most Holy Lord" (1 Tim.)
WS3026 "God Is Good All the Time" (1 Tim.)
         M45
WS3042 "Shout to the North" (1 Tim.)
         M99
WS3104 "Amazing Grace" ("My Chains Are Gone") (1 Tim.)
         M205
SP60 "To Him Who Sits on the Throne" (1 Tim.)

WS3187 "We Fall Down" (1 Tim.)
         M66
M74 "There Is Joy in the Lord" (1 Tim.)
S2258 "Sing Alleluia to the Lord" (1 Tim., Communion)
         SP93
S2266 "Here Is Bread, Here Is Wine" (1 Tim.,
        Communion)
S2056 "God Is So Good" (1 Tim., Luke)
M94 "That's Why We Praise Him" (Luke)
WS3040 "You Are My All in All" (Luke)
         SP220
WS3102 "You Are My King" ("Amazing Love") (Luke)
         M82
WS3023 "Forever" (Luke)
         M68
M106 "I Come to the Cross" (Luke)
M115 "When It's All Been Said and Done" (Luke)

Vocal Solos

"And Can It Be That I Should Gain" (1 Tim.)
         V-1   p. 29
"Amazing Grace" (1 Tim.)
         V-8   p. 56
"God, Our Ever Faithful Shepherd" (Luke)
         V-4   p. 15
"My Shepherd Will Supply My Need" (Luke)
         V-10   p. 4

Anthems

"A Debtor to Mercy Alone" (1 Tim.)
John Hudson; Beckenhorst BP1941
SATB, keyboard

"Rejoice, I Found the Lost" (Luke)
Wayne Wold; Augsburg 0800653548
Unison or two-part, keyboard

Other Suggestions

Visuals:
  O Desert, wind, mountains, earthquake, birds, ruins,
         mourning, darkness
  P Stray sheep, eating bread, 14:6, poor, joy
  E Christ, 1:15, Paul, glory, crown
  G One sheep, Jesus carrying lost sheep, ten coins,
         lamp, broom, woman rejoicing, one coin
Call to Worship: S2214. "Lead Me, Guide Me" (Luke)
Greeting: BOW454 (Luke)
Opening Prayer: BOW463 (1 Tim.) or BOW467 (Luke)
Prayer of Confession: BOW490 (Jer., Ps.)
Prayer: UM535. A Refuge amid Distraction (Ps.)
Affirmation of Faith: WSL76 or UM889 (1 Tim.)
Benediction: WSL159. Sisters and brothers (Luke)

EPTEMBER 22, 2013

Jeremiah 8:18–9:1

[18] My joy is gone, grief is upon me,
    my heart is sick.
[19] Hark, the cry of my poor people
    from far and wide in the land:
  "Is the LORD not in Zion?
    Is her King not in her?"
    ("Why have they provoked me to anger with their images,
    with their foreign idols?")
[20] "The harvest is past, the summer is ended,
    and we are not saved."
[21] For the hurt of my poor people I am hurt,
    I mourn, and dismay has taken hold of me.
[22] Is there no balm in Gilead?
    Is there no physician there?
  Why then has the health of my poor people
    not been restored?
9 [1] O that my head were a spring of water,
    and my eyes a fountain of tears,
  so that I might weep day and night
    for the slain of my poor people!

Psalm 79:1-9

[1] O God, the nations have come into your inheritance;
    they have defiled your holy temple;
    they have laid Jerusalem in ruins.
[2] They have given the bodies of your servants
    to the birds of the air for food,
    the flesh of your faithful to the wild animals of the earth.
[3] They have poured out their blood like water
    all around Jerusalem,
    and there was no one to bury them.
[4] We have become a taunt to our neighbors,
    mocked and derided by those around us.
[5] How long, O LORD? Will you be angry forever?
    Will your jealous wrath burn like fire?
[6] Pour out your anger on the nations
    that do not know you,
  and on the kingdoms
    that do not call on your name.
[7] For they have devoured Jacob
    and laid waste his habitation.
[8] Do not remember against us the iniquities of our ancestors;
    let your compassion come speedily to meet us,
    for we are brought very low.
[9] Help us, O God of our salvation,
    for the glory of your name;
  deliver us, and forgive our sins,
    for your name's sake.

1 Timothy 2:1-7

[1] First of all, then, I urge that supplications, prayers, intercessions, and thanksgivings be made for everyone, [2] for kings and all who are in high positions, so that we may lead a quiet and peaceable life in all godliness and dignity. [3] This is right and is acceptable in the sight of God our Savior, [4] who desires everyone to be saved and to come to the knowledge of the truth. [5] For
  there is one God;
    there is also one mediator between God and
        humankind,
  Christ Jesus, himself human,

[6] who gave himself a ransom for all
  —this was attested at the right time. [7] For this I was appointed a herald and an apostle (I am telling the truth, I am not lying), a teacher of the Gentiles in faith and truth.

Luke 16:1-13

[1] Then Jesus said to the disciples, "There was a rich man who had a manager, and charges were brought to him that this man was squandering his property. [2] So he summoned him and said to him, 'What is this that I hear about you? Give me an accounting of your management, because you cannot be my manager any longer.' [3] Then the manager said to himself, 'What will I do, now that my master is taking the position away from me? I am not strong enough to dig, and I am ashamed to beg. [4] I have decided what to do so that, when I am dismissed as manager, people may welcome me into their homes.' [5] So, summoning his master's debtors one by one, he asked the first, 'How much do you owe my master?' [6] He answered, 'A hundred jugs of olive oil.' He said to him, 'Take your bill, sit down quickly, and make it fifty.' [7] Then he asked another, 'And how much do you owe?' He replied, 'A hundred containers of wheat.' He said to him, 'Take your bill and make it eighty.' [8] And his master commended the dishonest manager because he had acted shrewdly; for the children of this age are more shrewd in dealing with their own generation than are the children of light. [9] And I tell you, make friends for yourselves by means of dishonest wealth so that when it is gone, they may welcome you into the eternal homes.

[10] "Whoever is faithful in a very little is faithful also in much; and whoever is dishonest in a very little is dishonest also in much. [11] If then you have not been faithful with the dishonest wealth, who will entrust to you the true riches? [12] And if you have not been faithful with what belongs to another, who will give you what is your own? [13] No slave can serve two masters; for a slave will either hate the one and love the other, or be devoted to the one and despise the other. You cannot serve God and wealth."

COLOR: GREEN

18th SUNDAY AFTER PENTECOST

Primary Hymns and Songs for the Day

2149	"Living for Jesus" (Luke) (O)	
375	"There Is a Balm in Gilead" (Jer.)	
	S-2 #21. Descant	
2209	"How Long, O Lord" (Ps.)	
85	"We Believe in One True God" (1 Tim.)	
	S-1 #278-279. Harmonizations	
2065	"More Precious than Silver" (Luke)	
	SP99	
373	"Nothing Between" (Luke)	
438	"Forth in Thy Name, O Lord" (Luke) (C)	
	H-3 Hbl-29, 57, 58; Chr-117; Desc-31; Org-31	
	S-1 #100-103. Various treatments	

Additional Hymn Suggestions

428	"For the Healing of the Nations" (Jer.)
443	"O God, Who Shaped Creation" (Jer.)
479	"Jesus, Lover of My Soul" (Jer.)
480	"O Love That Wilt Not Let Me Go" (Jer.)
2197	"Lord of All Hopefulness" (Jer.)
2174	"What Does the Lord Require of You" (Jer., Luke)
2177	"Wounded World That Cries for Healing" (Jer., Ps.)
2180	"Why Stand So Far Away, My God" (Jer., Ps.)
2217	"By the Babylonian Rivers" (Jer., Ps.)
358	"Dear Lord and Father of Mankind" (Jer., Ps.)
	(Alternate Text—"Parent of Us All")
410	"I Want a Principle Within" (Jer., Ps.)
	(see especially Stanza 3)
426	"Behold a Broken World" (Jer., Ps.)
518	"O Thou, in Whose Presence" (Jer., Ps.)
3141	"Holy Darkness" (Jer., Ps., Luke)
3142	"I Love the Lord" (Jer., Ps., Luke)
433	"All Who Love and Serve Your City" (Ps., Luke)
440	"Let There Be Light" (Ps., 1 Tim.)
105	"God of Many Names" (1 Tim.)
437	"This Is My Song" (1 Tim.)
2171	"Make Me a Channel of Your Peace" (1 Tim.)
2248	"Baptized in Water" (1 Tim., Baptism)
180	"Jesus Es Mi Rey Soberano" ("O Jesus, My King") (Luke)
206	"I Want to Walk as a Child of the Light" (Luke)
354	"I Surrender All" (Luke)
398	"Jesus Calls Us" (Luke)
441	"What Does the Lord Require" (Luke)
453	"More Love to Thee, O Christ" (Luke)
2044	"My Gratitude Now Accept, O God" ("Gracias, Señor") (Luke, Stewardship)
2172	"We Are Called" (Luke) (C)

Additional Contemporary Suggestions

WS3108	"Trading My Sorrows" (Jer., Ps.)
	M75
M267	"Hear Us from Heaven" (Jer., Ps.)
S2071	"Jesus, Name Above All Names" (1 Tim.)
	SP76
S2003	"Praise You" (Luke, Praise)
	M84
S2025	"As the Deer" (Luke)
	SP200
S2176	"Make Me a Servant" (Luke)
	SP193

UM405	"Seek Ye First" (Luke)
	SP182
M30	"Knowing You" ("All I Once Held Dear") (Luke)
M98	"Take This Life" (Luke, Stewardship)
M101	"These Hands" (Luke, Stewardship)
M152	"Be Glorified" (Luke, Stewardship)
S2150	"Lord, Be Glorified" (Luke, Stewardship)
	SP196

Vocal Solos

"Jesus, Lover of My Soul" (Jer.)
V-1   p. 37
"There Is a Balm in Gilead" (Jer.)
V-7   p. 44
"Maybe the Rain" (Luke)
V-5(2)   p. 27
"Seek First" (Luke)
V-8   p. 145
"Take My Life" (Luke, Stewardship)
V-8   p. 262
"Here I Am" (Luke, Stewardship)
V-11   p. 19

Anthems

"Prayer for Today" (Jer.)
Margaret Tucker; Choristers Guild CGA-358
Unison, keyboard (opt. flute)

"More Precious Than Silver" (Luke)
arr. Lloyd Larson; Hope C 5254
SATB, keyboard

Other Suggestions

Visuals:

O	Grief, heart, reaching, harvest, poor, heal, spring
P	Ruins, blood, fire, Ps. 79:9
E	Praying hands, judge, hand of God, Christ, cross
G	Ledger, shovel, tin cup, 100/50, oil, wheat, 100/80, darkness/light, symbols of wealth

A stewardship focus relates well to today's Luke reading.
Opening Prayer: UM677. Listen, Lord (Jer., Ps.)
Prayer of Confession: BOW486 (Jer., Ps.)
Prayer: BOW517. For the Nation (1 Tim.)
Prayer: WSL205. Loving God, we spend so much time (Luke)
Offertory Prayer: WSL146 or WSL147 (Luke)
Response: UM588. "All Things Come of Thee" (Luke)
Blessing: BOW544. For Leaders (1 Tim.)

SEPTEMBER 29, 2013

Jeremiah 32:1-3a, 6-15

¹The word that came to Jeremiah from the LORD in the tenth year of King Zedekiah of Judah, which was the eighteenth year of Nebuchadrezzar. ²At that time the army of the king of Babylon was besieging Jerusalem, and the prophet Jeremiah was confined in the court of the guard that was in the palace of the king of Judah, ³where King Zedekiah of Judah had confined him. . .

⁶Jeremiah said, The word of the LORD came to me: ⁷Hanamel son of your uncle Shallum is going to come to you and say, "Buy my field that is at Anathoth, for the right of redemption by purchase is yours." ⁸Then my cousin Hanamel came to me in the court of the guard, in accordance with the word of the LORD, and said to me, "Buy my field that is at Anathoth in the land of Benjamin, for the right of possession and redemption is yours; buy it for yourself." Then I knew that this was the word of the LORD.

⁹And I bought the field at Anathoth from my cousin Hanamel, and weighed out the money to him, seventeen shekels of silver. ¹⁰I signed the deed, sealed it, got witnesses, and weighed the money on scales. ¹¹Then I took the sealed deed of purchase, containing the terms and conditions, and the open copy; ¹²and I gave the deed of purchase to Baruch son of Neriah son of Mahseiah, in the presence of my cousin Hanamel, in the presence of the witnesses who signed the deed of purchase, and in the presence of all the Judeans who were sitting in the court of the guard. ¹³In their presence I charged Baruch, saying, ¹⁴Thus says the LORD of hosts, the God of Israel: Take these deeds, both this sealed deed of purchase and this open deed, and put them in an earthenware jar, in order that they may last for a long time. ¹⁵For thus says the LORD of hosts, the God of Israel: Houses and fields and vineyards shall again be bought in this land.

Psalm 91:1-6, 14-16

1 You who live in the shelter of the Most High,
   who abide in the shadow of the Almighty,
2 will say to the LORD, "My refuge and my fortress;
   my God, in whom I trust."
3 For he will deliver you from the snare of the fowler
   and from the deadly pestilence;
4 he will cover you with his pinions,
   and under his wings you will find refuge;
   his faithfulness is a shield and buckler.
5 You will not fear the terror of the night,
   or the arrow that flies by day,
6 or the pestilence that stalks in darkness,
   or the destruction that wastes at noonday.
. . . .
14 Those who love me, I will deliver;
   I will protect those who know my name.
15 When they call to me, I will answer them;
   I will be with them in trouble,
   I will rescue them and honor them.
16 With long life I will satisfy them,
   and show them my salvation.

1 Timothy 6:6-19

⁶Of course, there is great gain in godliness combined with contentment; ⁷for we brought nothing into the world, so that we can take nothing out of it; ⁸but if we have food and clothing, we will be content with these. ⁹But those who want to be rich fall into temptation and are trapped by many senseless and harmful desires that plunge people into ruin and destruction. ¹⁰For the love of money is a root of all kinds of evil, and in their eagerness to be rich some have wandered away from the faith and pierced themselves with many pains.

¹¹But as for you, man of God, shun all this; pursue righteousness, godliness, faith, love, endurance, gentleness. ¹²Fight the good fight of the faith; take hold of the eternal life, to which you were called and for which you made the good confession in the presence of many witnesses. ¹³In the presence of God, who gives life to all things, and of Christ Jesus, who in his testimony before Pontius Pilate made the good confession, I charge you ¹⁴to keep the commandment without spot or blame until the manifestation of our Lord Jesus Christ, ¹⁵which he will bring about at the right time—he who is the blessed and only Sovereign, the King of kings and Lord of lords. ¹⁶It is he alone who has immortality and dwells in unapproachable light, whom no one has ever seen or can see; to him be honor and eternal dominion. Amen.

¹⁷As for those who in the present age are rich, command them not to be haughty, or to set their hopes on the uncertainty of riches, but rather on God who richly provides us with everything for our enjoyment. ¹⁸They are to do good, to be rich in good works, generous, and ready to share, ¹⁹thus storing up for themselves the treasure of a good foundation for the future, so that they may take hold of the life that really is life.

Luke 16:19-31

¹⁹"There was a rich man who was dressed in purple and fine linen and who feasted sumptuously every day. ²⁰And at his gate lay a poor man named Lazarus, covered with sores, ²¹who longed to satisfy his hunger with what fell from the rich man's table; even the dogs would come and lick his sores. ²²The poor man died and was carried away by the angels to be with Abraham. The rich man also died and was buried. ²³In Hades, where he was being tormented, he looked up and saw Abraham far away with Lazarus by his side. ²⁴He called out, 'Father Abraham, have mercy on me, and send Lazarus to dip the tip of his finger in water and cool my tongue; for I am in agony in these flames.' ²⁵But Abraham said, 'Child, remember that during your lifetime you received your good things, and Lazarus in like manner evil things; but now he is comforted here, and you are in agony. ²⁶Besides all this, between you and us a great chasm has been fixed, so that those who might want to pass from here to you cannot do so, and no one can cross from there to us.' ²⁷He said, 'Then, father, I beg you to send him to my father's house—²⁸for I have five brothers—that he may warn them, so that they will not also come into this place of torment.' ²⁹Abraham replied, 'They have Moses and the prophets; they should listen to them.' ³⁰He said, 'No, father Abraham; but if someone goes to them from the dead, they will repent.' ³¹He said to him, 'If they do not listen to Moses and the prophets, neither will they be convinced even if someone rises from the dead.'"

COLOR: GREEN

19th SUNDAY AFTER PENTECOST

Primary Hymns and Songs for the Day
108	"God Hath Spoken by the Prophets" (Jer., Luke) (O)	
130	"God Will Take Care of You" (Ps.)	
143	"On Eagle's Wings" (Ps.)	
	S-2 #143 Stanzas for soloist	
502	"Thy Holy Wings, O Savior" (Ps.)	
	S-1 #47-49. Various treatments	
436	"The Voice of God Is Calling" (Luke)	
	S-2 #119-120. Descant and harmonization	
2036	"Give Thanks" (Luke)	
	SP170	
413	"A Charge to Keep I Have" (1 Tim.) (C)	
	S-1 #46. Choral harmonization	

Additional Hymn Suggestions
2008 "Let All Things Now Living" (Jer.)
729 "O Day of Peace That Dimly Shines" (Jer.)
518 "O Thou, in Whose Presence" (Jer., Ps.)
377 "It Is Well with My Soul" (Ps.)
498 "My Prayer Rises to Heaven" (Ps.)
523 "Saranam, Saranam" ("Refuge") (Ps.)
2001 "We Sing to You, O God" (Ps.)
2053 "If It Had Not Been for the Lord" (Ps.)
2121 "O Holy Spirit, Root of Life" (Ps.)
2142 "Blessed Quietness" (Ps.)
103 "Immortal, Invisible, God Only Wise" (1 Tim.)
399 "Take My Life, and Let It Be" (1 Tim.)
505 "When Our Confidence Is Shaken" (1 Tim.)
514 "Stand Up, Stand Up for Jesus" (1 Tim.)
530 "Are Ye Able" (1 Tim., Luke)
2211 "Faith Is Patience in the Night" (1 Tim.)
712 "I Sing a Song of the Saints of God" (1 Tim., Luke)
356 "Pues Si Vivimos" (1 Tim., Luke)
434 "Cuando El Pobre" ("When the Poor Ones") (Luke)
439 "We Utter Our Cry" (Luke)
441 "What Does the Lord Require" (Luke)
592 "When the Church of Jesus" (Luke)
655 "Fix Me, Jesus" (Luke)
2172 "We Are Called" (Luke)
2174 "What Does the Lord Require of You" (Luke)
2178 "Here Am I" (Luke)
2044 "My Gratitude Now Accept, O God" ("Gracias, Señor") (Luke, Stewardship)

Additional Contemporary Suggestions
S2002	"I Will Call Upon the Lord" (Ps.)	
	SP224	
S2055	"You Are My Hiding Place" (Ps.)	
S2054	"Nothing Can Trouble" (Ps.)	
S2145	"I've Got Peace Like a River" (Ps.)	
WS3021	"Everlasting God" (Ps.)	
WS3134	"Still" (Ps.)	
	M216	
M28	"Who Can Satisfy My Soul Like You?" (Ps.)	
M60	"Better Is One Day" (Ps.)	
M79	"I Stand Amazed" (Ps.)	
M92	"All Things Are Possible" (Ps.)	
M158	"Eagle's Wings" (Ps.)	
M22	"Crown Him King of Kings" (1 Tim.)	
M115	"When It's All Been Said and Done" (1 Tim.)	

S2069	"All Hail King Jesus" (1 Tim.)	
	SP63	
S2075	"King of Kings" (1 Tim.)	
	SP94	
S2087	"We Will Glorify" (1 Tim.)	
	SP68	
S2163	"He Who Began a Good Work in You" (1 Tim.)	
	SP180	
S2167	"More Like You" (1 Tim.)	
UM176	"Majesty" (1 Tim.)	
	SP73	
SP81	"Worthy, You Are Worthy" (1 Tim.)	
M176	"Worthy, You Are Worthy" (1 Tim.)	
WS3040	"You Are My All in All" (1 Tim., Luke)	
	SP220	
UM488	"Jesus, Remember Me" (Luke)	

Vocal Solos
"It Is Well with My Soul" (Ps.)
　V-5(2)　　p. 35
"Wings Like Eagles" (Ps.)
　V-11　　p. 9
"Sinner-Man So Hard to Believe" (Luke)
　V-7　　p. 48

Anthems
"Psalm 91" (Ps.)
Craig Courtney; Beckenhorst BP1500
SATB, keyboard, opt. flute and strings

"Poor Man Lazarus" (Luke)
arr. Jester Hairston; Bourne 2653-7
SATB *a cappella* (other voicings available)

Other Suggestions
Visuals:
O	War, field, scales, earthen jar, house
P	Shadow, refuge, fort, eagle, snare, shield/arrow
E	Newborn, coffin, money, 1 Tim. 6:11*b*, Jesus/Pilate, cross/ crown, generosity, treasure
G	Purple robe/linen, feast, sores, dogs, 5 men, angels, flames, water, Bible open to Exodus

Stewardship emphasis relates to New Testament lessons today.
Greeting: BOW457 (Ps.) or BOW424. One Great Hour (Luke)
Prayer for Healing: WSL204. God of compassion (Luke)
Prayer of Confession: WSL92 or WSL93 (Luke)
Response: S2277. "Lord, Have Mercy" (Luke)
Prayer: BOW423. Human Relations Day Litany (Luke)
Offertory Prayer: WSL104. O God, may our use of money (Luke)
Dismissal: BOW559 (1 Tim.)

OCTOBER 6, 2013
WORLD COMMUNION SUNDAY

Lamentations 1:1-6

1 How lonely sits the city
    that once was full of people!
  How like a widow she has become,
    she that was great among the nations!
  She that was a princess among the provinces
    has become a vassal.
2 She weeps bitterly in the night,
    with tears on her cheeks;
  among all her lovers
    she has no one to comfort her;
  all her friends have dealt treacherously with her,
    they have become her enemies.
3 Judah has gone into exile with suffering
    and hard servitude;
  she lives now among the nations,
    and finds no resting place;
  her pursuers have all overtaken her
    in the midst of her distress.
4 The roads to Zion mourn,
    for no one comes to the festivals;
  all her gates are desolate,
    her priests groan;
  her young girls grieve,
    and her lot is bitter.
5 Her foes have become the masters,
    her enemies prosper,
  because the LORD has made her suffer
    for the multitude of her transgressions;
  her children have gone away,
    captives before the foe.
6 From daughter Zion has departed
    all her majesty.
  Her princes have become like stags
    that find no pasture;
  they fled without strength
    before the pursuer.

Psalm 137

1 By the rivers of Babylon—
    there we sat down and there we wept
    when we remembered Zion.
2 On the willows there
    we hung up our harps.
3 For there our captors
    asked us for songs,
  and our tormentors asked for mirth, saying,
    "Sing us one of the songs of Zion!"
4 How could we sing the Lord's song
    in a foreign land?
5 If I forget you, O Jerusalem,
    let my right hand wither!
6 Let my tongue cling to the roof of my mouth,
    if I do not remember you,
  if I do not set Jerusalem
    above my highest joy.
7 Remember, O LORD, against the Edomites
    the day of Jerusalem's fall,

how they said, "Tear it down! Tear it down!
    Down to its foundations!"
8 O daughter Babylon, you devastator!
  Happy shall they be who pay you back
    what you have done to us!
9 Happy shall they be who take your little ones
    and dash them against the rock!

2 Timothy 1:1-14

1Paul, an apostle of Christ Jesus by the will of God, for the sake of the promise of life that is in Christ Jesus, 2To Timothy, my beloved child: Grace, mercy, and peace from God the Father and Christ Jesus our Lord.

3I am grateful to God—whom I worship with a clear conscience, as my ancestors did—when I remember you constantly in my prayers night and day. 4Recalling your tears, I long to see you so that I may be filled with joy. 5I am reminded of your sincere faith, a faith that lived first in your grandmother Lois and your mother Eunice and now, I am sure, lives in you. 6For this reason I remind you to rekindle the gift of God that is within you through the laying on of my hands; 7for God did not give us a spirit of cowardice, but rather a spirit of power and of love and of self-discipline. 8Do not be ashamed, then, of the testimony about our Lord or of me his prisoner, but join with me in suffering for the gospel, relying on the power of God, 9who saved us and called us with a holy calling, not according to our works but according to his own purpose and grace. This grace was given to us in Christ Jesus before the ages began, 10but it has now been revealed through the appearing of our Savior Christ Jesus, who abolished death and brought life and immortality to light through the gospel. 11For this gospel I was appointed a herald and an apostle and a teacher, 12and for this reason I suffer as I do. But I am not ashamed, for I know the one in whom I have put my trust, and I am sure that he is able to guard until that day what I have entrusted to him. 13Hold to the standard of sound teaching that you have heard from me, in the faith and love that are in Christ Jesus. 14Guard the good treasure entrusted to you, with the help of the Holy Spirit living in us.

Luke 17:5-10

5The apostles said to the Lord, "Increase our faith!" 6The Lord replied, "If you had faith the size of a mustard seed, you could say to this mulberry tree, 'Be uprooted and planted in the sea,' and it would obey you.

7"Who among you would say to your slave who has just come in from plowing or tending sheep in the field, 'Come here at once and take your place at the table'? 8Would you not rather say to him, 'Prepare supper for me, put on your apron and serve me while I eat and drink; later you may eat and drink'? 9Do you thank the slave for doing what was commanded? 10So you also, when you have done all that you were ordered to do, say, 'We are worthless slaves; we have done only what we ought to have done!' "

COLOR: GREEN　　　　　　　　　　　　　　　　　　**20th SUNDAY AFTER PENTECOST**

Primary Hymns and Songs for the Day

374	"Standing on the Promises" (2 Tim.) (O)
	H-3 Chr-177; Org-117
714	"I Know Whom I Have Believed" (2 Tim.)
2139	"I Know the Lord's Laid His Hands on Me" (2 Tim.)
2217	"By the Babylonian Rivers" (Ps.)
620	"One Bread, One Body" (World Communion)
	H-3 Chr-156
438	"Forth in Thy Name, O Lord" (1 Tim., Luke) (C)
	H-3 Hbl-29, 57, 58; Chr-117; Desc-31; Org-31
	S-1 #100-103. Various treatments

Additional Hymn Suggestions

352	"It's Me, It's Me, O Lord" (Ps.)
458	"Dear Lord, for All in Pain" (Ps.)
2238	"In the Midst of New Dimensions" (Ps., World Communion) (O)
540	"I Love Thy Kingdom, Lord" (Ps.)
2182	"When God Restored Our Common Life" (Ps.)
2216	"When We Are Called to Sing Your Praise" (Ps.)
465	"Holy Spirit, Truth Divine" (2 Tim.)
501	"O Thou Who Camest from Above" (2 Tim.)
617	"I Come with Joy" (2 Tim., World Communion)
632	"Draw Us in the Spirit's Tether" (2 Tim., Communion)
2255	"In the Singing" (2 Tim., Communion)
2266	"Here Is Bread, Here Is Wine" (2 Tim., Communion)
2211	"Faith Is Patience in the Night" (2 Tim., Luke)
452	"My Faith Looks Up to Thee" (2 Tim., Luke)
505	"When Our Confidence Is Shaken" (2 Tim., Luke)
517	"By Gracious Powers" (2 Tim., Luke)
275	"The Kingdom of God" (Luke)
385	"Let Us Plead for Faith Alone" (Luke)
578	"God of Love and God of Power" (Luke)
650	"Give Me the Faith Which Can Remove" (Luke)
2181	"We Need a Faith" (Luke, World Communion)
624	"Bread of the World" (World Communion)
630	"Become to Us the Living Bread" (Communion)
2117	"Spirit of God" (World Communion)
2221	"In Unity We Lift Our Song" (World Communion)
3120	"Amazing Abundance" (World Communion)

Additional Contemporary Suggestions

S2144	"Someone Asked the Question" (Ps.)
S2157	"Come and Fill Our Hearts" (Ps.)
WS3108	"Trading My Sorrows" (Ps.)
	M75
WS3168	"Come to the Table of Grace" (Ps., 2 Tim., Communion)
S2163	"He Who Began a Good Work in You" (2 Tim.)
	SP180
S2165	"Cry of My Heart" (2 Tim.)
	M39
M37	"He Is Able" (2 Tim.)
M101	"These Hands" (2 Tim.)
S2258	"Sing Alleluia to the Lord" (2 Tim., Communion)
	SP93
S2224	"Make Us One" (World Communion)
	SP137

S2226	"Bind Us Together" (World Communion)
	SP140
WS3154	"Draw the Circle Wide" (World Communion)

Vocal Solos

"Patiently Have I Waited for the Lord" (2 Tim.)
　　V-4　　　p. 24
"Here I Am" (2 Tim., Luke)
　　V-9　　　p. 19
"The Body of the Lord" (World Communion)
　　V-8　　　p. 344

Anthems

"In the Midst of New Dimensions" (Ps.)
arr. Jeremy Bankson; Paraclete Press MSM-60-6500
SATB, brass quintet, percussion, organ

"Bread of the World" (Communion)
Greg Scheer; Augsburg 0-8006-7793-5
SATB, piano

Other Suggestions

Visuals:

O	Empty city, widow, tiara/chains, weeping, stag
P	River, sitting/weeping, harp on willow
E	Letter, praying hands, tears/joy, women, flame, risen Christ, trumpet, treasure, Spirit
G	Mustard/mulberry trees, sea, plow, sheep, table/meal, chain/manacles

World Communion: Flags, nationalities, breads
Opening Prayer: WSL67. "Jesus Christ, Lord" (World Communion)
Prayer of Confession: BOW483 (2 Tim., Luke)
Prayer of Confession: BOW492 (World Communion)
Prayer: WSL151. O God, we are so grateful (2 Tim.)
Prayer: UM412 or UM564 (World Communion)
Prayer: BOW431, BOW502, BOW505 (World Communion)
Blessing: BOW545-547. Healing Prayers (Ps.)
Litany: UM556. Litany for Christian Unity (World Communion)
Offertory Prayer: WSL151. O God (World Communion)
Call to Communion: UM621. "Be Present at Our Table, Lord" (World Communion)
Great Thanksgiving for World Communion: BOW71-72.
Blessing: WS40. May the Spirit of God (2 Tim.)

OCTOBER 13, 2013

Jeremiah 29:1, 4-7

[1]These are the words of the letter that the prophet Jeremiah sent from Jerusalem to the remaining elders among the exiles, and to the priests, the prophets, and all the people, whom Nebuchadnezzar had taken into exile from Jerusalem to Babylon. . . . [4]Thus says the LORD of hosts, the God of Israel, to all the exiles whom I have sent into exile from Jerusalem to Babylon: [5]Build houses and live in them; plant gardens and eat what they produce. [6]Take wives and have sons and daughters; take wives for your sons, and give your daughters in marriage, that they may bear sons and daughters; multiply there, and do not decrease. [7]But seek the welfare of the city where I have sent you into exile, and pray to the LORD on its behalf, for in its welfare you will find your welfare.

Psalm 66:1-12

[1] Make a joyful noise to God, all the earth;
    [2]sing the glory of his name;
    give to him glorious praise.
[3] Say to God, "How awesome are your deeds!
    Because of your great power, your enemies cringe
    before you.
[4] All the earth worships you;
    they sing praises to you,
    sing praises to your name." *Selah*
[5] Come and see what God has done:
    he is awesome in his deeds among mortals.
[6] He turned the sea into dry land;
    they passed through the river on foot.
    There we rejoiced in him,
    [7]who rules by his might forever,
    whose eyes keep watch on the nations—
    let the rebellious not exalt themselves. *Selah*
[8] Bless our God, O peoples,
    let the sound of his praise be heard,
[9] who has kept us among the living,
    and has not let our feet slip.
[10] For you, O God, have tested us;
    you have tried us as silver is tried.
[11] You brought us into the net;
    you laid burdens on our backs;
[12] you let people ride over our heads;
    we went through fire and through water;
    yet you have brought us out to a spacious place.

2 Timothy 2:8-15

[8]Remember Jesus Christ, raised from the dead, a descendant of David—that is my gospel, [9]for which I suffer hardship, even to the point of being chained like a criminal. But the word of God is not chained. [10]Therefore I endure everything for the sake of the elect, so that they may also obtain the salvation that is in Christ Jesus, with eternal glory. [11]The saying is sure:

If we have died with him, we will also live with him;
[12] if we endure, we will also reign with him;
    if we deny him, he will also deny us;
[13] if we are faithless, he remains faithful—
    for he cannot deny himself.

[14]Remind them of this, and warn them before God that they are to avoid wrangling over words, which does no good but only ruins those who are listening. [15]Do your best to present yourself to God as one approved by him, a worker who has no need to be ashamed, rightly explaining the word of truth.

Luke 17:11-19

[11]On the way to Jerusalem Jesus was going through the region between Samaria and Galilee. [12]As he entered a village, ten lepers approached him. Keeping their distance, [13]they called out, saying, "Jesus, Master, have mercy on us!" [14]When he saw them, he said to them, "Go and show yourselves to the priests." And as they went, they were made clean. [15]Then one of them, when he saw that he was healed, turned back, praising God with a loud voice. [16]He prostrated himself at Jesus' feet and thanked him. And he was a Samaritan. [17]Then Jesus asked, "Were not ten made clean? But the other nine, where are they? [18]Was none of them found to return and give praise to God except this foreigner?" [19]Then he said to him, "Get up and go on your way; your faith has made you well."

COLOR: GREEN

21st SUNDAY AFTER PENTECOST

Primary Hymns and Songs for the Day

60 "I'll Praise My Maker While I've Breath (Luke, Ps.) (O)
      H-3 Chr-109; Org-105
      S-2 #141. Harmonization
2182 "When God Restored Our Common Life" (Jer.)
      H-3 Chr-139; Desc-90; Org-123
265 "O Christ, the Healer" (Luke)
2104 "An Outcast Among Outcasts" (Luke)
      H-3 Hbl-80; Chr-142; Desc-69; Org-78
      S-1 #215. Harmonization
2036 "Give Thanks" (Luke)
      SP170
3180 "As We Part for Towns and Cities" (Jer.) (C)
433 "All Who Love and Serve Your City" (Jer.) (C)
      H-3 Chr-26, 65; Org-19
      S-1 #62. Descant

Additional Hymn Suggestions

2181 "We Need a Faith" (Jer.)
2183 "Unsettled World" (Jer.)
3120 "Amazing Abundance" (Jer.)
518 "O Thou, in Whose Presence" (Jer., Ps.)
519 "Lift Every Voice and Sing" (Jer., Ps.)
81 "Canta, Debora, Canta!" (Ps.)
98 "To God Be the Glory" (Ps.)
2001 "We Sing to You, O God" (Ps.)
2006 "Lord God Almighty" (Ps.)
2011 "We Sing of Your Glory" ("Tuya Es la Gloria") (Ps.)
66 "Praise, My Soul, the King of Heaven" (Ps., Luke)
67 "We, Thy People, Praise Thee" (Ps., Luke)
140 "Great Is Thy Faithfulness" (Ps., Luke)
289 "Ah, Holy Jesus" (2 Tim.)
295 "In the Cross of Christ I Glory" (2 Tim.)
304 "Easter People, Raise Your Voices" (2 Tim.)
313 "Cristo Vive" ("Christ Is Risen") (2 Tim.)
356 "Pues si Vivimos" ("When We Are Living") (2 Tim.)
463 "Lord, Speak to Me" (2 Tim.)
532 "Jesus, Priceless Treasure" (2 Tim.)
610 "We Know That Christ Is Raised" (2 Tim., Baptism)
256 "We Would See Jesus" (Luke)
261 "Lord of the Dance" (Luke)
262 "Heal Me, Hands of Jesus" (Luke)
263 "When Jesus the Healer Passed Through Galilee" (Luke)
273 "Jesus' Hands Were Kind Hands" (Luke)
394 "Something Beautiful" (Luke)
458 "Dear Lord, for All in Pain" (Luke)

Additional Contemporary Suggestions

S2186 "Song of Hope" (Jer.)
UM99 "My Tribute" ("To God Be the Glory") (Ps.)
      SP118; V-8 p. 5 Vocal Solo
S2144 "Someone Asked the Question" (Ps.)
S2040 "Awesome God" (Ps.)
      SP11
SP10 "Awesome Power" (Ps.)
M47 "Come Just As You Are" (Ps.)
M50 "Refiner's Fire" (Ps.)
S2069 "All Hail King Jesus" (2 Tim.)
      SP63
SP208 "I Am Crucified with Christ" (2 Tim.)

UM507 "Through It All" (2 Tim., Luke)
UM84 "Thank You, Lord" (Luke)
S2064 "O Lord, You're Beautiful" (Luke)
S2081 "Thank You, Jesus" ("Tino tenda, Jesu") (Luke)
S2151 "I'm So Glad Jesus Lifted Me" (Luke)
S2244 "People Need the Lord" (Luke)
WS3037 "I Thank You, Jesus" (Luke)
M35 "White as Snow" (Luke)

Vocal Solos

"Great Day!" (Jer., Ps.)
      V-7   p. 14
"Now Thank We All Our God" (Luke)
      V-6   p. 8
"I Just Came to Praise the Lord" (Luke)
      V-8   p. 294

Anthems

"Shout with Joy!" (Ps.)
Mark Patterson; Choristers Guild CGA-1251
Unison, piano

"If I Forget, Yet God Remembers" (Luke)
Daniel Pederson; Augsburg 0-8006-7805-2
SATB, *a cappella*

Other Suggestions

Visuals:
    O   Letter, houses, garden, marriage, prayer/chain
    P   Praise, nations, awe, sea/desert, river, feet, refining, net, full backpack, fire/water, open space
    E   Christus Rex, chain, open manacles, cross
    G   Lepers, one prostrate, feet, praise, walking
Greeting: BOW379 (Jer., Ps.)
Opening Prayer: BOW464 (Jer., Ps.)
Greeting or Litany: WSL158. "Here in this sanctuary" (Jer.)
Prayer of Confession: BOW480 or 490 (2 Tim., Luke)
Response: S2275 "Kyrie" or S2277 "Lord, Have Mercy" (Luke)
Offertory Prayer: WSL142. "Heavenly Father, each day we witness" (Luke)
Prayer of Thanksgiving: BOW550 (Luke)
Closing Prayer: WSL171. "Thank you, God" (Jer., Communion)

OCTOBER 20, 2013

LAITY SUNDAY

Jeremiah 31:27-34

27The days are surely coming, says the LORD, when I will sow the house of Israel and the house of Judah with the seed of humans and the seed of animals. 28And just as I have watched over them to pluck up and break down, to over-throw, destroy, and bring evil, so I will watch over them to build and to plant, says the LORD. 29In those days they shall no longer say:

"The parents have eaten sour grapes,
and the children's teeth are set on edge."

30But all shall die for their own sins; the teeth of everyone who eats sour grapes shall be set on edge.

31The days are surely coming, says the LORD, when I will make a new covenant with the house of Israel and the house of Judah. 32It will not be like the covenant that I made with their ancestors when I took them by the hand to bring them out of the land of Egypt—a covenant that they broke, though I was their husband, says the LORD. 33But this is the covenant that I will make with the house of Israel after those days, says the LORD: I will put my law within them, and I will write it on their hearts; and I will be their God, and they shall be my people. 34No longer shall they teach one another, or say to each other, "Know the LORD," for they shall all know me, from the least of them to the greatest, says the LORD; for I will forgive their iniquity, and remember their sin no more.

Psalm 119:97-104

97 Oh, how I love your law!
It is my meditation all day long.
98 Your commandment makes me wiser than my enemies,
for it is always with me.
99 I have more understanding than all my teachers,
for your decrees are my meditation.
100I understand more than the aged,
for I keep your precepts.
101I hold back my feet from every evil way,
in order to keep your word.
102I do not turn away from your ordinances,
for you have taught me.
103How sweet are your words to my taste,
sweeter than honey to my mouth!
104Through your precepts I get understanding;
therefore I hate every false way.

2 Timothy 3:14–4:5

14But as for you, continue in what you have learned and firmly believed, knowing from whom you learned it, 15and how from childhood you have known the sacred writings that are able to instruct you for salvation through faith in Christ Jesus. 16All scripture is inspired by God and is useful for teaching, for reproof, for correction, and for training in righteousness, 17so that everyone who belongs to God may be proficient, equipped for every good work.

1In the presence of God and of Christ Jesus, who is to judge the living and the dead, and in view of his appear-ing and his kingdom, I solemnly urge you: 2proclaim the message; be persistent whether the time is favorable or unfavorable; convince, rebuke, and encourage, with the utmost patience in teaching. 3For the time is coming when people will not put up with sound doctrine, but having itching ears, they will accumulate for themselves teachers to suit their own desires, 4and will turn away from listening to the truth and wander away to myths. 5As for you, always be sober, endure suffering, do the work of an evangelist, carry out your ministry fully.

Luke 18:1-8

1Then Jesus told them a parable about their need to pray always and not to lose heart. 2He said, "In a certain city there was a judge who neither feared God nor had respect for people. 3In that city there was a widow who kept coming to him and saying, 'Grant me justice against my opponent.' 4For a while he refused; but later he said to himself, 'Though I have no fear of God and no respect for anyone, 5yet because this widow keeps bothering me, I will grant her justice, so that she may not wear me out by continually coming.' " 6And the Lord said, "Listen to what the unjust judge says. 7And will not God grant justice to his chosen ones who cry to him day and night? Will he delay long in helping them? 8I tell you, he will quickly grant justice to them. And yet, when the Son of Man comes, will he find faith on earth?"

COLOR: GREEN

22nd SUNDAY AFTER PENTECOST

Primary Hymns and Songs for the Day

384   "Love Divine, All Loves Excelling" (Jer.) (O)
        H-3 Chr-134; Desc-18; Org-13
        S-1 #41-42. Descant and harmonization

606   "Come, Let Us Use the Grace Divine" (Jer.)
        H-3 Hbl-15, 20, 34, 84; Chr-150; Org-67
        S-2 #100-103. Various treatments

2152   "Change My Heart, O God" (Jer.)
        SP195

601   "Thy Word Is a Lamp" (Ps., 2 Tim.)
        SP183

352   "Standing in the Need of Prayer" (Luke)
        H-3 Chr-177

593   "Here I Am, Lord" (Jer.) (C)
        H-3 Chr-97; Org-54

Additional Hymn Suggestions

383   "This Is a Day of New Beginnings" (Jer.)
388   "O Come and Dwell in Me" (Jer.)
583   "Sois la Semilla" ("You Are the Seed") (Jer.)
2060   "God the Sculptor of the Mountains" (Jer.)
2247   "Wonder of Wonders" (Jer., Baptism)
465   "Holy Spirit, Truth Divine" (Jer., 2 Tim., Luke)
500   "Spirit of God, Descend upon My Heart" (Jer., Luke)
501   "O Thou Who Camest from Above" (Jer., Luke)
596   "Blessed Jesus, at Thy Word" (Jer., Ps., 2 Tim.)
3115   "Covenant Prayer" (Jer., Ps., 2 Tim.)
600   "Wonderful Words of Life" (Ps.)
695   "O Lord, May Church and Home Combine" (Ps.)
430   "O Master, Let Me Walk with Thee" (Ps., 2 Tim.)
598   "O Word of God Incarnate" (Ps., 2 Tim.)
599   "Break Thou the Bread of Life" (Ps., 2 Tim., Communion)
507   "Through It All" (2 Tim.)
584   "Lord, You Give the Great Commission" (2 Tim.) (C)
714   "I Know Whom I Have Believed" (2 Tim.)
2004   "Praise the Source of Faith and Learning" (2 Tim.)
2246   "Deep in the Shadows of the Past" (2 Tim.)
463   "Lord, Speak to Me" (2 Tim., Luke)
451   "Be Thou My Vision" (Luke)
455   "Not So in Haste, My Heart" (Luke)
464   "I Will Trust in the Lord" (Luke)
3140   "Give Me Jesus" (Luke)
558   "We Are the Church" (Laity Sunday)

Additional Contemporary Suggestions

S2154   "Please Enter My Heart, Hosanna" (Jer.)
M49   "Refresh My Heart" (Jer.)
M85   "The Potter's Hand" (Jer.)
M30   "Knowing You" ("All I Once Held Dear") (Ps.)
M32   "Holy and Anointed One" (Ps.)
M38   "In the Secret" ("I Want to Know You") (Ps.)
WS3112   "Breathe" (Ps.)
        M61
M107   "Show Me Your Ways" (Ps.)
M149   "Ancient Words" (Ps.)
S2065   "More Precious Than Silver" (Ps.)
        SP99
S2025   "As the Deer" (Ps.)
        SP200

S2161   "To Know You More" (Ps.)
S2165   "Cry of My Heart" (Ps.)
        M39
S2163   "He Who Began a Good Work in You" (2 Tim.)
        SP180
S2193   "Lord, Listen to Your Children" (Luke)
S2207   "Lord, Listen to Your Children" (Luke)

Vocal Solos

"Gospel Train" (Jer.)
    V-7   p. 74
"Maybe the Rain" (Ps.)
    V-5(2)   p. 27
"If My People Will Pray" (Luke)
    V-8   p. 66

Anthems

"If with All Your Hearts" (Jer., Luke)
Mendelssohn, arr. Sherman; Hope C-5106
SATB, keyboard or handbells

"Thy Word Is Like a Garden, Lord" (Ps., 2 Tim.)
Dan Forrest; Hal Leonard 08745683
SATB, piano

Other Suggestions

Visuals:
    O   Sowing seeds, destruction, build/plant, torn document, Jer. 31:33*b*, heart, all ages, eraser
    P   Bible, meditation, feet, Ps. 119:103, honey
    E   Child, Bible, Christ, teacher, 2 Tim. 3:16, tools, gavel
    G   Prayer, gavel, scales of justice, woman pleading

Greeting: BOW326 (Ps.)
Opening Prayer: BOW461 or BOW468 (Ps., 2 Tim.)
Prayer of Confession: UM597. For the Spirit of Truth (2 Tim.)
Prayer of Confession: BOW478 (Ps., Luke)
Litany: BOW432 (Laity Sunday)
Prayer Response: S2200. "O Lord, Hear My Prayer" (Luke)
Prayer: UM392 (Jer., Ps.)
Prayer: BOW510 or BOW525 (Ps., 2 Tim.)
Prayer: S2201. "Prayers of the People" (Luke)
Song of Preparation: UM603. "Come, Holy Ghost" (Jer., Ps.)
Prayer of Preparation: WSL75 or UM602 (2 Tim.)
Benediction: BOW566. Sarum Blessing (Jer., Ps., 2 Tim.)

OCTOBER 27, 2013 — REFORMATION SUNDAY

Joel 2:23-32

²³ O children of Zion, be glad
    and rejoice in the LORD your God;
  for he has given the early rain for your vindication,
    he has poured down for you abundant rain,
    the early and the later rain, as before.
²⁴ The threshing floors shall be full of grain,
    the vats shall overflow with wine and oil.
²⁵ I will repay you for the years
    that the swarming locust has eaten,
  the hopper, the destroyer, and the cutter,
    my great army, which I sent against you.
²⁶ You shall eat in plenty and be satisfied,
    and praise the name of the LORD your God,
    who has dealt wondrously with you.
  And my people shall never again be put to shame.
²⁷ You shall know that I am in the midst of Israel,
    and that I, the LORD, am your God
      and there is no other.
  And my people shall never again
    be put to shame.
²⁸Then afterward
  I will pour out my spirit on all flesh;
    your sons and your daughters shall prophesy,
    your old men shall dream dreams,
    and your young men shall see visions.
²⁹ Even on the male and female slaves,
    in those days, I will pour out my spirit.

³⁰I will show portents in the heavens and on the earth, blood and fire and columns of smoke. ³¹The sun shall be turned to darkness, and the moon to blood, before the great and terrible day of the LORD comes. ³²Then everyone who calls on the name of the LORD shall be saved; for in Mount Zion and in Jerusalem there shall be those who escape, as the LORD has said, and among the survivors shall be those whom the LORD calls.

Psalm 65

¹ Praise is due to you,
    O God, in Zion;
  and to you shall vows be performed,
    ²O you who answer prayer!
  To you all flesh shall come.
³ When deeds of iniquity overwhelm us,
    you forgive our transgressions.
⁴ Happy are those whom you choose and bring near
    to live in your courts.
  We shall be satisfied with the goodness of your house,
    your holy temple.
⁵ By awesome deeds you answer us with deliverance,
    O God of our salvation;
  you are the hope of all the ends of the earth
    and of the farthest seas.
⁶ By your strength you established the mountains;
    you are girded with might.
⁷ You silence the roaring of the seas,
    the roaring of their waves,
    the tumult of the peoples.
⁸ Those who live at earth's farthest bounds are awed by
        your signs;
  you make the gateways of the morning and the
        evening shout for joy.

⁹ You visit the earth and water it,
    you greatly enrich it;
  the river of God is full of water;
    you provide the people with grain,
    for so you have prepared it.
¹⁰ You water its furrows abundantly,
    settling its ridges,
  softening it with showers,
    and blessing its growth.
¹¹ You crown the year with your bounty;
    your wagon tracks overflow with richness.
¹² The pastures of the wilderness overflow,
    the hills gird themselves with joy,
¹³ the meadows clothe themselves with flocks,
    the valleys deck themselves with grain,
    they shout and sing together for joy.

2 Timothy 4:6-8, 16-18

⁶As for me, I am already being poured out as a libation, and the time of my departure has come. ⁷I have fought the good fight, I have finished the race, I have kept the faith. ⁸From now on there is reserved for me the crown of righteousness, which the Lord, the righteous judge, will give me on that day, and not only to me but also to all who have longed for his appearing. . . .

¹⁶At my first defense no one came to my support, but all deserted me. May it not be counted against them! ¹⁷But the Lord stood by me and gave me strength, so that through me the message might be fully proclaimed and all the Gentiles might hear it. So I was rescued from the lion's mouth. ¹⁸The Lord will rescue me from every evil attack and save me for his heavenly kingdom. To him be the glory forever and ever.

Luke 18:9-14

⁹He also told this parable to some who trusted in themselves that they were righteous and regarded others with contempt: ¹⁰"Two men went up to the temple to pray, one a Pharisee and the other a tax collector. ¹¹The Pharisee, standing by himself, was praying thus, 'God, I thank you that I am not like other people: thieves, rogues, adulterers, or even like this tax collector. ¹²I fast twice a week; I give a tenth of all my income.' ¹³But the tax collector, standing far off, would not even look up to heaven, but was beating his breast and saying, 'God, be merciful to me, a sinner!' ¹⁴I tell you, this man went down to his home justified rather than the other; for all who exalt themselves will be humbled, but all who humble themselves will be exalted."

COLOR: GREEN　　　　　　　　　　　　　　**23rd SUNDAY AFTER PENTECOST**

Primary Hymns and Songs for the Day

110　"A Mighty Fortress Is Our God" (Joel, 2 Tim.,
　　　　Reformation) (O)
　　　　　　H-3　Chr-19; Desc-35; Org-34
　　　　　　S-1　#111-113. Various treatments
651　"Come, Holy Ghost, Our Souls Inspire" (Joel) (O)
　　　　　　H-3　Hbl-14, 52
　　　　　　S-2　#186. Handbell arrangement
2208　"Guide My Feet" (2 Tim.) (O)
　　　　　　H-3　Hbl-66; Chr-89
　　　　　　V-7　p. 15 Vocal Solo
2027　"Now Praise the Hidden God of Love" (Joel)
　　　　　　H-3　Chr-200; Org-45
357　"Just As I Am, Without One Plea" (Luke)
　　　　　　H-3　Chr-120; Org-186
2131　"Humble Thyself in the Sight of the Lord" (Luke)
　　　　　　SP223
2279　"The Trees of the Field" (Ps.) (C)

Additional Hymn Suggestions

67　"We, Thy People, Praise Thee" (Joel)
108　"God Hath Spoken by the Prophets" (Joel)
500　"Spirit of God, Descend Upon My Heart" (Joel)
538　"Wind Who Makes All Winds That Blow" (Joel)
541　"See How Great a Flame Aspires" (Joel)
543　"O Breath of Life" (Joel)
729　"O Day of Peace That Dimly Shines" (Joel)
2120　"Spirit, Spirit of Gentleness" (Joel)
2213　"Healer of Our Every Ill" (Joel)
2234　"Lead On, O Cloud of Presence" (Joel)
2246　"Deep in the Shadows of the Past" (Joel)
3145　"Breath of God, Breath of Peace" (Joel)
126　"Sing Praise to God Who Reigns Above" (Ps.)
77　"How Great Thou Art" (Ps., Luke)
128　"He Leadeth Me" (2 Tim.)
133　"Leaning on the Everlasting Arms" (2 Tim.)
505　"When Our Confidence Is Shaken" (2 Tim.)
507　"Through It All" (2 Tim.)
553　"And Are We Yet Alive" (2 Tim.)
2211　"Faith Is Patience in the Night" (2 Tim.)
407　"Close to Thee" (2 Tim., Luke)
479　"Jesus, Lover of My Soul" (2 Tim., Luke)
121　"There's a Wideness in God's Mercy" (Luke)
124　"Seek the Lord" (Luke)
351　"Pass Me Not, O Gentle Savior" (Luke)
355　"Depth of Mercy" (Luke)
3097　"Depth of Mercy" (Luke)
382　"Have Thine Own Way, Lord" (Luke)
402　"Lord, I Want to Be a Christian" (Luke)
410　"I Want a Principle Within" (Luke)
419　"I Am Thine, O Lord" (Luke)
2062　"The Lily of the Valley" (Luke)
2134　"Forgive Us, Lord" ("Perdon, Señor") (Luke)
3101　"Love Lifted Me" (Luke)

Additional Contemporary Suggestions

M26　"The Power of Your Love" (Joel)
WS3008　"Open the Eyes of My Heart" (Joel)
　　　　　　M57
S2002　"I Will Call Upon the Lord" (Joel)
　　　　　　SP224

S2086　"Open Our Eyes, Lord" (Joel)
　　　　　　SP199
S2040　"Awesome God" (Ps.)
　　　　　　SP11
SP158　"The Battle Belongs to the Lord" (2 Tim.)
S2163　"He Who Began a Good Work in You" (2 Tim.)
　　　　　　SP180
WS3042　"Shout to the North" (2 Tim.)
　　　　　　M99
M53　"Let It Be Said of Us" (2 Tim.)
M87　"Let the Peace of God Reign" (2 Tim.)
M34　"I Will Never Be (the Same Again)" (2 Tim., Luke)
S2162　"Grace Alone" (2 Tim., Luke)
　　　　　　M100
UM394　"Something Beautiful" (Luke)
S2151　"I'm So Glad Jesus Lifted Me" (Luke)
S2275　"Kyrie" (Luke)
WS3099　"Falling on My Knees" ("Hungry") (Luke)
　　　　　　M155

Vocal Solos

"Rejoice Greatly, O Daughter of Zion" (Joel)
　　V-2
"Spirit of God" (Joel)
　　V-8　　　p. 170
"Stan'in' In De Need of Prayer" (Luke)
　　V-7　　　p. 40

Anthems

"Guide My Feet" (2 Tim.)
Jacqueline B. Hairston; Fred Bock JG2287
SATB, *a cappella*

"O, My God, Bestow Thy Tender Mercy" (Luke)
Pergolesi/Hopson; Carl Fischer CM7974
Two-part mixed, keyboard

Other Suggestions

Visuals:
　　O　　Rain, thresh/grain, wine/oil, locusts, plenty,
　　　　　　people, manacles, blood/fire/smoke, eclipse, red
　　　　　　moon
　　P　　Praise, worship, sea/mountain, storm/calm,
　　　　　　sunrise/set, rain, river, harvest/wagon tracks, hills,
　　　　　　flocks
　　E　　Spilled wine, boxing gloves, open Bible, scales
　　G　　Two men (proud/humble), hands (raised/beating
　　　　　　chest), Luke 18:14*b*
　　Reformation Sunday: Luther, reformers, 95 theses
All Saints scriptures and ideas may be used today or next
　　week.
Greeting: BOW406 (Joel)
Opening Prayer: WSL37. Holy Spirit, rain down (Joel)
Hymn of Invocation: BOW223. "O Holy Spirit" (Joel)
Prayer of Confession: BOW490 (Luke)
Prayer: BOW315 or WSL38 (Joel)
Prayer: UM401. For Holiness of Heart (Luke)
Response: S2275 or S2277. "Lord, Have Mercy" (Luke)
Prayer: WSL190. Make my life a libation (2 Tim.)
Sung Benediction: BOW218. "Benediction for Pentecost"
　　(Joel)

25

NOVEMBER 1, 2013 (OR NOVEMBER 3, 2013)

Daniel 7:1-3, 15-18

[1]In the first year of King Belshazzar of Babylon, Daniel had a dream and visions of his head as he lay in bed. Then he wrote down the dream: [2]I, Daniel, saw in my vision by night the four winds of heaven stirring up the great sea, [3]and four great beasts came up out of the sea, different from one another. . . .

[15]As for me, Daniel, my spirit was troubled within me, and the visions of my head terrified me. [16]I approached one of the attendants to ask him the truth concerning all this. So he said that he would disclose to me the interpretation of the matter: [17]"As for these four great beasts, four kings shall arise out of the earth. [18]But the holy ones of the Most High shall receive the kingdom and possess the kingdom forever—forever and ever."

Psalm 149

[1] Praise the LORD!
Sing to the LORD a new song,
     his praise in the assembly of the faithful.
[2] Let Israel be glad in its Maker;
     let the children of Zion rejoice in their King.
[3] Let them praise his name with dancing,
     making melody to him with tambourine and lyre.
[4] For the LORD takes pleasure in his people;
     he adorns the humble with victory.
[5] Let the faithful exult in glory;
     let them sing for joy on their couches.
[6] Let the high praises of God be in their throats
     and two-edged swords in their hands,
[7] to execute vengeance on the nations and
     punishment on the peoples,
[8] to bind their kings with fetters and their nobles
     with chains of iron,
[9] to execute on them the judgment decreed.
     This is glory for all his faithful ones.
     Praise the LORD!

Ephesians 1:11-23

[11]In Christ we have also obtained an inheritance, having been destined according to the purpose of him who accomplishes all things according to his counsel and will, [12]so that we, who were the first to set our hope on Christ, might live for the praise of his glory. [13]In him you also, when you had heard the word of truth, the gospel of your salvation, and had believed in him, were marked with the seal of the promised Holy Spirit;[14]this is the pledge of our inheritance towards redemption as God's own people, to the praise of his glory.

[15]I have heard of your faith in the Lord Jesus and your love toward all the saints, and for this reason [16]I do not cease to give thanks for you as I remember you in my prayers. [17]I pray that the God of our Lord Jesus Christ, the Father of glory, may give you a spirit of wisdom and revelation as you come to know him, [18]so that, with the eyes of your heart enlightened, you may know what is the hope to which he has called you, what are the riches of his glorious inheritance among the saints, [19]and what is the immeasurable greatness of his power for us who believe, according to the working of his great power. [20]God put this power to work in Christ when he raised him from the dead and seated him at his right hand in the heavenly places, [21]far above all rule and authority and power and dominion, and above every name that is named, not only in this age but also in the age to come. [22]And he has put all things under his feet and has made him the head over all things for the church, [23]which is his body, the fullness of him who fills all in all.

Luke 6:20-31

[20] Then he looked up at his disciples and said:
     "Blessed are you who are poor,
          for yours is the kingdom of God.
[21] "Blessed are you who are hungry now,
          for you will be filled.
     "Blessed are you who weep now,
          for you will laugh.
[22] "Blessed are you when people hate you, and when they exclude you, revile you, and defame you on account of the Son of Man. [23]Rejoice on that day and leap for joy, for surely your reward is great in heaven; for that is what their ancestors did to the prophets.
[24] "But woe to you who are rich,
          for you have received your consolation.
[25] "Woe to you who are full now,
          for you will be hungry.
     "Woe to you who are laughing now,
          for you will mourn and weep.
[26] "Woe to you when all speak well of you, for that is what their ancestors did to the false prophets.
[27] "But I say to you that listen, Love your enemies, do good to those who hate you, [28]bless those who curse you, pray for those who abuse you. [29]If anyone strikes you on the cheek, offer the other also; and from anyone who takes away your coat do not withhold even your shirt.[30]Give to everyone who begs from you; and if anyone takes away your goods, do not ask for them again. [31]Do to others as you would have them do to you."

COLOR: WHITE

ALL SAINTS DAY

Primary Hymns and Songs for the Day

61	"Come, Thou Almighty King" (Dan.) (O)
	H-3 Hbl-28, 49, 53; Chr-56; Desc-57; Org-63
	S-1 #185-186. Descant and harmonization
368	"My Hope Is Built" (Eph.)
	H-3 Chr-191
	S-2 #171-172. Trumpet and vocal descants
2220	"We Are God's People" (Eph.)
2283	"For All the Saints" (Eph., Luke)
	H-3 Chr-200; Org-45
2155	"Blest Are They" (Luke)
711	"For All the Saints" (Dan., Eph.) (C)
	H-3 Hbl-58; Chr-65; Org-152
	S-1 #314-318. Various treatments

Additional Hymn Suggestions

139	"Praise to the Lord, the Almighty" (Dan., Ps.) (O)
149	"Cantemos al Señor" ("Let's Sing Unto the Lord") (Ps.)
2045	"Sing a New Song to the Lord" (Ps.)
3010	"Sing of the Lord's Goodness" (Ps., Luke)
709	"Come, Let Us Join Our Friends Above" (Eph.)
178	"Hope of the World" (Eph.)
2147	"There Are Some Things I May Not Know" (Eph.)
2261	"Life-Giving Bread" (Eph., Communion)
2269	"Come, Share the Lord" (Eph., Communion)
3035	"Bless Christ Through Whom All Things Are Made" (Eph., All Saints)
3140	"Give Me Jesus" (Eph., All Saints)
142	"If Thou But Suffer God to Guide Thee" (Eph., Luke)
519	"Lift Every Voice and Sing" (Eph., Luke)
710	"Faith of Our Fathers" (Eph., Luke)
520	"Nobody Knows the Trouble I See" (Luke)
529	"How Firm a Foundation" (Luke)
728	"Come Sunday" (Luke)
2019	"Holy" ("Santo") (Luke)
2219	"Goodness Is Stronger Than Evil" (Luke)
2042	"How Lovely, Lord, How Lovely" (All Saints)
2221	"In Unity We Lift Our Song" (All Saints)
2246	"Deep in the Shadows of the Past" (All Saints)
2268	"As We Gather at Your Table" (All Saints, Communion)
708	"Rejoice in God's Saints" (All Saints)
712	"I Sing a Song of the Saints of God" (All Saints)
614	"For the Bread Which You Have Broken" (All Saints, Communion)

Additional Contemporary Suggestions

UM171	"There's Something About That Name" (Dan.) SP89
M63	"I Could Sing of Your Love Forever" (Ps.)
S2028	"Clap Your Hands" (Ps.)
S2144	"Someone Asked the Question" (Ps., All Saints)
S2270	"I Will Enter" ("He Has Made Me Glad") (Ps.) SP168
SP23	"Sing Unto the Lord a New Song" (Ps.)
M46	"I Will Celebrate" (Ps.) SP147
M59	"Let Everything That Has Breath" (Ps.)
S2163	"He Who Began a Good Work in You" (Eph.) SP180

WS3008	"Open the Eyes of My Heart" (Eph.) M57
WS3105	"In Christ Alone" (Eph.) M138
M77	"Above All" (Eph.)
WS3023	"Forever" (Eph.) M68
S2036	"Give Thanks" (Luke) SP170
WS3187	"We Fall Down" (All Saints) M66

Vocal Solos

"In Bright Mansions Above" (All Saints)
  V-4   p. 39
"Borning Cry" (All Saints)
  V-5(1)   p. 10
"How Long Train Been Gone" (All Saints)
  V-7   p. 17

Anthems

"Beatitudes" (Luke)
Bob Chilcott; Oxford 9780193355477
SATB, organ

"Clouds of Witnesses Surround Us" (All Saints)
Robert A. Hobby; MorningStar 50-5205
SATB, organ, opt. brass quartet, timpani

Other Suggestions

Visuals:

O	Storm, bed, dreamscape, 4 beasts, terror, 4 crowns
P	Praise, new song, assembly, dance, instruments
E	Will, Christ, Bible, seal, flames/dove, jewelry box
G	Feeding/poor, smile through tears, leaping, prayer, turned cheek, shirt/coat, giving, warning

All Saints Day: Pictures of deceased members
Affirmation of Faith: WS83 (Luke, All Saints)
Prayer: UM713 or BOW415 or WSL44 (All Saints)
Prayer: WS200. "Show us, good Lord" (Luke)
Litany: BOW548. On the Anniversary of a Death (All Saints)
Canticle: UM652. "Canticle of Remembrance (Eph.)
Litany: WS49. For rebirth and resilience" (Luke, All Saints)
Offering Prayer: WS129. Blessed one, we discover (Luke)
Response: BOW219. "Beloved, Now We Are the Saints" (All Saints)
Great Thanksgiving for All Saints: BOW74-75.
Closing Prayer: WSL46. May God, who has given (All Saints)
Benediction: WSL167. Go! Never stop going out (Luke)

NOVEMBER 3, 2013

Habakkuk 1:1-4; 2:1-4

1 The oracle that the prophet Habakkuk saw.
2 O LORD, how long shall I cry for help,
    and you will not listen?
    Or cry to you "Violence!"
    and you will not save?
3 Why do you make me see wrong-doing
    and look at trouble?
    Destruction and violence are before me;
    strife and contention arise.
4 So the law becomes slack
    and justice never prevails.
    The wicked surround the righteous—
    therefore judgment comes forth perverted.
. . . .
2 1I will stand at my watchpost,
    and station myself on the rampart;
    I will keep watch to see what he will say to me,
    and what he will answer concerning my complaint.
2 Then the LORD answered me and said:
    Write the vision;
    make it plain on tablets,
    so that a runner may read it.
3 For there is still a vision for the appointed time;
    it speaks of the end, and does not lie.
    If it seems to tarry, wait for it;
    it will surely come, it will not delay.
4 Look at the proud!
    Their spirit is not right in them,
    but the righteous live by their faith.

Psalm 119:137-144

137 You are righteous, O LORD,
    and your judgments are right.
138 You have appointed your decrees in righteousness
    and in all faithfulness.
139 My zeal consumes me
    because my foes forget your words.
140 Your promise is well tried,
    and your servant loves it.
141 I am small and despised,
    yet I do not forget your precepts.
142 Your righteousness is an everlasting righteousness,
    and your law is the truth.
143 Trouble and anguish have come upon me,
    but your commandments are my delight.
144 Your decrees are righteous forever;
    give me understanding that I may live.

2 Thessalonians 1:1-4, 11-12

1Paul, Silvanus, and Timothy, To the church of the Thessalonians in God our Father and the Lord Jesus Christ:

2Grace to you and peace from God our Father and the Lord Jesus Christ.

3We must always give thanks to God for you, brothers and sisters, as is right, because your faith is growing abundantly, and the love of everyone of you for one another is increasing. 4Therefore we ourselves boast of you among the churches of God for your steadfastness and faith during all your persecutions and the afflictions that you are enduring. . . .

11To this end we always pray for you, asking that our God will make you worthy of his call and will fulfill by his power every good resolve and work of faith, 12so that the name of our Lord Jesus may be glorified in you, and you in him, according to the grace of our God and the Lord Jesus Christ.

Luke 19:1-10

1He entered Jericho and was passing through it. 2A man was there named Zacchaeus; he was a chief tax collector and was rich. 3He was trying to see who Jesus was, but on account of the crowd he could not, because he was short in stature. 4So he ran ahead and climbed a sycamore tree to see him, because he was going to pass that way. 5When Jesus came to the place, he looked up and said to him, "Zacchaeus, hurry and come down; for I must stay at your house today." 6So he hurried down and was happy to welcome him. 7All who saw it began to grumble and said, "He has gone to be the guest of one who is a sinner." 8Zacchaeus stood there and said to the Lord, "Look, half of my possessions, Lord, I will give to the poor; and if I have defrauded anyone of anything, I will pay back four times as much." 9Then Jesus said to him, "Today salvation has come to this house, because he too is a son of Abraham. 10For the Son of Man came to seek out and to save the lost."

COLOR: GREEN   **24th SUNDAY AFTER PENTECOST**

Primary Hymns and Songs for the Day

616   "Come, Sinners, to the Gospel Feast" (Luke) (O)
451   "Be Thou My Vision" (Hab.)
       H-3   Hbl-15, 48; Chr-36; Org-153
       S-1   #319. Arr. for organ/voices in canon
2150   "Lord, Be Glorified" (2 Thess.)
       SP196
591   "Rescue the Perishing" (Luke)
419   "I Am Thine, O Lord" (Luke) (C)

Additional Hymn Suggestions

505   "When Our Confidence Is Shaken" (Hab.)
534   "Be Still, My Soul" (Hab.)
730   "O Day of God, Draw Nigh" (Hab.)
726   "O Holy City, Seen of John" (Hab.)
727   "O What Their Joy and Their Glory Must Be" (Hab.)
2062   "The Lily of the Valley" (Hab.)
2255   "In the Singing" (Ps.)
107   "La Palabra Del Señor Es Recta" ("Righteous and Just Is the Word of the Lord") (Ps.)
695   "O Lord, May Church and Home Combine" (Ps.)
525   "We'll Understand It Better By and By" (Hab., 2 Thess.)
654   "How Blest Are They Who Trust" (2 Thess.)
662   "Stand Up and Bless the Lord" (2 Thess.)
2240   "One God and Father of Us All" (2 Thess.)
396   "O Jesus, I Have Promised" (2 Thess., Luke)
256   "We Would See Jesus" (Luke)
262   "Heal Me, Hands of Jesus" (Luke)
273   "Jesus' Hands Were Kind Hands" (Luke)
339   "Come, Sinners, to the Gospel Feast" (Luke)
340   "Come, Ye Sinners, Poor and Needy" (Luke)
378   "Amazing Grace" (Luke)
382   "Have Thine Own Way, Lord" (Luke)
383   "This Is a Day of New Beginnings" (Luke, Communion)
86   "Come, O Thou Traveler Unknown" (Luke)
389   "Freely, Freely" (Luke)
398   "Jesus Calls Us" (Luke)
399   "Take My Life, and Let It Be" (Luke)
434   "Cuando El Pobre" ("When the Poor Ones") (Luke)
617   "I Come with Joy" (Luke, Communion)
2149   "Living for Jesus" (Luke)
2182   "When God Restored our Common Life" (Luke)
3095   "Somebody's Knockin' at Your Door" (Luke)
3143   "Jesus, You Are the New Day" (Luke)

Additional Contemporary Suggestions

UM601   "Thy Word Is a Lamp" (Ps.)
       SP183
M38   "I Want to Know You" ("In the Secret") (Ps.)
S2161   "To Know You More" (Ps.)
M63   "I Could Sing of Your Love Forever" (Ps.)
S2165   "Cry of My Heart" (Ps., Luke)
       M39
S2163   "He Who Began a Good Work in You" (2 Thess.)
       SP180
S2150   "Lord, Be Glorified" (2 Thess.)
       SP196
M13   "Be Glorified" (2 Thess.)

M152   "Be Glorified" (2 Thess.)
M91   "Take My Life" (2 Thess., Luke)
S2036   "Give Thanks" (2 Thess., Luke)
       SP170
S2151   "I'm So Glad Jesus Lifted Me" (Luke)
UM394   "Something Beautiful" (Luke)
M34   "I Will Never Be (the Same Again)" (Luke)
M150   "Everyday" (Luke)
WS3042   "Shout to the North" (Luke)
       M99
WS3104   "Amazing Grace" ("My Chains Are Gone") (Luke)
       M205
WS3187   "We Fall Down" (Luke, All Saints)
       M66

Vocal Solos

"Be Thou My Vision" (Hab.)
     V-6   p. 13
"Here I Am" (1 Thess., Luke)
     V-11   p. 19
"Where Shall My Wondering Soul Begin?" (Luke)
     V-1   p. 59

Anthems

"Be Thou My Vision" (Hab.)
arr. Heather Sorenson; Shawnee Press 35028337
SATB, piano, opt. instrumental parts

"Zacchaeus" (Luke)
John D. Horman; Choristers Guild CGA1073
Unison/two-part, piano

Other Suggestions

Visuals:
    O   Praying hands, overturned scales, tower, tablets
    P   Open Bible, ten commandments
    E   Letter, embrace, love, persecution, prayer
    G   Tax form, small man (running, climbing tree), 1/2, 4x, Jesus, Luke 19:9a
All Saints scriptures and ideas may be used today or last week.
Greeting: WSL22. From Bethlehem to Nazareth (Luke)
Opening Prayer: WSL15. O God, you delight not (Luke)
Prayer of Confession: BOW489 or WSL189 (Luke)
Prayer: BOW525. For Wisdom (Hab., Ps.)
Prayer for Illumination: WSL71. Eternal God, in the reading (Ps.)
Offertory Prayer: WSL133. God of Grace and Glory (Luke)
Closing Prayer: WSL163. From where we are are (Luke)

NOVEMBER 10, 2013

Haggai 1:15b–2:9

[15]In the second year of King Darius,

[2] [1]in the seventh month, on the twenty-first day of the month, the word of the LORD came by the prophet Haggai, saying: [2]Speak now to Zerubbabel son of Shealtiel, governor of Judah, and to Joshua son of Jehozadak, the high priest, and to the remnant of the people, and say, [3]Who is left among you that saw this house in its former glory? How does it look to you now? Is it not in your sight as nothing? [4]Yet now take courage, O Zerubbabel, says the LORD; take courage, O Joshua, son of Jehozadak, the high priest; take courage, all you people of the land, says the LORD; work, for I am with you, says the LORD of hosts, [5]according to the promise that I made you when you came out of Egypt. My spirit abides among you; do not fear. [6]For thus says the LORD of hosts: Once again, in a little while, I will shake the heavens and the earth and the sea and the dry land; [7]and I will shake all the nations, so that the treasure of all nations shall come, and I will fill this house with splendor, says the LORD of hosts. [8]The silver is mine, and the gold is mine, says the LORD of hosts. [9]The latter splendor of this house shall be greater than the former, says the LORD of hosts; and in this place I will give prosperity, says the LORD of hosts.

Psalm 145:1-5, 17-21

[1] I will extol you, my God and King,
      and bless your name forever and ever.
[2] Every day I will bless you,
      and praise your name forever and ever.
[3] Great is the LORD, and greatly to be praised;
      his greatness is unsearchable.
[4] One generation shall laud your works to another,
      and shall declare your mighty acts.
[5] On the glorious splendor of your majesty,
      and on your wondrous works, I will meditate.
. . . .
[17] The LORD is just in all his ways,
      and kind in all his doings.
[18] The LORD is near to all who call on him,
      to all who call on him in truth.
[19] He fulfills the desire of all who fear him;
      he also hears their cry, and saves them.
[20] The LORD watches over all who love him,
      but all the wicked he will destroy.
[21] My mouth will speak the praise of the LORD,
      and all flesh will bless his holy name forever and ever.

2 Thessalonians 2:1-5, 13-17

[1]As to the coming of our Lord Jesus Christ and our being gathered together to him, we beg you, brothers and sisters, [2]not to be quickly shaken in mind or alarmed, either by spirit or by word or by letter, as though from us, to the effect that the day of the Lord is already here. [3]Let no one deceive you in any way; for that day will not come unless the rebellion comes first and the lawless one is revealed, the one destined for destruction. [4]He opposes and exalts himself above every so-called god or object of worship, so that he takes his seat in the temple of God, declaring himself to be God. [5]Do you not remember that I told you these things when I was still with you? . . .

[13]But we must always give thanks to God for you, brothers and sisters beloved by the Lord, because God chose you as the first fruits for salvation through sanctification by the Spirit and through belief in the truth. [14]For this purpose he called you through our proclamation of the good news, so that you may obtain the glory of our Lord Jesus Christ. [15]So then, brothers and sisters, stand firm and hold fast to the traditions that you were taught by us, either by word of mouth or by our letter.

[16]Now may our Lord Jesus Christ himself and God our Father, who loved us and through grace gave us eternal comfort and good hope, [17]comfort your hearts and strengthen them in every good work and word.

Luke 20:27-38

[27]Some Sadducees, those who say there is no resurrection, came to him [28]and asked him a question, "Teacher, Moses wrote for us that if a man's brother dies, leaving a wife but no children, the man shall marry the widow and raise up children for his brother. [29]Now there were seven brothers; the first married, and died childless; [30]then the second [31]and the third married her, and so in the same way all seven died childless. [32]Finally the woman also died. [33]In the resurrection, therefore, whose wife will the woman be? For the seven had married her." [34]Jesus said to them, "Those who belong to this age marry and are given in marriage; [35]but those who are considered worthy of a place in that age and in the resurrection from the dead neither marry nor are given in marriage. [36]Indeed they cannot die anymore, because they are like angels and are children of God, being children of the resurrection. [37]And the fact that the dead are raised Moses himself showed, in the story about the bush, where he speaks of the Lord as the God of Abraham, the God of Isaac, and the God of Jacob. [38]Now he is God not of the dead, but of the living; for to him all of them are alive."

COLOR: GREEN
25th SUNDAY AFTER PENTECOST

Primary Hymns and Songs for the Day

103	"Immortal, Invisible, God Only Wise" (Hag., Luke)
	H-3 Hbl-15, 71; Chr-65; Desc-93; Org-135
	S-1 #300. Harmonization
374	"Standing on the Promises" (Hag., Luke) (O)
	H-3 Chr-177; Org-117
93	"Let All the World in Every Corner Sing" (Ps.)
2022	"Great Is the Lord" (Ps.)
	SP30
664	"Sent Forth by God's Blessing" (Luke) (C)
	H-3 Chr-125; Org-9
	S-1 #327. Descant

Additional Hymn Suggestions

3189	"There is a Higher Throne" (Hag., Luke)
698	"God of the Ages" (Hag., Luke)
719	"My Lord, What a Morning" (Hag., 2 Thess.)
196	"Come, Thou Long-Expected Jesus" (Hag.) (O)
644	"Jesus, Joy of Our Desiring" (Hag.)
731	"Glorious Things of Thee Are Spoken" (Hag.)
117	"O God, Our Help in Ages Past" (Hag., Ps.) (O)
124	"Seek the Lord" (Hag., Ps.)
66	"Praise, My Soul, the King of Heaven" (Ps.)
77	"How Great Thou Art" (Ps.)
2044	"My Gratitude Now Accept, O God" (Ps.)
2008	"Let All Things Now Living" (Ps., Luke)
2267	"Taste and See" (Ps., Communion)
2255	"In the Singing" (2 Thess., Communion)
407	"Close to Thee" (2 Thess.)
430	"O Master, Let Me Walk With Thee" (2 Thess.)
479	"Jesus, Lover of My Soul" (2 Thess.)
480	"O Love That Wilt Not Let Me Go" (2 Thess.)
529	"How Firm a Foundation" (2 Thess.)
521	"I Want Jesus to Walk With Me" (2 Thess.)
710	"Faith of Our Fathers" (2 Thess.)
2123	"Loving Spirit" (2 Thess.)
2149	"Living for Jesus" (2 Thess., Luke)
315	"Come, Ye Faithful, Raise the Strain" (2 Thess., Luke)
660	"God Is Here" (2 Thess., Luke)
116	"The God of Abraham Praise" (Luke)
141	"Children of the Heavenly Father" (Luke)
307	"Christ Is Risen" (Luke)
356	"Pues Si Vivimos" ("When We Are Living") (Luke)
702	"Sing with All the Saints in Glory" (Luke) (C)

Additional Contemporary Suggestions

WS3188	"Hosanna" (Hag.)
M126	"Famous One" (Hag.)
SP207	"Be Bold, Be Strong" (Hag.)
SP58	"Great Is the Lord Almighty!" (Ps.)
SP78	"I Extol You" (Ps.)
M46	"I Will Celebrate" (Ps.)
	SP147
S2037	"I Sing Praises to Your Name" (Ps.)
	SP27
UM63	"Blessed Be the Name" (Ps.)
S2070	"He Is Exalted" (Ps.)
	SP66
S2003	"Praise You" (Ps.)
	M84

WS3014	"You Are Good" (Ps.)
	M124
WS3026	"God Is Good All the Time" (Ps.)
	M45
S2088	"Lord, I Lift Your Name on High" (Ps., Luke)
	M2
S2150	"Lord, Be Glorified" (2 Thess.)
	SP196
S2036	"Give Thanks" (2 Thess.)
	SP170
S2258	"Sing Alleluia to the Lord" (2 Thess., Communion)
	SP93
S2266	"Here Is Bread, Here Is Wine" (2 Thess., Communion)
UM393	"Spirit of the Living God" (2 Thess., Luke)
	SP131
	S-1 #212 Vocal descant idea
M201	"Alive Forever, Amen" (Luke)

Vocal Solos

"Thus Saith the Lord" (Hag.)
    V-2
"Come, Thou Long-Expected Jesus" (Hag.)
    V-10   p. 11
"Patiently Have I Waited for the Lord" (Hag., 2 Thess.)
    V-4   p. 24

Anthems

"O Spirit All-Embracing" (Hag.)
arr. Richard Proulx; GIA G-5321
SATB, organ, opt. brass and timpani

"Children of the Heavenly Father" (Luke)
arr. Daniel Kallman; Morningstar 50-8431
SATB, organ and children's choir

Other Suggestions

Visuals:

O	Church in ruins/restored, Exodus, quake, sea/desert
P	Crown, teach/learn, light, natural wonders, praise
E	Second Coming, fruit, preaching, letter, 2 Thess. 2:16-17
G	Coffin, wedding, 7 brothers, bride, resurrection, children in white robes, burning bush, 20:38a

Today's gospel reading lends itself well to dramatic re-enactment. Ask eight youth to play the parts of seven husbands and one wife, as one other youth or adult reads the scripture.

Prayer: UM721 or BOW421. Christ the King (Hag., 2 Thess.)

Response: WS3007. Laudate Dominum (Sing, praise) (Ps.)

Prayer of Thanksgiving: BOW554 (Hag., 2 Thess.)

Response: BOW219. "Beloved, Now We Are the Saints" (Luke)

See additional ideas in *The Abingdon Worship Annual 2013*.

NOVEMBER 17, 2013

Isaiah 65:17-25

[17]For I am about to create new heavens and a new earth; the former things shall not be remembered or come to mind. [18]But be glad and rejoice forever in what I am creating; for I am about to create Jerusalem as a joy, and its people as a delight. [19]I will rejoice in Jerusalem, and delight in my people; no more shall the sound of weeping be heard in it, or the cry of distress. [20]No more shall there be in it an infant that lives but a few days, or an old person who does not live out a lifetime; for one who dies at a hundred years will be considered a youth, and one who falls short of a hundred will be considered accursed. [21]They shall build houses and inhabit them; they shall plant vineyards and eat their fruit. [22]They shall not build and another inhabit; they shall not plant and another eat; for like the days of a tree shall the days of my people be, and my chosen shall long enjoy the work of their hands. [23]They shall not labor in vain, or bear children for calamity; for they shall be offspring blessed by the LORD— and their descendants as well. [24]Before they call I will answer, while they are yet speaking I will hear. [25]The wolf and the lamb shall feed together, the lion shall eat straw like the ox; but the serpent—its food shall be dust! They shall not hurt or destroy on all my holy mountain, says the LORD.

Isaiah 12

You will say in that day: I will give thanks to you, O LORD, for though you were angry with me, your anger turned away, and you comforted me. [2]Surely God is my salvation; I will trust, and will not be afraid, for the LORD GOD is my strength and my might; he has become my salvation. [3]With joy you will draw water from the wells of salvation.

[4]And you will say in that day: Give thanks to the LORD, call on his name; make known his deeds among the nations; proclaim that his name is exalted. [5]Sing praises to the LORD, for he has done gloriously; let this be known in all the earth. [6]Shout aloud and sing for joy, O royal Zion, for great in your midst is the Holy One of Israel.

2 Thessalonians 3:6-13

[6]Now we command you, beloved, in the name of our Lord Jesus Christ, to keep away from believers who are living in idleness and not according to the tradition that they received from us. [7]For you yourselves know how you ought to imitate us; we were not idle when we were with you, [8]and we did not eat anyone's bread without paying for it; but with toil and labour we worked night and day, so that we might not burden any of you. [9]This was not because we do not have that right, but in order to give you an example to imitate. [10]For even when we were with you, we gave you this command: Anyone unwilling to work should not eat. [11]For we hear that some of you are living in idleness, mere busybodies, not doing any work. [12]Now such persons we command and exhort in the Lord Jesus Christ to do their work quietly and to earn their own living. [13]Brothers and sisters, do not be weary in doing what is right.

Luke 21:5-19

[5]When some were speaking about the temple, how it was adorned with beautiful stones and gifts dedicated to God, he said, [6]"As for these things that you see, the days will come when not one stone will be left upon another; all will be thrown down." [7]They asked him, "Teacher, when will this be, and what will be the sign that this is about to take place?" [8]And he said, "Beware that you are not led astray; for many will come in my name and say, 'I am he!' and, 'The time is near!' Do not go after them. [9]"When you hear of wars and insurrections, do not be terrified; for these things must take place first, but the end will not follow immediately." [10]Then he said to them, "Nation will rise against nation, and kingdom against kingdom; [11]there will be great earthquakes, and in various places famines and plagues; and there will be dreadful portents and great signs from heaven. [12]"But before all this occurs, they will arrest you and persecute you; they will hand you over to synagogues and prisons, and you will be brought before kings and governors because of my name. [13]This will give you an opportunity to testify. [14]So make up your minds not to prepare your defense in advance; [15]for I will give you words and a wisdom that none of your opponents will be able to withstand or contradict. [16]You will be betrayed even by parents and brothers, by relatives and friends; and they will put some of you to death. [17]You will be hated by all because of my name. [18]But not a hair of your head will perish. [19]By your endurance you will gain your souls."

COLOR: GREEN   **26th SUNDAY AFTER PENTECOST**

Primary Hymns and Songs for the Day
2284	"Joy in the Morning" (Isa. 65) (O)
729	"O Day of Peace That Dimly Shines" (Isa. 65, Luke)
2030	"The First Song of Isaiah" (Isa. 12)
706	"Soon and Very Soon" (2 Thess., Luke)
	S-2 #187. Piano arrangement
438	"Forth in Thy Name, O Lord" (2 Thess.) (C)
	H-3 Hbl-29, 57, 58; Chr-117; Desc-31; Org-31
	S-1 #100-103. Various treatments.

Additional Hymn Suggestions
2210	"Joy Comes with the Dawn" (Isa. 65)
2282	"I'll Fly Away" (Isa. 65)
383	"This Is a Day of New Beginnings" (Isa. 65)
725	"Arise, Shine Out, Your Light Has Come" (Isa. 65)
727	"O What Their Joy and Their Glory Must Be" (Isa. 65)
3157	"Come, Let us Dream" (Isa. 65)
426	"Behold a Broken World" (Isa. 65, Luke)
724	"On Jordan's Stormy Banks I Stand" (Isa. 65, Luke)
732	"Come, We That Love the Lord" (Isa. 65, Luke) (same text as 733)
733	"Marching to Zion" (Isa. 65, Luke) (O)
110	"A Mighty Fortress Is Our God" (Isa. 12) (O)
2279	"The Trees of the Field" (Isa. 12)
410	"I Want a Principle Within" (2 Thess.)
550	"Christ, from Whom All Blessings Flow" (2 Thess.)
3043	"You, Lord, Are Both Lamb and Shepherd" (2 Thess.)
3115	"Covenant Prayer" (2 Thess.)
377	"It Is Well With My Soul" (2 Thess., Luke)
413	"A Charge to Keep I Have" (2 Thess., Luke)
433	"All Who Love and Serve Your City" (2 Thess., Luke)
722	"I Want to Be Ready" (2 Thess., Luke)
2142	"Blessed Quietness" (2 Thess., Luke)
425	"O Crucified Redeemer" (Luke)
427	"Where Cross the Crowded Ways of Life" (Luke)
439	"We Utter Our Cry" (Luke)
450	"Creator of the Earth and Skies" (Luke)
463	"Lord, Speak to Me" (Luke)
694	"Come, Ye Thankful People, Come" (Luke)
717	"The Battle Hymn of the Republic" (Luke)
719	"My Lord, What a Morning" (Luke)
730	"O Day of God, Draw Nigh" (Luke) (C)

Additional Contemporary Suggestions
S2270	"I Will Enter" ("He Has Made Me Glad") (Isa. 65)
	SP168
UM171	"There's Something About That Name" (Isa. 65)
	SP89
WS3108	"Trading My Sorrows" (Isa. 65)
	M75
WS3186	"Days of Elijah" (Isa. 65)
	M139
M64	"Hear our Praises" (Isa. 65, Isa. 12)
S2144	"Someone Asked the Question" (Isa. 65, Isa. 12)
SP18	"I Exalt You" (Isa. 12)
SP45	"Be Exalted, O God" ("I Will Give Thanks") (Isa. 12)
S2070	"He Is Exalted" (Isa. 12)
	SP66

S2074	"Shout to the Lord" (Isa. 12)
	M16
S2195	"In the Lord I'll Be Ever Thankful" (Isa. 12)
SP181	"God Is the Strength of My Heart" (Isa. 12)
WS3040	"You Are My All in All" (Isa. 12)
	SP220
M164	"Good to Me" (Isa. 12)
M31	"I See the Lord" (Isa. 12, Luke)
WS3117	"Rule of Life" (2 Thess.)
S2192	"Freedom Is Coming" (Luke)
S2194	"O Freedom" (Luke)
SP158	"The Battle Belongs to the Lord" (Luke)
M17	"This Kingdom" (Luke)
M69	"Did You Feel the Mountains Tremble?" (Luke)
WS3188	"Hosanna" (Luke)

Vocal Solos
"I'm Goin' Home" (Isa., Luke)
   V-8   p. 325
"It Is Well with My Soul" (2 Thess., Luke)
   V-5(2)   p. 35
"My Lord, What a Mornin'" (Luke)
   V-7   p. 68

Anthems
"New Heaven and Earth" (Isa. 65)
Marty Haugen; GIA 5757
SATB, keyboard, opt. two C-instruments

"The First Song of Isaiah" (Isa. 12)
Jack Noble White; Belwin-Mills CMR 3347
SATB, keyboard (opt. youth choir, dance, guitar, handbells, and percussion)

Other Suggestions
Visuals:
O	Space/earth, joy, building, grapes, work, wolf/lamb
P	Worship, anger/comfort, arm, water/well, joy
E	Idleness, bread, work, food
G	Temple, toppled rock, Jesus, war, whip/chain,

Introit: S2271, BOW199. "Come! Come! Everybody Worship" ("Vengan Todos Adoremos") (Isa. 12)
Greeting: BOW453 (Isa.)
Opening Prayer: BOW460 (2 Thess.)
Canticle: UM734. "Canticle of Hope" (Isa., Luke)
Prayer of Confession: WSL90. "You asked for my hands" (2 Thess.)
Prayer: UM409. For Grace to Labor (2 Thess.)
Prayer: UM705. For Direction (2 Thess.)
Prayer of Thanksgiving: BOW555 (2 Thess.)

NOVEMBER 24, 2013

Jeremiah 23:1-6

[1]Woe to the shepherds who destroy and scatter the sheep of my pasture! says the LORD. [2]Therefore thus says the LORD, the God of Israel, concerning the shepherds who shepherd my people: It is you who have scattered my flock, and have driven them away, and you have not attended to them. So I will attend to you for your evil doings, says the LORD. [3]Then I myself will gather the remnant of my flock out of all the lands where I have driven them, and I will bring them back to their fold, and they shall be fruitful and multiply. [4]I will raise up shepherds over them who will shepherd them, and they shall not fear any longer, or be dismayed, nor shall any be missing, says the LORD.

[5]The days are surely coming, says the LORD, when I will raise up for David a righteous Branch, and he shall reign as king and deal wisely, and shall execute justice and righteousness in the land. [6]In his days Judah will be saved and Israel will live in safety. And this is the name by which he will be called: "The LORD is our righteousness."

Luke 1:68-79

[68] "Blessed be the Lord God of Israel,
　　for he has looked favorably on his people and redeemed them.
[69] He has raised up a mighty savior for us
　　in the house of his servant David,
[70] as he spoke through the mouth of his holy prophets from of old,
[71] that we would be saved from our enemies and from the hand of all who hate us.
[72] Thus he has shown the mercy promised to our ancestors,
　　and has remembered his holy covenant,
[73] the oath that he swore to our ancestor Abraham,
　　to grant us [74]that we, being rescued from the hands of our enemies,
　　might serve him without fear, [75]in holiness and righteousness
　　before him all our days.
[76] And you, child, will be called the prophet of the Most High;
　　for you will go before the Lord to prepare his ways,
[77] to give knowledge of salvation to his people
　　by the forgiveness of their sins.
[78] By the tender mercy of our God,
　　the dawn from on high will break upon us,
[79] to give light to those who sit in darkness and in the shadow of death,
　　to guide our feet into the way of peace."

Colossians 1:11-20

[11]May you be made strong with all the strength that comes from his glorious power, and may you be prepared to endure everything with patience, while joyfully [12]giving thanks to the Father, who has enabled you to share in the inheritance of the saints in the light. [13]He has rescued us from the power of darkness and transferred us into the kingdom of his beloved Son, [14]in whom we have redemption, the forgiveness of sins.

[15]He is the image of the invisible God, the firstborn of all creation; [16]for in him all things in heaven and on earth were created, things visible and invisible, whether thrones or dominions or rulers or powers—all things have been created through him and for him. [17]He himself is before all things, and in him all things hold together. [18]He is the head of the body, the church; he is the beginning, the firstborn from the dead, so that he might come to have first place in everything. [19]For in him all the fullness of God was pleased to dwell, [20]and through him God was pleased to reconcile to himself all things, whether on earth or in heaven, by making peace through the blood of his cross.

Luke 23:33-43

[33]When they came to the place that is called The Skull, they crucified Jesus there with the criminals, one on his right and one on his left. [34]Then Jesus said, "Father, forgive them; for they do not know what they are doing." And they cast lots to divide his clothing. [35]And the people stood by, watching; but the leaders scoffed at him, saying, "He saved others; let him save himself if he is the Messiah of God, his chosen one!" [36]The soldiers also mocked him, coming up and offering him sour wine, [37]and saying, "If you are the King of the Jews, save yourself!" [38]There was also an inscription over him, "This is the King of the Jews." [39]One of the criminals who were hanged there kept deriding him and saying, "Are you not the Messiah? Save yourself and us!" [40]But the other rebuked him, saying, "Do you not fear God, since you are under the same sentence of condemnation? [41]And we indeed have been condemned justly, for we are getting what we deserve for our deeds, but this man has done nothing wrong." [42]Then he said, "Jesus, remember me when you come into your kingdom." [43]He replied, "Truly I tell you, today you will be with me in Paradise."

COLOR: WHITE   REIGN OF CHRIST / CHRIST THE KING SUNDAY

Primary Hymns and Songs for the Day

103   "Immortal, Invisible, God Only Wise" (Col.) (O)
        H-3 Hbl-15, 71; Chr-65; Desc-93; Org-135
        S-1 #300. Harmonization
188   "Christ Is the World's Light" (Luke 1, Col,)
        H-3 Hbl-57; Chr-64; Desc-22; Org-20
        S-1 #64. Descant
209   "Blessed Be the God of Israel" (Luke 1)
488   "Jesus, Remember Me" (Luke)
M77   "Above All" (Luke, Christ the King)
157   "Jesus Shall Reign" (Christ the King) (C)
        H-3 Hbl-29, 57, 58; Chr-117; Desc-31; Org-31
        S-1 #100-103. Various treatments

Additional Hymn Suggestions

2177   "Wounded World that Cries for Healing" (Jer.)
2183   "Unsettled World" (Jer.)
2184   "Sent Out in Jesus' Name" (Jer.)
211   "O Come, O Come, Emmanuel" (Luke 1)
2172   "We Are Called" (Luke 1, Christ the King)
2204   "Light of the World" (Luke 1)
2208   "Guide My Feet" (Luke 1)
2214   "Lead Me, Guide Me" (Luke 1)
2236   "Gather Us In" (Luke 1)
2255   "In the Singing" (Luke 1, Communion)
3043   "You, Lord, Are Both Lamb and Shepherd" (Luke
        1, Col.)
3035   "Bless Christ Through Whom All Things are Made"
        (Col.)
377   "It Is Well with My Soul" (Col.)
2145   "I've Got Peace Like a River" (Col.)
2181   "We Need a Faith" (Col.)
2195   "In the Lord I'll Be Ever Thankful" (Col.)
2220   "We Are God's People" (Col.)
2261   "Life-Giving Bread" (Col., Communion)
2269   "Come, Share the Lord" (Col., Communion)
2142   "Blessed Quietness" (Col., Luke 23)
296   "Sing, My Tongue, the Glorious Battle" (Col.,
        Luke 23)
297   "Beneath the Cross of Jesus" (Col., Luke 23)
301   "Jesus, Keep Me Near the Cross" (Col., Luke 23)
370   "Victory in Jesus" (Col., Luke 23)
325   "Hail, Thou Once Despised Jesus" (Luke 23)
2106   "When Jesus Wept" (Luke 23)
180   "Jesus Es Mi Rey Soberano" (Christ the King)
181   "Ye Servants of God" (Christ the King)
327   "Crown Him with Many Crowns" (Christ the King)

Additional Contemporary Suggestions

S2235   "We Are Marching" ("Siyahamba") (Luke 1)
S2266   "Here Is Bread, Here Is Wine" (Luke 1,
        Communion)
S2173   "Shine, Jesus, Shine" (Luke 1)
        SP142
M19   "Shine on Us" (Luke 1)
WS3177 "Here I Am to Worship" (Luke 1, Christ the King)
        M116
WS3032 "Across the Lands" (Col., Christ the King)
S2281   "May You Run and Not Be Weary" (Col.)
S2113   "Lamb of God" (Luke)
WS3085 "The Power of the Cross" (Luke, Christ the King)
        M222

SP64   "Our God Reigns" (Luke, Christ the King)
M21   "Blessing, Honour, Glory" (Luke, Christ the King)
M22   "Crown Him King of Kings" (Luke, Christ the
        King)
M24   "Jesus, We Crown You with Praise" (Luke)
S2088   "Lord, I Lift Your Name on High" (Luke, Christ the
        King)
        M2
S2040   "Awesome God" (Christ the King)
        SP11
S2063   "You Are Worthy" ("Eres Digno") (Christ the King)
S2069   "All Hail King Jesus" (Christ the King)
        SP63
S2075   "King of Kings" (Christ the King)
        SP94
S2091   "The King of Glory Comes" (Christ the King)

Vocal Solos

"Rejoice, The Lord Is King" (Christ the King)
        V-1   p. 66
"Ride On, Jesus" (Christ the King)
        V-7   p. 8
"King of Glory, King of Peace" (Christ the King)
        V-9   p. 24
"Holy is the Lamb" (Luke, Christ the King)
        V-5(1)   p. 5

Anthems

"There Shall a Star Come Out of Jacob" (Jer.)
Felix Mendelssohn; Schmitt, Hall, & McCreary SCHCH 1903
SATB, keyboard

"Sizohamba Naye (We Will Walk with God)" (Luke 1)
arr. Terry Taylor; Choristers Guild CGA-1250
Unison choir, opt. SATB, piano, opt. percussion

Other Suggestions

Visuals:
O   Scattered/herding sheep, today's shepherds,
        branch
P   Christus Rex, rescue, service, child, dawn, feet
E   Glory, joy, light/dark, rescue, creation, Christ
G   Skull, blood/lots/cross/clothes, INRI, wine,
        Luke 23:42
Christ the King: Crown, Christus Rex
Greeting: BOW456 (Col.) or BOW451 (Christ the King)
Canticle: UM205 (Col.) or UM208 (Luke 1)
Affirmation of Faith: WS76. "We believe in one God" (Col.)
Sung Confession: WS3084. "O Christ, You Hang upon a
        Cross" (Luke 23)
Prayer of Confession: BOW476 (Luke 1, Col.)
Prayer: UM466. An Invitation to Christ (Luke, Christ the
        King)
Prayer: UM721 or BOW421 or BOW511 (Christ the King)
Prayers: BOW506, 510, 522, 524, and 529 (Col.)
Prayer: WSL15. O God, you delight not in pomp (Luke 1)
Prayer: WSL34. Enlighten our hearts (Col.)
Prayers of the People: WSL26. Jesus, remember us (Luke 23)

NOVEMBER 28, 2013

Deuteronomy 26:1-11

[1]When you have come into the land that the LORD your God is giving you as an inheritance to possess, and you possess it, and settle in it, [2]you shall take some of the first of all the fruit of the ground, which you harvest from the land that the LORD your God is giving you, and you shall put it in a basket and go to the place that the LORD your God will choose as a dwelling for his name. [3]You shall go to the priest who is in office at that time, and say to him, "Today I declare to the LORD your God that I have come into the land that the LORD swore to our ancestors to give us." [4]When the priest takes the basket from your hand and sets it down before the altar of the LORD your God, [5]you shall make this response before the LORD your God: "A wandering Aramean was my ancestor; he went down into Egypt and lived there as an alien, few in number, and there he became a great nation, mighty and populous. [6]When the Egyptians treated us harshly and afflicted us, by imposing hard labor on us, [7]we cried to the LORD, the God of our ancestors; the LORD heard our voice and saw our affliction, our toil, and our oppression. [8]The LORD brought us out of Egypt with a mighty hand and an outstretched arm, with a terrifying display of power, and with signs and wonders; [9]and he brought us into this place and gave us this land, a land flowing with milk and honey. [10]So now I bring the first of the fruit of the ground that you, O LORD, have given me." You shall set it down before the LORD your God and bow down before the LORD your God. [11]Then you, together with the Levites and the aliens who reside among you, shall celebrate with all the bounty that the LORD your God has given to you and to your house.

Psalm 100

[1] Make a joyful noise to the LORD, all the earth.
[2]   Worship the LORD with gladness;
          come into his presence with singing.
[3] Know that the LORD is God.
          It is he that made us, and we are his;
          we are his people, and the sheep of his pasture.
[4] Enter his gates with thanksgiving,
          and his courts with praise.
          Give thanks to him, bless his name.
[5] For the LORD is good;
          his steadfast love endures forever,
          and his faithfulness to all generations.

Philippians 4:4-9

[4]Rejoice in the Lord always; again I will say, Rejoice. [5]Let your gentleness be known to everyone. The Lord is near. [6]Do not worry about anything, but in everything by prayer and supplication with thanksgiving let your requests be made known to God. [7]And the peace of God, which surpasses all understanding, will guard your hearts and your minds in Christ Jesus.

[8]Finally, beloved, whatever is true, whatever is honorable, whatever is just, whatever is pure, whatever is pleasing, whatever is commendable, if there is any excellence and if there is anything worthy of praise, think about these things. [9]Keep on doing the things that you have learned and received and heard and seen in me, and the God of peace will be with you.

John 6:25-35

[25]When they found him on the other side of the sea, they said to him, "Rabbi, when did you come here?" [26]Jesus answered them, "Very truly, I tell you, you are looking for me, not because you saw signs, but because you ate your fill of the loaves. [27]Do not work for the food that perishes, but for the food that endures for eternal life, which the Son of Man will give you. For it is on him that God the Father has set his seal." [28]Then they said to him, "What must we do to perform the works of God?" [29]Jesus answered them, "This is the work of God, that you believe in him whom he has sent." [30]So they said to him, "What sign are you going to give us then, so that we may see it and believe you? What work are you performing? [31]Our ancestors ate the manna in the wilderness; as it is written, 'He gave them bread from heaven to eat.' " [32]Then Jesus said to them, "Very truly, I tell you, it was not Moses who gave you the bread from heaven, but it is my Father who gives you the true bread from heaven. [33]For the bread of God is that which comes down from heaven and gives life to the world." [34]They said to him, "Sir, give us this bread always." [35]Jesus said to them, "I am the bread of life. Whoever comes to me will never be hungry, and whoever believes in me will never be thirsty."

COLOR: GREEN

THANKSGIVING DAY

Primary Hymns and Songs for the Day

694 "Come, Ye Thankful People, Come" (Deut., Ps.)
(O)
        H-3 Hbl-54; Chr-58; Desc-94; Org-137
        S-1 #302-303. Harmonizations with descant

2270 "I Will Enter His Gates" (Ps.)
        SP168

75 "All People That on Earth Do Dwell" (Ps.)
        H-3 Hbl-45; Chr-24; Desc-84, 85; Org-107
        S-1 #257-259. Various treatments
        S-2 #140. Descant

160 "Rejoice, Ye Pure in Heart" (Phil.)
        H-3 Hbl-17, 90; Chr-166; Desc-73; Org-85
        S-1 #228. Descant

161 "Rejoice, Ye Pure in Heart" (Phil.)

127 "Guide Me, O Thou Great Jehovah" (Deut., John)
(C)
        H-3 Hbl-25, 51, 58; Chr-89; Desc-26; Org-23
        S-1 #76-77. Descant and harmonization

Additional Hymn Suggestions

100 "God, Whose Love Is Reigning o'er Us" (Deut.)
(O)
2234 "Lead On, O Cloud of Presence" (Deut.) (O)
2238 "In the Midst of New Dimensions" (Deut., Advent)
87 "What Gift Can We Bring" (Deut.)
2009 "O God Beyond All Praising" (Deut.)
3009 "Praise God for This Holy Ground" (Deut.,
Thanksgiving)
102 "Now Thank We All Our God" (Ps.)
2274 "Come, All You People" ("Uyai Mose") (Ps.)
526 "What a Friend We Have in Jesus" (Phil.)
715 "Rejoice, the Lord Is King" (Phil.)
716 "Rejoice, the Lord Is King" (Phil.)
2197 "Lord of All Hopefulness" (Phil.)
2212 "My Life Flows On" (Phil., Thanksgiving)
2262 "Let Us Offer to the Father" (Phil., Thanksgiving)
2255 "In the Singing" (Phil., Communion)
3048 "View the Present through the Promise" (Phil.,
Advent)
2218 "You Are Mine" (Phil., John)
2060 "God the Sculptor of the Mountains" (John)
2204 "Light of the World" (John, Advent)
2062 "The Lily of the Valley" (John, Thanksgiving)
2236 "Gather Us In" (John, Thanksgiving)
563 "Father, We Thank You" (John, Thanksgiving)
565 "Father, We Thank You" (John, Thanksgiving)
628 "Eat This Bread" (John, Communion)
629 "You Satisfy the Hungry Heart" (John,
Communion)
631 "O Food to Pilgrims Given" (John, Communion)
2221 "In Unity We Lift Our Song" (John, Communion)
2261 "Life-Giving Bread" (John, Communion)
2008 "Let All Things Now Living" (Thanksgiving)
2061 "Praise Our God Above" (Thanksgiving)

Additional Contemporary Suggestions

S2031 "We Bring the Sacrifice of Praise" (Deut.)
        SP1
WS3002 "Blessed Be Your Name" (Deut., Thanksgiving)
WS3023 "Forever" (Deut., Ps.)
        M68

S2017 "Come, Rejoice in God" ("Jubilate") (Ps., Phil.)
WS3049 "Wait for the Lord" (Phil., Advent)
M177 "How Can I Keep from Singing" (Phil.)
WS3027 "Hallelujah" ("Your Love Is Amazing") (Ps., John)
        M118
M189 "Your Love, Oh Lord" (Ps., John)
UM186 "Alleluia" (John)
        SP108; S-2 #3-4
S2071 "Jesus, Name Above All Names" (John, Advent)
        SP76
S2132 "You Who Are Thirsty" (John)
        SP219
S2260 "Let Us Be Bread" (John, Communion)
UM628 "Eat This Bread" (John, Communion
WS3093 "Fill My Cup, Lord" (John, Communion)
        UM641 refrain; S-2 stanzas for soloist

Vocal Solos

"Now Thank We All Our God" (Thanksgiving)
        V-6   p. 8
"Life Indeed" (John, Communion)
        V-8   p. 271

Anthems

"What Gift Can We Bring" (Deut.)
Jane Marshall; Hope CY 3370
SSAB, keyboard

"O Be Joyful in God All Ye Lands" (Ps.)
Daniel Nelson; Paraclete Press PPM01205
SATB, piano

"Jubilate Deo" (Ps.)
Glenn L. Rudolph; Oxford 94.284
SATB, organ

Other Suggestions

Visuals:
  O   Produce, harvest, basket, altar, bricks, manacles
  P   Praise, singing, sheep, gates
  E   Rejoicing, Phil. 4:6, praying hands, Christ, Phil. 4:7
  G   Jesus teaching, loaves, John 6:27, manna, John 6:35
Call to Worship: WS3148. "There's a Spirit of L ove" (Phil.)
Opening Prayer: WSL55. "Almight God, you sustained"
(John)
Prayer of Confession: BOW485 or 494 (Deut., Thanksgiving)
Canticle: UM74. "Canticle of Thanksgiving (Ps.)
Thanksgiving Prayers: BOW418 and BOW507 or BOW557
Prayer: WSL203. God of all nations (Thanksgiving Day)
Communion Prayer: WSL81. Creator God, how lovely (John)
Offertory Prayer: WSL153. Exalted one, we joyfully rejoice
(Ps.)
Response: WS3007. Laudate Dominum (Sing, praise) (Ps.)
Great Thanksgiving for Thanksgiving Day: BOW76–77.
Prayer After Communion: WSL174. We have gathered (John)
Closing Prayer: WSL169. As you have been fed (John)

DECEMBER 1, 2013

UNITED METHODIST STUDENT SUNDAY

Isaiah 2:1-5

¹The word that Isaiah son of Amoz saw concerning Judah and Jerusalem.
² In days to come
the mountain of the Lord's house
shall be established as the highest of the mountains,
and shall be raised above the hills;
all the nations shall stream to it.
³ Many peoples shall come and say,
"Come, let us go up to the mountain of the LORD,
to the house of the God of Jacob;
that he may teach us his ways
and that we may walk in his paths."
For out of Zion shall go forth instruction,
and the word of the LORD from Jerusalem.
⁴ He shall judge between the nations,
and shall arbitrate for many peoples;
they shall beat their swords into plowshares,
and their spears into pruning hooks;
nation shall not lift up sword against nation,
neither shall they learn war any more.
⁵ O house of Jacob,
come, let us walk
in the light of the LORD!

Psalm 122

¹ I was glad when they said to me,
"Let us go to the house of the LORD!"
² Our feet are standing
within your gates, O Jerusalem.
³ Jerusalem—built as a city
that is bound firmly together.
⁴ To it the tribes go up,
the tribes of the LORD,
as was decreed for Israel,
to give thanks to the name of the LORD.
⁵ For there the thrones for judgment were set up,
the thrones of the house of David.
⁶ Pray for the peace of Jerusalem:
"May they prosper who love you.
⁷ Peace be within your walls,
and security within your towers."
⁸ For the sake of my relatives and friends
I will say, "Peace be within you."
⁹ For the sake of the house of the LORD our God,
I will seek your good.

Romans 13:11-14

¹¹Besides this, you know what time it is, how it is now the moment for you to wake from sleep. For salvation is nearer to us now than when we became believers; ¹²the night is far gone, the day is near. Let us then lay aside the works of darkness and put on the armor of light; ¹³let us live honorably as in the day, not in reveling and drunkenness, not in debauchery and licentiousness, not in quarreling and jealousy. ¹⁴Instead, put on the Lord Jesus Christ, and make no provision for the flesh, to gratify its desires.

Matthew 24:36-44

³⁶"But about that day and hour no one knows, neither the angels of heaven, nor the Son, but only the Father. ³⁷For as the days of Noah were, so will be the coming of the Son of Man. ³⁸For as in those days before the flood they were eating and drinking, marrying and giving in marriage, until the day Noah entered the ark, ³⁹and they knew nothing until the flood came and swept them all away, so too will be the coming of the Son of Man. ⁴⁰Then two will be in the field; one will be taken and one will be left. ⁴¹Two women will be grinding meal together; one will be taken and one will be left. ⁴²Keep awake therefore, for you do not know on what day your Lord is coming. ⁴³But understand this: if the owner of the house had known in what part of the night the thief was coming, he would have stayed awake and would not have let his house be broken into. ⁴⁴Therefore you also must be ready, for the Son of Man is coming at an unexpected hour."

COLOR: PURPLE OR BLUE   **1st SUNDAY OF ADVENT**

Primary Hymns and Songs for the Day
2172	"We Are Called" (Isa.) (O)
569	"We've a Story to Tell to the Nations" (Isa.) (O)
206	"I Want to Walk as a Child of the Light" (Isa., Rom.)
	S-2 #91. Descant
196	"Come, Thou Long-Expected Jesus" (Rom., Matt.)
	H-3 Hbl-46; Chr-26, 134; Desc-53; Org-56
	S-1 #168-171. Various treatments
720	"Wake, Awake, for Night Is Flying" (Rom., Matt.)
	H-3 Chr-174, 203; Org-172
626	"Let All Mortal Flesh Keep Silence" (Advent, Communion)
	H-3 Hbl-20, 74; Chr-124; Desc-37; Org-116
	S-1 #268-269. Handbell part and descant
706	"Soon and Very Soon" (Matt.) (C)
	S-2 #187. Piano arrangement

Additional Hymn Suggestions
426	"Behold a Broken World" (Isa.)
435	"O God of Every Nation" (Isa.) (C)
440	"Let There Be Light" (Isa.)
729	"O Day of Peace That Dimly Shines" (Isa.)
730	"O Day of God, Draw Nigh" (Isa.)
195	"Send Your Word" (Isa., Matt.)
433	"All Who Love and Serve Your City" (Isa., Matt.)
725	"Arise, Shine Out, Your Light Has Come" (Isa., Matt.)
732	"Come, We That Love the Lord" (Isa., Matt.)
733	"Marching to Zion" (Isa., Matt.)
2214	"Lead Me, Guide Me" (Isa., Rom., Advent)
551	"Awake, O Sleeper" (Rom.)
719	"My Lord, What a Morning" (Rom.)
634	"Now Let Us from This Table Rise" (Rom., Communion)
2092	"Like a Child" (Rom., Advent)
3179	"The Risen Christ"
202	"People, Look East" (Rom., Matt.)
722	"I Want to Be Ready" (Matt.)

Additional Contemporary Suggestions
M150	"Everyday" (Isa.)
S2144	"Someone Asked the Question" (Isa.)
S2204	"Light of the World" (Isa.)
S2232	"Come Now, O Prince of Peace" (Isa., Matt.)
S2235	"We Are Marching" ("Siyahamba") (Isa., Matt.)
WS3177	"Here I Am to Worship" (Isa., Matt., Advent)
	M116
S2270	"I Will Enter His Gates" (Ps.)
	SP168
S2195	"In the Lord I'll Be Ever Thankful" (Ps.)
WS3002	"Blessed Be Your Name" (Rom.)
	M163
SP158	"The Battle Belongs to the Lord" (Rom.)
M1	"Ancient of Days" (Rom., Matt.)
UM171	"There's Something About That Name" (Matt.)
	SP89
S2192	"Freedom Is Coming" (Matt.)
S2194	"O Freedom" (Matt.)
WS3186	"Days of Elijah" (Matt., Thanksgiving)
	M139

Vocal Solos
"Come, Thou Long Expected Jesus" (Matt., Rom., Advent)
V-1	p. 5
V-10	p. 11

"For Behold, Darkness Shall Cover the Earth" and
"The People That Walked in Darkness"
"Rejoice Greatly, O Daughter of Zion" (Isa.)
V-2	

"My Lord, What a Mornin'" (Rom., Matt., Advent)
V-7	p. 68

Anthems
"Come Now, O Prince of Peace" (Isa., Matt.)
arr. Joel Navarro; GIA G-7907
SATB, organ, opt. oboe and/or children's choir

"Processional on 'Let All Mortal Flesh Keep Silence'"
(Advent)
arr. Robert a. Hobby; MorningStar MSM-50-1950
SATB, brass, handbells, and organ

Other Suggestions
Visuals:
O	Mountain/hills/nations, paths, scales/justice, light
P	Ps. 122:1, feet/gates, Jerusalem, worship, wall/tower
E	Alarm clock, dawn, dark/light, armor, alb, Rom. 13:14
G	Clock, angels, Christ, Noah/ark/flood, one in field,

Introit: WS3044. "Make Way" (Matt., Advent)
Introit: WS3157. "Come, Let us Dream" (Isa.)
Introit: S2214. "Lead Me, Guide Me" (Matt., Advent)
Greeting: BOW243 (Rom.)
Opening Prayer: BOW254 (Rom.)
Blessing of the Advent Wreath: BOW261 (Advent)
Response: BOW208. "Come, Lord Jesus" (Advent)
Lighting of the Advent Candles: BOW262 (Advent)
Response: S2090, stanza 1. "Light the Advent Candle" (Advent)
Response: UM206, refrain."I Want to Walk as a Child of the Light" (Advent)
Response: UM211, stanza 1."O Come, O Come Emmanuel" (Rom., Matt., Advent)
Call to Prayer: WS3046. "Come, O Redeemer, Come" (Advent)
Litany: BOW433 (Student Sunday)
Offertory Prayer: WSL152. Father, John the Baptist (Advent)
Great Thanksgiving for Advent: BOW54-55

DECEMBER 8, 2013

Isaiah 11:1-10

1 A shoot shall come out from the stump of Jesse,
  and a branch shall grow out of his roots.
2 The spirit of the LORD shall rest on him,
  the spirit of wisdom and understanding,
  the spirit of counsel and might,
  the spirit of knowledge and the fear of the LORD.
3 His delight shall be in the fear of the LORD.
  He shall not judge by what his eyes see,
  or decide by what his ears hear;
4 but with righteousness he shall judge the poor,
  and decide with equity for the meek of the earth;
  he shall strike the earth with the rod of his mouth,
  and with the breath of his lips he shall kill the wicked.
5 Righteousness shall be the belt around his waist,
  and faithfulness the belt around his loins.
6 The wolf shall live with the lamb,
  the leopard shall lie down with the kid,
  the calf and the lion and the fatling together,
  and a little child shall lead them.
7 The cow and the bear shall graze,
  their young shall lie down together;
  and the lion shall eat straw like the ox.
8 The nursing child shall play over the hole of the asp,
  and the weaned child shall put its hand on the
  adder's den.
9 They will not hurt or destroy
  on all my holy mountain;
  for the earth will be full of the knowledge of the LORD
  as the waters cover the sea.
10 On that day the root of Jesse shall stand as a signal to the peoples; the nations shall inquire of him, and his dwelling shall be glorious.

Psalm 72:1-7, 18-19

1 Give the king your justice, O God,
  and your righteousness to a king's son.
2 May he judge your people with righteousness,
  and your poor with justice.
3 May the mountains yield prosperity for the people,
  and the hills, in righteousness.
4 May he defend the cause of the poor of the people,
  give deliverance to the needy,
  and crush the oppressor.
5 May he live while the sun endures,
  and as long as the moon, throughout all generations.
6 May he be like rain that falls on the mown grass,
  like showers that water the earth.
7 In his days may righteousness flourish
  and peace abound, until the moon is no more.
. . . .
18 Blessed be the LORD, the God of Israel,
  who alone does wondrous things.
19 Blessed be his glorious name forever;
  may his glory fill the whole earth.
    Amen and Amen.

Romans 15:4-13

4 For whatever was written in former days was written for our instruction, so that by steadfastness and by the encouragement of the scriptures we might have hope. 5 May the God of steadfastness and encouragement grant you to live in harmony with one another, in accordance with Christ Jesus, 6 so that together you may with one voice glorify the God and Father of our Lord Jesus Christ.

7 Welcome one another, therefore, just as Christ has welcomed you, for the glory of God. 8 For I tell you that Christ has become a servant of the circumcised on behalf of the truth of God in order that he might confirm the promises given to the patriarchs, 9 and in order that the Gentiles might glorify God for his mercy. As it is written,
"Therefore I will confess you among the Gentiles,
  and sing praises to your name";
10 and again he says,
  "Rejoice, O Gentiles, with his people";
11 and again,
  "Praise the Lord, all you Gentiles,
  and let all the peoples praise him";
12 and again Isaiah says,
  "The root of Jesse shall come,
  the one who rises to rule the Gentiles;
  in him the Gentiles shall hope."
13 May the God of hope fill you with all joy and peace in believing, so that you may abound in hope by the power of the Holy Spirit.

Matthew 3:1-12

In those days John the Baptist appeared in the wilderness of Judea, proclaiming, 2 "Repent, for the kingdom of heaven has come near." 3 This is the one of whom the prophet Isaiah spoke when he said,
  "The voice of one crying out in the wilderness:
  'Prepare the way of the Lord,
  make his paths straight.' "
4 Now John wore clothing of camel's hair with a leather belt around his waist, and his food was locusts and wild honey. 5 Then the people of Jerusalem and all Judea were going out to him, and all the region along the Jordan, 6 and they were baptized by him in the river Jordan, confessing their sins.

7 But when he saw many Pharisees and Sadducees coming for baptism, he said to them, "You brood of vipers! Who warned you to flee from the wrath to come? 8 Bear fruit worthy of repentance. 9 Do not presume to say to yourselves, 'We have Abraham as our ancestor'; for I tell you, God is able from these stones to raise up children to Abraham. 10 Even now the axe is lying at the root of the trees; every tree therefore that does not bear good fruit is cut down and thrown into the fire.

11 "I baptize you with water for repentance, but one who is more powerful than I is coming after me; I am not worthy to carry his sandals. He will baptize you with the Holy Spirit and fire. 12 His winnowing-fork is in his hand, and he will clear his threshing-floor and will gather his wheat into the granary; but the chaff he will burn with unquenchable fire."

COLOR: PURPLE OR BLUE   **2nd SUNDAY OF ADVENT**

Primary Hymns and Songs for the Day
203   "Hail to the Lord's Anointed" (Isa., Ps., Rom.) (O)
          H-3 Hbl-16, 22, 68; Chr-101; Desc-37
          S-1 #114. Descant
              #115. Harmonization
211   "O Come, O Come, Emmanuel" (Isa.)
          H-3 Hbl-14, 79; Chr-141; Org-168
          S-1 #342. Handbell accompaniment
216   "Lo, How a Rose E'er Blooming" (Isa.)
          H-3 Chr-129; Org-38
          S-2 #56-57. Various treatments
2089   "Wild and Lone the Prophet's Voice" (Matt.)
3045   "Down by the Jordan" (Matt.)
567   "Heralds of Christ" (Matt.) (C)
          H-3 Hbl-64; Chr-78; Desc-78; Org-96
          S-2 #131-132. Harmonization with descant

Additional Hymn Suggestions
3130   "Come, Emmanuel" (Isa., Advent)
214   "Savior of the Nations, Come" (Isa.)
617   "I Come With Joy" (Isa., Communion)
730   "O Day of God, Draw Nigh" (Isa.)
729   "O Day of Peace That Dimly Shines" (Isa.)
61   "Come, Thou Almighty King" (Isa., Ps.)
196   "Come, Thou Long-Expected Jesus" (Isa., Rom.)
2213   "Healer of Our Every Ill" (Isa., Rom.)
209   "Blessed Be the God of Israel" (Isa., Matt.)
210   "Toda la Tierra" ("All Earth Is Waiting") (Isa.,
          Matt.)
2177   "Wounded World that Cries for Healing" (Ps.)
2178   "Here Am I" (Ps.)
2180   "Why Stand So Far Away, My God?" (Ps.)
2182   "When God Restored our Common Life" (Ps.)
195   "Send Your Word" (Ps.)
213   "Lift Up Your Heads, Ye Mighty Gates" (Ps.)
247   "O Morning Star, How Fair and Bright" (Rom.)
347   "Spirit Song" (Rom.)
          SP134
560   "Help Us Accept Each Other" (Rom.) (C)
561   "Jesus, United by Thy Grace" (Rom., Communion)
2142   "Blessed Quietness" (Rom.)
2175   "Together We Serve" (Rom.)
2197   "Lord of All Hopefulness" (Rom.)
2218   "You Are Mine" (Rom.)
651   "Come, Holy Ghost, Our Souls Inspire" (Matt.)
2060   "God the Sculptor of the Mountains" (Matt.)

Additional Contemporary Suggestions
S2145   "I've Got Peace Like a River" (Isa., Rom.)
S2156   "Give Peace" ("Da Pacem Cordium") (Isa., Rom.)
S2157   "Come and Fill Our Hearts" (Isa., Rom.)
UM63   "Blessed Be the Name" (Ps.)
WS3002 "Blessed Be Your Name" (Ps.)
          M163
S2075   "King of Kings" (Ps., Advent)
          SP94
S2091   "The King of Glory Comes" (Ps., Advent)
S2118   "Holy Spirit, Come to Us" (Ps., Matt.)
S2016   "Glorify Thy Name" (Rom.)
          SP19
S2186   "Song of Hope" (Rom.)

S2162   "Grace Alone" (Rom.)
          M100
M63   "I Could Sing of Your Love Forever" (Rom.)
UM347   "Spirit Song" (Rom., Matt.)
          SP134
UM186   "Alleluia" (Matt.)
          SP108; S-2 #3-4
S2071   "Jesus, Name Above All Names" (Matt.)
          SP76
WS3044 "Make Way" (Matt.)
M34   "I Will Never Be" (the Same Again) (Matt.)
M50   "Refiner's Fire" (Matt.)
WS3112 "Breathe" (Matt.)
          M61

Vocal Solos
"Come, Let us Dream" (Isa.)
     WS3157
"I Wonder as I Wander" (Ps., Advent)
     V-8   p. 88
"Come Thou Long Expected Jesus" (Rom.)
     V-1   p. 5
     V-10   p. 11

Anthems
"O Come, O Come, Emmanuel" (Isa.)
David Cherwien; MorningStar MSM-50-0250
SATTBB, *a cappella*

"Prepare the Way, O Zion" (Matt.)
Kenneth Dake; MorningStar MSM-50-0425
SATB, violin, organ

Other Suggestions
Visuals:
   O   Stump/branch/roots, lamp, scales, belt, named
          animals, child, asp, adder's den, mountain/sea,
          nations
   P   Crown, scales, mountains/hills, poor/needy, sun/
          moon, rain, lunar eclipse, Ps. 72:18, 19
   E   Bible/OT, circle, welcome, nations/Christ, stump/
          root
   G   Baptism, ax/root/fire, sandals, fork/wheat/chaff/
          fire
Introit: UM207. "Prepare the Way of the Lord" (Matt.)
Greeting: BOW241 or BOW242 (Matt., Rom.)
Opening Prayer: BOW250 or BOW252 (Matt.)
Call or Response to Prayer: WS3046. "Come, O Redeemer,
     Come" (Advent)
Prayer: UM201. Advent (Isa., Matt.)
Offertory Prayer: WSL152. Father, John the Baptist (Matt.)
Lighting of the Advent Candles: BOW262 (Advent)
Response: S2090, stanza 2. "Light the Advent Candle"
Benediction: BOW561 (Rom.)

41

DECEMBER 15, 2013

Isaiah 35:1-10

1 The wilderness and the dry land shall be glad,
    the desert shall rejoice and blossom;
like the crocus 2it shall blossom abundantly,
    and rejoice with joy and singing.
 The glory of Lebanon shall be given to it,
    the majesty of Carmel and Sharon.
They shall see the glory of the LORD,
    the majesty of our God.
3 Strengthen the weak hands,
    and make firm the feeble knees.
4 Say to those who are of a fearful heart,
    "Be strong, do not fear!
Here is your God.
    He will come with vengeance,
 with terrible recompense.
    He will come and save you."
5 Then the eyes of the blind shall be opened,
    and the ears of the deaf unstopped;
6 then the lame shall leap like a deer,
    and the tongue of the speechless sing for joy.
For waters shall break forth in the wilderness,
    and streams in the desert;
7 the burning sand shall become a pool,
    and the thirsty ground springs of water;
the haunt of jackals shall become a swamp,
    the grass shall become reeds and rushes.
8 A highway shall be there,
    and it shall be called the Holy Way;
the unclean shall not travel on it,
    but it shall be for God's people;
    no traveler, not even fools, shall go astray.
9 No lion shall be there,
    nor shall any ravenous beast come up on it;
they shall not be found there,
    but the redeemed shall walk there.
10 And the ransomed of the LORD shall return,
    and come to Zion with singing;
everlasting joy shall be upon their heads;
    they shall obtain joy and gladness,
    and sorrow and sighing shall flee away.

Luke 1:47-55

47 "My soul magnifies the Lord,
    and my spirit rejoices in God my Savior,
48 for he has looked with favor on the lowliness of his servant.
    Surely, from now on all generations will call me blessed;
49 for the Mighty One has done great things for me,
    and holy is his name.
50 His mercy is for those who fear him
    from generation to generation.
51 He has shown strength with his arm;
    he has scattered the proud in the thoughts of their
        hearts.
52 He has brought down the powerful from their thrones,
    and lifted up the lowly;
53 he has filled the hungry with good things,
    and sent the rich away empty.
54 He has helped his servant Israel,
    in remembrance of his mercy,
55 according to the promise he made to our ancestors,
    to Abraham and to his descendants forever."

James 5:7-10

7Be patient, therefore, beloved, until the coming of the Lord. The farmer waits for the precious crop from the earth, being patient with it until it receives the early and the late rains. 8You also must be patient. Strengthen your hearts, for the coming of the Lord is near. 9Beloved, do not grumble against one another, so that you may not be judged. See, the Judge is standing at the doors! 10As an example of suffering and patience, beloved, take the prophets who spoke in the name of the Lord.

Matthew 11:2-11

2When John heard in prison what the Messiah was doing, he sent word by his disciples 3and said to him, "Are you the one who is to come, or are we to wait for another?" 4Jesus answered them, "Go and tell John what you hear and see: 5the blind receive their sight, the lame walk, the lepers are cleansed, the deaf hear, the dead are raised, and the poor have good news brought to them. 6And blessed is anyone who takes no offense at me." 7As they went away, Jesus began to speak to the crowds about John: "What did you go out into the wilderness to look at? A reed shaken by the wind? 8What then did you go out to see? Someone dressed in soft robes? Look, those who wear soft robes are in royal palaces. 9What then did you go out to see? A prophet? Yes, I tell you, and more than a prophet. 10This is the one about whom it is written,
    'See, I am sending my messenger ahead of you,
        who will prepare your way before you.'
11Truly I tell you, among those born of women no one has arisen greater than John the Baptist; yet the least in the kingdom of heaven is greater than he."

COLOR: PURPLE OR BLUE　　　　　　　　　**3rd SUNDAY OF ADVENT**

Primary Hymns and Songs for the Day

196　"Come, Thou Long-Expected Jesus" (James) (O)
　　　　H-3 Hbl-46; Chr-26, 134; Desc-53; Org-56
　　　　S-1 #168-171. Various treatments
198　"My Soul Gives Glory to My God" (Luke)
　　　　H-3 Chr-139, 145; Desc-77
　　　　S-1 #241-242. Orff arr. and descant
182　"Word of God, Come Down on Earth" (Matt.)
3001　"O For a Thousand Tongues to Sing (Matt.)
57　"O For a Thousand Tongues to Sing" (Matt.) (C)
　　　　H-3 Hbl-79; Chr-142; Desc-17; Org-12
　　　　S-1 #33-38. Various Treatments

Additional Hymn Suggestions

213　"Lift Up Your Heads, Ye Mighty Gates" (Isa.)
216　"Lo, How a Rose E'er Blooming" (Isa.)
233　"En el Frio Invernal" ("Cold December Flies Away")
　　　(Isa.)
2210　"Joy Comes with the Dawn" (Isa.)
206　"I Want to Walk as a Child of the Light" (Isa., James)
218　"It Came Upon the Midnight Clear" (Isa., James,
　　　Matt.)
142　"If Thou But Suffer God to Guide Thee" (James)
455　"Not So in Haste, My Heart" (James)
430　"O Master, Let Me Walk with Thee" (James)
2100　"Thou Didst Leave Thy Throne" (Isa., Matt.,
　　　Advent)
203　"Hail to the Lord's Anointed" (Isa., Matt.)
224　"Good Christian Friends, Rejoice" (Isa., Matt.)
241　"That Boy-Child of Mary" (Isa., Luke)
197　"Ye Who Claim the Faith of Jesus" (Luke)
200　"Tell Out, My Soul" (Luke)
215　"To a Maid Engaged to Joseph" (Luke)
2093　"The Snow lay on the Ground" (Luke)
2098　"The Virgin Mary Had a Baby Boy" (Luke)
2122　"She Comes Sailing on the Wind" (Luke)
2151　"I'm So Glad Jesus Lifted Me" (Luke)
2155　"Blest Are They" (Luke)
3157　"Come, Let us Dream" (Luke)
209　"Blessed Be the God of Israel" (Luke, Matt.) (C)
263　"When Jesus the Healer Passed Through Galilee"
　　　(Matt.)
505　"When Our Confidence Is Shaken" (Matt.)
2089　"Wild and Lone the Prophet's Voice" (Matt.,
　　　Advent)

Additional Contemporary Suggestions

WS3108　"Trading My Sorrows" (Isa.)
　　　　M75
M159　"All Who Are Thirsty" (Isa., Advent)
WS3046　"Come, O Redeemer, Come" (Isa., Advent)
S2005　"Arise, Shine" (Isa.)
S2144　"Someone Asked the Question" (Isa.)
S2036　"Give Thanks" (Isa., Luke)
　　　　SP170
M36　"Awesome in this Place" (Isa., Luke)
S2154　"Please Enter My Heart, Hosanna" (James, Advent)
WS3023　"Forever" (James, Luke)
　　　　M68
WS3042　"Shout to the North" (Luke)
　　　　M99
M164　"Good to Me" (Luke)

S2029　"Praise to the Lord" (Luke)
S2074　"Shout to the Lord" (Luke)
　　　　M16
WS3044　"Make Way" (Luke, Advent)
SP4　"Great and Mighty Is He" (Luke)
　　　　M11
WS3040　"You Are My All in All" (Luke, Matt.)
　　　　SP220
UM207　"Prepare the Way of the Lord" (Matt.)
WS3177　"Here I Am to Worship" (Matt.)
　　　　M116
UM204　"Emmanuel, Emmanuel" (Matt.)
　　　　SP75

Vocal Solos

"He Shall Feed His Flock Like a Shepherd" (Isa.)
　　V-2
"Prepare Thyself, Zion" (Isa., Advent)
　　V-9　　p. 2
"Lift Up Your Heads" (Isa., Advent)
　　V-10　　p. 38
"Patiently Have I Waited for the Lord" (James)
　　V-4　　p. 24
"O For a Thousand Tongues to Sing" (Matt.)
　　V-1　　p. 32

Anthems

"Dream A Dream" (Isa., Luke)
Lori True; GIA G-6653
SATB, keyboard, opt. C instrument and/or handbells

"Canticle of the Turning" (Luke)
Hal Hopson; MorningStar MSM-50-0057
SATB, flute, organ, opt. strings, harp, drum

Other Suggestions

Visuals:
　O　Blooms, healing, singing, river/stream, oasis,
　　　spring
　P　Mary, joy, arm/scatter, toppled throne, feeding,
　　　chest
　E　Second Coming, farmer/crops., gavel, scales, doors
　G　John, prison, Jesus with men, Matt. 11:5 imagery,
　　　prepare
Greeting: BOW244, 246, or 248 (Isa.) or BOW247 (James)
Opening Prayer: BOW252 (Matt.) or BOW 253 (James)
Opening Prayer: WSL1. O God, we are challenged (James)
Canticle: UM199. "Canticle of Mary" ("Magnificat") (Luke)
Lighting of the Advent Candles: BOW262 (Advent)
Response: S2090, stanza 3. "Light the Advent Candle"
Prayer: WSL148. Loving God you have blessed us (Luke)
Dismissal: BOW559 (James)
Movement or dance can enhance Luke 1 songs and readings.

DECEMBER 22, 2013

Isaiah 7:10-16

[10]Again the LORD spoke to Ahaz, saying, [11]Ask a sign of the LORD your God; let it be deep as Sheol or high as heaven. [12]But Ahaz said, I will not ask, and I will not put the LORD to the test. [13]Then Isaiah said: "Hear then, O house of David! Is it too little for you to weary mortals, that you weary my God also? [14]Therefore the Lord himself will give you a sign. Look, the young woman is with child and shall bear a son, and shall name him Immanuel. [15]He shall eat curds and honey by the time he knows how to refuse the evil and choose the good. [16]For before the child knows how to refuse the evil and choose the good, the land before whose two kings you are in dread will be deserted."

Psalm 80:1-7, 17-19

1   Give ear, O Shepherd of Israel,
        you who lead Joseph like a flock!
    You who are enthroned upon the cherubim, shine forth
[2]before Ephraim and Benjamin and Manasseh.
        Stir up your might,
            and come to save us!
3   Restore us, O God;
        let your face shine, that we may be saved.
4   O LORD God of hosts,
        how long will you be angry with your people's prayers?
5   You have fed them with the bread of tears,
        and given them tears to drink in full measure.
6   You make us the scorn of our neighbors;
        our enemies laugh among themselves.
7   Restore us, O God of hosts;
        let your face shine, that we may be saved.
. . . .
17   But let your hand be upon the one at your right hand,
        the one whom you made strong for yourself.
18   Then we will never turn back from you;
        give us life, and we will call on your name.
19   Restore us, O LORD God of hosts;
        let your face shine, that we may be saved.

Romans 1:1-7

[1]Paul, a servant of Jesus Christ, called to be an apostle, set apart for the gospel of God, [2]which he promised beforehand through his prophets in the holy scriptures, [3]the gospel concerning his Son, who was descended from David according to the flesh [4]and was declared to be Son of God with power according to the spirit of holiness by resurrection from the dead, Jesus Christ our Lord, [5]through whom we have received grace and apostleship to bring about the obedience of faith among all the Gentiles for the sake of his name, [6]including yourselves who are called to belong to Jesus Christ, [7]To all God's beloved in Rome, who are called to be saints: Grace to you and peace from God our Father and the Lord Jesus Christ.

Matthew 1:18-25

[18]Now the birth of Jesus the Messiah took place in this way. When his mother Mary had been engaged to Joseph, but before they lived together, she was found to be with child from the Holy Spirit. [19]Her husband Joseph, being a righteous man and unwilling to expose her to public disgrace, planned to dismiss her quietly. [20]But just when he had resolved to do this, an angel of the Lord appeared to him in a dream and said, "Joseph, son of David, do not be afraid to take Mary as your wife, for the child conceived in her is from the Holy Spirit. [21]She will bear a son, and you are to name him Jesus, for he will save his people from their sins." [22]All this took place to fulfill what had been spoken by the Lord through the prophet:
[23]   "Look, the virgin shall conceive and bear a son,
        and they shall name him Emmanuel,"
which means, "God is with us." [24]When Joseph awoke from sleep, he did as the angel of the Lord commanded him; he took her as his wife, [25]but had no marital relations with her until she had borne a son; and he named him Jesus.

COLOR: PURPLE OR BLUE　　　　　　　　　　**4th SUNDAY OF ADVENT**

Primary Hymns and Songs for the Day
204　"Emmanuel, Emmanuel" (Isa., Matt.) (O)
　　　　　SP75
211　"O Come, O Come, Emmanuel" (Isa., Matt.) (O)
　　　　　H-3　Hbl-14, 79; Chr-141; Org-168
　　　　　S-1　#342. Handbell accompaniment
250　"Once in Royal David's City" (Isa., Matt.)
　　　　　H-3　Hbl-83; Chr-68, 156; Desc-57; Org-63
　　　　　S-1　#182-184. Various treatments
215　"To a Maid Engaged to Joseph" (Matt.)
240　"Hark! the Herald Angels Sing" (Matt.)
　　　　　H-3　Hbl-26, 67; Chr-91; Desc-75; Org-89
　　　　　S-1　#234-6. Harmonizations and descant
2099　"Joseph Dearest, Joseph Mine" (Matt.)
2091　"The King of Glory Comes" (Matt.) (C)

Additional Hymn Suggestions
2172　"We Are Called" (Isa., Ps.)
206　"I Want to Walk as a Child of the Light" (Isa., Ps., Advent)
210　"Toda la Tierra" ("All Earth Is Waiting") (Isa., Matt.)
214　"Savior of the Nations, Come" (Isa., Matt.)
216　"Lo, How a Rose E'er Blooming" (Isa., Matt.)
3130　"Come, Emmanuel" (Isa., Matt.)
3046　"Come, O Redeemer, Come" (Ps., Advent)
2214　"Lead Me, Guide Me" (Ps., Advent)
202　"People, Look East" (Ps., Advent)
195　"Send Your Word" (Ps., Rom., Advent)
162　"Alleluia, Alleluia" (Rom.)
187　"Rise, Shine, You People" (Rom., Advent)
193　"Jesus! The Name High over All" (Rom.)
236　"While Shepherds Watched Their Flocks" (Rom.)
234　"O Come, All Ye Faithful" (Rom., Matt.)
196　"Come, Thou Long-Expected Jesus" (Matt.)
197　"Ye Who Claim the Faith of Jesus" (Matt.)
198　"My Soul Gives Glory to My God" (Matt.)
200　"Tell Out, My Soul" (Matt.)
220　"Angels From the Realms of Glory" (Matt.)
228　"He Is Born" ("Il Est Né") (Matt.)
230　"O Little Town of Bethlehem" (Matt.) (C)
276　"The First One Ever" (Matt.)
2092　"Like a Child" (Matt.)
2096　"Rise Up, Shepherd, and Follow" (Matt.)
2121　"O Holy Spirit, Root of Life" (Matt., Advent)
3051　"A Star Shone Bright" (Matt., Advent)

Additional Contemporary Suggestions
WS3046　"Come, O Redeemer, Come" (Advent)
S2069　"All Hail King Jesus" (Isa., Matt.)
　　　　　SP63
S2071　"Jesus, Name Above All Names" (Isa., Matt.)
　　　　　SP76
S2173　"Shine, Jesus, Shine" (Ps.)
　　　　　SP142
M26　"The Power of Your Love" (Ps.)
M49　"Refresh My Heart" (Rom., Advent)
M87　"Let the Peace of God Reign" (Rom.)
UM171　"There's Something About That Name" (Matt.)
　　　　　SP89
S2088　"Lord, I Lift Your Name on High" (Matt., Christmas)
　　　　　M2

M18　"Come and Behold Him" (Matt., Advent)
M24　"Jesus, We Crown You with Praise" (Matt.)

Vocal Solos
"Behold! A Virgin Shall Conceive" and
"O Thou That Tellest Good Tidings to Zion" (Isa., Matt.)
　　　　　V-2
"Glory Hallelujah to de New-Born King" (Isa., Matt.)
　　　　　V-7　　p. 80
"Lost in the Night" (Ps., Matt.)
　　　　　V-5(1)　　p. 18
"Hark! The Herald Angels Sing" (Matt.)
　　　　　V-1　　p. 13
"Who Is This Boy?" (Matt.)
　　　　　V-8　　p. 223

Anthems
"Hark! the Herald Angels Sing" (Matt.)
Matthew Culloton; MorningStar MSM-50-0070
SATB divisi, a cappella

"Sans Day Carol" (Matt.)
Stephen Caracciolo; MorningStar MSM-50-1119
SATB, organ, opt. tubular bells

"I Wonder as I Wander" (Matt.)
arr. John Rutter; Hinshaw HMC673
SATB, *a cappella*

Other Suggestions
Visuals:
　　O　　Test, pregnant woman, baby, Immanuel, curds/ honey
　　P　　Shepherd, seat, anger/ tears/laughter, returning
　　E　　Letter, Bible, resurrection, Rom. 1:7*b*
　　G　　Pregnant Mary, Joseph, Spirit symbol, birth, angel Emmanuel (God with us), "Jesus"
Use UM211 with the printed spoken antiphons. For processional, stop each time an antiphon is read, moving during the singing of each stanza.
Greeting: WSL4 (Matt.)
Opening Prayer: BOW249 (Isa.)
Call to Prayer: 2232. "Come Now, O Prince of Peace" ("O-So-So")
Prayer: BOW256. The Annunciation to Mary (Matt.)
Prayer: WSL6. Gracious God, your servant Mary (Matt.)
Lighting of the Advent Candles: BOW262 (Advent)
Response: S2090, stanza 4. "Light the Advent Candle" (Advent)
Prayer: WSL11. Radiant Morning Star (Matt.)
Offertory Prayer: WS125. Precious Lord, amid the twinkling lights (Matt., Advent)
Blessing: WSL7. The light that enlivens (Ps.)

DECEMBER 24/25, 2013

Isaiah 9:2-7

2 The people who walked in darkness
 have seen a great light;
those who lived in a land of deep darkness—
 on them light has shined.
3 You have multiplied the nation,
 you have increased its joy;
they rejoice before you
 as with joy at the harvest,
 as people exult when dividing plunder.
4 For the yoke of their burden,
 and the bar across their shoulders,
 the rod of their oppressor,
 you have broken as on the day of Midian.
5 For all the boots of the tramping warriors
 and all the garments rolled in blood
 shall be burned as fuel for the fire.
6 For a child has been born for us,
 a son given to us;
authority rests upon his shoulders;
 and he is named
Wonderful Counselor, Mighty God,
 Everlasting Father, Prince of Peace.
7 His authority shall grow continually,
 and there shall be endless peace
for the throne of David and his kingdom.
 He will establish and uphold it
with justice and with righteousness
 from this time onward and forevermore.
The zeal of the LORD of hosts will do this.

Psalm 96

1 O sing to the LORD a new song;
 sing to the LORD, all the earth.
2 Sing to the LORD, bless his name;
 tell of his salvation from day to day.
3 Declare his glory among the nations,
 his marvelous works among all the peoples.
4 For great is the LORD, and greatly to be praised;
 he is to be revered above all gods.
5 For all the gods of the peoples are idols,
 but the LORD made the heavens.
6 Honor and majesty are before him;
 strength and beauty are in his sanctuary.
7 Ascribe to the LORD, O families of the peoples,
 ascribe to the LORD glory and strength.
8 Ascribe to the LORD the glory due his name;
 bring an offering, and come into his courts.
9 Worship the LORD in holy splendor;
 tremble before him, all the earth.
10 Say among the nations, "The LORD is king!
 The world is firmly established; it shall never be moved.
 He will judge the peoples with equity."
11 Let the heavens be glad, and let the earth rejoice;
 let the sea roar, and all that fills it;
12 let the field exult, and everything in it.
 Then shall all the trees of the forest sing for joy
13 before the LORD; for he is coming,
 for he is coming to judge the earth.
He will judge the world with righteousness,
 and the peoples with his truth.

Titus 2:11-14

11For the grace of God has appeared, bringing salvation to all, 12training us to renounce impiety and worldly passions, and in the present age to live lives that are self-controlled, upright, and godly, 13while we wait for the blessed hope and the manifestation of the glory of our great God and Savior, Jesus Christ. 14He it is who gave himself for us that he might redeem us from all iniquity and purify for himself a people of his own who are zealous for good deeds.

Luke 2:1-20

1In those days a decree went out from Emperor Augustus that all the world should be registered. 2This was the first registration and was taken while Quirinius was governor of Syria. 3All went to their own towns to be registered. 4Joseph also went from the town of Nazareth in Galilee to Judea, to the city of David called Bethlehem, because he was descended from the house and family of David. 5He went to be registered with Mary, to whom he was engaged and who was expecting a child. 6While they were there, the time came for her to deliver her child. 7And she gave birth to her firstborn son and wrapped him in bands of cloth, and laid him in a manger, because there was no place for them in the inn.

8In that region there were shepherds living in the fields, keeping watch over their flock by night. 9Then an angel of the Lord stood before them, and the glory of the Lord shone around them, and they were terrified. 10But the angel said to them, "Do not be afraid; for see—I am bringing you good news of great joy for all the people: 11to you is born this day in the city of David a Savior, who is the Messiah, the Lord. 12This will be a sign for you: you will find a child wrapped in bands of cloth and lying in a manger." 13And suddenly there was with the angel a multitude of the heavenly host, praising God and saying,

14"Glory to God in the highest heaven,
 and on earth peace among those whom he favors!"

15When the angels had left them and gone into heaven, the shepherds said to one another, "Let us go now to Bethlehem and see this thing that has taken place, which the Lord has made known to us." 16So they went with haste and found Mary and Joseph, and the child lying in the manger. 17When they saw this, they made known what had been told them about this child; 18and all who heard it were amazed at what the shepherds told them. 19But Mary treasured all these words and pondered them in her heart. 20The shepherds returned, glorifying and praising God for all they had heard and seen, as it had been told them.

COLOR: WHITE   **CHRISTMAS EVE / CHRISTMAS DAY**

Primary Hymns and Songs for the Day
238 "Angels We Have Heard on High" (Luke) (O)
　　　H-3 Hbl-47; Chr-31; Desc-43; Org-45
3064 "On Christmas Night" (Isa., Luke)
239 "Silent Night, Holy Night" (Luke)
　　　H-3 Hbl-92; Chr-171; Desc-99; Org-159
　　　S-1 #322. Descant
　　　　　#323. Guitar/Autoharp chords
　　　S-2 #167. Handbell arrangement
246 "Joy to the World" (Titus, Luke) (C)
　　　S-1 #19-20. Trumpet descants
251 "Go, Tell it on the Mountain" (Luke) (C)
　　　H-3 Hbl-17; Chr-73; Desc-45; Org-46

Additional Hymn Suggestions
188 "Christ Is the World's Light" (Isa.)
223 "Break Forth, O Beauteous Heavenly Light" (Isa.)
247 "O Morning Star, How Fair and Bright" (Isa.)
2232 "Come Now, O Prince of Peace" (Isa.)
218 "It Came Upon the Midnight Clear" (Isa., Luke) (O)
3059 "Love Has Come" (Isa., Luke)
2001 "We Sing to You, O God" (Ps.)
66 "Praise, My Soul, the King of Heaven" (Ps.)
79 "Holy God, We Praise Thy Name" (Ps.)
221 "In the Bleak Midwinter" (Ps., Titus, Luke)
248 "On This Day Earth Shall Ring" (Ps., Titus, Luke) (O)
2011 "We Sing of Your Glory" (Ps., Luke)
217 "Away in a Manger" (Luke)
219 "What Child Is This" (Luke)
220 "Angels from the Realms of Glory" (Luke)
222 "Niño Lindo" ("Child So Lovely") (Luke)
227 "The Friendly Beasts" ("Jesus, Our Brother") (Luke)
229 "Infant Holy, Infant Lowly" (Luke)
232 "When Christmas Morn Is Dawning" (Luke)
234 "O Come, All Ye Faithful" (Luke)
240 "Hark! the Herald Angels Sing" (Luke) (O)
244 "'Twas in the Moon of Wintertime" (Luke)
250 "Once in Royal David's City" (Luke)
2092 "Like a Child" (Luke)
2096 "Rise Up, Shepherd, and Follow" (Luke)
2097 "One Holy Night in Bethlehem" (Luke)
2276 "Glory to God in the Highest" (Luke)
3063 "If I Could Visit Bethlehem" (Luke)
3066 "Still, Still, Still" (Luke)
636 "Christian People, Raise Your Song" (Communion)

Additional Contemporary Suggestions
UM174 "His Name Is Wonderful" (Isa.)
　　　SP90
S2023 "How Majestic Is Your Name" (Isa.)
　　　SP14
S2071 "Jesus, Name Above All Names" (Isa.)
　　　SP76
S2075 "King of Kings" (Isa.)
　　　SP94
WS3060 "Jesus, Jesus, Oh, What a Wonderful Child" (Isa., Luke)
WS3003 "How Great Is Our God" (Isa., Ps.)
　　　M117
UM176 "Majesty" (Ps.)
　　　SP73

SP23 "Sing Unto the Lord a New Song" (Ps.)
WS3042 "Shout to the North" (Ps.)
　　　M99
S2037 "I Sing Praises to Your Name" (Ps.)
　　　SP27
S2074 "Shout to the Lord" (Ps.)
　　　M16
S2258 "Sing Alleluia to the Lord" (Titus)
　　　SP93
S2088 "Lord, I Lift Your Name on High" (Luke)
　　　M2
WS3053 "Bethlehem" (Luke)
WS3057 "Glory in the highest" ("Gloria en las Alturas") (Luke)
WS3058 "Mary Had a Baby" (Luke)

Vocal Solos
"Hark! the Herald Angels Sing" (Luke)
　　　V-1　　　p. 13 (Use hymnal text)
"Welcome to Our World" (Luke)
　　　WS3067
　　　V-5(1)　　p. 34
"O Holy Night" (Luke)
　　　V-8　　　p. 93
"Sleep, Little Baby" (Luke)
　　　V-10　　　p. 27
"Sing Noel!" (Luke)
　　　V-11　　　p. 13
"Glory Hallelujah to de New-Born King" (Luke)
　　　V-7　　　p. 80

Anthems
"Still, Still, Still" (Luke)
arr. Robert A. Hobby; MorningStar MSM-50-1952
SATB, organ, opt. children's choir/solo

"In dulci Jubilo" (Luke)
Matthew Culloton; MorningStar MSM-50-0090
SATB divisi, *a cappella*

Other Suggestions
Visuals:
　　O　Darkness/light, joy, yoke, boots, fire, child, names
　　P　New song, nations, glory, Ps. 96:10*a*, gavel, nature images
　　E　Jesus, Second Coming, crucifix
　　G　Tax register, manger scene, shepherds, angels, Luke 2:14
Introit: S2045. "Sing a New Song to the Lord" (Ps.)
Introit: S2274. "Come, All You People" (Ps.)
Greeting: BOW271 (Luke) or BOW273 (Titus)
Greeting: WSL4. We gather in preparation (Luke, Christmas)
Opening Prayer: BOW277 or BOW278 (Isa., Luke)
Prayer Confession: WSL5. Merciful God (Luke)
Prayer of Preparation: WSL8. God of glory (Isa., Luke)
Prayer: UM231. Christmas (Luke)
Response: WS3190, stanza 1. "Mary Had a Little Lamb" (Luke)
Offertory Prayer: WSL127. Joy to the world (Luke)
Prayer of Thanksgiving and Intercession: BOW279 (Luke)
Great Thanksgiving for Christmas Eve: BOW56-57
Blessing: WSL7. The light that enlivens (Isa.)

47

DECEMBER 29, 2013

Isaiah 63:7-9

7 I will recount the gracious deeds of the Lord,
  the praiseworthy acts of the Lord,
 because of all that the Lord has done for us,
  and the great favor to the house of Israel
 that he has shown them according to his mercy,
  according to the abundance of his steadfast love.
8 For he said, "Surely they are my people,
  children who will not deal falsely";
 and he became their savior
9 in all their distress.
 It was no messenger or angel
  but his presence that saved them;
 in his love and in his pity he redeemed them;
  he lifted them up and carried them all the days of old.

Psalm 148

1 Praise the Lord!
 Praise the Lord from the heavens;
  praise him in the heights!
2 Praise him, all his angels;
  praise him, all his host!
3 Praise him, sun and moon;
  praise him, all you shining stars!
4 Praise him, you highest heavens,
  and you waters above the heavens!
5 Let them praise the name of the Lord,
  for he commanded and they were created.
6 He established them forever and ever;
  he fixed their bounds, which cannot be passed.
7 Praise the Lord from the earth,
  you sea monsters and all deeps,
8 fire and hail, snow and frost,
  stormy wind fulfilling his command!
9 Mountains and all hills,
  fruit trees and all cedars!
10 Wild animals and all cattle,
  creeping things and flying birds!
11 Kings of the earth and all peoples,
  princes and all rulers of the earth!
12 Young men and women alike,
  old and young together!
13 Let them praise the name of the Lord,
  for his name alone is exalted;
  his glory is above earth and heaven.
14 He has raised up a horn for his people,
  praise for all his faithful,
  for the people of Israel who are close to him.
 Praise the Lord!

Hebrews 2:10-18

10It was fitting that God, for whom and through whom all things exist, in bringing many children to glory, should make the pioneer of their salvation perfect through sufferings. 11For the one who sanctifies and those who are sanctified all have one Father. For this reason Jesus is not ashamed to call them brothers and sisters, 12saying,
 "I will proclaim your name to my brothers and sisters,
 in the midst of the congregation I will praise you."
13And again,
 "I will put my trust in him."
And again,

"Here am I and the children whom God has given me."
14Since, therefore, the children share flesh and blood, he himself likewise shared the same things, so that through death he might destroy the one who has the power of death, that is, the devil, 15and free those who all their lives were held in slavery by the fear of death. 16For it is clear that he did not come to help angels, but the descendants of Abraham. 17Therefore he had to become like his brothers and sisters in every respect, so that he might be a merciful and faithful high priest in the service of God, to make a sacrifice of atonement for the sins of the people. 18Because he himself was tested by what he suffered, he is able to help those who are being tested.

Matthew 2:13-23

13Now after they had left, an angel of the Lord appeared to Joseph in a dream and said, "Get up, take the child and his mother, and flee to Egypt, and remain there until I tell you; for Herod is about to search for the child, to destroy him." 14Then Joseph got up, took the child and his mother by night, and went to Egypt, 15and remained there until the death of Herod. This was to fulfill what had been spoken by the Lord through the prophet, "Out of Egypt I have called my son."

16When Herod saw that he had been tricked by the wise men, he was infuriated, and he sent and killed all the children in and around Bethlehem who were two years old or under, according to the time that he had learned from the wise men. 17Then was fulfilled what had been spoken through the prophet Jeremiah:
18 "A voice was heard in Ramah,
  wailing and loud lamentation,
 Rachel weeping for her children;
  she refused to be consoled, because they are no more."

19When Herod died, an angel of the Lord suddenly appeared in a dream to Joseph in Egypt and said, 20"Get up, take the child and his mother, and go to the land of Israel, for those who were seeking the child's life are dead." 21Then Joseph got up, took the child and his mother, and went to the land of Israel. 22But when he heard that Archelaus was ruling over Judea in place of his father Herod, he was afraid to go there. And after being warned in a dream, he went away to the district of Galilee. 23There he made his home in a town called Nazareth, so that what had been spoken through the prophets might be fulfilled, "He will be called a Nazorean."

COLOR: WHITE   **1st SUNDAY AFTER CHRISTMAS**

Primary Hymns and Songs for the Day
240   "Hark! the Herald Angels Sing" (Isa., Matt.) (O)
            H-3 Hbl-26, 67; Chr-91; Desc-75; Org-89
            S-1 #234-6. Harmonizations and descant
179   "O Sing a Song of Bethlehem" (Isa., Heb., Matt.)
            H-3 Hbl-15, 20, 34, 84; Chr-150; Org-67
            S-2 #100-103. Various treatments
219   "What Child Is This" (Matt.) (C)
            H-3 Hbl-102; Chr-210; Desc-46; Org-47
            S-1 #150. Guitar chords

Additional Hymn Suggestions
140   "Great Is Thy Faithfulness" (Isa.)
141   "Children of the Heavenly Father" (Isa.)
197   "Ye Who Claim the Faith of Jesus" (Isa.)
2011   "We Sing of Your Glory" (Isa., Christmas)
3064   "On Christmas Night" (Isa., Ps., Christmas)
69   "In Thee Is Gladness" (Isa., Heb.)
233   "En el Frío Invernal" ("Cold December Flies Away")
            (Isa., Heb., Matt.)
242   "Love Came Down at Christmas" (Isa., Matt.) (C)
62   "All Creatures of Our God and King" (Ps.) (O)
2008   "Let All Things Now Living" (Ps.)
2012   "Let Us with a Joyful Mind" (Ps.)
3018   "Creation Sings" (Ps.)
224   "Good Christian Friends, Rejoice" (Ps., Heb., Matt.)
153   "Thou Hidden Source of Calm Repose" (Heb.)
168   "At the Name of Jesus" (Heb.)
227   "The Friendly Beasts" (Heb.)
223   "Break Forth, O Beauteous Heavenly Light" (Heb.,
            Matt.)
229   "Infant Holy, Infant Lowly" (Heb., Matt.)
250   "Once in Royal David's City" (Heb., Matt.) (O)
222   "Niño Lindo" ("Child So Lovely") (Matt.)
235   "Rock-a-Bye, My Dear Little Boy" (Matt.)
237   "Sing We Now of Christmas" (Matt.) (C)
246   "Joy to the World" (Matt.)
447   "Our Parent, by Whose Name" (Matt.)
2095   "Star-Child" (Matt.)
2099   "Joseph Dearest, Joseph Mine" (Matt.)
3053   "Bethlehem" (Matt., Christmas)
3067   "Welcome to Our World" (Matt., Christmas)

Additional Contemporary Suggestions
S2022   "Great Is the Lord" (Isa.)
            SP30
SP185   "The Steadfast Love of the Lord" (Isa.)
S2033   "Glory to God" ("Gloria a Dios") (Ps., Christmas)
S2276   "Glory to God in the Highest" (Ps., Christmas)
S2087   "We Will Glorify" (Ps.)
            SP68
WS3034 "God of Wonders" (Ps.)
            M80
M59   "Let Everything That Has Breath" (Ps.)
WS3040 "You Are My All in All" (Heb.)
            SP220
M37   "He Is Able" (Heb.)
M65   "Before the Throne of God Above" (Heb.)
M78   "Once Again" (Heb.)
M81   "Amazing Love" (Heb.)
WS3102 "You Are My King" ("Amazing Love") (Heb.)
            M82

M94   "That's Why We Praise Him" (Heb.)
S2098   "The Virgin Mary Had a Baby Boy" (Matt.,
            Christmas)
WS3105 "In Christ Alone" (Christmas)
            M138

Vocal Solos
"Sing a Song of Joy" (Ps.)
    V-4   p. 2
"Gentle Jesus, Meek and Mild" (Matt.)
    V-1   p. 11
"Little Baby Jesus" (Matt., Christmas)
    V-8   p. 96
"Mary Had a Baby" (Matt., Christmas)
    V-7   p. 46
"To Touch His Tiny Hand" (Matt., Christmas)
    V-10   p. 22
"Sing Noel!" (Christmas)
    V-11   p. 13

Anthems
"Let Our Gladness Banish Sadness"
Michael Burkhardt; MorningStar MSM-50-1290
SATB, flute, keyboard

"Away in a Manger" (Matt., Christmas)
Matthew Culloton; Paraclete Press MSM-50-0095
SATBB, *a cappella*

Other Suggestions
Visuals:
    O   Salvation history, people, children, Christ
    P   Ps. 148:1*a*, angels, sun/moon/stars, nature
            imagery, horn
    E   Pioneer, crucifix, brothers/sisters, Jesus, manacles
    G   Angel/Joseph, escape, Herod/Wise Men, return
The New Year lections and suggestions for Dec. 31/Jan. 1
    may be used on this day.
Greeting: BOW275 (Isa., Christmas)
Opening Prayer: BOW278 (Isa., Ps., Heb., Christmas)
Prayer: BOW313 (Matt.)
Prayer: WSL11. Radiant Morning Star (Matt.)
For children: UM227. "The Friendly Beasts." Accompanying
    a soloist with guitar or piano. This tune is also
    recommended for 12/31, using another text.

DECEMBER 31, 2013 / JANUARY 1, 2014

Ecclesiastes 3:1-13

For everything there is a season, and a time for every matter under heaven: [2]a time to be born, and a time to die; a time to plant, and a time to pluck up what is planted; [3]a time to kill, and a time to heal; a time to break down, and a time to build up; [4]a time to weep, and a time to laugh; a time to mourn, and a time to dance; [5]a time to throw away stones, and a time to gather stones together; a time to embrace, and a time to refrain from embracing; [6]a time to seek, and a time to lose; a time to keep, and a time to throw away; [7]a time to tear, and a time to sew; a time to keep silence, and a time to speak; [8]a time to love, and a time to hate; a time for war, and a time for peace. [9]What gain have the workers from their toil? [10]I have seen the business that God has given to everyone to be busy with.

[11]He has made everything suitable for its time; moreover he has put a sense of past and future into their minds, yet they cannot find out what God has done from the beginning to the end. [12]I know that there is nothing better for them than to be happy and enjoy themselves as long as they live; [13]moreover, it is God's gift that all should eat and drink and take pleasure in all their toil.

Psalm 8

[1] O LORD, our Sovereign,
how majestic is your name in all the earth!
You have set your glory above the heavens.
[2]   Out of the mouths of babes and infants
you have founded a bulwark because of your foes,
to silence the enemy and the avenger.
[3] When I look at your heavens, the work of your fingers,
the moon and the stars that you have established;
[4] what are human beings that you are mindful of them,
mortals that you care for them?
[5] Yet you have made them a little lower than God,
and crowned them with glory and honor.
[6] You have given them dominion over the works of your
hands;
you have put all things under their feet,
[7] all sheep and oxen,
and also the beasts of the field,
[8] the birds of the air, and the fish of the sea,
whatever passes along the paths of the seas.
[9] O LORD, our Sovereign,
how majestic is your name in all the earth!

Revelation 21:1-6a

[1]Then I saw a new heaven and a new earth; for the first heaven and the first earth had passed away, and the sea was no more. [2]And I saw the holy city, the new Jerusalem, coming down out of heaven from God, prepared as a bride adorned for her husband. [3]And I heard a loud voice from the throne saying,

"See, the home of God is among mortals.
He will dwell with them as their God;
they will be his peoples,
and God himself will be with them;
[4] he will wipe every tear from their eyes.
Death will be no more;
mourning and crying and pain will be no more,
for the first things have passed away."

[5]And the one who was seated on the throne said, "See, I am making all things new." Also he said, "Write this, for these words are trustworthy and true." [6]Then he said to me, "It is done! I am the Alpha and the Omega, the beginning and the end."

Matthew 25:31-46

[31]"When the Son of Man comes in his glory, and all the angels with him, then he will sit on the throne of his glory. [32]All the nations will be gathered before him, and he will separate people one from another as a shepherd separates the sheep from the goats, [33]and he will put the sheep at his right hand and the goats at the left. [34]Then the king will say to those at his right hand, 'Come, you that are blessed by my Father, inherit the kingdom prepared for you from the foundation of the world; [35]for I was hungry and you gave me food, I was thirsty and you gave me something to drink, I was a stranger and you welcomed me, [36]I was naked and you gave me clothing, I was sick and you took care of me, I was in prison and you visited me.' [37]Then the righteous will answer him, 'Lord, when was it that we saw you hungry and gave you food, or thirsty and gave you something to drink? [38]And when was it that we saw you a stranger and welcomed you, or naked and gave you clothing? [39]And when was it that we saw you sick or in prison and visited you?' [40]And the king will answer them, 'Truly I tell you, just as you did it to one of the least of these who are members of my family, you did it to me.' [41]Then he will say to those at his left hand, 'You that are accursed, depart from me into the eternal fire prepared for the devil and his angels; [42]for I was hungry and you gave me no food, I was thirsty and you gave me nothing to drink, [43]I was a stranger and you did not welcome me, naked and you did not give me clothing, sick and in prison and you did not visit me.' [44]Then they also will answer, 'Lord, when was it that we saw you hungry or thirsty or a stranger or naked or sick or in prison, and did not take care of you?' [45]Then he will answer them, 'Truly I tell you, just as you did not do it to one of the least of these, you did not do it to me.' [46]And these will go away into eternal punishment, but the righteous into eternal life."

COLOR: WHITE

WATCH NIGHT / NEW YEAR

Primary Hymns and Songs for the Day

117	"O God, Our Help in Ages Past" (Eccles.) (O)
	H-3 Hbl-33, 80; Chr-60, 143; Desc-93;
	Org-132
	S-1 #293-296. Various treatments
2203	"In His Time" (Eccles.)
434	"Cuando El Pobre" ("When the Poor Ones")
	(Matt.)
2178	"Here Am I" (Matt.) (C)
3128	"Whatever You Do" (Matt.)
3115	"Covenant Prayer" (New Year, Covenant Service)
726	"O Holy City, Seen of John" (Rev.) (C)
	H-3 Chr-139, 145; Desc-77
	S-1 #241-242. Orff arr. and descant

Additional Hymn Suggestions

517	"By Gracious Powers" (Eccles.)
707	"Hymn of Promise" (Eccles.)
77	"How Great Thou Art" (Ps.)
97	"For the Fruits of This Creation" (Ps.) (O)
	(alternate tune #688)
141	"Children of the Heavenly Father" (Ps.)
383	"This Is a Day of New Beginnings" (Rev.)
428	"For the Healing of the Nations" (Rev.)
722	"I Want to Be Ready" (Rev.)
727	"O What Their Joy and Their Glory Must Be" (Rev.)
2142	"Blessed Quietness" (Rev.)
2210	"Joy Comes with the Dawn" (Rev.)
2284	"Joy in the Morning" (Rev.)
3109	"Living Spirit, Holy Fire" (Rev., Covenant Service)
3157	"Come, Let us Dream" (Rev.)
510	"Come, Ye Disconsolate" (Rev., Matt.)
638	"This Is the Feast of Victory" (Rev., Communion)
192	"There's a Spirit in the Air" (Matt.) (C)
427	"Where Cross the Crowded Ways of Life" (Matt.)
432	"Jesu, Jesu" (Matt.)
433	"All Who Love and Serve Your City" (Matt.)
568	"Christ for the World We Sing" (Matt.)
579	"Lord God, Your Love Has Called Us Here" (Matt.)
581	"Lord, Whose Love Through Humble Service" (Matt.)
591	"Rescue the Perishing" (Matt.)
617	"I Come With Joy" (Matt., New Year, Communion)
2048	"God Weeps" (Matt.)
2094	"Carol of the Epiphany" (Matt.)
2095	"Star-Child" (New Year, Matt.)
2126	"All Who Hunger" (Rev., Matt.)
2172	"We Are Called" (Matt., Epiphany)
2175	"Together We Serve" (Matt.)
2177	"Wounded World that Cries for Healing" (Matt.)
2187	"Now It Is Evening" (Matt.)
2254	"In Remembrance of Me" (Matt., Communion)

Additional Contemporary Suggestions

M63	"I Could Sing of Your Love Forever" (Eccles.)
M152	"Be Glorified" (Eccles.)
M13	"Be Glorified" (Eccles.)
M178	"Majestic" (Ps.)
S2023	"How Majestic Is Your Name" (Ps.)
	SP14
WS3015	"How Great You Are" (Ps.)
WS3027	"Hallelujah" ("Your Love Is Amazing") (Ps.)
	M118

WS3032	"Across the Lands" (Ps., Christmas)
WS3034	"God of Wonders" (Ps.)
	M80
UM171	"There's Something About That Name" (Rev.)
	SP89
UM347	"Spirit Song" (Rev.)
	SP134
UM706	"Soon and Very Soon" (Rev.)
	S-2 #187. Piano arrangement
S2132	"You Who Are Thirsty" (Rev.)
	SP219
S2194	"O Freedom" (Rev.)
S2087	"We Will Glorify" (Rev.)
	SP68
M32	"Holy and Anointed One" (Rev., Matt.)
SP60	"To Him Who Sits on the Throne" (Rev., Matt.)
S2244	"People Need the Lord" (Matt.)

Vocal Solos

"I Will Sing of Thy Great Mercies" (Eccles., Ps.)
V-4   p. 43
"Maybe the Rain" (Rev.)
V-5(2)   p. 27
"Sing for Christ Is Born" (Rev., Christmas)
V-10   p. 16
"Come to the Water" (Rev., Matt.)
WS3114
"Reach Out to Your Neighbor" (Matt.)
V-8   p. 372
"Covenant Prayer" (New Year)
V-11   p. 6

Anthems

"There Is a Season" (Eccles.)
Allen Petker; Pavanne 08301756
SATB, keyboard

"God has Work for Us to Do" (Matt.)
Mark Miller; Choristers Guild CGA-1288
SATB, piano

Other Suggestions

Visuals:

O	Clock, birth/death, plant/pluck up, etc.
P	Glory, newborns, fingers, moon/stars, humanity, earth,
E	Earth/space, heaven, bride, throne, wipe tears, Rev. 21:5a
G	Second Coming, nations, goats/sheep, feeding, etc.

These lections and ideas may be used on December 29.
Covenant Service Resources: BOW288, 291-294, UM607
Greeting: BOW294 (New Year) or BOW453 (Rev.)
Opening Prayer: WSL64. God of all creation (Ps., Covenant)
Prayer: WSL217. Lord of the morning (Matt., New Year)
Prayer: WSL199. O God of the crucified Christ (Matt.)
Canticle: UM734. "Canticle of Hope" (Rev.)
Offertory Prayer: WSL98 (Matt.) or WSL105 (Rev.)
Great Thanksgiving for New Year: BOW58-59
Litany: WSL158. Here in this sanctuary (Matt.)
Response: UM707, stanza 3. "Hymn of Promise" (Eccles.)
Blessing: WSL27 or WSL159 or WSL169 (Matt.)

JANUARY 5, 2014

Jeremiah 31:7-14

[7]For thus says the LORD: Sing aloud with gladness for Jacob, and raise shouts for the chief of the nations; proclaim, give praise, and say, "Save, O LORD, your people, the remnant of Israel." [8]See, I am going to bring them from the land of the north, and gather them from the farthest parts of the earth, among them the blind and the lame, those with child and those in labor, together; a great company, they shall return here. [9]With weeping they shall come, and with consolations I will lead them back, I will let them walk by brooks of water, in a straight path in which they shall not stumble; for I have become a father to Israel, and Ephraim is my firstborn.

[10]Hear the word of the LORD, O nations, and declare it in the coastlands far away; say, "He who scattered Israel will gather him, and will keep him as a shepherd a flock." [11]For the LORD has ransomed Jacob, and has redeemed him from hands too strong for him. [12]They shall come and sing aloud on the height of Zion, and they shall be radiant over the goodness of the LORD, over the grain, the wine, and the oil, and over the young of the flock and the herd; their life shall become like a watered garden, and they shall never languish again. [13]Then shall the young women rejoice in the dance, and the young men and the old shall be merry. I will turn their mourning into joy, I will comfort them, and give them gladness for sorrow. [14]I will give the priests their fill of fatness, and my people shall be satisfied with my bounty, says theLORD.

Psalm 147:12-20

[12] Praise the LORD, O Jerusalem! Praise your God, O Zion!

[13] For he strengthens the bars of your gates;
 he blesses your children within you.

[14] He grants peace within your borders;
 he fills you with the finest of wheat.

[15] He sends out his command to the earth;
 his word runs swiftly.

[16] He gives snow like wool; he scatters frost like ashes.

[17] He hurls down hail like crumbs—
 who can stand before his cold?

[18] He sends out his word, and melts them;
 he makes his wind blow, and the waters flow.

[19] He declares his word to Jacob,
 his statutes and ordinances to Israel.

[20] He has not dealt thus with any other nation;
 they do not know his ordinances.
 Praise the LORD!

Ephesians 1:3-14

[3]Blessed be the God and Father of our Lord Jesus Christ, who has blessed us in Christ with every spiritual blessing in the heavenly places,[4]just as he chose us in Christ before the foundation of the world to be holy and blameless before him in love. [5]He destined us for adoption as his children through Jesus Christ, according to the good pleasure of his will, [6]to the praise of his glorious grace that he freely bestowed on us in the Beloved. [7]In him we have redemption through his blood, the forgiveness of our trespasses, according to the riches of his grace [8]that he lavished on us. With all wisdom and insight [9]he has made known to us the mystery of his will, according to his good pleasure that he set forth in Christ, [10]as a plan for the fullness of time, to gather up all things in him, things in heaven and things on earth. [11]In Christ we have also obtained an inheritance, having been destined according to the purpose of him who accomplishes all things according to his counsel and will, [12]so that we, who were the first to set our hope on Christ, might live for the praise of his glory. [13]In him you also, when you had heard the word of truth, the gospel of your salvation, and had believed in him, were marked with the seal of the promised Holy Spirit; [14]this is the pledge of our inheritance toward redemption as God's own people, to the praise of his glory.

John 1: (1-9), 10-18

[1] In the beginning was the Word, and the Word was with God, and the Word was God. [2]He was in the beginning with God. [3]All things came into being through him, and without him not one thing came into being. What has come into being [4]in him was life, and the life was the light of all people. [5]The light shines in the darkness, and the darkness did not overcome it.

[6]There was a man sent from God, whose name was John. [7]He came as a witness to testify to the light, so that all might believe through him. [8]He himself was not the light, but he came to testify to the light. [9]The true light, which enlightens everyone, was coming into the world.

[10]He was in the world, and the world came into being through him; yet the world did not know him. [11]He came to what was his own, and his own people did not accept him. [12]But to all who received him, who believed in his name, he gave power to become children of God, [13]who were born, not of blood or of the will of the flesh or of the will of man, but of God.

[14]And the Word became flesh and lived among us, and we have seen his glory, the glory as of a father's only son, full of grace and truth. [15](John testified to him and cried out, "This was he of whom I said, 'He who comes after me ranks ahead of me because he was before me.'") [16]From his fullness we have all received, grace upon grace. [17]The law indeed was given through Moses; grace and truth came through Jesus Christ. [18]No one has ever seen God. It is God the only Son, who is close to the Father's heart, who has made him known.

COLOR: WHITE   **2nd SUNDAY AFTER CHRISTMAS**

Primary Hymns and Songs for the Day

240 "Hark! The Herald Angels Sing" (John) (O)
   H-3 Hbl-26, 67; Chr-91; Desc-75; Org-89
   S-1 #234-36. Harmonizations and descant
251 "Go, Tell It on the Mountain" (John) (O)
   H-3 Hbl-17; Chr-73; Desc-45; Org-46
223 "Break Forth, O Beauteous Heavenly Light" (Jer.)
186 "Alleluia" (Jer.)
   SP108; S-2 #3-4
261 "Lord of the Dance" (John)
   H-3 Chr-106; Org-81
246 "Joy to the World" (John, Christmas) (C)
   S-1 #19-20. Trumpet descants

Additional Hymn Suggestions

128 "He Leadeth Me: O Blessed Thought" (Jer.)
136 "The Lord's My Shepherd" (Jer.)
138 "The King of Love My Shepherd Is" (Jer.)
381 "Savior, Like a Shepherd Lead Us" (Jer.)
474 "Precious Lord, Take My Hand" (Jer.)
2058 "Shepherd Me, O God" (Jer.)
2236 "Gather Us In" (Jer.)
2279 "The Trees of the Field" (Jer.)
206 "I Want to Walk as a Child of the Light" (Jer., John)
160 "Rejoice, Ye Pure in Heart" (Ps.)
161 "Rejoice, Ye Pure in Heart" (Ps.)
103 "Immortal, Invisible, God Only Wise" (Eph.)
362 "Nothing But the Blood" (Eph., Communion)
369 "Blessed Assurance" (Eph.)
370 "Victory in Jesus" (Eph.)
377 "It Is Well with My Soul" (Eph.)
609 "You Have Put on Christ" (Eph.)
622 "There Is a Fountain Filled with Blood" (Eph., Communion)
2248 "Baptized in Water" (Eph.)
2276 "Glory to God in the Highest" (Eph.)
113 "Source and Sovereign, Rock and Cloud" (John)
145 "Morning Has Broken" (John)
152 "I Sing the Almighty Power of God" (John)
182 "Word of God, Come Down on Earth" (John)
195 "Send Your Word" (John)
214 "Savior of the Nations, Come" (John)
242 "Love Came Down at Christmas" (John)
596 "Blessed Jesus, at Thy Word" (John)
598 "O Word of God Incarnate" (John)
644 "Jesus, Joy of Our Desiring" (John, Communion)
2100 "Thou Didst Leave Thy Throne" (John)
2046 "Womb of Life" (John)
2121 "O Holy Spirit, Root of Life" (John)
2158 "Just a Closer Walk with Thee" (John)
2236 "Gather Us In" (John, Epiphany)

Additional Contemporary Suggestions

WS3042 "Shout to the North" (Jer.)
   M99
WS3096 "Gentle Shepherd" (Jer.)
WS3108 "Trading My Sorrows" (Jer.)
   M75
SP40 "God Will Make a Way" (Jer.)
S2144 "Someone Asked the Question" (Jer., Ps.)
UM99 "My Tribute" ("To God Be the Glory") (Eph.)
   SP118; V-8 p. 5 Vocal Solo

S2071 "Jesus, Name Above All Names" (John)
   SP76
S2173 "Shine, Jesus, Shine" (John, Epiphany)
   SP142
SP48 "Behold, What Manner of Love" (John)
S2204 "Light of the World" (John, Epiphany)
S2219 "Goodness Is Stronger than Evil" (John, Epiphany)
S2235 "We Are Marching" ("Siyahamba") (John, Epiphany)
WS3056 "Jesus, the Light of the World" (John, Epiphany)

Vocal Solos

"Sing a Song of Joy" (Ps.)
   V-4   p. 2
"And Can It Be That I Should Gain" (Eph.)
   V-1   p. 29
"Amazing Grace" (Eph.)
   V-8   p. 56
   V-10   p. 8

Anthems

"Love Came Down at Christmas" (John)
Nancy Frundahl: MorningStar MSM-50-1930
SATB divisi, opt. oboe

"Angels We Have Heard on High" (Christmas)
Taylor Davis; MorningStar MSM-50-1220
SATB, piano or harp, opt. children's choir and instruments

Other Suggestions

This Sunday may also be celebrated as Epiphany of the Lord Sunday using the ideas for January 6.
Visuals:
   O   Praise, singing, old and young dancing, blind, lame, children, pregnant woman
   P   Gates, children, wheat, runner, winter
   E   Christ, children, adoption certificate, wrapped gift, crucifix
   G   Creation, light/darkness, Christ (Word), John the Baptist
Introit: UM473. "Lead Me, Lord" (Ps.)
Greeting: BOW272 or 296 or 305 (John)
Opening Prayer: WSL8. God of glory (John, Christmas)
Prayer: BOW277 or 297 or 308 or 310 (John)
Blessing: WSL7. The light that enlivens (John)
Benediction: WSL167. Go! Never stop going out (John)
See more ideas in *The Abingdon Worship Annual 2014.*

53

JANUARY 6, 2014 (OR JANUARY 5, 2014)

Isaiah 60:1-6

1 Arise, shine; for your light has come,
   and the glory of the LORD has risen upon you.
2 For darkness shall cover the earth,
   and thick darkness the peoples;
  but the LORD will arise upon you,
   and his glory will appear over you.
3 Nations shall come to your light,
   and kings to the brightness of your dawn.
4 Lift up your eyes and look around;
   they all gather together, they come to you;
   your sons shall come from far away,
   and your daughters shall be carried on their
      nurses' arms.
5 Then you shall see and be radiant;
   your heart shall thrill and rejoice,
  because the abundance of the sea shall be brought to you,
   the wealth of the nations shall come to you.
6 A multitude of camels shall cover you,
   the young camels of Midian and Ephah;
   all those from Sheba shall come.
  They shall bring gold and frankincense,
   and shall proclaim the praise of the LORD.

Psalm 72:1-7, 10-14

1 Give the king your justice, O God,
   and your righteousness to a king's son.
2 May he judge your people with righteousness,
   and your poor with justice.
3 May the mountains yield prosperity for the people,
   and the hills, in righteousness.
4 May he defend the cause of the poor of the people,
   give deliverance to the needy,
   and crush the oppressor.
5 May he live while the sun endures,
   and as long as the moon, throughout all generations.
6 May he be like rain that falls on the mown grass,
   like showers that water the earth.
7 In his days may righteousness flourish
   and peace abound, until the moon is no more.
. . . .
10 May the kings of Tarshish and of the isles
   render him tribute,
  may the kings of Sheba and Seba bring gifts.
11 May all kings fall down before him,
   all nations give him service.
12 For he delivers the needy when they call,
   the poor and those who have no helper.
13 He has pity on the weak and the needy,
   and saves the lives of the needy.
14 From oppression and violence he redeems their life;
   and precious is their blood in his sight.

Ephesians 3:1-12

1This is the reason that I Paul am a prisoner for Christ Jesus for the sake of you Gentiles— 2for surely you have already heard of the commission of God's grace that was given me for you, 3and how the mystery was made known to me by revelation, as I wrote above in a few words, 4a reading of which will enable you to perceive my understanding of the mystery of Christ. 5In former generations this mystery was not made known to humankind, as it has now been revealed to his holy apostles and prophets by the Spirit: 6that is, the Gentiles have become fellow heirs, members of the same body, and sharers in the promise in Christ Jesus through the gospel.

7Of this gospel I have become a servant according to the gift of God's grace that was given me by the working of his power. 8Although I am the very least of all the saints, this grace was given to me to bring to the Gentiles the news of the boundless riches of Christ, 9and to make everyone see what is the plan of the mystery hidden for ages in God who created all things; 10so that through the church the wisdom of God in its rich variety might now be made known to the rulers and authorities in the heavenly places. 11This was in accordance with the eternal purpose that he has carried out in Christ Jesus our Lord, 12in whom we have access to God in boldness and confidence through faith in him.

Matthew 2:1-12

1In the time of King Herod, after Jesus was born in Bethlehem of Judea, wise men from the East came to Jerusalem, 2asking, "Where is the child who has been born king of the Jews? For we observed his star at its rising, and have come to pay him homage." 3When King Herod heard this, he was frightened, and all Jerusalem with him; 4and calling together all the chief priests and scribes of the people, he inquired of them where the Messiah was to be born. 5They told him, "In Bethlehem of Judea; for so it has been written by the prophet:
6 'And you, Bethlehem, in the land of Judah,
   are by no means least among the rulers of Judah;
   for from you shall come a ruler
   who is to shepherd my people Israel.' "
7Then Herod secretly called for the wise men and learned from them the exact time when the star had appeared. 8Then he sent them to Bethlehem, saying, "Go and search diligently for the child; and when you have found him, bring me word so that I may also go and pay him homage." 9When they had heard the king, they set out; and there, ahead of them, went the star that they had seen at its rising, until it stopped over the place where the child was. 10When they saw that the star had stopped, they were overwhelmed with joy. 11On entering the house, they saw the child with Mary his mother; and they knelt down and paid him homage. Then, opening their treasure chests, they offered him gifts of gold, frankincense, and myrrh. 12And having been warned in a dream not to return to Herod, they left for their own country by another road

COLOR: WHITE

EPIPHANY OF THE LORD

Primary Hymns and Songs for the Day

203	"Hail to the Lord's Anointed" (Ps.) (O)
	H-3 Hbl-16, 22, 68; Chr-101; Desc-37
	S-1 #114. Descant
	#115. Harmonization
2005	"Arise, Shine" (Isa.)
254	"We Three Kings" (Matt., Ps.)
	H-3 Chr-208; Org-65
	S-2 #97-98. Various treatments
2095	"Star-Child" (Matt.)
3051	"A Star Shone Bright" (Matt.)
251	"Go, Tell It on the Mountain" (Eph., Christmas) (C)
	H-3 Hbl-17, 28, 61; Chr-73; Desc-45; Org-46

Additional Hymn Suggestions

187	"Rise, Shine, You People" (Isa.)
209	"Blessed Be the God of Israel" (Isa., Christmas)
585	"This Little Light of Mine" (Isa.)
725	"Arise, Shine Out, Your Light has Come" (Isa.)
247	"O Morning Star, How Fair and Bright" (Isa., Ps., Matt.)
2172	"We Are Called" (Isa., Ps.)
2177	"Wounded World that Cries for Healing" (Ps.)
2178	"Here Am I" (Ps.)
2180	"Why Stand So Far Away, My God?" (Ps.)
2182	"When God Restored our Common Life" (Ps.)
157	"Jesus Shall Reign" (Ps.)
213	"Lift Up Your Heads, Ye Mighty Gates" (Ps.)
228	"He Is Born" ("Il Est Né") (Isa., Matt.)
249	"There's a Song in the Air" (Isa., Ps., Matt.)
188	"Christ Is the World's Light" (Eph.)
421	"Make Me a Captive, Lord" (Eph.) (C)
568	"Christ for the World We Sing" (Eph.)
233	"En el Frio Invernal" ("Cold December Flies Away") (Eph., Matt.)
246	"Joy to the World" (Eph., Matt.)
219	"What Child Is This" (Matt.)
220	"Angels from the Realms of Glory" (Matt.)
221	"In the Bleak Midwinter" (Matt.)
222	"Niño Lindo" ("Child So Lovely") (Matt.)
237	"Sing We Now of Christmas" (Matt.)
239	"Silent Night, Holy Night" (Matt.)
242	"Love Came Down at Christmas" (Matt.)
243	"De Tierra Lejana Venimos" ("From a Distant Home") (Matt.)
245	"The First Noel" (Matt.)
248	"On This Day Earth Shall Ring" (Matt.)
249	"There's a Song in the Air" (Matt.)
256	"We Would See Jesus" (Matt.)
627	"O the Depth of Love Divine" (Matt., Communion)
2094	"Carol of the Epiphany" (Matt.)
2096	"Rise Up, Shepherd, and Follow" (Matt.)
2098	"The Virgin Mary Had a Baby Boy" (Matt.)
3062	"Spirit-Child Jesus" (Matt., Epiphany)
3063	"If I Could Visit Bethlehem" (Matt., Epiphany)

Additional Contemporary Suggestions

S2173	"Shine, Jesus, Shine" (Isa., Epiphany)
	SP142
SP103	"We Worship and Adore You" (Isa.)
M4	"Let it Rise" (Isa.)
M19	"Shine on Us" (Isa., Epiphany)

SP176	"Arise Shine" (Isa.)
S2118	"Holy Spirit, Come to Us" (Ps.)
S2162	"Grace Alone" (Eph.)
	M100
S2069	"All Hail King Jesus" (Matt., Epiphany)
	SP63
WS3056	"Jesus, the Light of the World" (Matt., Epiphany)
UM186	"Alleluia" (Matt.)
	SP108; S-2 #3-4
M18	"Come and Behold Him" (Matt., Epiphany)

Vocal Solos

"For Behold, Darkness Shall Cover the Earth" and
"The People That Walked in Darkness" (Isa.)
  V-2
"Jesus, What a Wonderful Child" (Eph., Matt., Christmas)
  V-5(1)   p. 48
"Love Came Down at Christmas" (Matt.)
  V-8   p. 90
"Let De Heb'n-Light Shine on Me" (Matt., Epiphany)
  V-7   p. 66
"The Kings" (Matt., Epiphany)
  V-9   p. 13
"Fit for a King" (Matt., Epiphany)
  V-10   p. 32

Anthems

"O Nata Lux" (Isa.)
Guy Forbes; Pavane 08301844
SATB divisi, *a cappella*

"Three Kings" (Isa., Matt.)
Cornelius / Atkins; Oxford 9780193408487
SATB, soloist, *a cappella*

Other Suggestions

These ideas may be used on January 5 as Epiphany of the Lord Sunday.
Visuals:

O	Light, glory, darkness, daughters/nurses, sea, camels
P	Four scales of justice, Christ, mountains/hills, poor/needy
E	Manacles, letter, Christ, all nations
G	Herod, Wise Men, star, Bethlehem, Mary/baby, gifts

Introit: UM216. "Lo, How a Rose E'er Blooming" (Matt.)
Greeting: BOW296 (Epiphany) or BOW304 (Isa.)
Canticle: UM225. "Canticle of Simeon" (Ps., Matt.)
Prayer: BOW297 or UM255 (Isa., Epiphany)
Offertory Prayer: WSL150. *God of new beginnings* (New Year)
Great Thanksgiving for Epiphany: BOW58-59
Sung Benediction: WS3062. "Spirit-Child Jesus" (Matt.)

55

JANUARY 12, 2014

Isaiah 42:1-9

1 Here is my servant, whom I uphold,
   my chosen, in whom my soul delights;
   I have put my spirit upon him;
   he will bring forth justice to the nations.
2 He will not cry or lift up his voice,
   or make it heard in the street;
3 a bruised reed he will not break,
   and a dimly burning wick he will not quench;
   he will faithfully bring forth justice.
4 He will not grow faint or be crushed
   until he has established justice in the earth;
   and the coastlands wait for his teaching.
5 Thus says God, the LORD,
   who created the heavens and stretched them out,
   who spread out the earth and what comes from it,
   who gives breath to the people upon it
   and spirit to those who walk in it:
6 I am the LORD, I have called you in righteousness,
   I have taken you by the hand and kept you;
   I have given you as a covenant to the people,
   a light to the nations,
   7to open the eyes that are blind,
   to bring out the prisoners from the dungeon,
   from the prison those who sit in darkness.
8 I am the LORD, that is my name;
   my glory I give to no other,
   nor my praise to idols.
9 See, the former things have come to pass,
   and new things I now declare;
   before they spring forth,
   I tell you of them.

Psalm 29

1 Ascribe to the LORD, O heavenly beings,
   ascribe to the LORD glory and strength.
2 Ascribe to the LORD the glory of his name;
   worship the LORD in holy splendor.
3 The voice of the LORD is over the waters;
   the God of glory thunders,
   the LORD, over mighty waters.
4 The voice of the LORD is powerful;
   the voice of the LORD is full of majesty.
5 The voice of the LORD breaks the cedars;
   the LORD breaks the cedars of Lebanon.
6 He makes Lebanon skip like a calf,
   and Sirion like a young wild ox.
7 The voice of the LORD flashes forth flames of fire.
8 The voice of the LORD shakes the wilderness;
   the LORD shakes the wilderness of Kadesh.
9 The voice of the LORD causes the oaks to whirl,
   and strips the forest bare;
   and in his temple all say, "Glory!"
10 The LORD sits enthroned over the flood;
   the LORD sits enthroned as king forever.
11 May the LORD give strength to his people!
   May the LORD bless his people with peace!

Acts 10:34-43

34Then Peter began to speak to them: "I truly understand that God shows no partiality, 35but in every nation anyone who fears him and does what is right is acceptable to him. 36You know the message he sent to the people of Israel, preaching peace by Jesus Christ—he is Lord of all. 37That message spread throughout Judea, beginning in Galilee after the baptism that John announced: 38how God anointed Jesus of Nazareth with the Holy Spirit and with power; how he went about doing good and healing all who were oppressed by the devil, for God was with him. 39We are witnesses to all that he did both in Judea and in Jerusalem. They put him to death by hanging him on a tree; 40but God raised him on the third day and allowed him to appear, 41not to all the people but to us who were chosen by God as witnesses, and who ate and drank with him after he rose from the dead. 42He commanded us to preach to the people and to testify that he is the one ordained by God as judge of the living and the dead. 43All the prophets testify about him that everyone who believes in him receives forgiveness of sins through his name."

Matthew 3:13-17

13Then Jesus came from Galilee to John at the Jordan, to be baptized by him. 14John would have prevented him, saying, "I need to be baptized by you, and do you come to me?" 15But Jesus answered him, "Let it be so now; for it is proper for us in this way to fulfill all righteousness." Then he consented. 16And when Jesus had been baptized, just as he came up from the water, suddenly the heavens were opened to him and he saw the Spirit of God descending like a dove and alighting on him. 17And a voice from heaven said, "This is my Son, the Beloved, with whom I am well pleased."

COLOR: WHITE   **BAPTISM OF THE LORD**

Primary Hymns and Songs for the Day
189   "Fairest Lord Jesus" (Isa., Matt.) (O)
252   "When Jesus Came to Jordan" (Isa., Matt.)
            H-3 Chr-211
347   "Spirit Song" (Matt.)
            SP134
605   "Wash, O God, Our Sons and Daughters" (Matt.)
            H-3 Hbl-14, 64; Chr-132, 203
            S-2 #22. Descant
3045   "Down by the Jordan" (Matt.)
2186   "Canto de Esperanza" ("Song of Hope") (Isa.) (C)

Additional Hymn Suggestions
157   "Jesus Shall Reign" (Isa.)
182   "Word of God, Come Down on Earth" (Isa.)
589   "The Church of Christ, in Every Age" (Isa.) (C)
2172   "We Are Called" (Isa.)
2177   "Wounded World that Cries for Healing" (Isa.)
2218   "You Are Mine" (Isa.)
2236   "Gather Us In" (Isa.)
2241   "The Spirit Sends Us Forth to Serve" (Isa.)
428   "For the Healing of the Nations" (Isa., Acts)
3001   "O For a Thousand Tongues to Sing (Isa., Ps.)
57   "O For a Thousand Tongues to Sing" (Isa., Ps.) (O)
60   "I'll Praise My Maker While I've Breath" (Ps.) (O)
73   "O Worship the King" (Ps.)
604   "Praise and Thanksgiving Be to God" (Ps., Matt.,
            Baptism)
257   "We Meet You, O Christ" (Acts)
306   "The Strife is O'er, the Battle Done" (Acts)
315   "Come, Ye Faithful, Raise the Strain" (Acts)
437   "This Is My Song" (Acts)
537   "Filled with the Spirit's Power" (Acts)
617   "I Come With Joy" (Acts, Communion)
2089   "Wild and Lone the Prophet's Voice" (Acts, Matt.)
2114   "At the Font We Start Our Journey" (Acts, Baptism)
3164   "Down to the River to Pray" (Acts, Baptism)
610   "We Know That Christ Is Raised" (Acts, Baptism)
332   "Spirit of Faith, Come Down" (Acts, Matt.)
541   "See How Great a Flame Aspires" (Acts, Matt.)
543   "O Breath of Life" (Acts, Matt.)
334   "Sweet, Sweet Spirit" (Matt.)
            SP136
603   "Come, Holy Ghost, Our Hearts Inspire" (Matt.)
608   "This Is the Spirit's Entry Now" (Matt., Baptism)
2051   "I Was There to Hear Your Borning Cry" (Matt.,
            Baptism)
2052   "The Lone, Wild Bird" (Matt.)
2117   "Spirit of God" (Matt.)
2122   "She Comes Sailing on the Wind" (Matt.)
2123   "Loving Spirit" (Matt., Baptism)
2247   "Wonder of Wonders" (Matt., Baptism)
2248   "Baptized in Water" (Matt., Baptism)
2253   "Water, River, Spirit, Grace" (Matt., Baptism)

Additional Contemporary Suggestions
UM333   "I'm Goin'a Sing When the Spirit Says Sing" (Isa.,
            Matt.)
WS3186 "Days of Elijah" (Isa.)
            M139
S2019   "Holy" ("Santo") (Isa.)
S2204   "Light of the World" (Isa.)

S2235   "We Are Marching" (Isa.)
S2040   "Awesome God" (Ps.)
            SP11
SP181   "God Is the Strength of My Heart" (Ps.)
SP2   "Ah, Lord God" (Ps.)
SP4   "Great and Mighty Is He" (Ps., Matt.)
            M11
M32   "Holy and Anointed One" (Acts)
S2250   "I've Just Come from the Fountain" (Matt.,
            Baptism)
S2107   "Wade in the Water" (Matt., Baptism)
S2071   "Jesus, Name Above All Names" (Matt.)
            SP76
S2139   "I Know the Lord's Laid His Hands on Me" (Matt.)
WS3112 "Breathe" (Matt.)
            M61
UM328   "Surely the Presence of the Lord" (Matt.)
            SP243; S-2, #200 Stanzas for soloist

Vocal Solos
"Spirit of Faith, Come Down" (Matt.)
    V-1   p. 43
"Borning Cry" (Matt., Baptism)
    V-5(1)   p. 10
"Wash, O God, Our Sons and Daughters" (Matt., Baptism)
    V-5(1)   p. 64
"This Is De Healin' Water" (Matt., Baptism)
    V-7   p. 52

Anthems
"Wade in the Water" (Matt., Baptism)
Aaron David Miller; Morningstar MSM-50-2613
SATB, *a cappella*

"I Come With Joy" (Acts, Communion)
Kenneth Dake; MorningStar MSM-50-2825
SATB, *a cappella*

"Christ, When for Us You Were Baptized" (Matt.)
Michael Helman; Augsburg 800674057
SAB, keyboard

Other Suggestions
Visuals:
    O   Christ, dove, scales, bent reed, lighted wick, earth
    P   Ps. 29:1-2, worship, sea, storm, cedars, calf, ox,
            flames
    E   Jesus/baptism/dove, healing, risen Christ, witness
    G   John baptizing Jesus, dove, Matt. 3:17
For a congregational baptism reaffirmation, use Baptismal
    Covenant IV, UM50. Musical resources include:
UN608, S2252, S2249, WS3164, WS3165, BOW174
Call to Worship: WS3044. "Make Way" (Isa.)
Greeting: BOW300 (Ps.)
Sung Confession: WS3111. "Redemption" (Isa.)
Prayer: WSL12. Great God of waves (Isa., Matt., Baptism)
Prayer: UM253 or BOW301. Baptism of the Lord.
Dismissal: BOW559 (Ps., Acts)

JANUARY 19, 2014

HUMAN RELATIONS DAY

Isaiah 49:1-7

¹ Listen to me, O coastlands,
  pay attention, you peoples from far away!
  The LORD called me before I was born,
    while I was in my mother's womb he named me.
² He made my mouth like a sharp sword,
    in the shadow of his hand he hid me;
  he made me a polished arrow,
    in his quiver he hid me away.
³ And he said to me, "You are my servant,
    Israel, in whom I will be glorified."
⁴ But I said, "I have labored in vain,
    I have spent my strength for nothing and vanity;
  yet surely my cause is with the LORD,
    and my reward with my God."
⁵ And now the LORD says,
    who formed me in the womb to be his servant,
  to bring Jacob back to him,
    and that Israel might be gathered to him,
  for I am honored in the sight of the LORD,
    and my God has become my strength—
⁶ he says,
  "It is too light a thing that you should be my servant
    to raise up the tribes of Jacob
    and to restore the survivors of Israel;
  I will give you as a light to the nations,
    that my salvation may reach to the end of the earth."
⁷ Thus says the LORD,
    the Redeemer of Israel and his Holy One,
  to one deeply despised, abhorred by the nations,
    the slave of rulers,
  "Kings shall see and stand up,
    princes, and they shall prostrate themselves,
  because of the LORD, who is faithful,
    the Holy One of Israel, who has chosen you."

Psalm 40:1-11

¹ I waited patiently for the Lord;
    he inclined to me and heard my cry.
² He drew me up from the desolate pit,
    out of the miry bog,
  and set my feet upon a rock,
    making my steps secure.
³ He put a new song in my mouth,
    a song of praise to our God.
  Many will see and fear,
    and put their trust in the Lord.
⁴ Happy are those who make
    the Lord their trust,
  who do not turn to the proud,
    to those who go astray after false gods.
⁵ You have multiplied, O Lord my God,
    your wondrous deeds and your thoughts toward us;
    none can compare with you.
  Were I to proclaim and tell of them,
    they would be more than can be counted.
⁶ Sacrifice and offering you do not desire,
    but you have given me an open ear.
  Burnt offering and sin offering
    you have not required.
⁷ Then I said, "Here I am;
    in the scroll of the book it is written of me.
⁸ I delight to do your will, O my God;

your law is within my heart."
⁹ I have told the glad news of deliverance
    in the great congregation;
  see, I have not restrained my lips,
    as you know, O Lord.
¹⁰ I have not hidden your saving help within my heart,
    I have spoken of your faithfulness and your salvation;
  I have not concealed your steadfast love and your faithfulness
    from the great congregation.
¹¹ Do not, O Lord, withhold
    your mercy from me;
  let your steadfast love and your faithfulness
    keep me safe forever.

1 Corinthians 1:1-9

¹Paul, called to be an apostle of Christ Jesus by the will of God, and our brother Sosthenes,

²To the church of God that is in Corinth, to those who are sanctified in Christ Jesus, called to be saints, together with all those who in every place call on the name of our Lord Jesus Christ, both their Lord and ours:

³Grace to you and peace from God our Father and the Lord Jesus Christ.

⁴I give thanks to my God always for you because of the grace of God that has been given you in Christ Jesus, ⁵for in every way you have been enriched in him, in speech and knowledge of every kind— ⁶just as the testimony of Christ has been strengthened among you— ⁷so that you are not lacking in any spiritual gift as you wait for the revealing of our Lord Jesus Christ. ⁸He will also strengthen you to the end, so that you may be blameless on the day of our Lord Jesus Christ. ⁹God is faithful; by him you were called into the fellowship of his Son, Jesus Christ our Lord.

John 1:29-42

²⁹The next day he saw Jesus coming toward him and declared, "Here is the Lamb of God who takes away the sin of the world! ³⁰This is he of whom I said, 'After me comes a man who ranks ahead of me because he was before me.' ³¹I myself did not know him; but I came baptizing with water for this reason, that he might be revealed to Israel." ³²And John testified, "I saw the Spirit descending from heaven like a dove, and it remained on him. ³³I myself did not know him, but the one who sent me to baptize with water said to me, 'He on whom you see the Spirit descend and remain is the one who baptizes with the Holy Spirit.' ³⁴And I myself have seen and have testified that this is the Son of God."

³⁵The next day John again was standing with two of his disciples, ³⁶and as he watched Jesus walk by, he exclaimed, "Look, here is the Lamb of God!" ³⁷The two disciples heard him say this, and they followed Jesus. ³⁸When Jesus turned and saw them following, he said to them, "What are you looking for?" They said to him, "Rabbi" (which translated means Teacher), "where are you staying?" ³⁹He said to them, "Come and see." They came and saw where he was staying, and they remained with him that day. It was about four o"clock in the afternoon. ⁴⁰One of the two who heard John speak and followed him was Andrew, Simon Peter's brother. ⁴¹He first found his brother Simon and said to him, "We have found the Messiah" (which is translated Anointed). ⁴²He brought Simon to Jesus, who looked at him and said, "You are Simon son of John. You are to be called Cephas" (which is translated Peter).

COLOR: GREEN

2nd SUNDAY AFTER THE EPIPHANY

Primary Hymns and Songs for the Day

2172	"We Are Called" (Isa., Epiphany, Human Relations) (O)
140	"Great Is Thy Faithfulness" (1 Cor.)
	H-3 Chr-87; Desc-39; Org-39
	S-2 #59. Piano arrangement
579	"Lord God, Your Love Has Called Us Here" (1 Cor., John, Human Relations)
	S-1 #57-61. Various treatments
2235	"We Are Marching" (Isa., Human Relations) (C)

Additional Hymn Suggestions

79	"Holy God, We Praise Thy Name" (Isa.) (O)
103	"Immortal, Invisible, God Only Wise" (Isa.) (C)
188	"Christ Is the World's Light" (Isa.)
573	"O Zion, Haste" (Isa., Human Relations)
585	"This Little Light of Mine" (Isa., Epiphany)
686	"O Gladsome Light" (Isa.)
2050	"Mothering God, You Gave Me Birth" (Isa., Communion)
593	"Here I Am, Lord" (Ps.)
662	"Stand Up and Bless the Lord" (Ps.)
209	"Blessed Be the God of Israel" (1 Cor.)
331	"Holy Spirit, Come, Confirm Us" (1 Cor.)
336	"Of All the Spirit's Gifts to Me" (1 Cor.)
568	"Christ for the World We Sing" (1 Cor., John, Human Relations)
712	"I Sing a Song of the Saints of God" (1 Cor., John, Human Relations)
714	"I Know Whom I Have Believed" (1 Cor., John)
156	"I Love to Tell the Story" (John)
193	"Jesus! the Name High over All" (John)
344	"Tú Has Venido a la Orilla" ("Lord, You Have Come to the Lakeshore") (John)
357	"Just as I Am" (John)
532	"Jesus, Priceless Treasure" (John)
580	"Lead On, O King Eternal" (John)
591	"Rescue the Perishing" (John)
2089	"Wild and Lone the Prophet's Voice" (John)
2101	"Two Fishermen" (John)
2127	"Come and See" ("Kyrie") (John)
2130	"The Summons" (John)
2137	"Would I Have Answered When You Called" (John)
2276	"Glory to God in the Highest" (John)
3161	"Gracious Creator of Sea and of Land" (John)
2135	"When Cain Killed Abel" (Human Relations)
2170	"God Made from One Blood" (Human Relations)

Additional Contemporary Suggestions

S2150	"Lord, Be Glorified" (Isa.)
	SP196
M13	"Be Glorified" (Isa.)
M152	"Be Glorified" (Isa.)
WS3042	"Shout to the North" (Isa.)
	M99
M164	"Good to Me" (Isa.)
WS3040	"You Are My All in All" (Isa., John)
	SP220
S2204	"Light of the World" (Isa., Epiphany)
S2218	"You Are Mine" (Isa., John)
WS3023	"Forever" (Ps.)
	M68

WS3027	"Hallelujah" ("Your Love Is Amazing") (Ps.)
	M118
M189	"Your Love, Oh Lord" (Ps.)
S2055	"You Are My Hiding Place" (Ps.)
S2139	"I Know the Lord's Laid His Hands on Me" (1 Cor.)
M87	"Let the Peace of God Reign" (1 Cor.)
UM347	"Spirit Song" (John)
	SP134
S2071	"Jesus, Name Above All Names" (John)
	SP76
S2165	"Cry of My Heart" (John)
	M39
WS3081	"Now Behold the Lamb" (John)
WS3160	"We Will Follow" ("Somlandela") (John)
M15	"Agnus Dei" (John)
M47	"Come Just As You Are" (John)
WS3004	"Step By Step" (John)
	M51

Vocal Solos

"Ye Servants of God" (Isa., John)
    V-1   p. 41
"Patiently Have I Waited for the Lord" (Ps.)
    V-4   p. 24
"Holy is the Lamb" (John)
    V-5(1)   p. 5
"Leanin' on Dat Lamb" (John)
    V-7   p. 42

Anthems

"I Waited for the Lord" (Ps.)
F. Mendelssohn; Carl Fischer CM 6250
SATB, piano

"Agnus Dei" (John)
Mikael Carlsson; Santa Barbara Music SBMP1019
SATB, *a cappella*

Other Suggestions

Visuals:

O	Coast, pregnancy, hand, arrow, light, earth, Christ
P	Clasped hands, pit, bog, feet/rock, sing, preach
E	People, speak, learning, Bible, gifts, Second Coming
G	Jesus, Lamb, baptism, Spirit, John, witnessing

Greeting: BOW307 (1 Cor.)
Opening Prayer: WSL22. From Bethlehem to Nazareth (John)
Canticle: UM82 or UM83. "Canticle of God's Glory" (John)
Response: UM300. "O The Lamb" (John)
Prayer: BOW468 (Isa., Ps.)
Prayer: BOW435. Martin Luther King, Jr. Day
Prayer: WSL67, BOW515, and BOW526 (Isa.)
Litany: BOW423. Human Relations Day

JANUARY 26, 2014

Isaiah 9:1-4

¹But there will be no gloom for those who were in anguish. In the former time he brought into contempt the land of Zebulun and the land of Naphtali, but in the latter time he will make glorious the way of the sea, the land beyond the Jordan, Galilee of the nations.

² The people who walked in darkness
    have seen a great light;
those who lived in a land of deep darkness—
    on them light has shined.
³ You have multiplied the nation,
    you have increased its joy;
they rejoice before you
    as with joy at the harvest,
    as people exult when dividing plunder.
⁴ For the yoke of their burden,
    and the bar across their shoulders,
    the rod of their oppressor,
    you have broken as on the day of Midian.

Psalm 27:1, 4-9

¹ The LORD is my light and my salvation;
    whom shall I fear?
The LORD is the stronghold of my life;
    of whom shall I be afraid?
. . . .
⁴ One thing I asked of the LORD,
    that will I seek after:
to live in the house of the LORD
    all the days of my life,
to behold the beauty of the LORD,
    and to inquire in his temple.
⁵ For he will hide me in his shelter
    in the day of trouble;
he will conceal me under the cover of his tent;
    he will set me high on a rock.
⁶ Now my head is lifted up
    above my enemies all around me,
and I will offer in his tent
    sacrifices with shouts of joy;
I will sing and make melody to the LORD.
⁷ Hear, O LORD, when I cry aloud,
    be gracious to me and answer me!
⁸ "Come," my heart says, "seek his face!"
    Your face, LORD, do I seek.
⁹ Do not hide your face from me.
Do not turn your servant away in anger,
    you who have been my help.
Do not cast me off, do not forsake me,
    O God of my salvation!

1 Corinthians 1:10-18

¹⁰Now I appeal to you, brothers and sisters, by the name of our Lord Jesus Christ, that all of you be in agreement and that there be no divisions among you, but that you be united in the same mind and the same purpose. ¹¹For it has been reported to me by Chloe's people that there are quarrels among you, my brothers and sisters. ¹²What I mean is that each of you says, "I belong to Paul," or "I belong to Apollos," or "I belong to Cephas," or "I belong to Christ." ¹³Has Christ been divided? Was Paul crucified for you? Or were you baptized in the name of Paul?

¹⁴I thank God that I baptized none of you except Crispus and Gaius, ¹⁵so that no one can say that you were baptized in my name. ¹⁶(I did baptize also the household of Stephanas; beyond that, I do not know whether I baptized anyone else.) ¹⁷For Christ did not send me to baptize but to proclaim the gospel, and not with eloquent wisdom, so that the cross of Christ might not be emptied of its power.

¹⁸For the message about the cross is foolishness to those who are perishing, but to us who are being saved it is the power of God.

Matthew 4:12-23

¹²Now when Jesus heard that John had been arrested, he withdrew to Galilee. ¹³He left Nazareth and made his home in Capernaum by the sea, in the territory of Zebulun and Naphtali, ¹⁴so that what had been spoken through the prophet Isaiah might be fulfilled:

¹⁵ "Land of Zebulun, land of Naphtali,
    on the road by the sea, across the Jordan,
        Galilee of the Gentiles—
¹⁶ the people who sat in darkness
    have seen a great light,
and for those who sat in the region and shadow of death
    light has dawned."

¹⁷From that time Jesus began to proclaim, "Repent, for the kingdom of heaven has come near."

¹⁸As he walked by the Sea of Galilee, he saw two brothers, Simon, who is called Peter, and Andrew his brother, casting a net into the sea—for they were fishermen. ¹⁹And he said to them, "Follow me, and I will make you fish for people." ²⁰Immediately they left their nets and followed him. ²¹As he went from there, he saw two other brothers, James son of Zebedee and his brother John, in the boat with their father Zebedee, mending their nets, and he called them. ²²Immediately they left the boat and their father, and followed him.

²³Jesus went throughout Galilee, teaching in their synagogues and proclaiming the good news of the kingdom and curing every disease and every sickness among the people.

COLOR: GREEN

3rd SUNDAY AFTER THE EPIPHANY

Primary Hymns and Songs for the Day

545	"The Church's One Foundation" (1 Cor.) (O)	
	H-3 Hbl-94; Chr-180; Desc-16; Org-9	
	S-1 #25-26. Descant and harmonization	
344	"Tú Has Venido a la Orilla" ("Lord, You Have Come to the Lakeshore") (Matt.)	
	H-3 Chr-133; Org-114	
398	"Jesus Calls Us" (Matt.)	
	H-3 Chr-115	
	S-2 #65. Harmonization	
2101	"Two Fishermen" (Matt.)	
2129	"I Have Decided to Follow Jesus" (Matt.) (C)	

Additional Hymn Suggestions

173	"Christ, Whose Glory Fills the Skies" (Isa., Matt.)
206	"I Want to Walk as a Child of the Light" (Isa., Matt.)
247	"O Morning Star, How Fair and Bright" (Isa., Matt.)
2219	"Goodness Is Stronger than Evil" (Isa., Matt.)
2236	"Gather Us In" (Isa., Matt.)
2172	"We Are Called" (Isa., Ps., Matt.)
361	"Rock of Ages" (Ps.)
479	"Jesus, Lover of My Soul" (Ps.)
498	"My Prayer Rises to Heaven" (Ps.)
706	"Soon and Very Soon" (Ps.)
2053	"If It Had Not Been for the Lord" (Ps.)
2218	"You Are Mine" (Ps., Matt.)
132	"All My Hope Is Firmly Grounded" (1 Cor.)
298	"When I Survey the Wondrous Cross" (1 Cor.)
547	"O Church of God, United" (1 Cor.)
557	"Blest Be the Tie that Binds" (1 Cor.) (C)
558	"We Are the Church" (1 Cor.)
560	"Help Us Accept Each Other" (1 Cor.)
562	"Jesus, Lord, We Look to Thee" (1 Cor.)
566	"Blest Be the Dear Uniting Love" (1 Cor.)
261	"Lord of the Dance" (Matt.)
277	"Tell Me the Stories of Jesus" (Matt.)
348	"Softly and Tenderly Jesus Is Calling" (Matt.)
358	"Dear Lord and Father of Mankind" (Matt.)
	(Alternate Text—"Parent of Us All")
396	"O Jesus, I Have Promised" (Matt.)
430	"O Master, Let Me Walk with Thee" (Matt.)
2130	"The Summons" (Matt.)
2137	"Would I Have Answered When You Called" (Matt.)
3161	"Gracious Creator of Sea and of Land" (Matt.)

Additional Contemporary Suggestions

S2005	"Arise, Shine" (Isa., Matt.)
S2204	"Light of the World" (Isa., Matt.)
S2173	"Shine, Jesus, Shine" (Isa., Ps., Matt.)
	SP142
M19	"Shine on Us" (Isa., Matt., Epiphany)
WS3177	"Here I Am to Worship" (Isa., Epiphany)
	M116
S2002	"I Will Call Upon the Lord" (Ps.)
	SP224
S2064	"O Lord, You're Beautiful" (Ps.)
S2074	"Shout to the Lord" (Ps.)
	M16
M58	"All Heaven Declares" (Ps.)
M60	"Better Is One Day" (Ps.)
SP209	"The Lord Is My Light" (Ps.)

WS3004	"Step By Step" (Ps., Matt.)
	M51
M79	"I Stand Amazed" (Ps., Matt.)
M72	"Jesus, Lover of My Soul" ("It's All about You") (Ps., Matt.)
S2235	"We Are Singing" ("Siyahamba") (Ps., Matt.)
M53	"Let It Be Said of Us" (1 Cor.)
M76	"The Wonderful Cross" (1 Cor.)
M150	"Everyday" (Matt.)
S2165	"Cry of My Heart" (Matt.)
	M39
WS3160	"We Will Follow" ("Somlandela") (Matt.)

Vocal Solos

"The People That Walked in Darkness" (Isa.)
V-2
"The Lord Is My Light" (Ps.)
V-8 p. 57
"Softly and Tenderly" (Matt.)
V-5(3) p. 52

Anthems

"Dear Lord and Father of Mankind" (Matt.)
(Alt Text: "Dear Lord, creator of us all")
Charles H. H. Parry; Novello 14008506
SATB, keyboard

"Who At My Door Is Standing?" (Matt.)
arr. K. Lee Scott; Hinshaw HMC728
Two-part mixed, keyboard

Other Suggestions

Visuals:

O	Light/darkness, sea/land, joy, harvest, yoke, rod
P	Light, church, seekers, tent/rock, joy, singing
E	Walls torn down, baptism, crucifix, stone, Christus Rex
G	John, sea, light/darkess, dawn, fishnet, net with people, mending nets, boat, Jesus teaching

Introit: S2127. "Come and See" ("Kyrie") (Matt.)
Greeting: BOW306 or 456 (Isa., 1 Cor., Matt.)
Confession: WSL43. "We often act" (1 Cor.)
Confession: BOW488 or 492 (1 Cor.)
Confession: WSL97. Your light has filled our lives (Isa.)
Response: WS3137. "Lord Jesus Christ, Your Light Shines" (Isa., Ps.)
Canticle: UM205. "Canticle of Light and Darkness" (Isa.)
Prayer: BOW309 or 312 (Isa., 1 Cor., Matt.)
Prayer: BOW503 or 505. For the Church (1 Cor.)
Benediction: BOW560 (Ps.)
Blessing: WSL7. The light that enlivens (Isa.)

FEBRUARY 2, 2014

Micah 6:1-8

¹ Hear what the LORD says:
Rise, plead your case before the mountains,
and let the hills hear your voice.
² Hear, you mountains, the controversy of the LORD,
and you enduring foundations of the earth;
for the LORD has a controversy with his people,
and he will contend with Israel.
³ "O my people, what have I done to you?
In what have I wearied you? Answer me!
⁴ For I brought you up from the land of Egypt,
and redeemed you from the house of slavery;
and I sent before you Moses,
Aaron, and Miriam.
⁵ O my people, remember now what King Balak of Moab
devised,
what Balaam son of Beor answered him,
and what happened from Shittim to Gilgal,
that you may know the saving acts of the LORD."
⁶ With what shall I come before the LORD,
and bow myself before God on high?
Shall I come before him with burnt offerings,
with calves a year old?
⁷ Will the LORD be pleased with thousands of rams,
with ten thousands of rivers of oil?
Shall I give my firstborn for my transgression,
the fruit of my body for the sin of my soul?"
⁸ He has told you, O mortal, what is good;
and what does the LORD require of you
but to do justice, and to love kindness,
and to walk humbly with your God?

Psalm 15

¹ O LORD, who may abide in your tent?
Who may dwell on your holy hill?
² Those who walk blamelessly, and do what is right,
and speak the truth from their heart;
³ who do not slander with their tongue,
and do no evil to their friends,
nor take up a reproach against their neighbors;
⁴ in whose eyes the wicked are despised,
but who honor those who fear the LORD;
who stand by their oath even to their hurt;
⁵ who do not lend money at interest,
and do not take a bribe against the innocent.
Those who do these things shall never be moved.

1 Corinthians 1:18-31

¹⁸For the message about the cross is foolishness to those who are perishing, but to us who are being saved it is the power of God. ¹⁹For it is written,
"I will destroy the wisdom of the wise,
and the discernment of the discerning I will thwart."
²⁰Where is the one who is wise? Where is the scribe? Where is the debater of this age? Has not God made foolish the wisdom of the world? ²¹For since, in the wisdom of God, the world did not know God through wisdom, God decided, through the foolishness of our proclamation, to save those who believe. ²²For Jews demand signs and Greeks desire wisdom, ²³but we proclaim Christ crucified, a stumbling block to Jews and foolishness to Gentiles, ²⁴but to those who are the called, both Jews and Greeks, Christ the power of God and the wisdom of God. ²⁵For God's foolishness is wiser than human wisdom, and God's weakness is stronger than human strength.

²⁶Consider your own call, brothers and sisters: not many of you were wise by human standards, not many were powerful, not many were of noble birth. ²⁷But God chose what is foolish in the world to shame the wise; God chose what is weak in the world to shame the strong; ²⁸God chose what is low and despised in the world, things that are not, to reduce to nothing things that are, ²⁹so that no one might boast in the presence of God. ³⁰He is the source of your life in Christ Jesus, who became for us wisdom from God, and righteousness and sanctification and redemption, ³¹in order that, as it is written, "Let the one who boasts, boast in the Lord."

Matthew 5:1-12

¹When Jesus saw the crowds, he went up the mountain; and after he sat down, his disciples came to him. ²Then he began to speak, and taught them, saying:
³ "Blessed are the poor in spirit, for theirs is the kingdom of heaven.
⁴"Blessed are those who mourn, for they will be comforted.
⁵"Blessed are the meek, for they will inherit the earth.
⁶"Blessed are those who hunger and thirst for righteousness, for they will be filled.
⁷"Blessed are the merciful, for they will receive mercy.
⁸"Blessed are the pure in heart, for they will see God.
⁹"Blessed are the peacemakers, for they will be called children of God.
¹⁰"Blessed are those who are persecuted for righteousness sake, for theirs is the kingdom of heaven.
¹¹"Blessed are you when people revile you and persecute you and utter all kinds of evil against you falsely on my account. ¹²Rejoice and be glad, for your reward is great in heaven, for in the same way they persecuted the prophets who were before you.

COLOR: GREEN   **4th SUNDAY AFTER EPIPHANY**

Primary Hymns and Songs for the Day
2172 "We Are Called" (Mic.) (O)
451   "Be Thou My Vision" (1 Cor., Matt.)
        H-3 Hbl-15, 48; Chr-36; Org-153
        S-1 #319. Arr. for organ and voices in canon
708   "Rejoice in God's Saints" (Matt.) (O)
        H-3 Hbl-90, 105; Chr-221; Desc-49; Org-51
        S-2 #71-74. Introduction and
        harmonizations
2155 "Blest Are They" (Matt.)
2184 "Sent Out in Jesus' Name" (Mic.) (C)
584   "Lord, You Give the Great Commission" (Mic., Ps.) (C)
        H-3 Hbl-61; Chr-132; Org-2
        S-1 #4-5. Instrumental and vocal descants

Additional Hymn Suggestions
441   "What Does the Lord Require" (Mic.)
2106 "When Jesus Wept" (Mic.)
2174 "What Does the Lord Require of You" (Mic.)
2177 "Wounded World that Cries for Healing" (Mic.)
2213 "Healer of Our Every Ill" (Mic.)
2234 "Lead On, O Cloud of Presence" (Mic.)
3124 "How Shall I Come Before the Lord"
87   "What Gift Can We Bring" (Mic., Matt.)
433   "All Who Love and Serve Your City" (Mic., Matt.)
434   "Cuando El Pobre" ("When the Poor Ones") (Mic., Matt.)
439   "We Utter Our Cry" (Mic., Matt.)
464   "I Will Trust in the Lord" (Ps.)
213   "Lift Up Your Heads, Ye Mighty Gates" (Ps., Matt.)
132   "All My Hope Is Firmly Grounded" (1 Cor.)
163   "Ask Ye What Great Thing I Know" (1 Cor.)
298   "When I Survey the Wondrous Cross" (1 Cor.)
299   "When I Survey the Wondrous Cross" (1 Cor.)
308   "Thine Be the Glory" (1 Cor.)
450   "Creator of the Earth and Skies" (1 Cor.)
504   "The Old Rugged Cross" (1 Cor.)
3075 "Glory in the Cross" (1 Cor.)
452   "My Faith Looks Up to Thee" (1 Cor., Matt.)
465   "Holy Spirit, Truth Divine" (1 Cor., Matt.)
480   "O Love That Wilt Not Let Me Go" (1 Cor., Matt.)
506   "Wellspring of Wisdom" (1 Cor., Matt.)
402   "Lord, I Want to be a Christian" (Matt.)
467   "Trust and Obey" (Matt.)
469   "Jesus Is All the World to Me" (Matt.)
472   "Near to the Heart of God" (Matt.)
711   "For All the Saints" (Matt.)
712   "I Sing a Song of the Saints of God" (Matt.)
2019 "Holy" ("Santo") (Matt.)
2126 "All Who Hunger" (Matt.)
2140 "Since Jesus Came Into My Heart" (Matt.)
2219 "Goodness Is Stronger than Evil" (Matt.)
2262 "Let Us Offer to the Father" (Matt., Communion)
2264 "Come to the Table" (Matt., Communion)
2283 "For All the Saints" (Matt.)
3103 "Purify My Heart" (Matt.)
        M90

Additional Contemporary Suggestions
M71   "The Heart of Worship" (Mic.)
S2179 "Live in Charity" ("Ubi Caritas") (Mic.)
S2080 "All I Need Is You" (1 Cor.)

WS3040 "You Are My All in All" (1 Cor.)
        SP220
M53   "Let It Be Said of Us" (1 Cor.)
M76   "The Wonderful Cross" (1 Cor.)
WS3042 "Shout to the North" (1 Cor.)
        M99
S2266 "Here Is Bread, Here Is Wine" (1 Cor., Communion)
S2036 "Give Thanks" (1 Cor., Matt.)
        SP170
S2086 "Open Our Eyes, Lord" (Matt.)
        SP199
S2132 "You Who Are Thirsty" (Matt.)
        SP219
WS3008 "Open the Eyes of My Heart" (Matt.)
        M57
WS3108 "Trading My Sorrows" (Matt.)
        M75

Vocal Solos
"Fit for a King" (Mic.)
        V-10   p. 32
"Maybe the Rain" (Matt.)
        V-5(2)   p. 27
"This Is My Commandment" (Matt.)
        V-8   p. 284

Anthems
"With What Shall I Come?" (Mic.)
Ruth Elaine Schram; Lorenz 10/2849L
SATB, piano

"Blest Are They" (Matt.)
David Haas; GIA G-2958
SAB, keyboard

Other Suggestions
Visuals:
  O   Briefcase, Exodus, prayer, scales of justice, ministry
  P   Tent, hill, walking, speaking, destructive behavior, ministry, justice, money
  E   Empty cross, clown, debate, crucifix, block, Christ, world upside down
  G   Jesus teaching, examples of ministry described
Greeting: BOW449 (Ps.) or BOW453 (Matt.)
Opening Prayer: WSL60. As the sun rises (Mic.)
Opening Prayer: BOW460 or 465 (Mic., 1 Cor.)
Prayer of Confession: BOW479, 486, or 494 (Mic.)
Affirmation of Faith: WSL83. We believe (Matt.)
Litany: WSL49. For rebirth and resilience (Matt.)
Prayer: WSL199. O God of the crucified Christ (Matt.)
Prayer: WSL200. Show us, good Lord (Matt.)
Prayer: UM392 (Matt.) or BOW310 (1 Cor., Matt.)
Prayer: BOW513 or UM456 (Mic., 1 Cor.)
Response: WS3103. "Purify My Heart" (Matt.)
Offertory Prayer: WSL129. Blessed One (Matt.)
Blessing: WSL160. What does the Lord require (Mic.)

FEBRUARY 9, 2014

BOY SCOUT SUNDAY

Isaiah 58:1-9a (9b -12)

1 Shout out, do not hold back!
   Lift up your voice like a trumpet!
   Announce to my people their rebellion,
      to the house of Jacob their sins.
2 Yet day after day they seek me
      and delight to know my ways,
   as if they were a nation that practiced righteousness
      and did not forsake the ordinance of their God;
   they ask of me righteous judgments,
      they delight to draw near to God.
3 "Why do we fast, but you do not see?
      Why humble ourselves, but you do not notice?"
   Look, you serve your own interest on your fast day,
      and oppress all your workers.
4 Look, you fast only to quarrel and to fight
      and to strike with a wicked fist.
   Such fasting as you do today
      will not make your voice heard on high.
5 Is such the fast that I choose,
      a day to humble oneself?
   Is it to bow down the head like a bulrush,
      and to lie in sackcloth and ashes?
   Will you call this a fast,
      a day acceptable to the Lord?
6 Is not this the fast that I choose:
      to loose the bonds of injustice,
      to undo the thongs of the yoke,
   to let the oppressed go free,
      and to break every yoke?
7 Is it not to share your bread with the hungry,
      and bring the homeless poor into your house;
   when you see the naked, to cover them,
      and not to hide yourself from your own kin?
8 Then your light shall break forth like the dawn,
      and your healing shall spring up quickly;
   your vindicator shall go before you,
      the glory of the Lord shall be your rear guard.
9 Then you shall call, and the Lord will answer;
      you shall cry for help, and he will say, Here I am.
   If you remove the yoke from among you,
      the pointing of the finger, the speaking of evil,
10 if you offer your food to the hungry
      and satisfy the needs of the afflicted,
   then your light shall rise in the darkness
      and your gloom be like the noonday.
11 The Lord will guide you continually,
      and satisfy your needs in parched places,
      and make your bones strong;
   and you shall be like a watered garden,
      like a spring of water,
      whose waters never fail.
12 Your ancient ruins shall be rebuilt;
      you shall raise up the foundations of many generations;
   you shall be called the repairer of the breach,
      the restorer of streets to live in.

Psalm 112:1-10

1 Praise the Lord!
      Happy are those who fear the Lord,
      who greatly delight in his commandments.
2 Their descendants will be mighty in the land;
      the generation of the upright will be blessed.
3 Wealth and riches are in their houses,
      and their righteousness endures forever.
4 They rise in the darkness as a light for the upright;
      they are gracious, merciful, and righteous.
5 It is well with those who deal generously and lend,

who conduct their affairs with justice.
6 For the righteous will never be moved;
      they will be remembered forever.
7 They are not afraid of evil tidings;
      their hearts are firm, secure in the Lord.
8 Their hearts are steady, they will not be afraid;
      in the end they will look in triumph on their foes.
9 They have distributed freely, they have given to the poor;
      their righteousness endures forever; their horn is exalted in
         honor.
10 The wicked see it and are angry;
      they gnash their teeth and melt away;
      the desire of the wicked comes to nothing.

1 Corinthians 2:1-12 (13-16)

1 When I came to you, brothers and sisters, I did not come proclaiming the mystery of God to you in lofty words or wisdom. 2For I decided to know nothing among you except Jesus Christ, and him crucified. 3And I came to you in weakness and in fear and in much trembling. 4My speech and my proclamation were not with plausible words of wisdom, but with a demonstration of the Spirit and of power, 5so that your faith might rest not on human wisdom but on the power of God.

6Yet among the mature we do speak wisdom, though it is not a wisdom of this age or of the rulers of this age, who are doomed to perish. 7But we speak God's wisdom, secret and hidden, which God decreed before the ages for our glory. 8None of the rulers of this age understood this; for if they had, they would not have crucified the Lord of glory. 9But, as it is written,
   "What no eye has seen, nor ear heard,
      nor the human heart conceived,what God has prepared
         for those who love him"—
10these things God has revealed to us through the Spirit; for the Spirit searches everything, even the depths of God. 11For what human being knows what is truly human except the human spirit that is within? So also no one comprehends what is truly God's except the Spirit of God. 12Now we have received not the spirit of the world, but the Spirit that is from God, so that we may understand the gifts bestowed on us by God. 13And we speak of these things in words not taught by human wisdom but taught by the Spirit, interpreting spiritual things to those who are spiritual.

14Those who are unspiritual do not receive the gifts of God's Spirit, for they are foolishness to them, and they are unable to understand them because they are spiritually discerned. 15Those who are spiritual discern all things, and they are themselves subject to no one else's scrutiny.
16 "For who has known the mind of the Lord
      so as to instruct him?"
   But we have the mind of Christ.

Matthew 5:13-20

13"You are the salt of the earth; but if salt has lost its taste, how can its saltiness be restored? It is no longer good for anything, but is thrown out and trampled under foot.

14"You are the light of the world. A city built on a hill cannot be hid. 15No one after lighting a lamp puts it under the bushel basket, but on the lampstand, and it gives light to all in the house. 16In the same way, let your light shine before others, so that they may see your good works and give glory to your Father in heaven.

17"Do not think that I have come to abolish the law or the prophets; I have come not to abolish but to fulfill. 18For truly I tell you, until heaven and earth pass away, not one letter, not one stroke of a letter, will pass from the law until all is accomplished. 19Therefore, whoever breaks one of the least of these commandments, and teaches others to do the same, will be called least in the kingdom of heaven; but whoever does them and teaches them will be called great in the kingdom of heaven. 20For I tell you, unless your righteousness exceeds that of the scribes and Pharisees, you will never enter the kingdom of heaven.

COLOR: GREEN   **5th SUNDAY AFTER EPIPHANY**

Primary Hymns and Songs for the Day
2236	"Gather Us In" (Isa., Matt.) (O)
433	"All Who Love and Serve Your City" (Isa.)
	H-3 Chr-26, 65; Org-19
	S-1 #62. Descant
583	"Sois la Semilla" ("You Are the Seed") (Matt.)
585	"This Little Light of Mine" (Matt., Black History) (C)

Additional Hymn Suggestions
57	"O For a Thousand Tongues to Sing" (Isa.)
58	"Mil Voces Para Celebrar" (Isa.)
124	"Seek the Lord" (Isa.)
428	"For the Healing of the Nations" (Isa.)
434	"Cuando El Pobre" ("When the Poor Ones") (Isa.)
441	"What Does the Lord Require" (Isa.)
569	"We've a Story to Tell to the Nations" (Isa.)
593	"Here I Am, Lord" (Isa.)
632	"Draw Us in the Spirit's Tether" (Isa., Communion)
717	"The Battle Hymn of the Republic" (Isa.)
2208	"Guide My Feet" (Isa., Black History)
2172	"We Are Called" (Isa., Matt.)
411	"Dear Lord, Lead Me Day by Day" (Ps.)
463	"Lord, Speak to Me" (Ps.)
464	"I Will Trust in the Lord" (Ps., Black History)
708	"Rejoice in God's Saints" (Ps.)
163	"Ask Ye What Great Thing I Know" (1 Cor.)
438	"Forth in Thy Name, O Lord" (1 Cor.)
566	"Blest Be the Dear Uniting Love" (1 Cor.)
603	"Come, Holy Ghost, Our Hearts Inspire" (1 Cor.)
332	"Spirit of Faith, Come Down" (1 Cor.)
451	"Be Thou My Vision" (1 Cor.)
2082	"Woke Up This Morning" (1 Cor.)
2175	"Together We Serve" (Matt.)
2190	"Bring Forth the Kingdom" (Matt.)
2214	"Lead Me, Guide Me" (Matt.)
2218	"You Are Mine" (Matt.)
2237	"As a Fire Is Meant for Burning" (Matt.)
2261	"Life-Giving Bread" (Matt., Communion)

Additional Contemporary Suggestions
S2074	"Shout to the Lord" (Isa.)
	M16
WS3001	"O For a Thousand Tongues to Sing" (Isa.)
UM394	"Something Beautiful" (1 Cor.)
S2161	"To Know You More" (1 Cor.)
S2167	"More Like You" (1 Cor.)
M30	"Knowing You" ("All I Once Held Dear") (1 Cor.)
M33	"Jesus, You Are My Life" (1 Cor.)
M38	"In the Secret" ("I Want to Know You") (1 Cor.)
M53	"Let It Be Said of Us" (1 Cor.)
M91	"Take My Life" (1 Cor.)
M19	"Shine on Us" (Matt., Epiphany)
WS3177	"Here I Am to Worship" (Matt.)
	M116
WS3105	"In Christ Alone" (Matt.)
	M138
M150	"Everyday" (Matt.)
S2005	"Arise, Shine" (Matt.)
S2173	"Shine, Jesus, Shine" (Matt.)
	SP142
S2204	"Light of the World" (Matt.)

S2235	"We Are Marching" ("Siyahamba") (Matt.)
SP143	"Carry the Light" (Matt.)
SP144	"May We Be a Shining Light to the Nations" (Matt.)
WS3038	"Mighty to Save" (Matt.)
	M246

Vocal Solos
"God Will Make a Way" (with "He Leadeth Me") (Isa.)
    V-3   p. 9
"Shout to the Lord" (with "All Creatures of Our God and King") (Isa.)
    V-3   p. 32
"Jesus Revealed in Me" (1 Cor., Matt.)
    V-8   p. 347

Anthems
"Teach Me, O Lord" (Ps.)
Thomas Atwood; G. Schirmer ECS 372
SATB *a cappella*

"This Little Light of Mine" (Matt.)
David Bone; Hinshaw Music HMC-1966
SATB divisi, *a cappella*

Other Suggestions
Visuals:

O	Trumpet, fist, open shackles, yoke, bread, light, water,
P	Bible, light/dark, justice, heart, ministry to poor, horn, anger
E	Bible, heart, emotion, praise, walking
G	Salt/light, globe, city, lamp/basket/lampstand, Bible, teaching

Boy Scout Sunday is officially the Sunday before February 8, however the UMC celebrates it on the second Sunday of February.
Greeting: BOW306 or BOW326 (Isa., Matt.)
Opening Prayer: WSL218. Lord, set your blessing (Isa.)
Opening Prayer: BOW461 (1 Cor.)
Confession: WSL97. Your light has filled our lives (Matt.)
Prayer of Confession: BOW479 (Isa.)
Confession: WSL87. Almighty God (Isa.)
Canticle: UM125. Canticle of Covenant Faithfulness (Isa.)
Prayer: WSL57. Days pass and the years vanish (1 Cor.)
Prayer: UM456. For Courage to Do Justice (Isa.)
Prayer: BOW517. For the Nation (Isa.)
Prayer: BOW310 (Ps., 1 Cor.)
Prayer: BOW525. For Wisdom (1 Cor.)
Prayer: BOW308 (Matt.)
Prayer: BOW436 (Boy Scout Sunday)
Blessing: WSL59. You are the salt (Matt.)

FEBRUARY 16, 2014

Deuteronomy 30:15-20

[15]See, I have set before you today life and prosperity, death and adversity. [16]If you obey the commandments of the LORD your God that I am commanding you today, by loving the LORD your God, walking in his ways, and observing his commandments, decrees, and ordinances, then you shall live and become numerous, and the LORD your God will bless you in the land that you are entering to possess. [17]But if your heart turns away and you do not hear, but are led astray to bow down to other gods and serve them, [18]I declare to you today that you shall perish; you shall not live long in the land that you are crossing the Jordan to enter and possess. [19]I call heaven and earth to witness against you today that I have set before you life and death, blessings and curses. Choose life so that you and your descendants may live, [20]loving the LORD your God, obeying him, and holding fast to him; for that means life to you and length of days, so that you may live in the land that the LORD swore to give to your ancestors, to Abraham, to Isaac, and to Jacob.

Psalm 119:1-8

1   Happy are those whose way is blameless,
        who walk in the law of the LORD.
2   Happy are those who keep his decrees,
        who seek him with their whole heart,
3   who also do no wrong,
        but walk in his ways.
4   You have commanded your precepts
        to be kept diligently.
5   O that my ways may be steadfast
        in keeping your statutes!
6   Then I shall not be put to shame,
        having my eyes fixed on all your commandments.
7   I will praise you with an upright heart,
        when I learn your righteous ordinances.
8   I will observe your statutes;
        do not utterly forsake me.

1 Corinthians 3:1-9

[1] And so, brothers and sisters, I could not speak to you as spiritual people, but rather as people of the flesh, as infants in Christ. [2]I fed you with milk, not solid food, for you were not ready for solid food. Even now you are still not ready, [3]for you are still of the flesh. For as long as there is jealousy and quarreling among you, are you not of the flesh, and behaving according to human inclinations? [4]For when one says, "I belong to Paul," and another, "I belong to Apollos," are you not merely human?

[5]What then is Apollos? What is Paul? Servants through whom you came to believe, as the Lord assigned to each. [6]I planted, Apollos watered, but God gave the growth. [7]So neither the one who plants nor the one who waters is anything, but only God who gives the growth. [8]The one who plants and the one who waters have a common purpose, and each will receive wages according to the labor of each. [9]For we are God's servants, working together; you are God's field, God's building.

Matthew 5:21-37

[21]"You have heard that it was said to those of ancient times, 'You shall not murder'; and 'whoever murders shall be liable to judgment.' [22]But I say to you that if you are angry with a brother or sister, you will be liable to judgment; and if you insult a brother or sister, you will be liable to the council; and if you say, 'You fool,' you will be liable to the hell of fire. [23]So when you are offering your gift at the altar, if you remember that your brother or sister has something against you, [24]leave your gift there before the altar and go; first be reconciled to your brother or sister, and then come and offer your gift. [25]Come to terms quickly with your accuser while you are on the way to court with him, or your accuser may hand you over to the judge, and the judge to the guard, and you will be thrown into prison. [26]Truly I tell you, you will never get out until you have paid the last penny.

[27]"You have heard that it was said, 'You shall not commit adultery.' [28]But I say to you that everyone who looks at a woman with lust has already committed adultery with her in his heart. [29]If your right eye causes you to sin, tear it out and throw it away; it is better for you to lose one of your members than for your whole body to be thrown into hell. [30]And if your right hand causes you to sin, cut it off and throw it away; it is better for you to lose one of your members than for your whole body to go into hell.

[31]"It was also said, 'Whoever divorces his wife, let him give her a certificate of divorce.' [32]But I say to you that anyone who divorces his wife, except on the ground of unchastity, causes her to commit adultery; and whoever marries a divorced woman commits adultery.

[33]"Again, you have heard that it was said to those of ancient times, 'You shall not swear falsely, but carry out the vows you have made to the Lord.' [34]But I say to you, Do not swear at all, either by heaven, for it is the throne of God, [35]or by the earth, for it is his footstool, or by Jerusalem, for it is the city of the great King. [36]And do not swear by your head, for you cannot make one hair white or black. [37]Let your word be 'Yes, Yes' or 'No, No'; anything more than this comes from the evil one."

COLOR: GREEN

6th SUNDAY AFTER EPIPHANY

Primary Hymns and Songs for the Day

555   "Forward Through the Ages" (1 Cor.) (O)
         H-3 Hbl-59; Chr-156; Org-140

410   "I Want a Principle Within" (Matt.)

2169   "God, How Can We Forgive" (Matt.)
         H-3 Hbl-62, 95; Chr-59; Org-77
         S-1 #211. Harmonization

568   "Christ for the World We Sing" (1 Cor.) (C)
         H-3 Hbl-28, 49, 53; Chr-56; Desc-57; Org-63
         S-1 #185-186. Descant and harmonization

Additional Hymn Suggestions

439   "We Utter Our Cry" (Deut.)
2168   "Love the Lord Your God" (Deut.)
2268   "As We Gather at Your Table" (Deut., Communion)
3116   "Love the Lord" (Deut.)
3117   "Rule of Life" (Deut., Ps.)
430   "O Master, Let Me Walk With Thee" (Ps.)
695   "O Lord, May Church and Home Combine" (Ps.)
411   "Dear Lord, Lead Me Day by Day" (Ps., Matt.)
2242   "Walk with Me" (Ps., 1 Cor.)
546   "The Church's One Foundation" (1 Cor.)
547   "O Church of God, United" (1 Cor.)
548   "In Christ There Is No East or West" (1 Cor.)
566   "Blest Be the Dear Uniting Love" (1 Cor.)
567   "Heralds of Christ" (1 Cor.)
581   "Lord, Whose Love Through Humble Service" (1 Cor.)
583   "Sois la Semilla" ("You Are the Seed") (1 Cor.)
2175   "Together We Serve" (1 Cor.)
2181   "We Need a Faith" (1 Cor.)
2223   "They'll Know We Are Christians" (1 Cor.)
2240   "One God and Father of Us All" (1 Cor.)
2243   "We All Are One in Mission" (1 Cor.)
2135   "When Cain Killed Abel" (1 Cor., Matt.)
2170   "God Made from One Blood" (1 Cor., Matt.)
2269   "Come, Share the Lord" (1 Cor., Matt., Communion)
2138   "Sunday's Palms Are Wednesday's Ashes" (Matt.)
3070   "The Lord's Prayer" (Matt.) See also S2278, UM271, WS3068-WS3070.
3123   "Here Is Peace" (Matt.)
389   "Freely, Freely" (Matt.)
390   "Forgive Our Sins as We Forgive" (Matt.)
408   "The Gift of Love" (Matt.)
420   "Breathe on Me, Breath of God" (Matt.)
557   "Blest Be the Tie That Binds" (Matt.)
560   "Help Us Accept Each Other" (Matt.)

Additional Contemporary Suggestions

S2161   "To Know You More" (Deut.)
S2188   "The Family Prayer Song" ("As for Me and My House") (Deut.)
         M54
M40   "More Love, More Power" (Deut.)
M41   "You're Worthy of My Praise" (Deut.)
M62   "Rise Up and Praise Him" (Deut.)
M83   "Just Let Me Say" (Deut.)
M86   "With All of My Heart" (Deut.)
         SP187
M98   "Take This Life" (Deut.)
M53   "Let It Be Said of Us" (Deut., Matt.)

M38   "In the Secret" ("I Want to Know You") (Ps.)
WS3004   "Step By Step" (Ps.)
         M51
M107   "Show Me Your Ways" (Ps.)
M149   "Ancient Words" (Ps.)
UM601   "Thy Word Is a Lamp" (Ps.)
         SP183
S2165   "Cry of My Heart" (Ps.)
         M39
WS3154   "Draw the Circle Wide" (1 Cor., Matt.)
S2133   "Give Me a Clean Heart" (Matt.)
S2171   "Make Me a Channel of Your Peace" (Matt.)
UM405   "Seek Ye First" (Matt.)
         SP182

Vocal Solos

"My Heart Is Steadfast" (Ps.)
    V-5(2)   p. 40
"This Is My Commandment" (Matt.)
    V-8   p. 284
"He Breaks the Bread, He Pours the Wine" (Matt., Communion)
    V-10   p. 43

Anthems

"Walking With God" (Deut.)
Paul Basler; Colla Voce 36-22001
SATB, keyboard

"Breathe on Me, Breath of God" (Matt.)
Philip Wilby; GIA G-8197
SATB, organ

"Ubi Caritas" (1 Cor., Matt.)
Ola Gjeilo; Walton Music WW1386
a cappella

Other Suggestions

Visuals:
    O   Ten commandments, heart, river, "choose life"
    P   Bible, heart, devotion, praise, walking
    E   Infants, milk, quarrel, plant/water/growth, work, field, building
    G   Anger, fire, gift/altar, reconcile, jail, eye, hand, divorce certificate, stool

Opening Prayer: BOW466 (1 Cor., Matt.)
Prayer of Confession: UM892 (Deut.)
Prayer: UM894. The Lord's Prayer (Matt.)
Sung Prayer: UM270. "The Lord's Prayer" (Matt.) See also S2278, UM271, WS3068-WS3070.
Litany: BOW495. Litany for the Church and for the World (1 Cor., Matt.)
Prayer: BOW502. For the Church (1 Cor.)
For more ideas, see *The Abingdon Worship Annual 2014.*

FEBRUARY 23, 2014

Leviticus 19:1-2, 9-18

[1]The LORD spoke to Moses, saying:

[2]Speak to all the congregation of the people of Israel and say to them: You shall be holy, for I the LORD your God am holy. . . .

[9]When you reap the harvest of your land, you shall not reap to the very edges of your field, or gather the gleanings of your harvest. [10]You shall not strip your vineyard bare, or gather the fallen grapes of your vineyard; you shall leave them for the poor and the alien: I am the LORD your God.

[11]You shall not steal; you shall not deal falsely; and you shall not lie to one another. [12]And you shall not swear falsely by my name, profaning the name of your God: I am the LORD. [13]You shall not defraud your neighbor; you shall not steal; and you shall not keep for yourself the wages of a laborer until morning. [14]You shall not revile the deaf or put a stumbling block before the blind; you shall fear your God: I am the LORD. [15]You shall not render an unjust judgment; you shall not be partial to the poor or defer to the great: with justice you shall judge your neighbor. [16]You shall not go around as a slanderer among your people, and you shall not profit by the blood of your neighbor: I am the LORD. [17]You shall not hate in your heart anyone of your kin; you shall reprove your neighbor, or you will incur guilt yourself. [18]You shall not take vengeance or bear a grudge against any of your people, but you shall love your neighbor as yourself: I am the LORD.

Psalm 119:33-40

[33] Teach me, O LORD, the way of your statutes,
    and I will observe it to the end.
[34] Give me understanding, that I may keep your law
    and observe it with my whole heart.
[35] Lead me in the path of your commandments,
    for I delight in it.
[36] Turn my heart to your decrees,
    and not to selfish gain.
[37] Turn my eyes from looking at vanities;
    give me life in your ways.
[38] Confirm to your servant your promise,
    which is for those who fear you.
[39] Turn away the disgrace that I dread,
    for your ordinances are good.
[40] See, I have longed for your precepts;
    in your righteousness give me life.

1 Corinthians 3:10-11, 16-23

[10]According to the grace of God given to me, like a skilled master builder I laid a foundation, and someone else is building on it. Each builder must choose with care how to build on it. [11]For no one can lay any foundation other than the one that has been laid; that foundation is Jesus Christ. . . .

[16]Do you not know that you are God's temple and that God's Spirit dwells in you? [17]If anyone destroys God's temple, God will destroy that person. For God's temple is holy, and you are that temple.

[18]Do not deceive yourselves. If you think that you are wise in this age, you should become fools so that you may become wise. [19]For the wisdom of this world is foolishness with God. For it is written,

"He catches the wise in their craftiness,"
[20] and again,
    "The Lord knows the thoughts of the wise,
        that they are futile."

[21]So let no one boast about human leaders. For all things are yours, [22]whether Paul or Apollos or Cephas or the world or life or death or the present or the future—all belong to you, [23]and you belong to Christ, and Christ belongs to God.

Matthew 5:38-48

[38]"You have heard that it was said, 'An eye for an eye and a tooth for a tooth.' [39]But I say to you, Do not resist an evildoer. But if anyone strikes you on the right cheek, turn the other also; [40]and if anyone wants to sue you and take your coat, give your cloak as well; [41]and if anyone forces you to go one mile, go also the second mile. [42]Give to everyone who begs from you, and do not refuse anyone who wants to borrow from you.

[43]"You have heard that it was said, 'You shall love your neighbor and hate your enemy.' [44]But I say to you, Love your enemies and pray for those who persecute you, [45]so that you may be children of your Father in heaven; for he makes his sun rise on the evil and on the good, and sends rain on the righteous and on the unrighteous. [46]For if you love those who love you, what reward do you have? Do not even the tax collectors do the same? [47]And if you greet only your brothers and sisters, what more are you doing than others? Do not even the Gentiles do the same? [48]Be perfect, therefore, as your heavenly Father is perfect.

COLOR: GREEN   **7th SUNDAY AFTER EPIPHANY**

Primary Hymns and Songs for the Day

395   "Take Time to Be Holy" (Lev., Matt.) (O)
        H-3   Chr-178
        S-1   #159. Harmonization
2179   "Live in Charity" ("Ubi Caritas") (Lev., Matt.)
390   "Forgive Our Sins as We Forgive" (Matt.)
        H-3   Chr-68; Desc-28; Org-27
        S-1   #85. Choral harmonization
402   "Lord I Want to Be a Christian" (Matt.)
        H-3   Chr-130
559   "Christ Is Made the Sure Foundation" (1 Cor.) (C)
        H-3   Chr-49; Desc-103; Org-180
        S-1   #346. Descant

Additional Hymn Suggestions

399   "Take My Life, and Let It Be" (Lev.) (C)
404   "Every Time I Feel the Spirit" (Lev.)
428   "For the Healing of the Nations" (Lev.) (O)
440   "Let There Be Light" (Lev.)
432   "Jesu, Jesu" (Lev., Matt.)
        S-1 #63. Vocal part
434   "Cuando El Pobre" ("When the Poor Ones") (Lev., Matt.)
2168   "Love the Lord Your God" (Lev., Matt.)
2171   "Make Me a Channel of Your Peace" (Lev., Matt.)
2213   "Healer of Our Every Ill" (Lev., Matt.)
410   "I Want a Principle Within" (Lev., Ps.)
411   "Dear Lord, Lead Me Day by Day" (Lev., Ps.)
438   "Forth in Thy Name, O Lord" (Lev., Ps., 1 Cor.)
463   "Lord, Speak to Me" (Ps.)
473   "Lead Me, Lord" (Ps.)
474   "Precious Lord, Take My Hand" (Ps., Black History)
695   "O Lord, May Church and Home Combine" (Ps.)
2208   "Guide My Feet" (Ps., Black History)
2214   "Lead Me, Guide Me" (Ps.)
3030   "Eternal God Transcending Time" (Ps.)
451   "Be Thou My Vision" (Ps., 1 Cor.)
454   "Open My Eyes, That I May See" (Ps., 1 Cor.)
546   "The Church's One Foundation" (1 Cor.)
566   "Blest Be the Dear Uniting Love" (1 Cor.)
2220   "We Are God's People" (1 Cor.)
2228   "Sacred the Body" (1 Cor.)
2243   "We All Are One in Mission" (1 Cor.)
2138   "Sunday's Palms Are Wednesday's Ashes" (Matt.)
2169   "God, How Can We Forgive" (Matt.)
389   "Freely, Freely" (Matt.)
408   "The Gift of Love" (Matt.)
417   "O For a Heart to Praise My God" (Matt.)
431   "Let There Be Peace on Earth" (Matt.)
444   "O Young and Fearless Prophet" (Matt.)
447   "Our Parent, By Whose Name" (Matt.)
549   "Where Charity and Love Prevail" (Matt.)
551   "Awake, O Sleeper" (Matt.)
560   "Help Us Accept Each Other" (Matt.)
2269   "Come, Share the Lord" (Matt., Communion)

Additional Contemporary Suggestions

M53   "Let It Be Said of Us" (Lev., Matt.)
M40   "More Love, More Power" (Lev.)
UM405   "Seek Ye First" (Lev., Ps.)
        SP182

UM349   "Turn Your Eyes Upon Jesus" (Ps.)
        SP218
S2025   "As the Deer" (Ps.)
        SP200
S2032   "My Life Is in You, Lord" (Ps.)
        SP204
S2165   "Cry of My Heart" (Ps.)
        M39
WS3005   "Fill Us with Your Love, O Lord" (Ps.)
WS3008   "Open the Eyes of My Heart" (Ps.)
        M57
M38   "In the Secret" ("I Want to Know You") (Ps.)
WS3004   "Step By Step" (Ps.)
        M51
M107   "Show Me Your Ways" (Ps.)
M108   "Lead Me, Lord" (Ps.)
M30   "Knowing You" (Ps., 1 Cor.)
S2161   "To Know You More" (Ps., Matt.)
S2162   "Grace Alone" (1 Cor.)
        M100
S2164   "Sanctuary" (1 Cor.)
        M52
S2039   "Holy, Holy" (Matt.)
        SP141

Vocal Solos

"Here I Am" (Lev.)
   V-11   p. 19
"Maybe the Rain" (Ps.)
   V-5(2)   p. 27
"The Gift of Love" (Matt.)
   V-8   p. 120

Anthems

"The Best of Rooms" (1 Cor.)
Z. Randall Stroope; Morningstar 50-5808
SATB, organ

"Lord I Want to Be a Christian" (Matt.)
Moses Hogan; Hal Leonard 08703140
SATB divisi, *a cappella*

Other Suggestions

Visuals:
    O   Ten Commandments, wheat/grapes, block, scales
    P   Bible, heart, path, eyes, turning
    E   Builder, foundation, Christ, temple, people
    G   Eye tooth, cheeks, coat/cloak, second mile, heart, prayer, sun/rain
Greeting and Prayers: BOW456, 503, 525 (1 Cor.)
Opening Prayer: BOW461 (Ps.)
Song of Confession: UM450. "Creator of the Earth and Skies" (Lev., Ps.)
Prayer of Confession: BOW476 or BOW488 (Matt.)
Prayer: UM392. Prayer for a New Heart (Matt.)
Response: WS3043, stanzas 1 and 3. "You, Lord Are Both Lamb and Shepherd" (Matt.)
Litany: BOW496. The Ten Commandments (Lev.)

69

MARCH 2, 2014

Exodus 24:12-18

¹²The LORD said to Moses, "Come up to me on the mountain, and wait there; and I will give you the tablets of stone, with the law and the commandment, which I have written for their instruction." ¹³So Moses set out with his assistant Joshua, and Moses went up into the mountain of God. ¹⁴To the elders he had said, "Wait here for us, until we come to you again; for Aaron and Hur are with you; whoever has a dispute may go to them." ¹⁵Then Moses went up on the mountain, and the cloud covered the mountain. ¹⁶The glory of the LORD settled on Mount Sinai, and the cloud covered it for six days; on the seventh day he called to Moses out of the cloud. ¹⁷Now the appearance of the glory of the LORD was like a devouring fire on the top of the mountain in the sight of the people of Israel. ¹⁸Moses entered the cloud, and went up on the mountain. Moses was on the mountain for forty days and forty nights.

Psalm 99

¹The LORD is king; let the peoples tremble!
    He sits enthroned upon the cherubim;
        let the earth quake!
² The LORD is great in Zion;
    he is exalted over all the peoples.
³ Let them praise your great and awesome name.
    Holy is he!
⁴ Mighty King, lover of justice,
    you have established equity;
you have executed justice
    and righteousness in Jacob.
⁵ Extol the LORD our God;
    worship at his footstool.
    Holy is he!
⁶ Moses and Aaron were among his priests,
    Samuel also was among those who called on his name.
    They cried to the LORD, and he answered them.
⁷ He spoke to them in the pillar of cloud;
    they kept his decrees,
    and the statutes that he gave them.
⁸ O LORD our God, you answered them;
    you were a forgiving God to them,
    but an avenger of their wrongdoings.
⁹ Extol the LORD our God,
    and worship at his holy mountain;
    for the LORD our God is holy.

2 Peter 1:16-21

¹⁶For we did not follow cleverly devised myths when we made known to you the power and coming of our Lord Jesus Christ, but we had been eyewitnesses of his majesty. ¹⁷For he received honor and glory from God the Father when that voice was conveyed to him by the Majestic Glory, saying, "This is my Son, my Beloved, with whom I am well pleased." ¹⁸We ourselves heard this voice come from heaven, while we were with him on the holy mountain.

¹⁹So we have the prophetic message more fully confirmed. You will do well to be attentive to this as to a lamp shining in a dark place, until the day dawns and the morning star rises in your hearts. ²⁰First of all you must understand this, that no prophecy of scripture is a matter of one's own interpretation, ²¹because no prophecy ever came by human will, but men and women moved by the Holy Spirit spoke from God.

Matthew 17:1-9

¹ Six days later, Jesus took with him Peter and James and his brother John and led them up a high mountain, by themselves. ²And he was transfigured before them, and his face shone like the sun, and his clothes became dazzling white. ³Suddenly there appeared to them Moses and Elijah, talking with him. ⁴Then Peter said to Jesus, "Lord, it is good for us to be here; if you wish, I will make three dwellings here, one for you, one for Moses, and one for Elijah." ⁵While he was still speaking, suddenly a bright cloud overshadowed them, and from the cloud a voice said, "This is my Son, the Beloved; with him I am well pleased; listen to him!" ⁶When the disciples heard this, they fell to the ground and were overcome by fear. ⁷But Jesus came and touched them, saying, "Get up and do not be afraid." ⁸And when they looked up, they saw no one except Jesus himself alone.

⁹As they were coming down the mountain, Jesus ordered them, "Tell no one about the vision until after the Son of Man has been raised from the dead.

COLOR: WHITE   TRANSFIGURATION SUNDAY

Primary Hymns and Songs for the Day

173   "Christ, Whose Glory Fills the Skies" (2 Pet., Matt.) (O)
>H-3 Hbl-51; Chr-206; Desc-89; Org-120
>S-1 #278-279. Harmonizations

258   "O Wondrous Sight! O Vision Fair" (2 Pet., Matt.)
>H-3 Hbl-47; Chr-32; Desc-102; Org-175
>S-2 #191. Harmonization

2272   "Holy Ground" (Matt.)
>SP86

3043   "You, Lord, Are Both Lamb and Shepherd" (Matt.)

2102   "Swiftly Pass the Clouds of Glory" (Matt.)
>H-3 Chr-98; Org-43

103   "Immortal, Invisible, God Only Wise" (Exod.) (C)
>H-3 Hbl-15, 71; Chr-65; Desc-93; Org-135
>S-1 #300. Harmonization

Additional Hymn Suggestions

73   "O Worship the King" (Exod.)
127   "Guide Me, O Thou Great Jehovah" (Exod.)
731   "Glorious Things of Thee Are Spoken" (Exod.)
2077   "You Alone Are Holy" (Exod., Transfiguration)
2120   "Spirit, Spirit of Gentleness" (Exod.)
3009   "Praise God for This Holy Ground" (Exod., Matt.)
116   "The God of Abraham Praise" (Exod., Matt.)
404   "Every Time I Feel the Spirit" (Exod., Matt.)
451   "Be Thou My Vision" (Exod., Matt., Transfiguration)
107   "La Palabra Del Señor Es Recta" ("Righteous and Just Is the Word of the Lord") (Ps.)
139   "Praise to the Lord, the Almighty" (Ps.)
2177   "Wounded World that Cries for Healing" (Ps.)
2183   "Unsettled World" (Ps.)
2246   "Deep in the Shadows of the Past" (2 Pet.)
3056   "Jesus, the Light of the World" (2 Pet.)
506   "Wellspring of Wisdom" (2 Pet.)
247   "O Morning Star, How Fair and Bright" (2 Pet., Matt.)
260   "Christ, Upon the Mountain Peak" (2 Pet., Matt.)
371   "I Stand Amazed in the Presence" (Matt.)
644   "Jesus, Joy of Our Desiring" (Matt., Communion)
623   "Here, O My Lord, I See Thee" (Matt., Communion)
2012   "Let Us with a Joyful Mind" (Matt.)
2103   "We Have Come at Christ's Own Bidding" (Matt.)
2202   "Come Away with Me" (Matt., Transfiguration)

Additional Contemporary Suggestions

S2040   "Awesome God" (Exod., Ps.)
>SP11

UM176   "Majesty, Worship His Majesty" (Ps.)
>SP73

M126   "Famous One" (Ps., 2 Pet.)
M149   "Ancient Words" (2 Pet.)
S2069   "All Hail King Jesus" (Matt., Transfiguration)
>SP63

S2070   "He Is Exalted" (Matt., Transfiguration)
>SP66

UM349   "Turn Your Eyes upon Jesus" (Matt.)
>SP218

M36   "Awesome in this Place" (Matt., Transfiguration)
M43   "We Declare Your Majesty" (Matt., Transfiguration)

SP171   "When I Look Into Your Holiness" (Matt., Transfiguration)
SP4   "Great and Mighty Is He" (Transfiguration)
>M11

S2018   "Honor and Praise" (Transfiguration)

Vocal Solos

"Be Thou My Vision" (Exod., Matt., Transfiguration)
>V-6   p. 13

"I Saw the Lord, and All Beside Was Darkness" (Exod., Matt.)
>V-8   p. 268

"Ev'ry Time I Feel De Spirit" (Exod., Matt.)
>V-7   p. 78

Anthems

"Praise to the Lord, the Almighty" (Ps.)
Arr. Robert J. Powell; GIA G-6856
SATB, organ, brass quartet

"My God, How Wonderful Thou Art" (Exod., Matt.)
arr. René Clausen; Augsburg 0-8006-7699-8
SATB, *a cappella*

"Christ Upon the Mountain Peak" (Matt.)
John Bertalot; Augsburg 11-10499
Two-part, keyboard and C instrument

Other Suggestions

Visuals:
>**O**   Exod. 24:12*b*, mountain, tablets, cloud, glory, volcano
>**P**   Throne, quake, Ps. 99:3, scales, footstool, cloud, tablet
>**E**   Majesty, 2 Pet. 1:17*b*, mountain, lamp, dawn, star, Bible
>**G**   Mountain, three figures/booths, cloud, Matt. 17:5*b*, fear

Introit: S2274. "Come, All You People" ("Uyai Mose") (Ps.)
Greeting: BOW318 (Exod., Transfiguration)
Opening Prayer: BOW462 (Ps.)
Prayer of Confession: BOW481 (Exod.) or BOW483 (Matt.)
Sung Confession: UM82 "Canticle of God's Glory" (Exod., Matt.)
Call to Prayer: S2273, BOW187. "Jesus, We Are Here" (Matt.)
Prayer: UM259, WSL13 or BOW319 (Matt., Transfiguration)
Prayer: WSL11 (2 Pet.)
Litany: BOW496. The Ten Commandments (Exod.)
Benediction: BOW562 (Matt.)
See additional ideas in *The Abingdon Worship Annual 2014*.

MARCH 5, 2014

Joel 2:1-2, 12-17

1 Blow the trumpet in Zion;
  sound the alarm on my holy mountain!
Let all the inhabitants of the land tremble,
  for the day of the LORD is coming, it is near—
2 a day of darkness and gloom,
  a day of clouds and thick darkness!
Like blackness spread upon the mountains
  a great and powerful army comes;
their like has never been from of old,
  nor will be again after them
  in ages to come.
. . . .
12 Yet even now, says the LORD,
  return to me with all your heart,
with fasting, with weeping, and with mourning;
  13rend your hearts and not your clothing.
Return to the LORD, your God,
  for he is gracious and merciful,
slow to anger, and abounding in steadfast love,
  and relents from punishing.
14 Who knows whether he will not turn and relent,
  and leave a blessing behind him,
a grain offering and a drink offering
  for the LORD, your God?

15 Blow the trumpet in Zion;
  sanctify a fast;
call a solemn assembly;
  16gather the people.
Sanctify the congregation;
  assemble the aged;
gather the children,
  even infants at the breast.
Let the bridegroom leave his room,
  and the bride her canopy.
17 Between the vestibule and the altar
  let the priests, the ministers of the LORD, weep.
Let them say, "Spare your people, O LORD,
  and do not make your heritage a mockery,
  a byword among the nations.
Why should it be said among the peoples,
  'Where is their God?' "

Psalm 51:1-17

1 Have mercy on me, O God,
  according to your steadfast love;
according to your abundant mercy
  blot out my transgressions.
2 Wash me thoroughly from my iniquity,
  and cleanse me from my sin.
3 For I know my transgressions,
  and my sin is ever before me.
4 Against you, you alone, have I sinned,
  and done what is evil in your sight,
so that you are justified in your sentence
  and blameless when you pass judgment.
5 Indeed, I was born guilty,
  a sinner when my mother conceived me.
6 You desire truth in the inward being;
  therefore teach me wisdom in my secret heart.
7 Purge me with hyssop, and I shall be clean;
  wash me, and I shall be whiter than snow.
8 Let me hear joy and gladness;
  let the bones that you have crushed rejoice.
9 Hide your face from my sins,
  and blot out all my iniquities.
10 Create in me a clean heart, O God,
  and put a new and right spirit within me.
11 Do not cast me away from your presence,
  and do not take your holy spirit from me.
12 Restore to me the joy of your salvation,
  and sustain in me a willing spirit.
13 Then I will teach transgressors your ways,
  and sinners will return to you.
14 Deliver me from bloodshed, O God,
  O God of my salvation,
  and my tongue will sing aloud of your deliverance.
15 O Lord, open my lips,
  and my mouth will declare your praise.
16 For you have no delight in sacrifice;
  if I were to give a burnt offering, you would not be pleased.
17 The sacrifice acceptable to God is a broken spirit;
  a broken and contrite heart, O God, you will not despise.

2 Corinthians 5:20b–6:10

20So we are ambassadors for Christ, since God is making his appeal through us; we entreat you on behalf of Christ, be reconciled to God. 21For our sake he made him to be sin who knew no sin, so that in him we might become the righteousness of God.

6As we work together with him, we urge you also not to accept the grace of God in vain. 2For he says,
  "At an acceptable time I have listened to you,
  and on a day of salvation I have helped you."
See, now is the acceptable time; see, now is the day of salvation! 3We are putting no obstacle in anyone's way, so that no fault may be found with our ministry, 4but as servants of God we have commended ourselves in every way: through great endurance, in afflictions, hardships, calamities, 5beatings, imprisonments, riots, labors, sleepless nights, hunger; 6by purity, knowledge, patience, kindness, holiness of spirit, genuine love, 7truthful speech, and the power of God; with the weapons of righteousness for the right hand and for the left; 8in honor and dishonor, in ill repute and good repute. We are treated as impostors, and yet are true; 9as unknown, and yet are well known; as dying, and see—we are alive; as punished, and yet not killed; 10as sorrowful, yet always rejoicing; as poor, yet making many rich; as having nothing, and yet possessing everything.

Matthew 6:1-6, 16-21

1"Beware of practicing your piety before others in order to be seen by them; for then you have no reward from your Father in heaven. 2"So whenever you give alms, do not sound a trumpet before you, as the hypocrites do in the synagogues and in the streets, so that they may be praised by others. Truly I tell you, they have received their reward. 3But when you give alms, do not let your left hand know what your right hand is doing, 4so that your alms may be done in secret; and your Father who sees in secret will reward you. 5"And whenever you pray, do not be like the hypocrites; for they love to stand and pray in the synagogues and at the street corners, so that they may be seen by others. Truly I tell you, they have received their reward. 6But whenever you pray, go into your room and shut the door and pray to your Father who is in secret; and your Father who sees in secret will reward you. . . .

16"And whenever you fast, do not look dismal, like the hypocrites, for they disfigure their faces so as to show others that they are fasting. Truly I tell you, they have received their reward. 17But when you fast, put oil on your head and wash your face, 18so that your fasting may be seen not by others but by your Father who is in secret; and your Father who sees in secret will reward you.

19"Do not store up for yourselves treasures on earth, where moth and rust consume and where thieves break in and steal; 20but store up for yourselves treasures in heaven, where neither moth nor rust consumes and where thieves do not break in and steal. 21For where your treasure is, there your heart will be also.

COLOR: PURPLE   **ASH WEDNESDAY**

Primary Hymns and Songs for the Day
395   "Take Time to Be Holy" (Matt.) (O)
        H-3 Chr-178
        S-1 #159. Harmonization
2133   "Give Me a Clean Heart" (Ps., Ash Wednesday)
2138   "Sunday's Palms Are Wednesday's Ashes" (Ps., Ash Wednesday)
        H-3 Hbl-14, 64; Chr-132, 203
        S-2 #22. Descant
        Please note that 2128 and 2138 use the same tune.
3098   "Dust and Ashes" (Ash Wednesday)
402   "Lord, I Want to Be a Christian" (Joel, Matt.) (C)
        H-3 Chr-130

Additional Hymn Suggestions
121   "There's a Wideness in God's Mercy" (Joel)
296   "Sing, My Tongue, the Glorious Battle" (Joel)
343   "Come Back Quickly to the Lord" (Joel)
379   "Blow Ye the Trumpet, Blow" (Joel)
2206   "Without Seeing You" (Joel, Ash Wednesday)
351   "Pass Me Not, O Gentle Savior" (Ps.)
355   "Depth of Mercy" (Ps.)
417   "O For a Heart to Praise My God" (Ps.)
502   "Thy Holy Wings, O Savior" (Ps.)
3140   "Give Me Jesus" (Ps.)
2134   "Forgive Us, Lord" ("Perdon, Senor") (Ps.)
2140   "Since Jesus Came Into My Heart" (Ps., Matt.)
292   "What Wondrous Love Is This" (2 Cor.)
294   "Alas! and Did My Savior Bleed" (2 Cor., Lent)
359   "Alas! and Did My Savior Bleed" (2 Cor., Lent)
337   "Only Trust Him" (2 Cor.)
384   "Love Divine, All Loves Excelling" (2 Cor.)
407   "Close to Thee" (2 Cor.)
450   "Creator of the Earth and Skies" (2 Cor.)
546   "The Church's One Foundation" (2 Cor.)
2255   "In the Singing" (2 Cor., Communion)
453   "More Love to Thee, O Christ" (Matt.)
492   "Prayer Is the Soul's Sincere Desire" (Matt.)
496   "Sweet Hour of Prayer" (Matt.)
2128   "Come and Find the Quiet Center" (Matt., Ash Wednesday)
2169   "God, How Can We Forgive" (Matt.)
2202   "Come Away with Me" (Matt.)
2205   "The Fragrance of Christ" (Matt.)
3070   "The Lord's Prayer" (Matt.)
        See also S2278, UM271, WS3068-WS3070

Additional Contemporary Suggestions
S2206   "Without Seeing You" (Joel)
S2055   "You Are My Hiding Place" (Ps.)
S2154   "Please Enter My Heart, Hosanna" (Ps.)
S2152   "Change My Heart, O God" (Ps.)
        SP195
M49   "Refresh My Heart" (Ps.)
M50   "Refiner's Fire" (Ps.)
S2086   "Open Our Eyes, Lord" (Ps.)
        SP199
M26   "The Power of Your Love" (Ps.)
M35   "White as Snow" (Ps.)
WS3008 "Open the Eyes of My Heart" (Ps.)
        M57

M89   "Purified" (Ps.)
WS3103 "Purify My Heart" (Ps.)
        M90
M97   "I Give You My Heart" (Ps.)
M153   "Give Us Clean Hands" (Ps.)
WS3130 "Come, Emmanuel" (Ps., 2 Cor, Ash Wednesday)
M67   "We Want to See Jesus Lifted High" (2 Cor.)
M94   "That's Why We Praise Him" (2 Cor.)
SP158   "The Battle Belongs to the Lord" (2 Cor.)
M38   "I Want to Know You" ("In the Secret") (Matt.)
M115   "When It's All Been Said and Done" (Matt.)
WS3040 "You Are My All in All" (Matt., Lent)
        SP220

Vocal Solos
"If With All Your Hearts" (Joel)
    V-8   p. 277
"A Contrite Heart" (Ps.)
    V-4   p. 10
"Turn My Heart to You" (Ps., Ash Wednesday)
    V-5(2)   p. 14
"Clean Before My Lord" (Ps.)
    V-8   p. 233

Anthems
"Now Is the Healing Time Decreed" (Ash Wednesday)
arr. Stuart Forster; Paraclete Press PPM01208
SAB, organ

"Create in Me a Clean Heart" (Ps.)
Mark Burrows; Abingdon Press 0687491649
SATB, piano

Other Suggestions
Visuals:
  O   Black cloth, grain, trumpet, empty plate, weeping
  P   Water, snow, rejoicing, Ps. 51:10, 15, 17, heart
  E   Clock, calendar with today's date, rejoicing, black/gold
  G   Praying hands, oil/water, closed door, empty plate, rusty items, Matt. 6:21, ashes of last year's palms, oil
  Ash Wednesday: Ashes, rough fabrics
Suggested Service: BOW321-324
Greeting: BOW328 or BOW331 (Joel)
Opening Prayer: BOW460 (Matt.)
Call to Prayer: S2157. "Come and Fill Our Hearts" (Ps.)
Confession: WSL14 or BOW475 (Joel, Ps., Ash Wednesday)
Confession: WSL93. Renewing God (Ps., Healing)
Response: WS3122. "Christ Has Broken Down the Wall" (2 Cor.)
Prayer: UM353. Ash Wednesday (Ps.)
Prayer: WSL15. O God, you delight not in pomp (Matt., Ps.)
Response: BOW217. "Remember That You Are Dust" (Joel)
Isaiah 58:1-12 gives another interpretation of fasting.
Offertory Prayer: WSL109. O great and holy God (2 Cor.)
Offertory Prayer: WSL123. Gracious God (Matt.)
Meditative Songs in Taizé Style: S2057, S2058, S2118, S2133, S2156, S2157, S2159, S2200, S2275

73

MARCH 9, 2014

GIRL SCOUT SUNDAY

Genesis 2:15-17; 3:1-7

[15]The Lord God took the man and put him in the garden of Eden to till it and keep it. [16]And the Lord God commanded the man, "You may freely eat of every tree of the garden; [17]but of the tree of the knowledge of good and evil you shall not eat, for in the day that you eat of it you shall die." . . .

[1]Now the serpent was more crafty than any other wild animal that the Lord God had made. He said to the woman, "Did God say, 'You shall not eat from any tree in the garden'?" [2]The woman said to the serpent, "We may eat of the fruit of the trees in the garden; [3]but God said, 'You shall not eat of the fruit of the tree that is in the middle of the garden, nor shall you touch it, or you shall die.'" [4]But the serpent said to the woman, "You will not die; [5]for God knows that when you eat of it your eyes will be opened, and you will be like God, knowing good and evil." [6]So when the woman saw that the tree was good for food, and that it was a delight to the eyes, and that the tree was to be desired to make one wise, she took of its fruit and ate; and she also gave some to her husband, who was with her, and he ate. [7]Then the eyes of both were opened, and they knew that they were naked; and they sewed fig leaves together and made loincloths for themselves.

Psalm 32

[1] Happy are those whose transgression is forgiven,
       whose sin is covered.
[2] Happy are those to whom the Lord imputes no iniquity,
       and in whose spirit there is no deceit.
[3] While I kept silence, my body wasted away
       through my groaning all day long.
[4] For day and night your hand was heavy upon me;
           my strength was dried up as by the heat of summer.
                                                              Selah
[5] Then I acknowledged my sin to you,
       and I did not hide my iniquity;
     I said, "I will confess my transgressions to the Lord,"
       and you forgave the guilt of my sin. *Selah*
[6] Therefore let all who are faithful
       offer prayer to you;
     at a time of distress, the rush of mighty waters
       shall not reach them.
[7] You are a hiding place for me;
       you preserve me from trouble;
     you surround me with glad cries of deliverance. *Selah*
[8] I will instruct you and teach you the way you should go;
       I will counsel you with my eye upon you.
[9] Do not be like a horse or a mule, without understanding,
       whose temper must be curbed with bit and bridle,
       else it will not stay near you.
[10] Many are the torments of the wicked,
       but steadfast love surrounds those who trust in
         the Lord.
[11] Be glad in the Lord and rejoice, O righteous,
       and shout for joy, all you upright in heart.

Romans 5:12-19

[12]Therefore, just as sin came into the world through one man, and death came through sin, and so death spread to all because all have sinned— [13]sin was indeed in the world before the law, but sin is not reckoned when there is no law.

[14]Yet death exercised dominion from Adam to Moses, even over those whose sins were not like the transgression of Adam, who is a type of the one who was to come.

[15]But the free gift is not like the trespass. For if the many died through the one man's trespass, much more surely have the grace of God and the free gift in the grace of the one man, Jesus Christ, abounded for the many. [16]And the free gift is not like the effect of the one man's sin. For the judgment following one trespass brought condemnation, but the free gift following many trespasses brings justification. [17]If, because of the one man's trespass, death exercised dominion through that one, much more surely will those who receive the abundance of grace and the free gift of righteousness exercise dominion in life through the one man, Jesus Christ.

[18]Therefore just as one man's trespass led to condemnation for all, so one man's act of righteousness leads to justification and life for all. [19]For just as by the one man's disobedience the many were made sinners, so by the one man's obedience the many will be made righteous.

Matthew 4:1-11

[1]Then Jesus was led up by the Spirit into the wilderness to be tempted by the devil. [2]He fasted forty days and forty nights, and afterwards he was famished. [3]The tempter came and said to him, "If you are the Son of God, command these stones to become loaves of bread." [4]But he answered, "It is written,

 'One does not live by bread alone,
   but by every word that comes from the mouth of God.'"
[5]Then the devil took him to the holy city and placed him on the pinnacle of the temple, [6]saying to him, "If you are the Son of God, throw yourself down; for it is written,

 'He will command his angels concerning you,'
   and 'On their hands they will bear you up,
 so that you will not dash your foot against a stone.'"
[7]Jesus said to him, "Again it is written, 'Do not put the Lord your God to the test.'"

[8]Again, the devil took him to a very high mountain and showed him all the kingdoms of the world and their splendor; [9]and he said to him, "All these I will give you, if you will fall down and worship me." [10]Jesus said to him, "Away with you, Satan! for it is written,

 'Worship the Lord your God,
   and serve only him.'"
[11]Then the devil left him, and suddenly angels came and waited on him.

COLOR: PURPLE

1st SUNDAY IN LENT

Primary Hymns and Songs for the Day

269 "Lord, Who Throughout These Forty Days" (Matt.)
(O)
> H-3 Hbl-129; Chr-106; Desc-65; Org-72
> S-2 #105. Flute/violin descant
> #106. Harmonization

2112 "Jesus Walked This Lonesome Valley" (Matt.)
2105 "Jesus, Tempted in the Desert" (Matt.)
> H-3 Chr-53; Org-33
> S-1 #109-10. Descant and harmonization

378 "Amazing Grace" (Ps., Rom.) (C)
> H-3 Hbl-14, 46; Chr-27; Desc-14; Org-4
> S-2 #5-7. Various treatments

Additional Hymn Suggestions

120 "Your Love, O God" (Gen.)
132 "All My Hope Is Firmly Grounded" (Gen.)
150 "God Who Stretched the Spangled Heavens"
(Gen.)
692 "Creator of the Stars of Night" (Gen.)
2170 "God Made from One Blood" (Gen.)
73 "O Worship the King" (Gen., Rom.)
140 "Great Is Thy Faithfulness" (Ps.)
391 "O Happy Day, That Fixed My Choice" (Ps.)
2279 "The Trees of the Field" (Ps.)
2267 "Taste and See" (Ps., Communion)
365 "Grace Greater than Our Sin" (Ps., Rom.)
287 "O Love Divine, What Hast Thou Done" (Rom.)
294 "Alas! And Did My Savior Bleed" (Rom.)
359 "Alas! And Did My Savior Bleed" (Rom.)
313 "Cristo Vive" ("Christ Is Risen") (Rom.)
363 "And Can It Be That I Should Gain" (Rom.)
364 "Because He Lives" (Rom.,)
505 "When Our Confidence Is Shaken" (Rom.)
671 "Lord, Dismiss Us With Thy Blessing" (Rom.) (C)
2255 "In the Singing" (Rom., Communion)
267 "O Love, How Deep" (Matt.)
377 "It Is Well With My Soul" (Matt.)
534 "Be Still, My Soul" (Matt.)
2051 "I Was There to Hear Your Borning Cry" (Matt.)
3072 "Cast Out, O Christ" (Matt., Lent)
3098 "Dust and Ashes" (Matt., Lent)
2083 "My Song Is Love Unknown" (Matt., Lent)
2089 "Wild and Lone the Prophet's Voice" (Lent)
616 "Come, Sinners, to the Gospel Feast"
(Communion)
622 "There Is a Fountain Filled With Blood"
(Communion)

Additional Contemporary Suggestions

S2055 "You Are My Hiding Place" (Ps.)
S2074 "Shout to the Lord"
> M16
M92 "All Things Are Possible" (Ps.)
M73 "My Redeemer Lives" (Ps., Lent)
WS3027 "Hallelujah" ("Your Love Is Amazing") (Ps., Lent)
> M118
WS3104 "Amazing Grace" ("My Chains Are Gone") (Ps.,
Rom.)
> M205
WS3187 "We Fall Down" (Rom.)
> M66

S2064 "O Lord, You're Beautiful" (Rom.)
S2258 "Sing Alleluia to the Lord" (Rom.)
> SP93
S2113 "Lamb of God" (Matt., Lent)
S2088 "Lord, I Lift Your Name on High" (Matt., Lent)
> M2
WS3073 "We Walk His Way" (Matt., Lent)

Vocal Solos

"In the Image of God" (Gen., Rom., Lent)
> V-8   p. 362
"And Can It Be That I Should Gain" (Rom.)
> V-1   p. 29
"Amazing Grace" (Rom.)
> V-8   p. 56
"Grace Greater Than Our Sin" (Rom.)
> V-8   p. 180
"Holy is the Lamb" (Matt.)
> V-5(1)   p. 5

Anthems

"Lord, Who Throughout These Forty Days" (Matt.)
Robert Powell; Concordia 98-4119
SATB, keyboard

"Oh, Love, How Deep" (Matt.)
arr. Bradley Ellingboe; Kjos 8831
Two-part mixed, organ and percussion

Other Suggestions

Visuals:
> **O**   Garden, fruit tree, serpent, fig leaves/loin cloth
> **P**   Hand, dry/heat, praying hands, waterfall, hiding place, teaching, bit/bridle, joy, Ps. 32:11
> **E**   Target/arrows (sin), gift, Christ, crucifix
> **G**   Dove/flames, 40/40, stones/bread, Bible, pinnacle, angels ministering, Matt. 4:7, mountain, vista

Introit: WS3043, stanza 3. "You, Lord, are Both Lamb and Shepherd" (Matt., Lent)
Greeting: BOW331 (Ps.)
Call to Prayer: UM330. "Daw-Kee, Aim Daw-Tis-Taw" ("Great Spirit, Now I Pray") (Matt.)
Act of Congregational Centering: BOW470 (Gen., Rom., Matt.)
Prayer of Confession: BOW478 or BOW487 (Gen.)
Prayer: UM366. For Guidance (Gen., Rom.)
Prayer: BOW333 (Matt.)
Prayer: WSL16 or WSL19 (Matt., Lent)
Canticle: UM167. "Canticle of Christ's Obedience" (Rom., Matt.)
Invitation to Lenten Discipline: BOW322 (Matt.)
Prayer of Thanksgiving: BOW552 (Gen., Rom.)
Prayer: BOW436 (Girl Scout Sunday)
Blessing: WSL18. May the blessing of God (Matt., Lent)

MARCH 16, 2014

Genesis 12:1-4a

[1]Now the LORD said to Abram, "Go from your country and your kindred and your father's house to the land that I will show you. [2]I will make of you a great nation, and I will bless you, and make your name great, so that you will be a blessing. [3]I will bless those who bless you, and the one who curses you I will curse; and in you all the families of the earth shall be blessed."

[4]So Abram went, as the LORD had told him; and Lot went with him. Abram was seventy-five years old when he departed from Haran.

Psalm 121

[1] I lift up my eyes to the hills—
    from where will my help come?
[2] My help comes from the LORD,
    who made heaven and earth.
[3] He will not let your foot be moved;
    he who keeps you will not slumber.
[4] He who keeps Israel
    will neither slumber nor sleep.
[5] The LORD is your keeper;
    the LORD is your shade at your right hand.
[6] The sun shall not strike you by day,
    nor the moon by night.
[7] The LORD will keep you from all evil;
    he will keep your life.
[8] The LORD will keep
    your going out and your coming in
    from this time on and forevermore.

Romans 4:1-5, 13-17

[1]What then are we to say was gained by Abraham, our ancestor according to the flesh? [2]For if Abraham was justified by works, he has something to boast about, but not before God. [3]For what does the scripture say? "Abraham believed God, and it was reckoned to him as righteousness." [4]Now to one who works, wages are not reckoned as a gift but as something due. [5]But to one who without works trusts him who justifies the ungodly, such faith is reckoned as righteousness.

. . . .

[13]For the promise that he would inherit the world did not come to Abraham or to his descendants through the law but through the righteousness of faith. [14]If it is the adherents of the law who are to be the heirs, faith is null and the promise is void. [15]For the law brings wrath; but where there is no law, neither is there violation.

[16]For this reason it depends on faith, in order that the promise may rest on grace and be guaranteed to all his descendants, not only to the adherents of the law but also to those who share the faith of Abraham (for he is the father of all of us, [17]as it is written, "I have made you the father of many nations") —in the presence of the God in whom he believed, who gives life to the dead and calls into existence the things that do not exist.

John 3:1-17

[1]Now there was a Pharisee named Nicodemus, a leader of the Jews. [2]He came to Jesus by night and said to him, "Rabbi, we know that you are a teacher who has come from God; for no one can do these signs that you do apart from the presence of God." [3]Jesus answered him, "Very truly, I tell you, no one can see the kingdom of God without being born from above." [4]Nicodemus said to him, "How can anyone be born after having grown old? Can one enter a second time into the mother's womb and be born?" [5]Jesus answered, "Very truly, I tell you, no one can enter the kingdom of God without being born of water and Spirit. [6]What is born of the flesh is flesh, and what is born of the Spirit is spirit. [7]Do not be astonished that I said to you, 'You must be born from above.' [8]The wind blows where it chooses, and you hear the sound of it, but you do not know where it comes from or where it goes. So it is with everyone who is born of the Spirit." [9]Nicodemus said to him, "How can these things be?" [10]Jesus answered him, "Are you a teacher of Israel, and yet you do not understand these things?

[11]"Very truly, I tell you, we speak of what we know and testify to what we have seen; yet you do not receive our testimony. [12]If I have told you about earthly things and you do not believe, how can you believe if I tell you about heavenly things? [13]No one has ascended into heaven except the one who descended from heaven, the Son of Man. [14]And just as Moses lifted up the serpent in the wilderness, so must the Son of Man be lifted up, [15]that whoever believes in him may have eternal life.

[16]"For God so loved the world that he gave his only Son, so that everyone who believes in him may not perish but may have eternal life.

[17]"Indeed, God did not send the Son into the world to condemn the world, but in order that the world might be saved through him."

COLOR: PURPLE   **2nd SUNDAY IN LENT**

Primary Hymns and Songs for the Day
116   "The God of Abraham Praise" (Gen.) (O)
        H-3 Hbl-62, 95; Chr-59; Org-77
        S-1 #211. Harmonization
98   "To God Be the Glory" (John)
        H-3 Chr-201
        S-2 #176. Piano arrangement
369   "Blessed Assurance" (John)
        H-3 Chr-39
        S-1 #24. Harmonization
159   "Lift High the Cross" (John)
        H-3 Hbl-75; Chr-128; Desc-25; Org-21
        S-1 #71-75. Various treatments
389   "Freely, Freely" (John) (C)

Additional Hymn Suggestions
2246   "Deep in the Shadows of the Past" (Gen.)
100   "God, Whose Love Is Reigning o'er Us" (Gen.)
117   "O God, Our Help in Ages Past" (Gen., Ps.)
142   "If Thou But Suffer God to Guide Thee" (Gen., Ps.)
508   "Faith, While Trees Are Still in Blossom" (Gen., Rom.)
2211   "Faith Is Patience in the Night" (Gen., Rom.)
129   "Give to the Winds Thy Fears" (Ps.)
479   "Jesus, Lover of My Soul" (Ps.)
2166   "Christ Beside Me" (Ps.)
3131   "Hear My Prayer, O God" (Ps.)
385   "Let Us Plead for Faith Alone" (Rom.)
541   "See How Great a Flame Aspires" (Rom.)
710   "Faith of Our Fathers" (Rom.)
2196   "We Walk by Faith" (Rom.)
2255   "In the Singing" (Rom., Communion)
184   "Of the Father's Love Begotten" (John)
364   "Because He Lives" (John)
605   "Wash, O God, Our Sons and Daughters" (John, Baptism)
610   "We Know That Christ Is Raised" (John, Baptism)
654   "How Blest Are They Who Trust in Christ" (John)
2046   "Womb of Life" (John, Communion)
2050   "Mothering God, You Gave Me Birth" (John, Communion)
2084   "Come, Let Us with Our Lord Arise" (John)
2092   "Like a Child" (John)
2121   "O Holy Spirit, Root of Life" (John)
2149   "Living for Jesus" (John)
2220   "We Are God's People" (John)
2236   "Gather Us In" (John)
2259   "Victim Divine" (John, Lent, Communion)

Additional Contemporary Suggestions
S2118 "Holy Spirit, Come to Us" (Ps.)
S2258 "Sing Alleluia to the Lord" (Rom.)
        SP93
S2266 "Here Is Bread, Here Is Wine" (Rom., Communion)
S2073 "Celebrate Love" (John)
S2108 "O How He Loves You and Me!" (John)
        SP113
S2085 "He Came Down" (John)
S2088 "Lord, I Lift Your Name on High" (John, Lent)
        M2
SP111 "There Is a Redeemer" (John)

WS3040 "You Are My All in All" (John)
        SP220
M7   "I Believe in Jesus" (John)
M25   "No Greater Love" (John, Lent)
WS3026 "God Is Good All the Time" (John)
        M45
M63   "I Could Sing of Your Love Forever" (John)
M77   "Above All" (John)
WS3102 "You Are My King" ("Amazing Love") (John)
        M82
M94   "That's Why We Praise Him" (John)
M106   "I Come to the Cross" (John, Lent)

Vocal Solos
"Jesus, Lover of My Soul" (Ps.)
    V-1   p. 37
"I Will Lift Up Mine Eyes" (Ps.)
    V-11   p. 27
"Redeeming Grace" (Rom.)
    V-4   p. 47
"Oh, What Love!" (Rom., John)
    V-8   p. 144
"Wash Me in Your Water" (John, Baptism)
    V-5(2) p. 18
"Born Again" (John)
    V-8   p. 8

Anthems
"I Will Look to the Hills" (Ps.)
Charles Garner; GIA G-6338
SATB, *a cappella*

"For God So Loved the World" (John)
Allen Pote; Hope C5386
SATB, piano

Other Suggestions
Visuals:
    O   Luggage, multitude, farewell, walking
    P   Hills, foot, sleep, sun/moon, evils, open door
    E   Abraham, paycheck, will, trust
    G   Cloak/night, newborn, water/Spirit, wind, serpent lifted, crucifix, #16, Ascension
The scripture from John makes today an excellent day to schedule baptisms. Baptismal Covenant III (BOW 106) directly refers to today's reading from John.
Greeting: BOW327 (Ps.)
Opening Prayer: BOW251 or BOW392 (John)
Call to Prayer: WS3131, stanza 1. "Hear My Prayer, O God" (Ps.)
Prayer of Confession: BOW489 (John) or BOW494 (Gen.)
Prayer: BOW335 (Rom., Lent)
Prayer: BOW373-374. Abraham's Trust in God (Gen.)
Litany: BOW432. Laity Sunday (Gen., Baptism)
Song of Thanksgiving: BOW182. "Doxology" (John)

MARCH 23, 2014

Exodus 17:1-7

[1]From the wilderness of Sin the whole congregation of the Israelites journeyed by stages, as the LORD commanded. They camped at Rephidim, but there was no water for the people to drink. [2]The people quarreled with Moses, and said, "Give us water to drink." Moses said to them, "Why do you quarrel with me? Why do you test the LORD?" [3]But the people thirsted there for water; and the people complained against Moses and said, "Why did you bring us out of Egypt, to kill us and our children and livestock with thirst?" [4]So Moses cried out to the LORD, "What shall I do with this people? They are almost ready to stone me." [5]The LORD said to Moses, "Go on ahead of the people, and take some of the elders of Israel with you; take in your hand the staff with which you struck the Nile, and go. [6]I will be standing there in front of you on the rock at Horeb. Strike the rock, and water will come out of it, so that the people may drink." Moses did so, in the sight of the elders of Israel. [7]He called the place Massah and Meribah, because the Israelites quarreled and tested the LORD, saying, "Is the LORD among us or not?"

Psalm 95

[1] O come, let us sing to the LORD;
   let us make a joyful noise to the rock of our salvation!
[2] Let us come into his presence with thanksgiving;
   let us make a joyful noise to him with songs of praise!
[3] For the LORD is a great God,
   and a great King above all gods.
[4] In his hand are the depths of the earth;
   the heights of the mountains are his also.
[5] The sea is his, for he made it,
   and the dry land, which his hands have formed.
[6] O come, let us worship and bow down,
   let us kneel before the LORD, our Maker!
[7] For he is our God,
   and we are the people of his pasture,
   and the sheep of his hand.
 O that today you would listen to his voice!
[8] Do not harden your hearts,
   as at Meribah, as on the day at Massah in the wilderness,
[9] when your ancestors tested me,
   and put me to the proof, though they had seen my work.
[10] For forty years I loathed that generation
   and said, "They are a people whose hearts go astray,
   and they do not regard my ways."
[11] Therefore in my anger I swore,
   "They shall not enter my rest."

Romans 5:1-11

[1]Therefore, since we are justified by faith, we have peace with God through our Lord Jesus Christ, [2]through whom we have obtained access to this grace in which we stand; and we boast in our hope of sharing the glory of God. [3]And not only that, but we also boast in our sufferings, knowing that suffering produces endurance, [4]and endurance produces character, and character produces hope, [5]and hope does not disappoint us, because God's love has been poured into our hearts through the Holy Spirit that has been given to us.

[6]For while we were still weak, at the right time Christ died for the ungodly. [7]Indeed, rarely will anyone die for a righteous person—though perhaps for a good person someone might actually dare to die. [8]But God proves his love for us in that while we still were sinners Christ died for us. [9]Much more surely then, now that we have been justified by his blood, will we be saved through him from the wrath of God. [10]For if while we were enemies, we were reconciled to God through the death of his Son, much more surely, having been reconciled, will we be saved by his life. [11]But more than that, we even boast in God through our Lord Jesus Christ, through whom we have now received reconciliation.

John 4:5-42

[5]So he came to a Samaritan city called Sychar, near the plot of ground that Jacob had given to his son Joseph. [6]Jacob's well was there, and Jesus, tired out by his journey, was sitting by the well. It was about noon.

[7]A Samaritan woman came to draw water, and Jesus said to her, "Give me a drink." [8](His disciples had gone to the city to buy food.) [9]The Samaritan woman said to him, "How is it that you, a Jew, ask a drink of me, a woman of Samaria?" (Jews do not share things in common with Samaritans.) [10]Jesus answered her, "If you knew the gift of God, and who it is that is saying to you, 'Give me a drink,' you would have asked him, and he would have given you living water." [11]The woman said to him, "Sir, you have no bucket, and the well is deep. Where do you get that living water? [12]Are you greater than our ancestor Jacob, who gave us the well, and with his sons and his flocks drank from it?" [13]Jesus said to her, "Everyone who drinks of this water will be thirsty again, [14]but those who drink of the water that I will give them will never be thirsty. The water that I will give will become in them a spring of water gushing up to eternal life." [15]The woman said to him, "Sir, give me this water, so that I may never be thirsty or have to keep coming here to draw water."

[16]Jesus said to her, "Go, call your husband, and come back." [17]The woman answered him, "I have no husband." Jesus said to her, "You are right in saying, 'I have no husband'; [18]for you have had five husbands, and the one you have now is not your husband. What you have said is true!" [19]The woman said to him, "Sir, I see that you are a prophet. [20]Our ancestors worshiped on this mountain, but you say that the place where people must worship is in Jerusalem." [21]Jesus said to her, "Woman, believe me, the hour is coming when you will worship the Father neither on this mountain nor in Jerusalem. [22]You worship what you do not know; we worship what we know, for salvation is from the Jews. [23]But the hour is coming, and is now here, when the true worshipers will worship the Father in spirit and truth, for the Father seeks such as these to worship him. [24]God is spirit, and those who worship him must worship in spirit and truth." [25]The woman said to him, "I know that Messiah is coming" (who is called Christ). "When he comes, he will proclaim all things to us." [26]Jesus said to her, "I am he, the one who is speaking to you."

[27]Just then his disciples came. They were astonished that he was speaking with a woman, but no one said, "What do you want?" or, "Why are you speaking with her?" [28]Then the woman left her water jar and went back to the city. She said to the people, [29]"Come and see a man who told me everything I have ever done! He cannot be the Messiah, can he?" [30]They left the city and were on their way to him.

[31]Meanwhile the disciples were urging him, "Rabbi, eat something." [32]But he said to them, "I have food to eat that you do not know about." [33]So the disciples said to one another, "Surely no one has brought him something to eat?" [34]Jesus said to them, "My food is to do the will of him who sent me and to complete his work. [35]Do you not say, 'Four months more, then comes the harvest'? But I tell you, look around you, and see how the fields are ripe for harvesting. [36]The reaper is already receiving wages and is gathering fruit for eternal life, so that sower and reaper may rejoice together. [37]For here the saying holds true, 'One sows and another reaps.' [38]I sent you to reap that for which you did not labor. Others have labored, and you have entered into their labor."

[39]Many Samaritans from that city believed in him because of the woman's testimony, "He told me everything I have ever done." [40]So when the Samaritans came to him, they asked him to stay with them; and he stayed there two days. [41]And many more believed because of his word. [42]They said to the woman, "It is no longer because of what you said that we believe, for we have heard for ourselves, and we know that this is truly the Savior of the world."

COLOR: PURPLE

3rd SUNDAY IN LENT

Primary Hymns and Songs for the Day

127   "Guide Me, O Thou Great Jehovah" (Exod., John) (O)
> H-3   Hbl-25, 51, 58; Chr-89; Desc-26; Org-23
> S-1   #76-77. Descant and harmonization

2132   "You Who Are Thirsty" (Exod., John)
> SP219

2108   "O How He Loves You and Me!" (Rom.)
> SP113

298   "When I Survey the Wondrous Cross" (Rom.) (C)
> H-3   Hbl-6, 102; Chr-213; Desc-49; Org-49
> S-1   #155. Descant

Additional Hymn Suggestions

132   "All My Hope Is Firmly Grounded" (Exod.)
731   "Glorious Things of Thee Are Spoken" (Exod.)
413   "A Charge to Keep I Have" (Exod., John)
631   "O Food to Pilgrims Given" (Exod., John, Communion)
2211   "Faith Is Patience in the Night" (Exod., Rom.)
89   "Joyful, Joyful, We Adore Thee" (Ps., John)
282   "'Tis Finished! The Messiah Dies" (Rom.)
422   "Jesus, Thine All-Victorious Love" (Rom.)
480   "O Love That Wilt Not Let Me Go" (Rom.)
505   "When Our Confidence Is Shaken" (Rom.)
591   "Rescue the Perishing" (Rom.)
2196   "We Walk by Faith" (Rom.)
2255   "In the Singing" (Rom., Communion)
3043   "You, Lord, are Both Lamb and Shepherd" (Rom., Lent)
3072   "Cast Out, O Christ" (Rom.)
627   "O the Depth of Love Divine" (Rom., Communion)
2213   "Healer of Our Every Ill" (Rom., John)
113   "Source and Sovereign, Rock and Cloud" (John)
138   "The King of Love, My Shepherd Is" (John)
188   "Christ Is the World's Light" (John)
274   "Woman in the Night" (John)
276   "The First One Ever" (John)
350   "Come, All of You" (John)
479   "Jesus, Lover of My Soul" (John)
644   "Jesus, Joy of Our Desiring" (John)
629   "You Satisfy the Hungry Heart" (John, Communion)
2236   "Gather Us In" (John)
2126   "All Who Hunger" (John, Communion)
2261   "Life-Giving Bread" (John, Communion)
2264   "Come to the Table" (John, Communion)
3098   "Dust and Ashes" (John, Lent)

Additional Contemporary Suggestions

S2002   "I Will Call Upon the Lord" (Ps.)
> SP224

S2022   "Great Is the Lord" (Ps.)
> SP30

S2274   "Come, All You People" ("Uyai Mose") (Ps.)
M77   "Above All" (Ps., Lent)
M93   "Rock of Ages" (Ps.)
SP103   "We Worship and Adore You" (Ps.)
WS3177   "Here I Am to Worship" (Ps., John)
> M116

M63   "I Could Sing of Your Love Forever" (Ps., Rom.)

S2073   "Celebrate Love" (Rom.)
S2143   "O Lord, Your Tenderness" (Rom.)
S2156   "Give Peace" ("Da Pacem Cordium") (Rom.)
S2258   "Sing Alleluia to the Lord" (Rom.)
> SP93

UM394   "Something Beautiful" (Rom.)
WS3102   "You Are My King" ("Amazing Love") (Rom.)
> M82

M94   "That's Why We Praise Him" (Rom.)
S2266   "Here Is Bread, Here Is Wine" (Rom., John, Communion)
S2071   "Jesus, Name Above All Names" (John)
> SP76

M5   "The River Is Here" (John)
M28   "Who Can Satisfy My Soul Like You?" (John)
M40   "More Love, More Power" (John)
M47   "Come Just As You Are" (John)
WS3176   "Come, Now Is the Time to Worship" (John)
> M56

WS3099   "Falling on My Knees" ("Hungry") (John)
> M155

M159   "All Who Are Thirsty" (John)
WS3093   "Fill My Cup, Lord" (John, Communion)
> UM641 refrain; S-2 stanzas for soloist

WS3162   "Stand in Awe" (John)

Vocal Solos

"Redeeming Grace" (Rom.)
> V-4   p. 47

"Maybe the Rain" (John)
> V-5(2)   p. 27

"Life Indeed" (John)
> V-8   p. 271

Anthems

"Jesus, Lover of My Soul" (John)
arr. David Huntsinger; Alfred 29371
SATB, keyboard

"Just as I Am" (John)
Bob Chilcott; Oxford 9780193511491
SATB, organ

Other Suggestions

Visuals:
> **O**   Wilderness, quarrel, stones, staff, rock, water, Exod. 17:7c
> **P**   Singing, rock, instruments, mountain, sea, dry land
> **E**   Christ, glory/suffering, hearts/Spirit, crucifix
> **G**   Well, noon, water jar, living water, clock

Opening Prayer: WSL63. Our hearts are full of praise (John)
Canticle: UM91. "Canticle of Praise to God" (Ps.)
Prayer of Confession: BOW485 (Exod.)
Words of Assurance: Romans 5:8
Prayer: WSL57. Days pass and the years vanish (Exod.)
Prayer: WSL52. O God, you pour out (John)
Litany: WSL53. We also boast in our sufferings (Rom.)
Benediction: BOW564 (Exod., John) or BOW561 (Rom.)
Benediction: WSL167. Go! Never stop going out (John)

MARCH 30, 2014

ONE GREAT HOUR OF SHARING

1 Samuel 16:1-13

[1]The Lord said to Samuel, "How long will you grieve over Saul? I have rejected him from being king over Israel. Fill your horn with oil and set out; I will send you to Jesse the Bethlehemite, for I have provided for myself a king among his sons." [2]Samuel said, "How can I go? If Saul hears of it, he will kill me." And the Lord said, "Take a heifer with you, and say, 'I have come to sacrifice to the Lord.' [3]Invite Jesse to the sacrifice, and I will show you what you shall do; and you shall anoint for me the one whom I name to you." [4]Samuel did what the Lord commanded, and came to Bethlehem. The elders of the city came to meet him trembling, and said, "Do you come peaceably?" [5]He said, "Peaceably; I have come to sacrifice to the Lord; sanctify yourselves and come with me to the sacrifice." And he sanctified Jesse and his sons and invited them to the sacrifice.

[6]When they came, he looked on Eliab and thought, "Surely the Lord's anointed is now before the Lord." [7]But the Lord said to Samuel, "Do not look on his appearance or on the height of his stature, because I have rejected him; for the Lord does not see as mortals see; they look on the outward appearance, but the Lord looks on the heart." [8]Then Jesse called Abinadab, and made him pass before Samuel. He said, "Neither has the Lord chosen this one." [9]Then Jesse made Shammah pass by. And he said, "Neither has the Lord chosen this one." [10]Jesse made seven of his sons pass before Samuel, and Samuel said to Jesse, "The Lord has not chosen any of these." [11]Samuel said to Jesse, "Are all your sons here?" And he said, "There remains yet the youngest, but he is keeping the sheep." And Samuel said to Jesse, "Send and bring him; for we will not sit down until he comes here." [12]He sent and brought him in. Now he was ruddy, and had beautiful eyes, and was handsome. The Lord said, "Rise and anoint him; for this is the one." [13]Then Samuel took the horn of oil, and anointed him in the presence of his brothers; and the spirit of the Lord came mightily upon David from that day forward. Samuel then set out and went to Ramah.

Psalm 23

[1] The Lord is my shepherd, I shall not want.
  [2]He makes me lie down in green pastures;
he leads me beside still waters;
  [3]he restores my soul.
He leads me in right paths
for his name's sake.
[4] Even though I walk through the darkest valley,
  I fear no evil;
for you are with me;
  your rod and your staff—
they comfort me.
[5] You prepare a table before me
  in the presence of my enemies;
you anoint my head with oil;
  my cup overflows.
[6] Surely goodness and mercy shall follow me
  all the days of my life,
and I shall dwell in the house of the Lord
  my whole life long.

Ephesians 5:8-14

[8]For once you were darkness, but now in the Lord you are light. Live as children of light— [9]for the fruit of the light is found in all that is good and right and true. [10]Try to find out what is pleasing to the Lord. [11]Take no part in the unfruitful works of darkness, but instead expose them. [12]For it is shameful even to mention what such people do secretly; [13]but everything exposed by the light becomes visible, [14]for everything that becomes visible is light. Therefore it says,
"Sleeper, awake!
Rise from the dead,
and Christ will shine on you."

John 9:1-41

[1]As he walked along, he saw a man blind from birth. [2]His disciples asked him, "Rabbi, who sinned, this man or his parents, that he was born blind?" [3]Jesus answered, "Neither this man nor his parents sinned; he was born blind so that God's works might be revealed in him. [4]We must work the works of him who sent me while it is day; night is coming when no one can work. [5]As long as I am in the world, I am the light of the world." [6]When he had said this, he spat on the ground and made mud with the saliva and spread the mud on the man's eyes, [7]saying to him, "Go, wash in the pool of Siloam" (which means Sent). Then he went and washed and came back able to see.

[8]The neighbors and those who had seen him before as a beggar began to ask, "Is this not the man who used to sit and beg?" [9]Some were saying, "It is he." Others were saying, "No, but it is someone like him." He kept saying, "I am the man." [10]But they kept asking him, "Then how were your eyes opened?" [11]He answered, "The man called Jesus made mud, spread it on my eyes, and said to me, 'Go to Siloam and wash.' Then I went and washed and received my sight." [12]They said to him, "Where is he?" He said, "I do not know."

[13]They brought to the Pharisees the man who had formerly been blind. [14]Now it was a sabbath day when Jesus made the mud and opened his eyes. [15]Then the Pharisees also began to ask him how he had received his sight. He said to them, "He put mud on my eyes. Then I washed, and now I see." [16]Some of the Pharisees said, "This man is not from God, for he does not observe the sabbath." But others said, "How can a man who is a sinner perform such signs?" And they were divided. [17]So they said again to the blind man, "What do you say about him? It was your eyes he opened." He said, "He is a prophet."

[18]The Jews did not believe that he had been blind and had received his sight until they called the parents of the man who had received his sight [19]and asked them, "Is this your son, who you say was born blind? How then does he now see?" [20]His parents answered, "We know that this is our son, and that he was born blind; [21]but we do not know how it is that now he sees, nor do we know who opened his eyes. Ask him; he is of age. He will speak for himself." [22]His parents said this because they were afraid of the Jews; for the Jews had already agreed that anyone who confessed Jesus to be the Messiah would be put out of the synagogue. [23]Therefore his parents said, "He is of age; ask him."

[24]So for the second time they called the man who had been blind, and they said to him, "Give glory to God! We know that this man is a sinner." [25]He answered, "I do not know whether he is a sinner. One thing I do know, that though I was blind, now I see." [26]They said to him, "What did he do to you? How did he open your eyes?" [27]He answered them, "I have told you already, and you would not listen. Why do you want to hear it again? Do you also want to become his disciples?" [28]Then they reviled him, saying, "You are his disciple, but we are disciples of Moses. [29]We know that God has spoken to Moses, but as for this man, we do not know where he comes from." [30]The man answered, "Here is an astonishing thing! You do not know where he comes from, and yet he opened my eyes. [31]We know that God does not listen to sinners, but he does listen to one who worships him and obeys his will. [32]Never since the world began has it been heard that anyone opened the eyes of a person born blind. [33]If this man were not from God, he could do nothing." [34]They answered him, "You were born entirely in sins, and are you trying to teach us?" And they drove him out.

[35]Jesus heard that they had driven him out, and when he found him, he said, "Do you believe in the Son of Man?" [36]He answered, "And who is he, sir? Tell me, so that I may believe in him." [37]Jesus said to him, "You have seen him, and the one speaking with you is he." [38]He said, "Lord, I believe." And he worshiped him. [39]Jesus said, "I came into this world for judgment so that those who do not see may see, and those who do see may become blind." [40]Some of the Pharisees near him heard this and said to him, "Surely we are not blind, are we?" [41]Jesus said to them, "If you were blind, you would not have sin. But now that you say, 'We see,' your sin remains."

COLOR: PURPLE

4th SUNDAY IN LENT

Primary Hymns and Songs for the Day

454	"Open My Eyes, That I May See" (John) (O)
	H-3 Chr-157; Org-108
138	"The King of Love My Shepherd Is" (Ps.)
2058	"Shepherd Me, O God" (Ps.)
2086	"Open Our Eyes, Lord" (John)
	SP199
206	"I Want to Walk as a Child of the Light" (Eph., John)
	S-2 #91. Descant
128	"He Leadeth Me: O Blessed Thought" (1 Sam, Ps.) (C)

Additional Hymn Suggestions

578	"God of Love and God of Power" (1 Sam., One Great Hour)
407	"Close to Thee" (1 Sam., Ps.)
474	"Precious Lord, Take My Hand" (1 Sam., Ps.)
136	"The Lord's My Shepherd" (Ps.)
381	"Savior, Like a Shepherd Lead Us" (Ps.)
650	"Give Me the Faith Which Can Remove" (Ps.)
2113	"Lamb of God" (Ps.)
2140	"Since Jesus Came Into My Heart" (Ps.)
2206	"Without Seeing You" (Ps.)
2112	"Jesus Walked This Lonesome Valley" (Ps., Lent)
518	"O Thou, in Whose Presence" (Ps., John)
2214	"Lead Me, Guide Me" (Ps., Eph.)
551	"Awake, O Sleeper" (Eph.)
573	"O Zion, Haste" (Eph., One Great Hour)
2172	"We Are Called" (Eph.)
2218	"You Are Mine" (Eph., John)
2236	"Gather Us In" (Eph., Communion)
2237	"As a Fire Is Meant for Burning" (Eph., John)
57	"O For a Thousand Tongues to Sing" (John, One Great Hour)
263	"When Jesus the Healer Passed Through Galilee" (John)
265	"O Christ, the Healer" (John)
451	"Be Thou My Vision" (John)
2199	"Stay with Us" (John)
2254	"In Remembrance of Me" (John, Communion)
581	"Lord, Whose Love Through Humble Service" (John, One Great Hour)

Additional Contemporary Suggestions

S2054	"Nothing Can Trouble" ("Nada Te Turbe") (Ps.)
S2113	"Lamb of God" (Ps., Lent)
SP40	"God Will Make a Way" (Ps.)
WS3026	"God Is Good All the Time" (Ps.)
	M45
WS3096	"Gentle Shepherd" (Ps., Lent)
WS3106	"Your Grace Is Enough (Ps., Lent)
	M191
M72	"Jesus, Lover of My Soul" ("It's All about You") (Ps.)
M79	"I Stand Amazed" (Ps., Lent)
M19	"Shine on Us" (Eph.)
M150	"Everyday" (Eph.)
S2235	"We Are Marching" ("Siyahamba") (Eph.)
S2173	"Shine, Jesus, Shine" (Eph., John)
	SP142
S2204	"Light of the World" (Eph., John)

S2253	"Water, River, Spirit, Grace" (John)
WS3177	"Here I Am to Worship" (Eph., John)
	M116
WS3105	"In Christ Alone" (Eph., John)
	M138
UM349	"Turn Your Eyes upon Jesus" (John)
	SP218
M26	"The Power of Your Love" (John)
WS3008	"Open the Eyes of My Heart" (John)
	M57
M77	"Above All" (John)
M164	"Good to Me" (John)
SP111	"There Is a Redeemer" (John, Communion)
3001	"O For a Thousand Tongues to Sing (John, One Great Hour)

Vocal Solos

"God, Our Ever Faithful Shepherd" (Ps.)
V-4   p. 15
"The Lord is My Shepherd" (Ps.)
V-5(3)   p. 30
"Shepherd of Love" (Ps.)
V-8   p. 142
"My Shepherd Will Supply My Need" (Ps.)
V-10   p. 4
"Patiently Have I Waited for the Lord" (John)
V-4   p. 24

Anthems

"The Lord Is My Shepherd" (Ps.)
Howard Goodall; Alfred 0571520480
SATB, keyboard, opt. strings

"I Believe" (John)
Mark Miller; Choristers Guild CGA-1310
SATB, piano

Other Suggestions

Visuals:

O	Oil/horn, crown, heifer, washing hands, 7 sons, boy
P	Shepherd/sheep, pasture, water, path, dark valley, rod/ staff, banquet, oil, overflowing cup, house of God
E	Dark/light, children, ministry, waking, Christ
G	Mud, dark glasses, day/night, light/dark, water

Service of Healing I: BOW615-621 (John)
Introit: UM473. "Lead Me, Lord" (Ps.)
Greeting: BOW306 or BOW326 (Eph.)
Litany: BOW424 (One Great Hour)
Prayer of Confession and Pardon: BOW476 (Eph.)
Unison Reading of Psalm 23: BOW145 (Ps.)
Canticle: UM137 (Ps.)
Prayer: WSL17. A wilderness beckons (Ps., Lent)
Prayer: UM446 or UM456 (One Great Hour)
Prayer: UM489. For God's Gifts (Eph.)
Prayer of Intercession: BOW397 (Eph., One Great Hour)

APRIL 6, 2014

Ezekiel 37:1-14

[1]The hand of the LORD came upon me, and he brought me out by the spirit of the LORD and set me down in the middle of a valley; it was full of bones. [2]He led me all around them; there were very many lying in the valley, and they were very dry. [3]He said to me, "Mortal, can these bones live?" I answered, "O Lord GOD, you know." [4]Then he said to me, "Prophesy to these bones, and say to them: O dry bones, hear the word of the LORD. [5]Thus says the Lord GOD to these bones: I will cause breath to enter you, and you shall live. [6]I will lay sinews on you, and will cause flesh to come upon you, and cover you with skin, and put breath in you, and you shall live; and you shall know that I am the LORD."

[7]So I prophesied as I had been commanded; and as I prophesied, suddenly there was a noise, a rattling, and the bones came together, bone to its bone. [8]I looked, and there were sinews on them, and flesh had come upon them, and skin had covered them; but there was no breath in them. [9]Then he said to me, "Prophesy to the breath, prophesy, mortal, and say to the breath: Thus says the Lord GOD: Come from the four winds, O breath, and breathe upon these slain, that they may live." [10]I prophesied as he commanded me, and the breath came into them, and they lived, and stood on their feet, a vast multitude.

[11]Then he said to me, "Mortal, these bones are the whole house of Israel. They say, 'Our bones are dried up, and our hope is lost; we are cut off completely.' [12]Therefore prophesy, and say to them, Thus says the Lord GOD: I am going to open your graves, and bring you up from your graves, O my people; and I will bring you back to the land of Israel. [13]And you shall know that I am the LORD, when I open your graves, and bring you up from your graves, O my people. [14]I will put my spirit within you, and you shall live, and I will place you on your own soil; then you shall know that I, the LORD, have spoken and will act," says the LORD.

Psalm 130

[1] Out of the depths I cry to you, O LORD.
[2] Lord, hear my voice!
 Let your ears be attentive
  to the voice of my supplications!
[3] If you, O LORD, should mark iniquities,
  Lord, who could stand?
[4] But there is forgiveness with you,
  so that you may be revered.
[5] I wait for the LORD, my soul waits,
  and in his word I hope;
[6] my soul waits for the Lord
  more than those who watch for the morning,
  more than those who watch for the morning.
[7] O Israel, hope in the LORD!
 For with the LORD there is steadfast love,
  and with him is great power to redeem.
[8] It is he who will redeem Israel
  from all its iniquities.

Romans 8:6-11

[6]To set the mind on the flesh is death, but to set the mind on the Spirit is life and peace. [7]For this reason the mind that is set on the flesh is hostile to God; it does not submit to God's law—indeed it cannot, [8]and those who are in the flesh cannot please God.

[9]But you are not in the flesh; you are in the Spirit, since the Spirit of God dwells in you. Anyone who does not have the Spirit of Christ does not belong to him. [10]But if Christ is in you, though the body is dead because of sin, the Spirit is life because of righteousness. [11]If the Spirit of him who raised Jesus from the dead dwells in you, he who raised Christ from the dead will give life to your mortal bodies also through his Spirit that dwells in you.

John 11:1-45

[1]Now a certain man was ill, Lazarus of Bethany, the village of Mary and her sister Martha. [2]Mary was the one who anointed the Lord with perfume and wiped his feet with her hair; her brother Lazarus was ill. [3]So the sisters sent a message to Jesus, "Lord, he whom you love is ill." [4]But when Jesus heard it, he said, "This illness does not lead to death; rather it is for God's glory, so that the Son of God may be glorified through it." [5]Accordingly, though Jesus loved Martha and her sister and Lazarus, [6]after having heard that Lazarus was ill, he stayed two days longer in the place where he was.

[7]Then after this he said to the disciples, "Let us go to Judea again." [8]The disciples said to him, "Rabbi, the Jews were just now trying to stone you, and are you going there again?" [9]Jesus answered, "Are there not twelve hours of daylight? Those who walk during the day do not stumble, because they see the light of this world. [10]But those who walk at night stumble, because the light is not in them." [11]After saying this, he told them, "Our friend Lazarus has fallen asleep, but I am going there to awaken him." [12]The disciples said to him, "Lord, if he has fallen asleep, he will be all right." [13]Jesus, however, had been speaking about his death, but they thought that he was referring merely to sleep. [14]Then Jesus told them plainly, "Lazarus is dead. [15]For your sake I am glad I was not there, so that you may believe. But let us go to him." [16]Thomas, who was called the Twin, said to his fellow disciples, "Let us also go, that we may die with him."

[17]When Jesus arrived, he found that Lazarus had already been in the tomb four days. [18]Now Bethany was near Jerusalem, some two miles away, [19]and many of the Jews had come to Martha and Mary to console them about their brother. [20]When Martha heard that Jesus was coming, she went and met him, while Mary stayed at home. [21]Martha said to Jesus, "Lord, if you had been here, my brother would not have died. [22]But even now I know that God will give you whatever you ask of him." [23]Jesus said to her, "Your brother will rise again." [24]Martha said to him, "I know that he will rise again in the resurrection on the last day." [25]Jesus said to her, "I am the resurrection and the life. Those who believe in me, even though they die, will live, [26]and everyone who lives and believes in me will never die. Do you believe this?" [27]She said to him, "Yes, Lord, I believe that you are the Messiah, the Son of God, the one coming into the world."

[28]When she had said this, she went back and called her sister Mary, and told her privately, "The Teacher is here and is calling for you." [29]And when she heard it, she got up quickly and went to him. [30]Now Jesus had not yet come to the village, but was still at the place where Martha had met him. [31]The Jews who were with her in the house, consoling her, saw Mary get up quickly and go out. They followed her because they thought that she was going to the tomb to weep there. [32]When Mary came where Jesus was and saw him, she knelt at his feet and said to him, "Lord, if you had been here, my brother would not have died." [33]When Jesus saw her weeping, and the Jews who came with her also weeping, he was greatly disturbed in spirit and deeply moved. [34]He said, "Where have you laid him?" They said to him, "Lord, come and see." [35]Jesus began to weep. [36]So the Jews said, "See how he loved him!" [37]But some of them said, "Could not he who opened the eyes of the blind man have kept this man from dying?"

[38]Then Jesus, again greatly disturbed, came to the tomb. It was a cave, and a stone was lying against it. [39]Jesus said, "Take away the stone." Martha, the sister of the dead man, said to him, "Lord, already there is a stench because he has been dead four days." [40]Jesus said to her, "Did I not tell you that if you believed, you would see the glory of God?" [41]So they took away the stone. And Jesus looked upward and said, "Father, I thank you for having heard me. [42]I knew that you always hear me, but I have said this for the sake of the crowd standing here, so that they may believe that you sent me." [43]When he had said this, he cried with a loud voice, "Lazarus, come out!" [44]The dead man came out, his hands and feet bound with strips of cloth, and his face wrapped in a cloth. Jesus said to them, "Unbind him, and let him go."

[45]Many of the Jews therefore, who had come with Mary and had seen what Jesus did, believed in him.

COLOR: PURPLE   **5th SUNDAY IN LENT**

Primary Hymns and Songs for the Day
261   "Lord of the Dance" (John, Lent) (O)
311   "Now the Green Blade Riseth" (Ezek., John)
383   "This Is a Day of New Beginnings" (Ezek., John)
        H-3 Chr-196
393   "Spirit of the Living God" (Rom.)
        SP131; S-1 #212 Vocal descant idea
2110   "Why Has God Forsaken Me?" (Ps., John)
        H-3 Chr-220
420   "Breathe on Me, Breath of God" (Ezek.) (C)

Additional Hymn Suggestions
503   "Let It Breathe on Me" (Ezek.)
178   "Hope of the World" (Ezek., John)
266   "Heal us, Emmanuel, Hear Our Prayer" (Ezek., John)
303   The Day of Resurrection (Ezek., John)
305   "Camina, Pueblo de Dios" ("Walk On, O People of God") (Ezek., John)
307   "Christ Is Risen" (Ezek., John)
315   "Come, Ye Faithful, Raise the Strain" (Ezek., John)
331   "Holy Spirit, Come, Confirm Us" (Ezek., Rom., John)
332   "Spirit of Faith, Come Down" (Ezek., Rom., John)
515   "Out of the Depths I Cry to You" (Ps.)
2136   "Out of the Depths" (Ps.)
3131   "Hear My Prayer, O God" (Ps.)
3141   "Holy Darkness" (Ps., Lent)
2209   "How Long, O Lord" (Ps., John)
465   "Holy Spirit, Truth Divine" (Rom.)
359   "Alas! and Did My Savior Bleed" (Rom.)
294   "Alas! and Did My Savior Bleed" (Rom.)
467   "Trust and Obey" (Rom., John)
500   "Spirit of God, Descend Upon My Heart" (Rom., John)
180   "Jesús Es Mi Rey Soberano" ("O Jesus, My King") (John)
262   "Heal Me, Hands of Jesus" (John)
265   "O Christ, the Healer" (John)
273   "Jesus' Hands Were Kind Hands" (John)
274   "Woman in the Night" (John)
300   "O The Lamb" (John)
304   "Easter People, Raise Your Voices" (John)
310   "He Lives" (John)
313   "Cristo Vive" ("Christ Is Risen") (John)
314   "In the Garden" (John)
319   "Christ Jesus Lay in Death's Strong Bonds" (John)
322   "Up from the Grave He Arose" (John)
384   "Love Divine, All Loves Excelling" (John)
2046   "Womb of Life" (John, Communion)
2106   "When Jesus Wept" (John)
2172   "We Are Called" (John)
2158   "Just a Closer Walk with Thee" (John, Lent)
2214   "Lead Me, Guide Me" (John, Lent)
3017   "Come, Join the Dance of Trinity" (John, Lent)

Additional Contemporary Suggestions
S2118   "Holy Spirit, Come to Us" (Ezek.)
WS3186 "Days of Elijah" (Ezek.)
         M139
S2139   "Oh, I Know the Lord's Laid His Hands on Me" (Ezek., John)

S2088   "Lord, I Lift Your Name on High" (Ezek., Rom., John, Lent)
         M2
SP235   "Let Your Spirit Rise" (Ezek., Rom., John)
WS3099 "Falling on My Knees" ("Hungry") (Ps.)
         M155
WS3094 "Come to Me" (Ps., John)
S2150   "Lord, Be Glorified" (Rom., John)
         SP196
S2215   "Cares Chorus" (John)
         SP221
S2026   "Halle, Halle, Halleluja" (John)
S2204   "Light of the World" (John)
S2235   "We Are Marching" ("Siyahamba") (John)
M7   "I Believe in Jesus" (John)
M150   "Everyday" (John)

Vocal Solos
"Out of the Depths I Cry to Thee" (Ps.)
    V-9   p. 16
"Spirit of Faith Come Down" (John, Rom.)
    V-1   p. 43
"Just a Closer Walk With Thee" (John, Lent)
    V-5(2)   p. 31
    V-8   p. 323

Anthems
"Psalm 130" (Ps.)
John Ferguson; Augsburg 0800656075
SATB, keyboard

"Lazarus" (John)
Robert Tanner; GIA Publications G-5851
SATB, *a cappella*

Other Suggestions
Visuals:
    O   Valley/bones, wilderness, multitude, open graves
    P   Listening, praying hands/waiting, rescue
    E   Coffin, Spirit symbols, Christ, open tomb
    G   Jar/woman, hair/feet, message, night/stumbling block, woman/Jesus/kneeling, tears, tomb, strips of cloth
Plan this service so that it moves from the quietness of the tomb and the Psalm to the joy of Lazarus' resurrection.
Opening Prayer: WSL52. O God, you pour out (Ezek., Rom.)
Call to Prayer: WS3111. "Redemption" (Rom., Lent)
Confession: BOW486 (Ezek.)
Assurance: BOW375. New Life for God's People (Ezek.)
Canticle: UM516. "Canticle of Redemption" (Ps.)
Prayer: UM461. For Those Who Mourn (John)

APRIL 13, 2014

Matthew 21:1-11 (Palms Text)

[1]When they had come near Jerusalem and had reached Bethphage, at the Mount of Olives, Jesus sent two disciples, [2]saying to them, "Go into the village ahead of you, and immediately you will find a donkey tied, and a colt with her; untie them and bring them to me. [3]If anyone says anything to you, just say this, 'The Lord needs them.' And he will send them immediately." [4]This took place to fulfill what had been spoken through the prophet, saying,

[5] "Tell the daughter of Zion,
Look, your king is coming to you,
    humble, and mounted on a donkey,
        and on a colt, the foal of a donkey."

[6]The disciples went and did as Jesus had directed them; [7]they brought the donkey and the colt, and put their cloaks on them, and he sat on them. [8]A very large crowd spread their cloaks on the road, and others cut branches from the trees and spread them on the road. [9]The crowds that went ahead of him and that followed were shouting,

"Hosanna to the Son of David!
    Blessed is the one who comes in the name of the Lord!
Hosanna in the highest heaven!"

[10]When he entered Jerusalem, the whole city was in turmoil, asking, "Who is this?" [11]The crowds were saying, "This is the prophet Jesus from Nazareth in Galilee."

Psalm 118:1-2, 19-29 (Palms Text)

[1] O give thanks to the LORD, for he is good;
        his steadfast love endures forever!
[2] Let Israel say,
        "His steadfast love endures forever."
. . . .
[19] Open to me the gates of righteousness,
        that I may enter through them
        and give thanks to the LORD.
[20] This is the gate of the LORD;
        the righteous shall enter through it.
[21] I thank you that you have answered me
        and have become my salvation.
[22] The stone that the builders rejected
        has become the chief cornerstone.
[23] This is the Lord's doing;
        it is marvelous in our eyes.
[24] This is the day that the LORD has made;
        let us rejoice and be glad in it.
[25] Save us, we beseech you, O LORD!
        O LORD, we beseech you, give us success!
[26] Blessed is the one who comes in the name of the LORD.
        We bless you from the house of the LORD.
[27] The LORD is God,
        and he has given us light.
    Bind the festal procession with branches,
        up to the horns of the altar.
[28] You are my God, and I will give thanks to you;
        you are my God, I will extol you.
[29] O give thanks to the LORD, for he is good,
        for his steadfast love endures forever.

Isaiah 50:4-9a (Passion Text)

[4] The Lord GOD has given me
        the tongue of a teacher,
    that I may know how to sustain
        the weary with a word.
    Morning by morning he wakens—
        wakens my ear
        to listen as those who are taught.

[5] The Lord GOD has opened my ear,
        and I was not rebellious,
        I did not turn backward.
[6] I gave my back to those who struck me,
        and my cheeks to those who pulled out the beard;
    I did not hide my face
        from insult and spitting.
[7] The Lord GOD helps me;
        therefore I have not been disgraced;
    therefore I have set my face like flint,
        and I know that I shall not be put to shame;
        [8]he who vindicates me is near.
    Who will contend with me?
        Let us stand up together.
    Who are my adversaries?
        Let them confront me.
[9] It is the Lord GOD who helps me;
        who will declare me guilty?
    All of them will wear out like a garment;
        the moth will eat them up.

Psalm 31:9-16 (Passion Text)

[9] Be gracious to me, O LORD, for I am in distress;
        my eye wastes away from grief,
        my soul and body also.
[10] For my life is spent with sorrow,
        and my years with sighing;
    my strength fails because of my misery,
        and my bones waste away.
[11] I am the scorn of all my adversaries,
        a horror to my neighbors,
    an object of dread to my acquaintances;
        those who see me in the street flee from me.
[12] I have passed out of mind like one who is dead;
        I have become like a broken vessel.
[13] For I hear the whispering of many—
        terror all around!—
    as they scheme together against me,
        as they plot to take my life.
[14] But I trust in you, O LORD;
        I say, "You are my God."
[15] My times are in your hand;
        deliver me from the hand of my enemies and persecutors.
[16] Let your face shine upon your servant;
        save me in your steadfast love.

Philippians 2:5-11 (Passion Text)

[5] Let the same mind be in you that was in Christ Jesus,
[6] who, though he was in the form of God,
        did not regard equality with God
        as something to be exploited,
[7] but emptied himself,
        taking the form of a slave,
        being born in human likeness.
    And being found in human form,
        [8]he humbled himself
        and became obedient to the point of death—
        even death on a cross.
[9] Therefore God also highly exalted him
        and gave him the name
        that is above every name,
[10] so that at the name of Jesus
        every knee should bend,
        in heaven and on earth and under the earth,
[11] and every tongue should confess

84

COLOR: PURPLE   **PALM/PASSION SUNDAY**

that Jesus Christ is Lord,
to the glory of God the Father.

Matthew 26:14–27:66 (27:11-54) (Passion Text)

[14]Then one of the twelve, who was called Judas Iscariot, went to the chief priests [15]and said, "What will you give me if I betray him to you?" They paid him thirty pieces of silver. [16]And from that moment he began to look for an opportunity to betray him.

[17]On the first day of Unleavened Bread the disciples came to Jesus, saying, "Where do you want us to make the preparations for you to eat the Passover?" [18]He said, "Go into the city to a certain man, and say to him, 'The Teacher says, My time is near; I will keep the Passover at your house with my disciples.'" [19]So the disciples did as Jesus had directed them, and they prepared the Passover meal.

[20]When it was evening, he took his place with the twelve; [21]and while they were eating, he said, "Truly I tell you, one of you will betray me." [22]And they became greatly distressed and began to say to him one after another, "Surely not I, Lord?" [23]He answered, "The one who has dipped his hand into the bowl with me will betray me. [24]The Son of Man goes as it is written of him, but woe to that one by whom the Son of Man is betrayed! It would have been better for that one not to have been born." [25]Judas, who betrayed him, said, "Surely not I, Rabbi?" He replied, "You have said so."

[26]While they were eating, Jesus took a loaf of bread, and after blessing it he broke it, gave it to the disciples, and said, "Take, eat; this is my body." [27]Then he took a cup, and after giving thanks he gave it to them, saying, "Drink from it, all of you; [28]for this is my blood of the covenant, which is poured out for many for the forgiveness of sins. [29]I tell you, I will never again drink of this fruit of the vine until that day when I drink it new with you in my Father's kingdom."

[30]When they had sung the hymn, they went out to the Mount of Olives.

[31]Then Jesus said to them, "You will all become deserters because of me this night; for it is written,

'I will strike the shepherd,
and the sheep of the flock will be scattered.'

[32]But after I am raised up, I will go ahead of you to Galilee." [33]Peter said to him, "Though all become deserters because of you, I will never desert you." [34]Jesus said to him, "Truly I tell you, this very night, before the cock crows, you will deny me three times." [35]Peter said to him, "Even though I must die with you, I will not deny you." And so said all the disciples.

[36]Then Jesus went with them to a place called Gethsemane; and he said to his disciples, "Sit here while I go over there and pray." [37]He took with him Peter and the two sons of Zebedee, and began to be grieved and agitated. [38]Then he said to them, "I am deeply grieved, even to death; remain here, and stay awake with me." [39]And going a little farther, he threw himself on the ground and prayed, "My Father, if it is possible, let this cup pass from me; yet not what I want but what you want." [40]Then he came to the disciples and found them sleeping; and he said to Peter, "So, could you not stay awake with me one hour? [41]Stay awake and pray that you may not come into the time of trial; the spirit indeed is willing, but the flesh is weak." [42]Again he went away for the second time and prayed, "My Father, if this cannot pass unless I drink it, your will be done." [43]Again he came and found them sleeping, for their eyes were heavy. [44]So leaving them again, he went away and prayed for the third time, saying the same words. [45]Then he came to the disciples and said to them, "Are you still sleeping and taking your rest? See, the hour is at hand, and the Son of Man is betrayed into the hands of sinners. [46]Get up, let us be going. See, my betrayer is at hand."

[47]While he was still speaking, Judas, one of the twelve, arrived; with him was a large crowd with swords and clubs, from the chief priests and the elders of the people. [48]Now the betrayer had given them a sign, saying, "The one I will kiss is the man; arrest him." [49]At once he came up to Jesus and said, "Greetings, Rabbi!" and kissed him. [50]Jesus said to him, "Friend, do what you are here to do." Then they came and laid hands on Jesus and arrested him. [51]Suddenly, one of those with Jesus put his hand on his sword, drew it, and struck the slave of the high priest, cutting off his ear. [52]Then Jesus said to him, "Put your sword back into its place; for all who take the sword will perish by the sword. [53]Do you think that I cannot appeal to my Father, and he will at once send me more than twelve legions of angels? [54]But how then would the scriptures be fulfilled, which say it must happen in this way?" [55]At that hour Jesus said to the crowds, "Have you come out with swords and clubs to arrest me as though I were a bandit? Day after day I sat in the temple teaching, and you did not arrest me. [56]But all this has taken place, so that the scriptures of the prophets may be fulfilled." Then all the disciples deserted him and fled.

[57]Those who had arrested Jesus took him to Caiaphas the high priest, in whose house the scribes and the elders had gathered. [58]But Peter was following him at a distance, as far as the courtyard of the high priest; and going inside, he sat with the guards in order to see how this would end. [59]Now the chief priests and the whole council were looking for false testimony against Jesus so that they might put him to death, [60]but they found none, though many false witnesses came forward. At last two came forward [61]and said, "This fellow said, 'I am able to destroy the temple of God and to build it in three days.'" [62]The high priest stood up and said, "Have you no answer? What is it that they testify against you?" [63]But Jesus was silent. Then the high priest said to him, "I put you under oath before the living God, tell us if you are the Messiah, the Son of God." [64]Jesus said to him, "You have said so. But I tell you,

From now on you will see the Son of Man
seated at the right hand of Power
and coming on the clouds of heaven."

[65]Then the high priest tore his clothes and said, "He has blasphemed! Why do we still need witnesses? You have now heard his blasphemy. [66]What is your verdict?" They answered, "He deserves death." [67]Then they spat in his face and struck him; and some slapped him, [68]saying, "Prophesy to us, you Messiah! Who is it that struck you?"

[69]Now Peter was sitting outside in the courtyard. A servant-girl came to him and said, "You also were with Jesus the Galilean." [70]But he denied it before all of them, saying, "I do not know what you are talking about." [71]When he went out to the porch, another servant-girl saw him, and she said to the bystanders, "This man was with Jesus of Nazareth." [72]Again he denied it with an oath, "I do not know the man." [73]After a little while the bystanders came up and said to Peter, "Certainly you are also one of them, for your accent betrays you." [74]Then he began to curse, and he swore an oath, "I do not know the man!" At that moment the cock crowed. [75]Then Peter remembered what Jesus had said: "Before the cock crows, you will deny me three times." And he went out and wept bitterly.

27When morning came, all the chief priests and the elders of the people conferred together against Jesus in order to bring about his death. [2]They bound him, led him away, and handed him over to Pilate the governor.

[3]When Judas, his betrayer, saw that Jesus was condemned, he repented and brought back the thirty pieces of silver to the chief priests and the elders. [4]He said, "I have sinned by betraying innocent blood." But they said, "What is that to us? See to it yourself." [5]Throwing down the pieces of silver in the temple,

85

APRIL 13, 2014

he departed; and he went and hanged himself. [6]But the chief priests, taking the pieces of silver, said, "It is not lawful to put them into the treasury, since they are blood money." [7]After conferring together, they used them to buy the potter's field as a place to bury foreigners. [8]For this reason that field has been called the Field of Blood to this day. [9]Then was fulfilled what had been spoken through the prophet Jeremiah, "And they took the thirty pieces of silver, the price of the one on whom a price had been set, on whom some of the people of Israel had set a price, [10]and they gave them for the potter's field, as the Lord commanded me."

[11]Now Jesus stood before the governor; and the governor asked him, "Are you the King of the Jews?" Jesus said, "You say so." [12]But when he was accused by the chief priests and elders, he did not answer. [13]Then Pilate said to him, "Do you not hear how many accusations they make against you?" [14]But he gave him no answer, not even to a single charge, so that the governor was greatly amazed.

[15]Now at the festival the governor was accustomed to release a prisoner for the crowd, anyone whom they wanted. [16]At that time they had a notorious prisoner, called Jesus Barabbas. [17]So after they had gathered, Pilate said to them, "Whom do you want me to release for you, Jesus Barabbas or Jesus who is called the Messiah?" [18]For he realized that it was out of jealousy that they had handed him over. [19]While he was sitting on the judgment seat, his wife sent word to him, "Have nothing to do with that innocent man, for today I have suffered a great deal because of a dream about him." [20]Now the chief priests and the elders persuaded the crowds to ask for Barabbas and to have Jesus killed. [21]The governor again said to them, "Which of the two do you want me to release for you?" And they said, "Barabbas." [22]Pilate said to them, "Then what should I do with Jesus who is called the Messiah?" All of them said, "Let him be crucified!" [23]Then he asked, "Why, what evil has he done?" But they shouted all the more, "Let him be crucified!"

[24]So when Pilate saw that he could do nothing, but rather that a riot was beginning, he took some water and washed his hands before the crowd, saying, "I am innocent of this man's blood; see to it yourselves." [25]Then the people as a whole answered, "His blood be on us and on our children!" [26]So he released Barabbas for them; and after flogging Jesus, he handed him over to be crucified.

[27]Then the soldiers of the governor took Jesus into the governor's headquarters, and they gathered the whole cohort around him. [28]They stripped him and put a scarlet robe on him, [29]and after twisting some thorns into a crown, they put it on his head. They put a reed in his right hand and knelt before him and mocked him, saying, "Hail, King of the Jews!" [30]They spat on him, and took the reed and struck him on the head. [31]After mocking him, they stripped him of the robe and put his own clothes on him. Then they led him away to crucify him.

[32]As they went out, they came upon a man from Cyrene named Simon; they compelled this man to carry his cross. [33]And when they came to a place called Golgotha (which means Place of a Skull), [34]they offered him wine to drink, mixed with gall; but when he tasted it, he would not drink it. [35]And when they had crucified him, they divided his clothes among themselves by casting lots; [36]then they sat down there and kept watch over him. [37]Over his head they put the charge against him, which read, "This is Jesus, the King of the Jews."

[38]Then two bandits were crucified with him, one on his right and one on his left. [39]Those who passed by derided him, shaking their heads [40]and saying, "You who would destroy the temple and build it in three days, save yourself! If you are the Son of God, come down from the cross." [41]In the same way the chief priests also, along with the scribes and elders, were mocking

him, saying, [42]"He saved others; he cannot save himself. He is the King of Israel; let him come down from the cross now, and we will believe in him. [43]He trusts in God; let God deliver him now, if he wants to; for he said, 'I am God's Son.'" [44]The bandits who were crucified with him also taunted him in the same way.

[45]From noon on, darkness came over the whole land until three in the afternoon. [46]And about three o"clock Jesus cried with a loud voice, "Eli, Eli, lema sabachthani?" that is, "My God, my God, why have you forsaken me?" [47]When some of the bystanders heard it, they said, "This man is calling for Elijah." [48]At once one of them ran and got a sponge, filled it with sour wine, put it on a stick, and gave it to him to drink. [49]But the others said, "Wait, let us see whether Elijah will come to save him." [50]Then Jesus cried again with a loud voice and breathed his last. [51]At that moment the curtain of the temple was torn in two, from top to bottom. The earth shook, and the rocks were split. [52]The tombs also were opened, and many bodies of the saints who had fallen asleep were raised. [53]After his resurrection they came out of the tombs and entered the holy city and appeared to many. [54]Now when the centurion and those with him, who were keeping watch over Jesus, saw the earthquake and what took place, they were terrified and said, "Truly this man was God's Son!"

[55]Many women were also there, looking on from a distance; they had followed Jesus from Galilee and had provided for him. [56]Among them were Mary Magdalene, and Mary the mother of James and Joseph, and the mother of the sons of Zebedee.

[57]When it was evening, there came a rich man from Arimathea, named Joseph, who was also a disciple of Jesus. [58]He went to Pilate and asked for the body of Jesus; then Pilate ordered it to be given to him. [59]So Joseph took the body and wrapped it in a clean linen cloth [60]and laid it in his own new tomb, which he had hewn in the rock. He then rolled a great stone to the door of the tomb and went away. [61]Mary Magdalene and the other Mary were there, sitting opposite the tomb.

[62]The next day, that is, after the day of Preparation, the chief priests and the Pharisees gathered before Pilate [63]and said, "Sir, we remember what that impostor said while he was still alive, 'After three days I will rise again.' [64]Therefore command the tomb to be made secure until the third day; otherwise his disciples may go and steal him away, and tell the people, 'He has been raised from the dead,' and the last deception would be worse than the first." [65]Pilate said to them, "You have a guard of soldiers; go, make it as secure as you can." [66]So they went with the guard and made the tomb secure by sealing the stone.

COLOR: PURPLE

PALM/PASSION SUNDAY

Primary Hymns and Songs for the Day

3082   "Who Is He" (Palms Gospel) (O)
       H-3   Hbl-25, 74; Chr-120; Desc-54; Org-58
       S-1   #173-176. Various treatments
277   "Tell Me the Stories of Jesus" (Palms Gospel)
279   "Mantos y Palmas" ("Filled with Excitement")
     (Palms Gospel)
       S-2   #90. Performance note
            #89. Harmonization
2113   "Lamb of God" (Passion Gospel)
286   "O Sacred Head, Now Wounded" (Passion)
       H-3   Hbl-82; Chr-148; Desc-86; Org-111
581   "Lord Whose Love Through Humble Service" (C)
     (Passion)

Additional Hymn Suggestions

278   "Hosanna, Loud Hosanna" (Palms Gospel)
280   "All Glory, Laud, and Honor" (Palms Gospel) (O)
2019   "Holy" ("Santo") (Palms Gospel)
2047   "Bring Many Names" (Palms)
2109   "Hosanna! Hosanna!" (Palms Gospel)
2256   "Holy, Holy, Holy Lord" (Palms Gospel)
161   "Rejoice, Ye Pure in Heart" (Phil., Palms Closing)
166   "All Praise to Thee, for Thou, O King Divine"
     (Phil.)
168   "At the Name of Jesus" (Phil.)
193   "Jesus! the Name High Over All" (Phil.)
3075   "Glory in the Cross" (Phil., Passion)
285   "To Mock Your Reign, O Dearest Lord" (Passion)
287   "O Love Divine, What Hast Thou Done" (Passion)
291   "He Never Said a Mumbalin' Word" (Isa., Passion)
296   "Sing, My Tongue, the Glorious Battle" (Passion)
355   "Depth of Mercy" (Passion, Holy Week)
3097   "Depth of Mercy" (Passion, Holy Week)
2083   "My Song Is Love Unknown" (Palms/Passion)
2100   "Thou Didst Leave Thy Throne" (Phil., Passion)
2104   "An Outcast Among Outcasts" (Passion Gospel)
2110   "Why Has God Forsaken Me?" (Passion Gospel)
2111   "We Sang Our Glad Hosannas" (Palms/Passion)
2137   "Would I Have Answered When You Called"
     (Passion Gospel)
2138   "Sunday's Palms Are Wednesday's Ashes" (Passion)
2209   "How Long, O Lord" (Passion Gospel)
2261   "Life-Giving Bread" (Passion Gospel, Communion)
3043   "You, Lord, are Both Lamb and Shepherd"
     (Passion)
3080   "Lord, Is It I?" (Passion Gospel, Holy Week)
633   "The Bread of Life for All Is Broken" (Passion,
     Communion)

Additional Contemporary Suggestions

WS3078   "Hosanna" (Palms Gospel, Ps. 118)
WS3079   "Hosanna" (Palms Gospel, Ps. 118)
WS3188   "Hosanna" (Palms Gospel)
       M268
S2069   "All Hail King Jesus" (Palms Gospel)
       SP63
S2075   "King of Kings" (Palms Gospel)
       SP94
S2091   "The King of Glory Comes" (Palms Gospel)
SP82   "Hosanna" (Palms Gospel)
WS3044   "Make Way" (Palms Gospel)

S2043   "Alleluia" (Ps. 118)
S2270   "I Will Enter His Gates" (Ps. 118)
       SP168
WS3023   "Forever" (Ps. 118)
       M68
WS3027   "Hallelujah" ("Your Love Is Amazing") (Ps.)
       M118
UM177   "He Is Lord" (Phil.)
       SP122
M111   "The Heavens Shall Declare" (Phil., Palms)
S2023   "How Majestic Is Your Name" (Phil.)
       SP14
SP18   "I Exalt You" (Phil.)
M1   "Ancient of Days" (Phil.)
M178   "Majestic" (Phil.)
M24   "Jesus, We Crown You with Praise" (Passion Gospel)
M77   "Above All" (Passion Gospel)
M78   "Once Again" (Passion Gospel)
S2198   "Stay With Me" (Passion Gospel)
WS3083   "We Adore You, Jesus Christ" ("Adoremus te
     Christe") (Passion Gospel, Holy Week)

Vocal Solos

"Ride On, Ride On in Majesty!" (Palm Sunday)
     V-5(2)   p. 57
"Ride On, Jesus" (Palm Sunday)
     V-7   p. 8
"Lamb of God" (Passion Gospel)
     V-5(2)   p. 5
"The Shepherd Became a Lamb" (Palm/Passion)
     V-10   p. 48

Anthems

"A Festive Hosanna" (Palms Liturgy)
Victor Johnson; Choristers Guild CGA-1259
SATB, piano, opt., trumpet

"We Sang Our Glad Hosannas" (Passion Liturgy)
John Horman; Abingdon Press 024099
Children and SATB, keyboard

Other Suggestions

Visuals:

Palms	Donkey, colt/cloaks/crowd/branches
Ps. 118	Gate, cornerstone, branches, joy
O	Jesus teaching, morning, Christ, passion, flint
Ps. 31	Tears, praying/comforting hands, broken pottery
E	Manacles, wood cross, crucifix, resurrection,
Passion	Thirty coins, praying hands, sword, robe, crucifix, crown of thorns, INRI, dice/robe, tombstone

Greeting: WSL21. Hosanna! (Palms Gospel, Ps. 118)
Canticle: UM167. "Canticle of Christ's Obedience" (Phil.)
Affirmation of Faith: WSL76 or WSL 80. We believe (Phil.)
Prayer: UM281. Passion/Palm Sunday
Offertory Prayer: WSL141. Holy One (Holy Week)
Prayer of Thanksgiving: BOW550 (Phil., Luke)

APRIL 17, 2014

Exodus 12:1-4 (5-10) 11-14

¹The LORD said to Moses and Aaron in the land of Egypt: ²This month shall mark for you the beginning of months; it shall be the first month of the year for you. ³Tell the whole congregation of Israel that on the tenth of this month they are to take a lamb for each family, a lamb for each household. ⁴If a household is too small for a whole lamb, it shall join its closest neighbor in obtaining one; the lamb shall be divided in proportion to the number of people who eat of it. ⁵Your lamb shall be without blemish, a year-old male; you may take it from the sheep or from the goats. ⁶You shall keep it until the fourteenth day of this month; then the whole assembled congregation of Israel shall slaughter it at twilight. ⁷They shall take some of the blood and put it on the two doorposts and the lintel of the houses in which they eat it. ⁸They shall eat the lamb that same night; they shall eat it roasted over the fire with unleavened bread and bitter herbs. ⁹Do not eat any of it raw or boiled in water, but roasted over the fire, with its head, legs, and inner organs. ¹⁰You shall let none of it remain until the morning; anything that remains until the morning you shall burn. ¹¹This is how you shall eat it: your loins girded, your sandals on your feet, and your staff in your hand; and you shall eat it hurriedly. It is the passover of the LORD. ¹²For I will pass through the land of Egypt that night, and I will strike down every firstborn in the land of Egypt, both human beings and animals; on all the gods of Egypt I will execute judgments: I am the LORD. ¹³The blood shall be a sign for you on the houses where you live: when I see the blood, I will pass over you, and no plague shall destroy you when I strike the land of Egypt.

¹⁴This day shall be a day of remembrance for you. You shall celebrate it as a festival to the LORD; throughout your generations you shall observe it as a perpetual ordinance.

Psalm 116:1-4, 12-19

¹ I love the LORD, because he has heard
      my voice and my supplications.
² Because he inclined his ear to me,
      therefore I will call on him as long as I live.
³ The snares of death encompassed me;
      the pangs of Sheol laid hold on me;
      I suffered distress and anguish.
⁴ Then I called on the name of the LORD:
      'O LORD, I pray, save my life!'
. . . .
¹² What shall I return to the LORD
      for all his bounty to me?
¹³ I will lift up the cup of salvation
      and call on the name of the LORD,
¹⁴ I will pay my vows to the LORD
      in the presence of all his people.
¹⁵ Precious in the sight of the LORD
      is the death of his faithful ones.
¹⁶ O LORD, I am your servant;
      I am your servant, the child of your serving girl.
      You have loosed my bonds.
¹⁷ I will offer to you a thanksgiving sacrifice
      and call on the name of the LORD.
¹⁸ I will pay my vows to the LORD
      in the presence of all his people,
¹⁹ in the courts of the house of the LORD,
      in your midst, O Jerusalem.
    Praise the LORD!

1 Corinthians 11:23-26

²³For I received from the Lord what I also handed on to you, that the Lord Jesus on the night when he was betrayed took a loaf of bread, ²⁴and when he had given thanks, he broke it and said, "This is my body that is for you. Do this in remembrance of me." ²⁵In the same way he took the cup also, after supper, saying, "This cup is the new covenant in my blood. Do this, as often as you drink it, in remembrance of me." ²⁶For as often as you eat this bread and drink the cup, you proclaim the Lord's death until he comes.

John 13:1-17, 31b -35

¹Now before the festival of the Passover, Jesus knew that his hour had come to depart from this world and go to the Father. Having loved his own who were in the world, he loved them to the end. ²The devil had already put it into the heart of Judas son of Simon Iscariot to betray him. And during supper ³Jesus, knowing that the Father had given all things into his hands, and that he had come from God and was going to God, ⁴got up from the table, took off his outer robe, and tied a towel around himself. ⁵Then he poured water into a basin and began to wash the disciples' feet and to wipe them with the towel that was tied around him. ⁶He came to Simon Peter, who said to him, "Lord, are you going to wash my feet?" ⁷Jesus answered, "You do not know now what I am doing, but later you will understand." ⁸Peter said to him, "You will never wash my feet." Jesus answered, "Unless I wash you, you have no share with me." ⁹Simon Peter said to him, "Lord, not my feet only but also my hands and my head!" ¹⁰Jesus said to him, "One who has bathed does not need to wash, except for the feet, but is entirely clean. And you are clean, though not all of you." ¹¹For he knew who was to betray him; for this reason he said, "Not all of you are clean."

¹²After he had washed their feet, had put on his robe, and had returned to the table, he said to them, "Do you know what I have done to you? ¹³You call me Teacher and Lord—and you are right, for that is what I am. ¹⁴So if I, your Lord and Teacher, have washed your feet, you also ought to wash one another's feet. ¹⁵For I have set you an example, that you also should do as I have done to you. ¹⁶Very truly, I tell you, servants are not greater than their master, nor are messengers greater than the one who sent them. ¹⁷If you know these things, you are blessed if you do them. . . .

³¹When he had gone out, Jesus said, "Now the Son of Man has been glorified, and God has been glorified in him. ³²If God has been glorified in him, God will also glorify him in himself and will glorify him at once. ³³Little children, I am with you only a little longer. You will look for me; and as I said to the Jews so now I say to you, 'Where I am going, you cannot come.' ³⁴I give you a new commandment, that you love one another. Just as I have loved you, you also should love one another. ³⁵By this everyone will know that you are my disciples, if you have love for one another."

COLOR: PURPLE   **HOLY THURSDAY**

Primary Hymns and Songs for the Day
292   "What Wondrous Love Is This" (Ps., John) (O)
           H-3 Hbl-102; Chr-212; Org-185
           S-1 #347. Harmonization
2254   "In Remembrance of Me" (Ps., 1 Cor, Communion)
432   "Jesu, Jesu" (John, footwashing) (C)
           S-1 #63. Vocal part

Additional Hymn Suggestions
117   "O God, Our Help in Ages Past" (Exod.)
2060   "God the Sculptor of the Mountains" (Exod.)
2246   "Deep in the Shadows of the Past" (Exod.)
523   "Saranam, Saranam" ("Refuge") (Exod., Ps.)
3142   "I Love the Lord" (Ps.)
3093   "Fill My Cup, Lord" (Ps., Communion)
           UM641 refrain; S-2 stanzas for soloist
589   "The Church of Christ, in Every Age" (1 Cor.)
590   "Christ Loves the Church" (1 Cor.)
614   "For the Bread Which You Have Broken (1 Cor., Communion)
615   "For the Bread Which You Have Broken" (1 Cor., Communion)
619   "Now The Silence" (Communion)
637   "Una Espiga" ("Sheaves of Summer") (1 Cor., Communion.)
2050   "Mothering God, You Gave Me Birth" (1 Cor., Communion)
2255   "In the Singing" (1 Cor., Communion)
2260   "Let Us Be Bread" (1 Cor., John, Communion)
2261   "Life-Giving Bread" (1 Cor., Communion)
2263   "Broken for Me" (1 Cor., Lent, Communion)
2265   "Time Now to Gather" (1 Cor., Communion)
2269   "Come, Share the Lord" (1 Cor., Communion)
289   "Ah, Holy Jesus" (John)
292   "What Wondrous Love Is This" (John, Holy Week)
421   "Make Me a Captive, Lord" (John)
430   "O Master, Let Me Walk with Thee" (John)
579   "Lord God, Your Love has Called Us Here" (John)
710   (Alternate tune for #579)
632   "Draw Us in the Spirit's Tether" (John, Communion)
2111   "We Sang Our Glad Hosannas" (John, Holy Week)
2175   "Together We Serve" (John)
2177   "Wounded World that Cries for Healing" (John)
2213   "Healer of Our Every Ill" (John)
2268   "As We Gather at Your Table" (John, Communion)
3074   "Jesus Is a Rock in a Weary Land" (John, Holy Week)

Additional Contemporary Suggestions
S2002   "I Will Call Upon the Lord" (Ps.)
           SP224
S2031   "We Bring the Sacrifice of Praise" (Ps.)
           SP1
S2068   "I Love You, Lord" (Ps.)
           SP72
M71   "The Heart of Worship" (Ps.)
M79   "I Stand Amazed" (Ps., Lent)
M211   "I Will Not Forget You" (Ps.)
UM628 "Eat This Bread" (1 Cor., Communion)
UM640 "Take Our Bread" (1 Cor., John, Communion)

S2266   "Here Is Bread, Here Is Wine" (1 Cor., Communion)
S2176   "Make Me a Servant" (John)
           SP193
S2222   "The Servant Song"
           SP193
S2223   "They'll Know We Are Christians" (John)
S2224   "Make Us One" (John)
           SP137
S2226   "Bind Us Together" (John)
           SP140
S2179   "Live in Charity" ("Ubi Caritas") (John)
S2038   "Father, I Adore You" (John)
           SP194
WS3148 "There's a Spirit of Love in This Place" (John)
WS3151 "The Jesus in Me" (John)
WS3154 "Draw the Circle Wide" (John)
M86   "With All of My Heart" (John)
           SP187

Vocal Solos
"Author of Life Divine" (1 Cor., John)
    V-1   p. 39
"In Remembrance" (John, Communion)
    V-5(2)   p. 7
"He Breaks the Bread, He Pours the Wine" (John)
    V-10   p. 43

Anthems
"What Wondrous Love Is This" (Ps., John)
arr. Austin C. Lovelace; Paraclete Press PPM01212
SATB, organ

"O Master, Let Me Walk with Thee" (John)
Hal H. Hopson; MorningStar MSM-50-9212
SATB, keyboard, opt. violin, viola, or cello

Other Suggestions
Visuals:
    O   Goat/lamb, blood/doorposts, unleavened bread, sandals, staff, Exod. 12:11*b*, 14*a*
    P   Praying hands, lifted cup, death, open manacles
    E   Broken loaf, cup, Last Supper
    G   Robe/towel/water/basin, John 13:12*b*, Last Supper, Jesus speaking, 13:34a,b, acts of love
For a quiet service of acoustic or *a cappella* music, consider:
    UM292, UM432, UM618, UM620, UM625, S2157, S2179, S2258, S2260, S2261, S2264, S2267, WS3168
Suggested Service of Worship: BOW351
Prayer: UM283 or BOW349. Holy Thursday
Offertory Prayer: WSL154. Heavenly Father (John)
Invitation to Communion: WS3152. "Welcome" (John)
Great Thanksgiving for Holy Thursday Evening: BOW64–65

APRIL 18, 2014

Isaiah 52:13–53:12

13 See, my servant shall prosper;
    he shall be exalted and lifted up,
    and shall be very high.
14 Just as there were many who were astonished at him—
    so marred was his appearance,
        beyond human semblance,
    and his form beyond that of mortals—
15 so he shall startle many nations;
    kings shall shut their mouths because of him;
    for that which had not been told them they shall see,
        and that which they had not heard they
        shall contemplate.
53 Who has believed what we have heard?
    And to whom has the arm of the LORD been revealed?
2 For he grew up before him like a young plant,
    and like a root out of dry ground;
    he had no form or majesty that we should look at him,
        nothing in his appearance that we should desire him.
3 He was despised and rejected by others;
    a man of suffering and acquainted with infirmity;
    and as one from whom others hide their faces
        he was despised, and we held him of no account.
4 Surely he has borne our infirmities
    and carried our diseases;
    yet we accounted him stricken,
        struck down by God, and afflicted.
5 But he was wounded for our transgressions,
    crushed for our iniquities;
    upon him was the punishment that made us whole,
        and by his bruises we are healed.
6 All we like sheep have gone astray;
    we have all turned to our own way,
    and the LORD has laid on him
        the iniquity of us all.
7 He was oppressed, and he was afflicted,
    yet he did not open his mouth;
    like a lamb that is led to the slaughter,
        and like a sheep that before its shearers is silent,
        so he did not open his mouth.
8 By a perversion of justice he was taken away.
    Who could have imagined his future?
    For he was cut off from the land of the living,
        stricken for the transgression of my people.
9 They made his grave with the wicked
    and his tomb with the rich,
    although he had done no violence,
        and there was no deceit in his mouth.
10 Yet it was the will of the LORD to crush him with pain.
    When you make his life an offering for sin,
        he shall see his offspring, and shall prolong his days;
    through him the will of the LORD shall prosper.
11   Out of his anguish he shall see light;
    he shall find satisfaction through his knowledge.
        The righteous one, my servant,
        shall make many righteous,
        and he shall bear their iniquities.
12 Therefore I will allot him a portion with the great,
    and he shall divide the spoil with the strong;
    because he poured out himself to death,
        and was numbered with the transgressors;
    yet he bore the sin of many,
        and made intercession for the transgressors.

Psalm 22

1 My God, my God, why have you forsaken me?
    Why are you so far from helping me,
        from the words of my groaning?
2 O my God, I cry by day, but you do not answer;
    and by night, but find no rest.
3 Yet you are holy,
    enthroned on the praises of Israel.
4 In you our ancestors trusted;
    they trusted, and you delivered them.
5 To you they cried, and were saved;
    in you they trusted, and were not put to shame.
6 But I am a worm, and not human;
    scorned by others, and despised by the people.
7 All who see me mock at me;
    they make mouths at me, they shake their heads;
8 "Commit your cause to the LORD; let him deliver—
    let him rescue the one in whom he delights!"
9 Yet it was you who took me from the womb;
    you kept me safe on my mother's breast.
10 On you I was cast from my birth,
    and since my mother bore me you have been my God.
11 Do not be far from me,
    for trouble is near
    and there is no one to help.
12 Many bulls encircle me,
    strong bulls of Bashan surround me;
13 they open wide their mouths at me,
    like a ravening and roaring lion.
14 I am poured out like water,
    and all my bones are out of joint;
    my heart is like wax;
        it is melted within my breast;
15 my mouth is dried up like a potsherd,
    and my tongue sticks to my jaws;
    you lay me in the dust of death.
16 For dogs are all around me;
    a company of evildoers encircles me.
    My hands and feet have shriveled;
17 I can count all my bones.
    They stare and gloat over me;
18 they divide my clothes among themselves,
    and for my clothing they cast lots.
19 But you, O LORD, do not be far away!
    O my help, come quickly to my aid!
20 Deliver my soul from the sword,
    my life from the power of the dog!
    21Save me from the mouth of the lion!
    From the horns of the wild oxen you have rescued me.
22 I will tell of your name to my brothers and sisters;
    in the midst of the congregation I will praise you:
23 You who fear the LORD, praise him!
    All you offspring of Jacob, glorify him;
    stand in awe of him, all you offspring of Israel!
24 For he did not despise or abhor
    the affliction of the afflicted;
    he did not hide his face from me,
        but heard when I cried to him.
25 From you comes my praise in the great congregation;
    my vows I will pay before those who fear him.
26 The poor shall eat and be satisfied;
    those who seek him shall praise the LORD.
    May your hearts live forever!

COLOR: NONE

GOOD FRIDAY

27 All the ends of the earth shall remember
    and turn to the LORD;
  and all the families of the nations
    shall worship before him.
28 For dominion belongs to the LORD,
    and he rules over the nations.
29 To him, indeed, shall all who sleep in the earth bow down;
    before him shall bow all who go down to the dust,
    and I shall live for him.
30 Posterity will serve him;
    future generations will be told about the Lord,
31 and proclaim his deliverance to a people yet unborn,
    saying that he has done it.

Hebrews 10:16-25

16 "This is the covenant that I will make with them
    after those days, says the Lord:
  I will put my laws in their hearts,
    and I will write them on their minds,"
17 he also adds,
  "I will remember their sins and their lawless deeds
      no more."
18 Where there is forgiveness of these, there is no longer any offering for sin.

19 Therefore, my friends, since we have confidence to enter the sanctuary by the blood of Jesus, 20 by the new and living way that he opened for us through the curtain (that is, through his flesh), 21 and since we have a great priest over the house of God, 22 let us approach with a true heart in full assurance of faith, with our hearts sprinkled clean from an evil conscience and our bodies washed with pure water. 23 Let us hold fast to the confession of our hope without wavering, for he who has promised is faithful. 24 And let us consider how to provoke one another to love and good deeds, 25 not neglecting to meet together, as is the habit of some, but encouraging one another, and all the more as you see the Day approaching.

John 18:1–19:42

1 After Jesus had spoken these words, he went out with his disciples across the Kidron valley to a place where there was a garden, which he and his disciples entered. 2 Now Judas, who betrayed him, also knew the place, because Jesus often met there with his disciples. 3 So Judas brought a detachment of soldiers together with police from the chief priests and the Pharisees, and they came there with lanterns and torches and weapons. 4 Then Jesus, knowing all that was to happen to him, came forward and asked them, "Whom are you looking for?" 5 They answered, "Jesus of Nazareth." Jesus replied, "I am he." Judas, who betrayed him, was standing with them. 6 When Jesus said to them, "I am he," they stepped back and fell to the ground. 7 Again he asked them, "Whom are you looking for?" And they said, "Jesus of Nazareth." 8 Jesus answered, "I told you that I am he. So if you are looking for me, let these men go." 9 This was to fulfill the word that he had spoken, "I did not lose a single one of those whom you gave me." 10 Then Simon Peter, who had a sword, drew it, struck the high priest's slave, and cut off his right ear. The slave's name was Malchus. 11 Jesus said to Peter, "Put your sword back into its sheath. Am I not to drink the cup that the Father has given me?"

12 So the soldiers, their officer, and the Jewish police arrested Jesus and bound him. 13 First they took him to Annas, who was the father-in-law of Caiaphas, the high priest that year. 14 Caiaphas was the one who had advised the Jews that it was better to have one person die for the people.

15 Simon Peter and another disciple followed Jesus. Since that disciple was known to the high priest, he went with Jesus into the courtyard of the high priest, 16 but Peter was standing outside at the gate. So the other disciple, who was known to the high priest, went out, spoke to the woman who guarded the gate, and brought Peter in. 17 The woman said to Peter, "You are not also one of this man's disciples, are you?" He said, "I am not." 18 Now the slaves and the police had made a charcoal fire because it was cold, and they were standing around it and warming themselves. Peter also was standing with them and warming himself.

19 Then the high priest questioned Jesus about his disciples and about his teaching. 20 Jesus answered, "I have spoken openly to the world; I have always taught in synagogues and in the temple, where all the Jews come together. I have said nothing in secret. 21 Why do you ask me? Ask those who heard what I said to them; they know what I said." 22 When he had said this, one of the police standing nearby struck Jesus on the face, saying, "Is that how you answer the high priest?" 23 Jesus answered, "If I have spoken wrongly, testify to the wrong. But if I have spoken rightly, why do you strike me?" 24 Then Annas sent him bound to Caiaphas the high priest.

25 Now Simon Peter was standing and warming himself. They asked him, "You are not also one of his disciples, are you?" He denied it and said, "I am not." 26 One of the slaves of the high priest, a relative of the man whose ear Peter had cut off, asked, "Did I not see you in the garden with him?" 27 Again Peter denied it, and at that moment the cock crowed.

28 Then they took Jesus from Caiaphas to Pilate's headquarters. It was early in the morning. They themselves did not enter the headquarters, so as to avoid ritual defilement and to be able to eat the Passover. 29 So Pilate went out to them and said, "What accusation do you bring against this man?" 30 They answered, "If this man were not a criminal, we would not have handed him over to you." 31 Pilate said to them, "Take him yourselves and judge him according to your law." The Jews replied, "We are not permitted to put anyone to death." 32 (This was to fulfill what Jesus had said when he indicated the kind of death he was to die.)

33 Then Pilate entered the headquarters again, summoned Jesus, and asked him, "Are you the King of the Jews?" 34 Jesus answered, "Do you ask this on your own, or did others tell you about me?" 35 Pilate replied, "I am not a Jew, am I? Your own nation and the chief priests have handed you over to me. What have you done?" 36 Jesus answered, "My kingdom is not from this world. If my kingdom were from this world, my followers would be fighting to keep me from being handed over to the Jews. But as it is, my kingdom is not from here." 37 Pilate asked him, "So you are a king?" Jesus answered, "You say that I am a king. For this I was born, and for this I came into the world, to testify to the truth. Everyone who belongs to the truth listens to my voice." 38 Pilate asked him, "What is truth?"

After he had said this, he went out to the Jews again and told them, "I find no case against him. 39 But you have a custom that I release someone for you at the Passover. Do you want me to release for you the King of the Jews?" 40 They

APRIL 18, 2014

shouted in reply, "Not this man, but Barabbas!" Now Barabbas was a bandit.

[19]Then Pilate took Jesus and had him flogged. [2]And the soldiers wove a crown of thorns and put it on his head, and they dressed him in a purple robe. [3]They kept coming up to him, saying, "Hail, King of the Jews!" and striking him on the face. [4]Pilate went out again and said to them, "Look, I am bringing him out to you to let you know that I find no case against him." [5]So Jesus came out, wearing the crown of thorns and the purple robe. Pilate said to them, "Here is the man!" [6]When the chief priests and the police saw him, they shouted, "Crucify him! Crucify him!" Pilate said to them, "Take him yourselves and crucify him; I find no case against him." [7]The Jews answered him, "We have a law, and according to that law he ought to die because he has claimed to be the Son of God."

[8]Now when Pilate heard this, he was more afraid than ever. [9]He entered his headquarters again and asked Jesus, "Where are you from?" But Jesus gave him no answer. [10]Pilate therefore said to him, "Do you refuse to speak to me? Do you not know that I have power to release you, and power to crucify you?" [11]Jesus answered him, "You would have no power over me unless it had been given you from above; therefore the one who handed me over to you is guilty of a greater sin." [12]From then on Pilate tried to release him, but the Jews cried out, "If you release this man, you are no friend of the emperor. Everyone who claims to be a king sets himself against the emperor."

[13]When Pilate heard these words, he brought Jesus outside and sat on the judge's bench at a place called The Stone Pavement, or in Hebrew Gabbatha. [14]Now it was the day of Preparation for the Passover; and it was about noon. He said to the Jews, "Here is your King!" [15]They cried out, "Away with him! Away with him! Crucify him!" Pilate asked them, "Shall I crucify your King?" The chief priests answered, "We have no king but the emperor." [16]Then he handed him over to them to be crucified.

So they took Jesus; [17]and carrying the cross by himself, he went out to what is called The Place of the Skull, which in Hebrew is called Golgotha. [18]There they crucified him, and with him two others, one on either side, with Jesus between them.

[19]Pilate also had an inscription written and put on the cross. It read, "Jesus of Nazareth, the King of the Jews." [20]Many of the Jews read this inscription, because the place where Jesus was crucified was near the city; and it was written in Hebrew, in Latin, and in Greek. [21]Then the chief priests of the Jews said to Pilate, "Do not write, 'The King of the Jews,' but, 'This man said, I am King of the Jews.'" [22]Pilate answered, "What I have written I have written." [23]When the soldiers had crucified Jesus, they took his clothes and divided them into four parts, one for each soldier. They also took his tunic; now the tunic was seamless, woven in one piece from the top. [24]So they said to one another, "Let us not tear it, but cast lots for it to see who will get it." This was to fulfill what the scripture says,

"They divided my clothes among themselves,
and for my clothing they cast lots."

[25]And that is what the soldiers did. Meanwhile, standing near the cross of Jesus were his mother, and his mother's sister, Mary the wife of Clopas, and Mary Magdalene. [26]When Jesus saw his mother and the disciple whom he loved standing beside her, he said to his mother, "Woman, here is your son." [27]Then he said to the disciple, "Here is your mother." And from that hour the disciple took her into his own home.

[28]After this, when Jesus knew that all was now finished, he said (in order to fulfill the scripture), "I am thirsty." [29]A jar full of sour wine was standing there. So they put a sponge full of the wine on a branch of hyssop and held it to his mouth. [30]When Jesus had received the wine, he said, "It is finished." Then he bowed his head and gave up his spirit.

[31]Since it was the day of Preparation, the Jews did not want the bodies left on the cross during the sabbath, especially because that sabbath was a day of great solemnity. So they asked Pilate to have the legs of the crucified men broken and the bodies removed. [32]Then the soldiers came and broke the legs of the first and of the other who had been crucified with him. [33]But when they came to Jesus and saw that he was already dead, they did not break his legs. [34]Instead, one of the soldiers pierced his side with a spear, and at once blood and water came out. [35](He who saw this has testified so that you also may believe. His testimony is true, and he knows that he tells the truth.) [36]These things occurred so that the scripture might be fulfilled, "None of his bones shall be broken." [37]And again another passage of scripture says, "They will look on the one whom they have pierced."

[38]After these things, Joseph of Arimathea, who was a disciple of Jesus, though a secret one because of his fear of the Jews, asked Pilate to let him take away the body of Jesus. Pilate gave him permission; so he came and removed his body. [39]Nicodemus, who had at first come to Jesus by night, also came, bringing a mixture of myrrh and aloes, weighing about a hundred pounds. [40]They took the body of Jesus and wrapped it with the spices in linen cloths, according to the burial custom of the Jews. [41]Now there was a garden in the place where he was crucified, and in the garden there was a new tomb in which no one had ever been laid. [42]And so, because it was the Jewish day of Preparation, and the tomb was nearby, they laid Jesus there.

COLOR: NONE   GOOD FRIDAY

Primary Hymns and Songs for the Day
165   "Hallelujah! What a Savior" (Isa.) (O)
        H-3 Chr-134
286   "O Sacred Head, Now Wounded" (John)
        H-3 Hbl-82; Chr-148; Desc-86; Org-111
288   "Were You There" (John)
        H-3 Hbl-101; Chr-209
        S-2 #195-196. Descant and harmonization
        V-7 p. 60 Vocal solo
298   "When I Survey the Wondrous Cross" (John) (C)
        H-3 Hbl-6, 102; Chr-213; Desc-49; Org-49
        S-1 #155. Descant

Additional Hymn Suggestions
285   "To Mock Your Reign, O Dearest Lord" (Isa., John)
291   "He Never Said a Mumbalin' Word" (Isa., John)
294   "Alas! and Did My Savior Bleed" (Isa., John)
515   "Out of the Depths I Cry to You" (Ps.)
520   "Nobody Knows the Trouble I See" (Ps.)
2180   "Why Stand So Far Away, My God?" (Ps., John)
2209   "How Long, O Lord" (Ps., Good Friday)
2267   "Taste and See" (Ps., Communion)
2140   "Since Jesus Came Into My Heart" (Heb.)
419   "I Am Thine, O Lord" (Heb.)
472   "Near to the Heart of God" (Heb.)
2149   "Living for Jesus" (Heb., John, Good Friday)
2259   "Victim Divine" (Heb., Communion)
282   "'Tis Finished! The Messiah Dies" (John)
289   "Ah, Holy Jesus" (John)
290   "Go to Dark Gethsemane" (John)
355   "Depth of Mercy" (John)
3097   "Depth of Mercy" (John)
424   "Must Jesus Bear the Cross Alone" (John)
425   "O Crucified Redeemer" (John)
470   "My God, I Love Thee" (John)
633   "The Bread of Life for All Is Broken" (John)
2083   "My Song Is Love Unknown" (Good Friday)
2100   "Thou Didst Leave Thy Throne" (John)
2106   "When Jesus Wept" (John)
2110   "Why Has God Forsaken Me?" (John)
2111   "We Sang Our Glad Hosannas" (John)
2112   "Jesus Walked This Lonesome Valley" (John)
2263   "Broken for Me" (Good Friday, Communion)
3084   "O Christ, You Hang upon a Cross" (John)
3105   "In Christ Alone" (John, Good Friday)
        M138

Additional Contemporary Suggestions
SP64   "Our God Reigns" (Isa.)
S2108   "O How He Loves You and Me!" (Isa., John)
        SP113
SP111   "There Is a Redeemer" (Isa., John)
UM640   "Take Our Bread" (Heb., Communion)
M35   "White as Snow" (Heb.)
M65   "Before the Throne of God Above" (Heb.)
M81   "Amazing Love" (Heb., Good Friday)
WS3102   "You Are My King" ("Amazing Love") (Heb.)
        M82
M106   "I Come to the Cross" (Heb., Good Friday)
UM488   "Jesus, Remember Me" (John)
WS3085   "The Power of the Cross" (John, Good Friday)
        M222

S2198   "Stay With Me" ("Nohu pu") (Good Friday)
S2113   "Lamb of God" (Good Friday)
M24   "Jesus, We Crown You with Praise" (John)
M76   "The Wonderful Cross" (Good Friday)
M77   "Above All" (John, Good Friday)
WS3105   "In Christ Alone" (Good Friday)
        M138

Vocal Solos
"He Was Cut Off Out of the Land of the Living" (recitative)
and "But Thou Didst Not Leave His Soul in Hell" (aria)
    V-2
"'Tis Finished! The Messiah Dies" (John)
    V-1   p. 63
"Lamb of God" (John, Good Friday)
    V-5(2)   p. 5
"Ah, Holy Jesus" (John, Good Friday)
    V-6   p. 24
"They Led Him Away" (John)
    V-8   p. 245

Anthems
"I See His Blood Upon the Rose" (John)
Michael Bedford; GIA G-6420
SATB, *a cappella*

"Behold the Lamb of God" (John)
John Helgen; Kjos 9026
SATB, organ

Other Suggestions
Visuals:
    O   Plant, root, suffering, crucifix, lamb/shears
    P   Crucifix, Exodus, nursing, water, bones, sword,
        dog/lion/ox, feeding the poor
    E   Heb. 10:16*b*, eraser, crucifix, curtain, worship
    G   Sword, fire, cock, whip, robe, rugged cross, crucifix
        nails, crown (thorns), ladder, sponge, spear, shroud
    Good Friday: Black-draped cross, altar stripped
Suggested Services of Worship: BOW362, 365, or 366
Greeting: BOW329 or BOW384 (Heb.)
Opening Prayer: WSL25. Today the carpenter's hands (John)
Confession: WSL24. Holy Savior (John)
Prayer: UM284. Good Friday (John)
Offertory Prayer: WSL155. God of the Crucified Jesus (John)
Reading: UM293. Behold the Savior of Mankind (John)
Hymn UM290. "Go to Dark Gethsemane." Use this hymn
    to supplement the reading of the John passage. Stanza
    1 before beginning 18:1. Sing stanza 2 after 19:3.
    Sing stanza 3 after 19:30. Sing UM288, stanza 5 at the
    conclusion of the reading.
Closing Prayer: WSL28. Eternal God (Good Friday)

APRIL 20, 2014

Acts 10:34-43

[34]Then Peter began to speak to them: "I truly understand that God shows no partiality, [35]but in every nation anyone who fears him and does what is right is acceptable to him. [36]You know the message he sent to the people of Israel, preaching peace by Jesus Christ—he is Lord of all. [37]That message spread throughout Judea, beginning in Galilee after the baptism that John announced: [38]how God anointed Jesus of Nazareth with the Holy Spirit and with power; how he went about doing good and healing all who were oppressed by the devil, for God was with him. [39]We are witnesses to all that he did both in Judea and in Jerusalem. They put him to death by hanging him on a tree; [40]but God raised him on the third day and allowed him to appear, [41]not to all the people but to us who were chosen by God as witnesses, and who ate and drank with him after he rose from the dead. [42]He commanded us to preach to the people and to testify that he is the one ordained by God as judge of the living and the dead. [43]All the prophets testify about him that everyone who believes in him receives forgiveness of sins through his name."

Psalm 118:1-2, 14-24

1 O give thanks to the LORD, for he is good;
    his steadfast love endures forever!
2 Let Israel say,
    "His steadfast love endures forever."

. . . .

14 The LORD is my strength and my might;
    he has become my salvation.
15 There are glad songs of victory in the tents of
    the righteous:
    "The right hand of the LORD does valiantly;
16 the right hand of the LORD is exalted;
    the right hand of the LORD does valiantly."
17 I shall not die, but I shall live,
    and recount the deeds of the LORD.
18 The LORD has punished me severely,
    but he did not give me over to death.
19 Open to me the gates of righteousness,
    that I may enter through them
    and give thanks to the LORD.
20 This is the gate of the LORD;
    the righteous shall enter through it.
21 I thank you that you have answered me
    and have become my salvation.
22 The stone that the builders rejected
    has become the chief cornerstone.
23 This is the Lord's doing;
    it is marvelous in our eyes.
24 This is the day that the LORD has made;
    let us rejoice and be glad in it.

Colossians 3:1-4

[1]So if you have been raised with Christ, seek the things that are above, where Christ is, seated at the right hand of God. [2]Set your minds on things that are above, not on things that are on earth, [3]for you have died, and your life is hidden with Christ in God. [4]When Christ who is your life is revealed, then you also will be revealed with him in glory.

John 20:1-18

[1]Early on the first day of the week, while it was still dark, Mary Magdalene came to the tomb and saw that the stone had been removed from the tomb. [2]So she ran and went to Simon Peter and the other disciple, the one whom Jesus loved, and said to them, "They have taken the Lord out of the tomb, and we do not know where they have laid him." [3]Then Peter and the other disciple set out and went toward the tomb. [4]The two were running together, but the other disciple outran Peter and reached the tomb first. [5]He bent down to look in and saw the linen wrappings lying there, but he did not go in. [6]Then Simon Peter came, following him, and went into the tomb. He saw the linen wrappings lying there, [7]and the cloth that had been on Jesus' head, not lying with the linen wrappings but rolled up in a place by itself. [8]Then the other disciple, who reached the tomb first, also went in, and he saw and believed; [9]for as yet they did not understand the scripture, that he must rise from the dead. [10]Then the disciples returned to their homes.

[11]But Mary stood weeping outside the tomb. As she wept, she bent over to look into the tomb; [12]and she saw two angels in white, sitting where the body of Jesus had been lying, one at the head and the other at the feet. [13]They said to her, "Woman, why are you weeping?" She said to them, "They have taken away my Lord, and I do not know where they have laid him." [14]When she had said this, she turned around and saw Jesus standing there, but she did not know that it was Jesus. [15]Jesus said to her, "Woman, why are you weeping? Whom are you looking for?" Supposing him to be the gardener, she said to him, "Sir, if you have carried him away, tell me where you have laid him, and I will take him away." [16]Jesus said to her, "Mary!" She turned and said to him in Hebrew, "Rabbouni!" (which means Teacher). [17]Jesus said to her, "Do not hold on to me, because I have not yet ascended to the Father. But go to my brothers and say to them, 'I am ascending to my Father and your Father, to my God and your God.'" [18]Mary Magdalene went and announced to the disciples, "I have seen the Lord"; and she told them that he had said these things to her.

COLOR: WHITE   **EASTER SUNDAY**

Primary Hymns and Songs for the Day
302   "Christ the Lord Is Risen Today" (John) (O)
              H-3 Hbl-8, 51; Chr-49; Desc-31; Org-32
              S-1 #104-108. Various treatments
2115   "Christ Has Risen" (John)
              H-3 Chr-80; Desc-52
              S-1 #160-162. Various treatments
              S-2 #87-88. Brass/timpani intro. and arr.
3090   "The Easter Song" (John, Easter)
327   "Crown Him with Many Crowns" (John) (C)
              H-3 Hbl-55; Chr-60; Desc-30; Org-27
              S-1 #86-88. Various treatments

Additional Hymn Suggestions
2114   "At the Font We Start Our Journey" (Acts, Baptism)
3164   "Down to the River" (Acts, Baptism)
261   "Lord of the Dance" (Acts)
306   "The Strife Is O'er, the Battle Done" (Acts)
444   "O Young and Fearless Prophet" (Acts)
658   "This Is the Day" (Ps.)
662   "Stand Up and Bless the Lord" (Ps.)
2084   "Come, Let Us with Our Lord Arise" (Ps., Easter)
3079   "Hosanna" (Ps., Easter)
3117   "Rule of Life" (Ps.)
317   "O Sons and Daughters, Let Us Sing" (Ps., John)
2082   "Woke Up This Morning" (Col.)
2276   "Glory to God in the Highest" (Col.)
307   "Christ Is Risen" (Col., John, Communion)
2077   "You Alone Are Holy" (John, Easter)
2111   "We Sang Our Glad Hosannas" (John)
2242   "Walk with Me" (John)
134   "O Mary, Don't You Weep" (John)
274   "Woman in the Night" (John)
276   "The First One Ever" (John)
303   "The Day of Resurrection" (John)
308   "Thine Be the Glory" (John)
310   "He Lives" (John)
313   "Cristo Vive" ("Christ Is Risen") (John)
314   "In the Garden" (John)
315   "Come, Ye Faithful, Raise the Strain" (John)
316   "He Rose" (John)
318   "Christ Is Alive" (John)
322   "Up from the Grave He Arose" (John)
3043   "You, Lord, Are Both Lamb and Shepherd" (John)
3088   "Easter Alleluia" (John, Easter)
3143   "Jesus, You Are the New Day" (John)

Additional Contemporary Suggestions
S2026   "Halle, Halle, Halleluja" (Easter, Opening)
S2195   "In the Lord I'll Be Ever Thankful" (Ps.)
S2270   "I Will Enter His Gates" (Ps.)
              SP168
WS3040   "You Are My All in All" (Ps.)
              SP220
WS3023   "Forever" (Ps.)
              M68
WS3027   "Hallelujah" ("Your Love Is Amazing") (Ps.)
              M118
M32   "Holy and Anointed One" (Acts)
S2161   "To Know You More" (Col.)
S2088   "Lord, I Lift Your Name on High" (Col., Easter)
              M2

S2116   "Christ the Lord Is Risen" (John, Easter)
SP121   "Celebrate Jesus" (John, Easter)
UM186   "Alleluia" (John)
              SP108; S-2 #3-4
M20   "Jesus Is Alive" (John, Easter)
M21   "Blessing, Honour and Glory" (Easter)
M73   "My Redeemer Lives" (Easter)
M201   "Alive Forever, Amen" (Easter)
S2039   "Holy, Holy" (Easter)
              SP141
S2043   "Alleluia" (Easter)
              See also S2078
S2258   "Sing Alleluia to the Lord" (Easter, Communion)
              SP93
S2072   "Amen, Amen" (Easter, Closing)

Vocal Solos
"Jesus Christ Is Risen Today" (John, Easter)
    V-1   p. 50
"I Know That My Redeemer Liveth" (Easter)
    V-2
    V-8   p. 202
"I Know That My Redeemer Lives" (Easter)
    V-5(2)   p. 22
"The First Day of My Life" (John, Easter)
    V-11   p. 22

Anthems
"Crown Him with Many Crowns" (John)
arr. Carlton Young; GIA G-7412
SATB, keyboard, trumpet

"A Hymn of Resurrection" (John)
Gwyneth Walker; E.C. Schirmer 7199
SATB, organ, opt. brass and timpani

"Easter Alleluia!" (John)
Mark A. Miller; Abingdon Press 9780687644209
SATB, piano (opt. children's choir)

Other Suggestions
Visuals:
    O   Crucifix, resurrection, Acts 10:39*a*
    P   Ps. 118:29, singing, tents, gates, cornerstone
    E   Butterfly, empty cross, open tomb, Christ returning
    G   Basket/spices, open tomb, grave clothes, napkin,
               runners, tears, risen Christ, "I have seen..."
Introit: UM657. "This Is the Day" (Ps.)
Call to Worship: WSL22. From Bethlehem (Acts, Easter)
Call to Worship: WSL29 or BOW386. Christ is risen (John, Easter)
Opening Prayer: WSL28. Eternal God, rock (John, Easter)
Litany: WSL36. When the world divides us (Acts)
Prayer of Thanksgiving and Intercession: BOW395 (John)
Response: UM84. "Thank You, Lord" (Ps.)
Blessing: WSL27. May the Christ who walks (John, Easter)

APRIL 27, 2014

Acts 2:14a, 22-32

[14]But Peter, standing with the eleven, raised his voice and addressed them, "Men of Judea and all who live in Jerusalem, let this be known to you, and listen to what I say. . . .

[22]"You that are Israelites, listen to what I have to say: Jesus of Nazareth, a man attested to you by God with deeds of power, wonders, and signs that God did through him among you, as you yourselves know— [23]this man, handed over to you according to the definite plan and foreknowledge of God, you crucified and killed by the hands of those outside the law. [24]But God raised him up, having freed him from death, because it was impossible for him to be held in its power.
[25] For David says concerning him,
  'I saw the Lord always before me,
    for he is at my right hand so that I will not be shaken;
[26] therefore my heart was glad, and my tongue rejoiced;
    moreover my flesh will live in hope.
[27] For you will not abandon my soul to Hades,
    or let your Holy One experience corruption.
[28] You have made known to me the ways of life;
    you will make me full of gladness with your presence.'
[29]"Fellow Israelites, I may say to you confidently of our ancestor David that he both died and was buried, and his tomb is with us to this day. [30]Since he was a prophet, he knew that God had sworn with an oath to him that he would put one of his descendants on his throne. [31]Foreseeing this, David spoke of the resurrection of the Messiah, saying,
  'He was not abandoned to Hades,
    nor did his flesh experience corruption.'
[32]This Jesus God raised up, and of that all of us are witnesses.

Psalm 16

[1] Protect me, O God, for in you I take refuge.
[2] I say to the LORD, "You are my Lord;
    I have no good apart from you."
[3] As for the holy ones in the land, they are the noble,
    in whom is all my delight.
[4] Those who choose another god multiply their sorrows;
    their drink offerings of blood I will not pour out
    or take their names upon my lips.
[5] The LORD is my chosen portion and my cup;
    you hold my lot.
[6] The boundary lines have fallen for me in pleasant places;
    I have a goodly heritage.
[7] I bless the LORD who gives me counsel;
    in the night also my heart instructs me.
[8] I keep the LORD always before me;
    because he is at my right hand, I shall not be moved.
[9] Therefore my heart is glad, and my soul rejoices;
    my body also rests secure.
[10] For you do not give me up to Sheol,
    or let your faithful one see the Pit.
[11] You show me the path of life.
    In your presence there is fullness of joy;
    in your right hand are pleasures forevermore.

1 Peter 1:3-9

[3]Blessed be the God and Father of our Lord Jesus Christ! By his great mercy he has given us a new birth into a living hope through the resurrection of Jesus Christ from the dead, [4]and into an inheritance that is imperishable, undefiled, and unfading, kept in heaven for you, [5]who are being protected by the power of God through faith for a salvation ready to be revealed in the last time. [6]In this you rejoice, even if now for a little while you have had to suffer various trials, [7]so that the genuineness of your faith—being more precious than gold that, though perishable, is tested by fire—may be found to result in praise and glory and honor when Jesus Christ is revealed. [8]Although you have not seen him, you love him; and even though you do not see him now, you believe in him and rejoice with an indescribable and glorious joy, [9]for you are receiving the outcome of your faith, the salvation of your souls.

John 20:19-31

[19]When it was evening on that day, the first day of the week, and the doors of the house where the disciples had met were locked for fear of the Jews, Jesus came and stood among them and said, "Peace be with you." [20]After he said this, he showed them his hands and his side. Then the disciples rejoiced when they saw the Lord. [21]Jesus said to them again, "Peace be with you. As the Father has sent me, so I send you." [22]When he had said this, he breathed on them and said to them, "Receive the Holy Spirit. [23]If you forgive the sins of any, they are forgiven them; if you retain the sins of any, they are retained."

[24]But Thomas (who was called the Twin), one of the twelve, was not with them when Jesus came. [25]So the other disciples told him, "We have seen the Lord." But he said to them, "Unless I see the mark of the nails in his hands, and put my finger in the mark of the nails and my hand in his side, I will not believe."

[26]A week later his disciples were again in the house, and Thomas was with them. Although the doors were shut, Jesus came and stood among them and said, "Peace be with you." [27]Then he said to Thomas, "Put your finger here and see my hands. Reach out your hand and put it in my side. Do not doubt but believe." [28]Thomas answered him, "My Lord and my God!" [29]Jesus said to him, "Have you believed because you have seen me? Blessed are those who have not seen and yet have come to believe."

[30]Now Jesus did many other signs in the presence of his disciples, which are not written in this book. [31]But these are written so that you may come to believe that Jesus is the Messiah, the Son of God, and that through believing you may have life in his name.

COLOR: WHITE   2nd SUNDAY OF EASTER

Primary Hymns and Songs for the Day
304   "Easter People, Raise Your Voices" (1 Pet.) (O)
           H-3 Chr-30, 48, 62; Desc-89; Org-121
           S-1 #280. Descant and harmonization
162   "Alleluia, Alleluia" (Acts)
           H-3 Hbl-46; Chr-26
           S-1 #14. Descant
2206   "Without Seeing You" (1 Pet., John)
308   "Thine Be the Glory" (Acts, John) (C)
           H-3 Hbl-98; Chr-195; Desc-59
           S-1 #190. Arrangement
           S-2 #95. Various treatments

Additional Hymn Suggestions
312   "Hail the Day That Sees Him Rise" (Acts)
336   "Of All the Spirit's Gifts to Me" (Acts, John)
3009   "Praise God for This Holy Ground" (Acts, John)
2043   "Alleluia" (Ps., Easter)
175   "Jesus, the Very Thought of Thee" (1 Pet.)
508   "Faith, While Trees Are Still in Blossom" (1 Pet.)
2050   "Mothering God, You Gave Me Birth" (1 Pet., Communion)
2147   "There Are Some Things I May Not Know" (1 Pet.)
355   "Depth of Mercy" (1 Pet., John)
3097   "Depth of Mercy" (1 Pet., John)
3105   "In Christ Alone" (1 Pet.)
303   "The Day of Resurrection" (1 Pet., John)
317   "O Sons and Daughters, Let Us Sing" (John)
319   "Christ Jesus Lay in Death's Strong Band" (John)
331   "Holy Spirit, Come, Confirm Us" (John)
332   "Spirit of Faith, Come Down" (John)
384   "Love Divine, All Loves Excelling" (John, Communion)
420   "Breathe on Me, Breath of God" (John)
465   "Holy Spirit, Truth Divine" (John)
475   "Come Down, O Love Divine" (John)
503   "Let it Breathe on Me" (John)
543   "O Breath of Life" (John)
2004   "Praise the Source of Faith and Learning" (John)
2046   "Womb of Life" (John, Communion)
2115   "Christ Has Risen" (John)
2117   "Spirit of God" (John)
2169   "God, How Can We Forgive" (John)
2187   "Now It Is Evening" (John)
2196   "We Walk by Faith" (John)
2211   "Faith Is Patience in the Night" (John)
2242   "Walk with Me" (John)
2255   "In the Singing" (John, Communion)
2269   "Come, Share the Lord" (John, Communion)
3089   "O Living God" (John)
3145   "Breath of God, Breath of Peace" (John)

Additional Contemporary Suggestions
UM328 "Surely the Presence of the Lord (Acts, John)
           SP243; S-2, #200 Stanzas for soloist
S2270   "I Will Enter" ("He Has Made Me Glad") (Acts)
           SP168
S2272   "Holy Ground" (Acts, John)
           SP86
M36   "Awesome In This Place" (Acts, John)
M7   "I Believe In Jesus" (Acts, John)
M92   "All Things Are Possible" (Ps.)

S2043   "Alleluia" (Ps., Easter)
           SP122
S2065   "More Precious than Silver" (Ps., 1 Pet.)
           SP99
M30   "Knowing You" (Ps., 1 Pet., John)
WS3108 "Trading My Sorrows" (Ps., John)
           M75
UM99   "My Tribute" ("To God Be the Glory") (1 Pet.)
           SP118; V-8 p. 5 Vocal Solo
S2154   "Please Enter My Heart, Hosanna" (1 Pet., John)
S2151   "I'm So Glad Jesus Lifted Me" (1 Pet.)
M21   "Blessing, Honour and Glory" (1 Pet.)
SP111   "There Is a Redeemer" (1 Pet., John)
SP64   "Our God Reigns" (John)
S2032   "My Life Is in You, Lord" (John)
           SP204
S2086   "Open Our Eyes, Lord" (John)
           SP199
S2119   "Where the Spirit of the Lord Is" (John, Communion)
S2266   "Here Is Bread, Here Is Wine" (John, Communion)
M26   "The Power of Your Love" (John)
M38   "I Want to Know You" ("In the Secret") (John)
WS3008 "Open the Eyes of My Heart" (John)
           M57
M88   "Holy Spirit, Rain Down" (John)

Vocal Solo
"Spirit of Faith, Come Down" (Acts, John)
    V-1   p. 43

Anthems
"A Better Resurrection" (1 Pet., John)
Craig Courtney; Beckenhorst CU-1000
SATB divisi, *a cappella*

"Grieve Not the Holy Spirit of God " (John)
Tertius Noble; H.W. Gray GCMR00409
SATB, keyboard

"Although the Doors Were Closed" (John)
James Clemens; Concordia: 98-3394U75
SATB, keyboard

Other Suggestions
Visuals:
  O   Eleven men, preaching, crucifix, open tomb, heart, joy
  P   Cup, boundary line, prayer, joy, rest, path, hand
  E   Newborn, butterfly/chrysalis, gold/fire, joy
  G   Locked door, Jesus, "Peace. . .," wind, wounds, John 20:29*b*
Greeting: BOW456 (1 Pet.)
Litany: WSL33. This is the good news (1 Pet., Easter)
Opening Prayer: WSL37. Holy Spirit, rain down (John)
Prayer: BOW394 (1 Pet.)
Prayer or Blessing: BOW396 (John, Easter)
Offertory: WSL131. Blessed One, the resurrection (1 Pet.)
Blessing: WSL27. May the Christ who walks (John, Easter)
Response: UM376. Dona Nobis Pacem (John)
Benediction: WSL161. Sisters and brothers (John)

MAY 4, 2014

NATIVE AMERICAN AWARENESS SUNDAY

Acts 2:14a, 36-41

[14]But Peter, standing with the eleven, raised his voice and addressed them, "Men of Judea and all who live in Jerusalem, let this be known to you, and listen to what I say. . . .

[36]Therefore let the entire house of Israel know with certainty that God has made him both Lord and Messiah, this Jesus whom you crucified."

[37]Now when they heard this, they were cut to the heart and said to Peter and to the other apostles, "Brothers, what should we do?" [38]Peter said to them, "Repent, and be baptized every one of you in the name of Jesus Christ so that your sins may be forgiven; and you will receive the gift of the Holy Spirit. [39]For the promise is for you, for your children, and for all who are far away, everyone whom the Lord our God calls to him." [40]And he testified with many other arguments and exhorted them, saying, "Save yourselves from this corrupt generation." [41]So those who welcomed his message were baptized, and that day about three thousand persons were added.

Psalm 116:1-4, 12-19

1 I love the LORD, because he has heard
    my voice and my supplications.
2 Because he inclined his ear to me,
    therefore I will call on him as long as I live.
3 The snares of death encompassed me;
    the pangs of Sheol laid hold on me;
    I suffered distress and anguish.
4 Then I called on the name of the LORD:
    "O LORD, I pray, save my life!"
. . . .
12 What shall I return to the LORD
    for all his bounty to me?
13 I will lift up the cup of salvation
    and call on the name of the LORD,
14 I will pay my vows to the LORD
    in the presence of all his people.
15 Precious in the sight of the LORD
    is the death of his faithful ones.
16 O LORD, I am your servant;
    I am your servant, the child of your serving girl.
    You have loosed my bonds.
17 I will offer to you a thanksgiving sacrifice
    and call on the name of the LORD.
18 I will pay my vows to the LORD
    in the presence of all his people,
19 in the courts of the house of the LORD,
    in your midst, O Jerusalem.
    Praise the LORD!

1 Peter 1:17-23

[17]If you invoke as Father the one who judges all people impartially according to their deeds, live in reverent fear during the time of your exile. [18]You know that you were ransomed from the futile ways inherited from your ancestors, not with perishable things like silver or gold, [19]but with the precious blood of Christ, like that of a lamb without defect or blemish. [20]He was destined before the foundation of the world, but was revealed at the end of the ages for your sake. [21]Through him you have come to trust in God, who raised him from the dead and gave him glory, so that your faith and hope are set on God.

[22]Now that you have purified your souls by your obedience to the truth so that you have genuine mutual love, love one another deeply from the heart. [23]You have been born anew, not of perishable but of imperishable seed, through the living and enduring word of God.

Luke 24:13-35

[13]Now on that same day two of them were going to a village called Emmaus, about seven miles from Jerusalem, [14]and talking with each other about all these things that had happened. [15]While they were talking and discussing, Jesus himself came near and went with them, [16]but their eyes were kept from recognizing him. [17]And he said to them, "What are you discussing with each other while you walk along?" They stood still, looking sad. [18]Then one of them, whose name was Cleopas, answered him, "Are you the only stranger in Jerusalem who does not know the things that have taken place there in these days?" [19]He asked them, "What things?" They replied, "The things about Jesus of Nazareth, who was a prophet mighty in deed and word before God and all the people, [20]and how our chief priests and leaders handed him over to be condemned to death and crucified him. [21]But we had hoped that he was the one to redeem Israel. Yes, and besides all this, it is now the third day since these things took place. [22]Moreover, some women of our group astounded us. They were at the tomb early this morning, [23]and when they did not find his body there, they came back and told us that they had indeed seen a vision of angels who said that he was alive. [24]Some of those who were with us went to the tomb and found it just as the women had said; but they did not see him." [25]Then he said to them, "Oh, how foolish you are, and how slow of heart to believe all that the prophets have declared! [26]Was it not necessary that the Messiah should suffer these things and then enter into his glory?" [27]Then beginning with Moses and all the prophets, he interpreted to them the things about himself in all the scriptures.

[28]As they came near the village to which they were going, he walked ahead as if he were going on. [29]But they urged him strongly, saying, "Stay with us, because it is almost evening and the day is now nearly over." So he went in to stay with them. [30]When he was at the table with them, he took bread, blessed and broke it, and gave it to them. [31]Then their eyes were opened, and they recognized him; and he vanished from their sight. [32]They said to each other, "Were not our hearts burning within us while he was talking to us on the road, while he was opening the scriptures to us?" [33]That same hour they got up and returned to Jerusalem; and they found the eleven and their companions gathered together. [34]They were saying, "The Lord has risen indeed, and he has appeared to Simon!" [35]Then they told what had happened on the road, and how he had been made known to them in the breaking of the bread.

COLOR: WHITE　　　　　　　　　　　　　　　　　　　　　　　　**3rd SUNDAY OF EASTER**

Primary Hymns and Songs for the Day

610　　"We Know That Christ Is Raised" (Acts) (O)
　　　　　　H-3　Hbl-100; Chr-214; Desc- ; Org-37
　　　　　　S-1　#118-127. Various treatments
2199　　"Stay with Us" (Luke)
3086　　"Day of Arising" (Luke, Communion)
　　　　　　H-3　Hbl-77; Chr-136; Desc-21; Org-16
　　　　　　S-1　#50-51. Flute and vocal descants
309　　"On the Day of Resurrection" (Luke)
　　　　　　S-2　#55. Trumpet descant
434　　"Cuando El Pobre" ("When the Poor Ones")
　　　　(Luke)
613　　"O Thou, Who This Mysterious Bread" (Luke) (C)
　　　　　　H-3　Hbl-129; Chr-106; Desc-65; Org-72
　　　　　　S-2　#105. Flute/violin descant
　　　　　　　　#106. Harmonization

Additional Hymn Suggestions

539　　"O Spirit of the Living God" (Acts)
604　　"Praise and Thanksgiving Be to God" (Acts)
605　　"Wash, O God, Our Sons and Daughters" (Acts)
606　　"Come, Let Us Use the Grace Divine" (Acts)
608　　"This Is the Spirit's Entry Now" (Acts)
2114　　"At the Font We Start Our Journey" (Acts, Baptism)
2247　　"Wonder of Wonders" (Acts, Baptism)
2251　　"We Were Baptized in Christ Jesus" (Acts, Baptism)
3093　　"Fill My Cup, Lord" (Ps.)
3142　　"I Love You, Lord" (Ps.)
357　　"Just As I Am, Without One Plea" (1 Pet.)
362　　"Nothing but the Blood" (1 Pet.)
369　　"Blessed Assurance" (1 Pet.)
370　　"Victory in Jesus" (Acts, 1 Pet.)
377　　"It Is Well with My Soul" (1 Pet.)
378　　"Amazing Grace" (1 Pet.)
452　　"My Faith Looks Up to Thee" (1 Pet.)
532　　"Jesus, Priceless Treasure" (1 Pet.)
545　　"The Church's One Foundation" (1 Pet.)
2142　　"Blessed Quietness" (1 Pet.)
2213　　"Healer of Our Every Ill" (1 Pet.)
2264　　"Come to the Table" (1 Pet., Communion)
133　　"Leaning on the Everlasting Arms" (Luke)
257　　"We Meet You, O Christ" (Luke)
318　　"Christ Is Alive" (Luke)
454　　"Open My Eyes, That I May See" (Luke)
633　　"The Bread of Life for All Is Broken" (Luke)
635　　"Because Thou Hast Said" (Luke, Communion)
700　　"Abide with Me" (Luke)
2060　　"God the Sculptor of the Mountains" (Luke)
2115　　"Christ Has Risen" (Luke)
2242　　"Walk with Me" (Luke)
2269　　"Come, Share the Lord" (Luke, Communion)
3089　　"O Living God" (Luke)
3167　　"Feed Us, Lord" (Luke, Communion)
3179　　"The Risen Christ" (Luke) (O)

Additional Contemporary Suggestions

S2252　　"Come, Be Baptized" (Acts, Baptism)
S2002　　"I Will Call Upon the Lord" (Ps.)
　　　　　　SP224
S2031　　"We Bring the Sacrifice of Praise" (Ps.)
　　　　　　SP1

S2068　　"I Love You, Lord" (Ps.)
　　　　　　SP72
UM640　　"Take Our Bread" (1 Pet., Communion)
WS3104　　"Amazing Grace" ("My Chains Are Gone") (1 Pet.)
　　　　　　M205
S2065　　"More Precious than Silver" (1 Pet.)
　　　　　　SP99
S2179　　"Live in Charity" ("Ubi Caritas") (1 Pet.)
S2223　　"They'll Know We Are Christians" (1 Pet.)
S2226　　"Bind Us Together" (1 Pet.)
　　　　　　SP140
S2260　　"Let Us Be Bread" (1 Pet., Luke, Communion)
M15　　"Agnus Dei" (1 Pet., Easter)
M23　　"Hallelujah to the Lamb" (1 Pet., Easter)
M27　　"We Will Worship the Lamb" (1 Pet., Easter)
UM349　　"Turn Your Eyes upon Jesus" (Luke)
　　　　　　SP218
UM661　　"Jesus, We Want to Meet" (Luke)
S2086　　"Open Our Eyes, Lord" (Luke)
　　　　　　SP199
S2222　　"The Servant Song" (Luke)
　　　　　　SP193
WS3008　　"Open the Eyes of My Heart" (Luke)
　　　　　　M57

Vocal Solos

"Wash, O God, Our Sons and Daughters" (Acts, Baptism)
　　　V-5(1)　　p. 64
"Worthy Is the Lamb" (1 Pet., Easter)
　　　V-8　　p. 228
"The First Day of my Life" (Luke, Easter)
　　　V-11　　p. 22

Anthems

"Blessed Assurance" (1 Pet.)
arr. Keith Hampton; Choristers Guild CGA-1238
SATB, piano, opt. solo

"As We Gather At Your Table" (Communion)
K. Lee Scott; Augsburg 0-8006-7808-7
SAB, organ

Other Suggestions

Visuals:
　O　　Christus Rex, repent, baptism, gift, Spirit, 3000
　P　　Ear, snare, anguish, prayer, cup, shackles, gifts
　E　　Silver/gold, blood, lamb, Jesus, baptism, Bible
　G　　Jesus, 3 men walking, Bible, broken bread, burning
　　　　　heart, blindness/vision
Introit: S2273, BOW187. "Jesus, We Are Here" (Luke)
Call to Worship: WSL31. The Risen Savior (1 Pet.)
Native American Resources: BOW425, BOW468, UM329.
Prayer: WSL72. Loving God (Luke)
Response: UM300. "O the Lamb" (1 Pet., Easter)
Prayer or Blessing: BOW396 (Luke, Easter)
Benediction: BOW562 (Luke, Native American)

MAY 11, 2014
FESTIVAL OF THE CHRISTIAN HOME/MOTHER'S DAY

Acts 2:42-47

[42]They devoted themselves to the apostles' teaching and fellowship, to the breaking of bread and the prayers.

[43]Awe came upon everyone, because many wonders and signs were being done by the apostles. [44]All who believed were together and had all things in common; [45]they would sell their possessions and goods and distribute the proceeds to all, as any had need. [46]Day by day, as they spent much time together in the temple, they broke bread at home and ate their food with glad and generous hearts, [47]praising God and having the goodwill of all the people. And day by day the Lord added to their number those who were being saved.

Psalm 23

[1] The Lord is my shepherd, I shall not want.
[2]   He makes me lie down in green pastures;
  he leads me beside still waters;
    [3]he restores my soul.
  He leads me in right paths
    for his name's sake.
[4] Even though I walk through the darkest valley,
    I fear no evil;
  for you are with me;
    your rod and your staff—
    they comfort me.
[5] You prepare a table before me
    in the presence of my enemies;
  you anoint my head with oil;
    my cup overflows.
[6] Surely goodness and mercy shall follow me
    all the days of my life,
  and I shall dwell in the house of the Lord
    my whole life long.

1 Peter 2:19-25

[19]For it is a credit to you if, being aware of God, you endure pain while suffering unjustly. [20]If you endure when you are beaten for doing wrong, what credit is that? But if you endure when you do right and suffer for it, you have God's approval. [21]For to this you have been called, because Christ also suffered for you, leaving you an example, so that you should follow in his steps.

[22]"He committed no sin,
  and no deceit was found in his mouth."

[23]When he was abused, he did not return abuse; when he suffered, he did not threaten; but he entrusted himself to the one who judges justly. [24]He himself bore our sins in his body on the cross, so that, free from sins, we might live for righteousness; by his wounds you have been healed. [25]For you were going astray like sheep, but now you have returned to the shepherd and guardian of your souls.

John 10:1-10

[1]"Very truly, I tell you, anyone who does not enter the sheepfold by the gate but climbs in by another way is a thief and a bandit. [2]The one who enters by the gate is the shepherd of the sheep. [3]The gatekeeper opens the gate for him, and the sheep hear his voice. He calls his own sheep by name and leads them out. [4]When he has brought out all his own, he goes ahead of them, and the sheep follow him because they know his voice. [5]They will not follow a stranger, but they will run from him because they do not know the voice of strangers." [6]Jesus used this figure of speech with them, but they did not understand what he was saying to them.

[7]So again Jesus said to them, "Very truly, I tell you, I am the gate for the sheep. [8]All who came before me are thieves and bandits; but the sheep did not listen to them. [9]I am the gate. Whoever enters by me will be saved, and will come in and go out and find pasture. [10]The thief comes only to steal and kill and destroy. I came that they may have life, and have it abundantly."

COLOR: WHITE   **4th SUNDAY OF EASTER**

Primary Hymns and Songs for the Day
136   "The Lord's My Shepherd, I'll Not Want" (Ps., John)
       (O)
549   "Where Charity and Love Prevail" (Acts, Christian
       Home)
              H-3 Hbl-71, 104; Chr-111; Desc-95; Org-143
              S-2 #162. Harmonization
138   "The King of Love My Shepherd Is" (Ps., 1 Pet.)
              S-1 #298-299. Harmonizations
2058   "Shepherd Me, O God" (Ps., John)
2223   "They'll Know We Are Christians" (Acts) (C)

Additional Hymn Suggestions
334   "Sweet, Sweet Spirit" (Acts)
              SP136
537   "Filled with the Spirit's Power" (Acts)
557   "Blest Be the Tie That Binds (Acts, Christian
       Home)
561   "Jesus, United by Thy Grace" (Acts)
562   "Jesus, Lord, We Look to Thee" (Acts)
618   "Let Us Break Bread Together" (Acts, Communion)
2136   "Out of the Depths" (Acts)
2175   "Together We Serve" (Acts)
2181   "We Need a Faith" (Acts)
2182   "When God Restored our Common Life" (Acts)
2238   "In the Midst of New Dimensions" (Acts)
2242   "Walk with Me" (Acts)
2243   "We All Are One in Mission" (Acts)
2269   "Come, Share the Lord" (Acts, Communion)
3012   "When Words Alone Cannot Express" (Acts)
3167   "Feed Us, Lord" (Acts, Communion)
128   "He Leadeth Me: O Blessed Thought" (Ps.)
407   "Close to Thee" (Ps.)
474   "Precious Lord, Take My Hand" (Ps.)
497   "Send Me, Lord" (Ps.)
2112   "Jesus Walked This Lonesome Valley" (Ps.)
2206   "Without Seeing You" (Ps.)
2140   "Since Jesus Came Into My Heart" (Ps., 1 Pet.)
3031   "God Leads Us Along" (Ps., John)
3088   "Easter Alleluia" (Ps., Easter)
381   "Savior, Like a Shepherd Lead Us" (Ps., John) (O)
2214   "Lead Me, Guide Me" (Ps., John)
2218   "You Are Mine" (Ps., John)
518   "O Thou, in Whose Presence" (Ps., John)
650   "Give Me the Faith Which Can Remove" (Ps., John)
318   "Christ Is Alive" (1 Pet.)
2101   "Two Fishermen" (1 Pet.)
3100   "Jesus Paid It All" (1 Pet.)
115   "How Like a Gentle Spirit" (John)
261   "Lord of the Dance" (John, Easter)
629   "You Satisfy the Hungry Heart" (John,
       Communion)

Additional Contemporary Suggestions
WS3121 "If You Believe and I Believe" (Acts)
UM620   "One Bread, One Body" (Acts, Communion)
S2224   "Make Us One" (Acts)
               SP137
S2240   "One God and Father of Us All" (Acts)
S2054   "Nothing Can Trouble" ("Nada Te Turbe") (Ps.)
S2113   "Lamb of God" (Ps.)

WS3026 "God Is Good All the Time" (Ps.)
               M45
WS3096 "Gentle Shepherd" (Ps.)
WS3106 "Your Grace Is Enough" (Ps.)
SP40   "God Will Make a Way" (Ps.)
M79   "I Stand Amazed" (Ps.)
M108   "Lead Me, Lord" (Ps., 1 Pet.)
M72   "Jesus, Lover of My Soul" (Ps., John)
UM174   "His Name Is Wonderful" (Ps., John)
               SP90
S2071   "Jesus, Name Above All Names" (1 Pet.)
               SP76
S2072   "Amen, Amen" (1 Pet.)
S2244   "People Need the Lord" (John)
M28   "Who Can Satisfy My Soul Like You?" (John)

Vocal Solos
"God, Our Ever Faithful Shepherd" (Ps., John)
    V-4   p. 15
"My Shepherd Will Supply My Need" (Ps., John)
    V-10   p. 4
"Maybe the Rain" (Ps., John)
    V-5(2)   p. 27
"Come, Praise the Lord!" (Ps., Easter)
    V-8   p. 304
"In the Image of God" (1 Pet.)
    V-8   p. 362

Anthems
"Draw Us in the Spirit's Tether" (Acts)
Harold Friedell; H.W. Gray GCMR02472
SATB, keyboard

"The King of Love My Shepherd Is" (Ps.)
Michael McCarthy; MorningStar 50-7600
Unison voices and SATB divisi, keyboard

"The Good Shepherd" (John)
Zebulon Highben; GIA G-7483
SAB, piano, C instrument

Other Suggestions
Visuals:
    O   Teaching, fellowship, broken bread, prayer, meal
    P   Shepherd/sheep, pasture, lake, path, valley, rod,
             staff, banquet table, cup, sanctuary
    E   Whip/club, Passion, crucifix, healing, sheep
    G   Sheepfold, gate, robber's mask, sheep/shepherd
Opening Prayer: BOW393 (John)
Canticle: UM137. Psalm 23 (Ps., John)
Prayer: BOW399, Week 4 (Ps., John)
Prayer: BOW518 (Acts)
Prayer: WSL201. God our Creator (Mother's Day)
Litany: UM556. Litany for Christian Unity (Acts)
Additional prayers, calls to worship, and benedictions are
    available in *The Abingdon Worship Annual 2014.*

MAY 18, 2014

HERITAGE SUNDAY

Acts 7:55-60

[55]But filled with the Holy Spirit, he gazed into heaven and saw the glory of God and Jesus standing at the right hand of God. [56]"Look," he said, "I see the heavens opened and the Son of Man standing at the right hand of God!" [57]But they covered their ears, and with a loud shout all rushed together against him. [58]Then they dragged him out of the city and began to stone him; and the witnesses laid their coats at the feet of a young man named Saul. [59]While they were stoning Stephen, he prayed, "Lord Jesus, receive my spirit." [60]Then he knelt down and cried out in a loud voice, "Lord, do not hold this sin against them." When he had said this, he died.

Psalm 31:1-5, 15-16

[1] In you, O LORD, I seek refuge;
    do not let me ever be put to shame;
    in your righteousness deliver me.
[2] Incline your ear to me;
    rescue me speedily.
  Be a rock of refuge for me,
    a strong fortress to save me.
[3] You are indeed my rock and my fortress;
    for your name's sake lead me and guide me,
[4] take me out of the net that is hidden for me,
    for you are my refuge.
[5] Into your hand I commit my spirit;
    you have redeemed me, O LORD, faithful God.
. . . .
[15] My times are in your hand;
    deliver me from the hand of my enemies and
        persecutors.
[16] Let your face shine upon your servant;
    save me in your steadfast love.

1 Peter 2:2-10

[2]Like newborn infants, long for the pure, spiritual milk, so that by it you may grow into salvation— [3]if indeed you have tasted that the Lord is good.

[4]Come to him, a living stone, though rejected by mortals yet chosen and precious in God's sight, and [5]like living stones, let yourselves be built into a spiritual house, to be a holy priesthood, to offer spiritual sacrifices acceptable to God through Jesus Christ.
[6] For it stands in scripture:
    "See, I am laying in Zion a stone,
      a cornerstone chosen and precious;
    and whoever believes in him will not be put to shame."
[7]To you then who believe, he is precious; but for those who do not believe,
    "The stone that the builders rejected
      has become the very head of the corner,"
[8]and
    "A stone that makes them stumble,
      and a rock that makes them fall."
They stumble because they disobey the word, as they were destined to do.
[9]But you are a chosen race, a royal priesthood, a holy nation, God's own people, in order that you may proclaim the mighty acts of him who called you out of darkness into his marvelous light.
[10] Once you were not a people,
    but now you are God's people;
    once you had not received mercy,
    but now you have received mercy.

John 14:1-14

[1]"Do not let your hearts be troubled. Believe in God, believe also in me. [2]In my Father's house there are many dwelling places. If it were not so, would I have told you that I go to prepare a place for you? [3]And if I go and prepare a place for you, I will come again and will take you to myself, so that where I am, there you may be also.

[4]And you know the way to the place where I am going." [5]Thomas said to him, "Lord, we do not know where you are going. How can we know the way?" [6]Jesus said to him, "I am the way, and the truth, and the life. No one comes to the Father except through me. [7]If you know me, you will know my Father also. From now on you do know him and have seen him."

[8]Philip said to him, "Lord, show us the Father, and we will be satisfied." [9]Jesus said to him, "Have I been with you all this time, Philip, and you still do not know me? Whoever has seen me has seen the Father. How can you say, 'Show us the Father'? [10]Do you not believe that I am in the Father and the Father is in me? The words that I say to you I do not speak on my own; but the Father who dwells in me does his works. [11]Believe me that I am in the Father and the Father is in me; but if you do not, then believe me because of the works themselves. [12]Very truly, I tell you, the one who believes in me will also do the works that I do and, in fact, will do greater works than these, because I am going to the Father. [13]I will do whatever you ask in my name, so that the Father may be glorified in the Son. [14]If in my name you ask me for anything, I will do it."

COLOR: WHITE

5th SUNDAY OF EASTER

Primary Hymns and Songs for the Day
545   "The Church's One Foundation" (1 Pet., John) (O)
       H-3   Hbl-94; Chr-180; Desc-16; Org-9
       S-1   #25-26. Descant and harmonization
534   "Be Still, My Soul" (Acts, Ps.)
       H-3   Chr-36
2146   "His Eye Is on the Sparrow" (John)
559   "Christ Is Made the Sure Foundation" (1 Pet.) (C)
       H-3   Chr-49; Desc-103; Org-180
       S-1   #346. Descant

Additional Hymn Suggestions
577   "God of Grace and God of Glory" (Acts)
326   "The Head That Once Was Crowned" (Acts)
60   "I'll Praise My Maker While I've Breath" (Acts)
2135   "When Cain Killed Abel" (Acts)
2216   "When We Are Called to Sing Your Praise" (Acts)
2246   "Deep in the Shadows of the Past" (Acts)
2208   "Guide My Feet" (Acts, Ps.)
2214   "Lead Me, Guide Me" (Acts, Ps.)
523   "Saranam, Saranam" ("Refuge") (Acts, Ps.)
411   "Dear Lord, Lead Me Day by Day" (Ps.)
497   "Send Me, Lord" (Ps.)
337   "Only Trust Him" (Ps., John)
529   "How Firm a Foundation" (1 Pet.)
558   "We Are the Church" (1 Pet.)
2220   "We Are God's People" (1 Pet.)
3020   "God of the Bible" (1 Pet.)
3105   "In Christ Alone" (1 Pet.)
3147   "Built on a Rock" (1 Pet.)
113   "Source and Sovereign, Rock and Cloud" (John)
164   "Come, My Way, My Truth, My Life" (John)
172   "My Jesus, I Love Thee" (John)
188   "Christ Is the World's Light" (John)
370   "Victory in Jesus" (John)
492   "Prayer Is the Soul's Sincere Desire" (John)
701   "When We All Get to Heaven" (John)
2046   "Womb of Life" (John, Communion)
2127   "Come and See" ("Kyrie") (John)
2213   "Healer of Our Every Ill" (John)
2254   "In Remembrance of Me" (John, Communion)
2282   "I'll Fly Away" (John)
3089   "O Living God" (John)
3115   "Covenant Prayer" (Heritage Sunday)
3117   "Rule of Life" (Heritage Sunday)

Additional Contemporary Suggestions
S2272   "Holy Ground" (Acts)
       SP86
S2208   "Guide My Feet" (Acts, Ps.)
S2002   "I Will Call Upon the Lord" (Ps.)
       SP224
S2066   "Praise the Name of Jesus" (Ps.)
       SP87
M93   "Rock of Ages" (Ps.)
M108   "Lead Me, Lord" (Ps.)
SP40   "God Will Make a Way" (Ps.)
S2065   "More Precious than Silver" (1 Pet.)
       SP99
S2162   "Grace Alone" (1 Pet.)
       M100
S2204   "Light of the World" (1 Pet.)

SP177   "Cornerstone" (1 Pet.)
M30   "Knowing You" ("All I Once Held Dear") (1 Pet.)
WS3177   "Here I Am to Worship" (1 Pet.)
       M116
WS3105   "In Christ Alone" (1 Pet.)
       M138
M13   "Be Glorified" (John)
M152   "Be Glorified" (John)
SP48   "Behold, What Manner of Love" (John)
S2144   "Someone Asked the Question" (John)
S2244   "People Need the Lord" (John)
S2026   "Halle, Halle, Halleluja" (John, Easter)
M94   "That's Why We Praise Him" (John, Easter)

Vocal Solos
"How Firm a Foundation" (1 Pet.)
     V-6   p. 31
"The Call" (John)
     V-4   p. 31
"In Bright Mansions Above" (John)
     V-4   p. 39
"They Led Him Away" (John, Easter)
     V-8   p. 245
"Here, O Lord, Your Servants Gather" (John)
     UM552

Anthems
"Psalm 146 - I'll Praise My Maker While I've Breath" (Acts)
Hal H. Hopson; MorningStar MSM-50-3901
SATBB, organ

"Christ Is Made the Sure Foundation" (1 Pet.)
Dale Wood; Alfred SCHCH05904
SATB, organ

Other Suggestions
Visuals:
     O   Spirit/flames/dove, Christ, heavens opened, stones, coats, Acts 7:59b, 60b, life/death
     P   Rock, Ps. 31:3a, fortress, net, hands, Ps. 31:16a, b
     E   Newborn, milk, stone(s), cornerstone, stumbling blocks, 1 Pet. 2:9a, crowd, nations, dark/light
     G   Hearts, mourning, dwellings, Christ, works, John 14:13, 14
Greeting: BOW456 (1 Pet.)
Call to Worship: WSL73. "We come broken" (John)
Prayer: UM466. An Invitation to Christ (John)
Prayer: UM535. A Refuge amid Distraction (Acts, Ps.)
Prayer: UM607. "Covenant Prayer" (Heritage Sunday)
Wesleyan Hymns: List on UMH 922 (Heritage Sunday)
Celebration of New Faith Beginnings: BOW588-590 (1 Pet.)
Benediction: BOW563 (John)

MAY 25, 2014

Acts 17:22-31

[22]Then Paul stood in front of the Areopagus and said, "Athenians, I see how extremely religious you are in every way. [23]For as I went through the city and looked carefully at the objects of your worship, I found among them an altar with the inscription, 'To an unknown god.' What therefore you worship as unknown, this I proclaim to you. [24]The God who made the world and everything in it, he who is Lord of heaven and earth, does not live in shrines made by human hands, [25]nor is he served by human hands, as though he needed anything, since he himself gives to all mortals life and breath and all things. [26]From one ancestor he made all nations to inhabit the whole earth, and he allotted the times of their existence and the boundaries of the places where they would live, [27]so that they would search for God and perhaps grope for him and find him—though indeed he is not far from each one of us. [28]For 'In him we live and move and have our being'; as even some of your own poets have said,

'For we too are his offspring.'

[29]Since we are God's offspring, we ought not to think that the deity is like gold, or silver, or stone, an image formed by the art and imagination of mortals. [30]While God has overlooked the times of human ignorance, now he commands all people everywhere to repent, [31]because he has fixed a day on which he will have the world judged in righteousness by a man whom he has appointed, and of this he has given assurance to all by raising him from the dead."

Psalm 66:8-20

8   Bless our God, O peoples,
    let the sound of his praise be heard,
9   who has kept us among the living,
    and has not let our feet slip.
10   For you, O God, have tested us;
    you have tried us as silver is tried.
11   You brought us into the net;
    you laid burdens on our backs;
12   you let people ride over our heads;
    we went through fire and through water;
    yet you have brought us out to a spacious place.
13   I will come into your house with burnt offerings;
    I will pay you my vows,
14   those that my lips uttered
    and my mouth promised when I was in trouble.
15   I will offer to you burnt offerings of fatlings,
    with the smoke of the sacrifice of rams;
    I will make an offering of bulls and goats. *Selah*
16   Come and hear, all you who fear God,
    and I will tell what he has done for me.
17   I cried aloud to him,
    and he was extolled with my tongue.
18   If I had cherished iniquity in my heart,
    the Lord would not have listened.
19   But truly God has listened;
    he has given heed to the words of my prayer.
20   Blessed be God,
    because he has not rejected my prayer
    or removed his steadfast love from me.

1 Peter 3:13-22

[13]Now who will harm you if you are eager to do what is good? [14]But even if you do suffer for doing what is right, you are blessed. Do not fear what they fear, and do not be intimidated, [15]but in your hearts sanctify Christ as Lord. Always be ready to make your defense to anyone who demands from you an accounting for the hope that is in you; [16]yet do it with gentleness and reverence. Keep your conscience clear, so that, when you are maligned, those who abuse you for your good conduct in Christ may be put to shame. [17]For it is better to suffer for doing good, if suffering should be God's will, than to suffer for doing evil. [18]For Christ also suffered for sins once for all, the righteous for the unrighteous, in order to bring you to God. He was put to death in the flesh, but made alive in the spirit, [19]in which also he went and made a proclamation to the spirits in prison, [20]who in former times did not obey, when God waited patiently in the days of Noah, during the building of the ark, in which a few, that is, eight persons, were saved through water. [21]And baptism, which this prefigured, now saves you—not as a removal of dirt from the body, but as an appeal to God for a good conscience, through the resurrection of Jesus Christ, [22]who has gone into heaven and is at the right hand of God, with angels, authorities, and powers made subject to him.

John 14:15-21

[15]"If you love me, you will keep my commandments. [16]And I will ask the Father, and he will give you another Advocate, to be with you forever. [17]This is the Spirit of truth, whom the world cannot receive, because it neither sees him nor knows him. You know him, because he abides with you, and he will be in you.

[18]"I will not leave you orphaned; I am coming to you. [19]In a little while the world will no longer see me, but you will see me; because I live, you also will live. [20]On that day you will know that I am in my Father, and you in me, and I in you. [21]They who have my commandments and keep them are those who love me; and those who love me will be loved by my Father, and I will love them and reveal myself to them."

COLOR: WHITE   **6th SUNDAY OF EASTER**

Primary Hymns and Songs for the Day

152 "I Sing the Almighty Power of God" (Acts, John) (O)
       H-3 Hbl-44; Chr-21; Desc-40; Org-40
       S-1 #131-132. Introduction and descant

393 "Spirit of the Living God" (Acts, John)
       SP131
       S-1#212 Vocal descant idea

384 "Love Divine, All Loves Excelling" (John) (C)
       H-3 Chr-134; Desc-18; Org-13
       S-1 #41-42. Descant and harmonization

Additional Hymn Suggestions

62	"All Creatures of Our God and King" (Acts)
88	"Maker, in Whom We Live" (Acts)
92	"For the Beauty of the Earth" (Acts, Communion)
369	"Blessed Assurance" (Acts)
541	"See How Great a Flame Aspires" (Acts)
573	"O Zion, Haste" (Acts)
632	"Draw Us in the Spirit's Tether" (Acts, Communion)
660	"God Is Here" (Acts)
2027	"Now Praise the Hidden God of Love" (Acts)
2170	"God Made from One Blood" (Acts)
3153	"O God in Whom We Live" (Acts)
304	"Easter People, Raise Your Voices" (Acts, 1 Pet.)
2001	"We Sing to You, O God" (Ps.)
2006	"Lord God Almighty" (Ps.)
2011	"We Sing of Your Glory" (Ps.)
142	"If Thou But Suffer God to Guide Thee" (1 Pet.)
417	"O For a Heart to Praise My God" (1 Pet.)
502	"Thy Holy Wings, O Savior" (1 Pet.)
605	"Wash, O God, Our Sons and Daughters" (1 Pet., Baptism)
610	"We Know That Christ Is Raised" (1 Pet., Baptism)
2247	"Wonder of Wonders" (1 Pet., Baptism)
2248	"Baptized in Water" (1 Pet., Baptism)
2251	"We Were Baptized in Christ Jesus" (1 Pet., Baptism)
113	"Source and Sovereign, Rock and Cloud" (John)
153	"Thou Hidden Source of Calm Repose" (John)
312	"Hail the Day That Sees Him Rise" (John, Easter)
331	"Holy Spirit, Come, Confirm Us" (John)
356	"Pues Si Vivimos" ("When We Are Living") (John)
364	"Because He Lives" (John, Easter)
380	"There's Within My Heart a Melody" (John)
402	"Lord, I Want to Be a Christian" (John)
408	"The Gift of Love" (John)
414	"Thou Hidden Love of God" (John)
465	"Holy Spirit, Truth Divine" (John)
539	"O Spirit of the Living God" (John)
700	"Abide With Me" (John)
2117	"Spirit of God" (John)
2142	"Blessed Quietness" (John, Communion)
2168	"Love the Lord Your God" (John)
2213	"Healer of Our Every Ill" (John)
3089	"O Living God" (John)
3145	"Breath of God, Breath of Peace" (John)

Additional Contemporary Suggestions

UM328 "Surely the Presence of the Lord" (Acts, John)
       SP243; S-2, #200 Stanzas for soloist

M36 "Awesome in this Place" (Acts, John)

S2065	"More Precious than Silver" (Acts)
	SP99
S2031	"We Bring the Sacrifice of Praise" (Ps.)
	SP1
S2144	"Someone Asked the Question" (Ps.)
M47	"Come Just As You Are" (Ps.)
M50	"Refiner's Fire" (Ps.)
M58	"All Heaven Declares" (Ps., Easter)
SP10	"Awesome Power" (Ps.)
S2249	"God Claims You" (1 Pet., Baptism)
S2118	"Holy Spirit, Come to Us" (John)
S2119	"Where the Spirit of the Lord Is" (John)
S2179	"Live in Charity" ("Ubi Caritas") (John)
SP48	"Behold, What Manner of Love" (John)
SP235	"Let Your Spirit Rise Within Me" (John)
M26	"The Power of Your Love" (John)
M32	"Holy and Anointed One" (John, Easter)
M88	"Holy Spirit, Rain Down" (John)
M154	"Dwell" (John)

Vocal Solos

"Rejoice, The Lord Is King" (Acts, 1 Pet.)
    V-1   p. 66
"Wash, O God, Our Sons and Daughters" (1 Pet., Baptism)
    V-5(1)   p. 64

Anthems

"In The Seasons of Our Silence" (Acts)
Sandra T. Ford; Hinshaw HMC2088
SATB, keyboard, flute or violin

"If Thou But Suffer God to Guide Thee" (1 Pet.)
arr. James Woodward; GIA G-7201
Two-part mixed, keyboard

"If You Love Me, Keep My Commandments" (John)
Tallis/arr. Hopson; MorningStar 50-5550
Two-part mixed, keyboard

Other Suggestions

Visuals:
    O   Preaching, globe, Acts 17:28*a*, risen Christ
    P   Feet, refine silver, fire/water, offering, prayer
    E   Hearts, readiness, briefcase, accounting, Christ, crucifix, prisoners, resurrection
    G   Advocate (briefcase), Spirit, open Bible, child

Greeting: BOW390 (John)
Prayer: WSL42. God, whose fingers sculpt (Acts)
Litany: BOW426 (Heritage Sunday)
Prayer of Intercession: BOW397 or BOW545 (1 Pet.)
Blessing: WSL40. May the Spirit of God (John)
See additional ideas in *The Abingdon Worship Annual 2014*

MAY 25, 2014 (OR JUNE 1, 2014)

Acts 1:1-11

In the first book, Theophilus, I wrote about all that Jesus did and taught from the beginning [2]until the day when he was taken up to heaven, after giving instructions through the Holy Spirit to the apostles whom he had chosen. [3]After his suffering he presented himself alive to them by many convincing proofs, appearing to them during forty days and speaking about the kingdom of God. [4]While staying with them, he ordered them not to leave Jerusalem, but to wait there for the promise of the Father. "This," he said, "is what you have heard from me; [5]for John baptized with water, but you will be baptized with the Holy Spirit not many days from now."

[6]So when they had come together, they asked him, "Lord, is this the time when you will restore the kingdom to Israel?" [7]He replied, "It is not for you to know the times or periods that the Father has set by his own authority. [8]But you will receive power when the Holy Spirit has come upon you; and you will be my witnesses in Jerusalem, in all Judea and Samaria, and to the ends of the earth." [9]When he had said this, as they were watching, he was lifted up, and a cloud took him out of their sight. [10]While he was going and they were gazing up toward heaven, suddenly two men in white robes stood by them. [11]They said, "Men of Galilee, why do you stand looking up toward heaven? This Jesus, who has been taken up from you into heaven, will come in the same way as you saw him go into heaven."

Psalm 47

1 Clap your hands, all you peoples;
   shout to God with loud songs of joy.
2 For the LORD, the Most High, is awesome,
   a great king over all the earth.
3 He subdued peoples under us,
   and nations under our feet.
4 He chose our heritage for us,
   the pride of Jacob whom he loves.   *Selah*

5 God has gone up with a shout,
   the LORD with the sound of a trumpet.
6 Sing praises to God, sing praises;
   sing praises to our King, sing praises.
7 For God is the king of all the earth;
   sing praises with a psalm.

8 God is king over the nations;
   God sits on his holy throne.
9 The princes of the peoples gather
   as the people of the God of Abraham.
   For the shields of the earth belong to God;
   he is highly exalted.

Ephesians 1:15-23

[15]I have heard of your faith in the Lord Jesus and your love toward all the saints, and for this reason [16]I do not cease to give thanks for you as I remember you in my prayers. [17]I pray that the God of our Lord Jesus Christ, the Father of glory, may give you a spirit of wisdom and revelation as you come to know him, [18]so that, with the eyes of your heart enlightened, you may know what is the hope to which he has called you, what are the riches of his glorious inheritance among the saints, [19]and what is the immeasurable greatness of his power for us who believe, according to the working of his great power. [20]God put this power to work in Christ when he raised him from the dead and seated him at his right hand in the heavenly places, [21]far above all rule and authority and power and dominion, and above every name that is named, not only in this age but also in the age to come. [22]And he has put all things under his feet and has made him the head over all things for the church, [23]which is his body, the fullness of him who fills all in all.

Luke 24:44-53

[44]Then he said to them, "These are my words that I spoke to you while I was still with you—that everything written about me in the law of Moses, the prophets, and the psalms must be fulfilled." [45]Then he opened their minds to understand the scriptures, [46]and he said to them, "Thus it is written, that the Messiah is to suffer and to rise from the dead on the third day, [47]and that repentance and forgiveness of sins is to be proclaimed in his name to all nations, beginning from Jerusalem. [48]You are witnesses of these things. [49]And see, I am sending upon you what my Father promised; so stay here in the city until you have been clothed with power from on high."

[50]Then he led them out as far as Bethany, and, lifting up his hands, he blessed them. [51]While he was blessing them, he withdrew from them and was carried up into heaven. [52]And they worshiped him, and returned to Jerusalem with great joy; [53]and they were continually in the temple blessing God.

COLOR: WHITE   **ASCENSION DAY**

Primary Hymns and Songs for the Day

312   "Hail the Day That Sees Him Rise" (Acts, Luke) (O)
          H-3   Hbl-72; Chr-50; Desc-69; Org-78
          S-1   #213-214. Transposition with descant
          S-1   #213. Descant
325   "Hail, Thou Once Despised Jesus" (Eph., Luke)
          H-3   Chr-90; Desc-54; Org-60
          S-1   #178-179. Harmonizations
3087   "O Christ, When You Ascended" (Acts, Luke)
2070   "He Is Exalted" (Acts, Ps., Luke, Ascension) (C)
          SP66

Additional Hymn Suggestions

541   "See How Great a Flame Aspires" (Acts)
603   "Come, Holy Ghost, Our Hearts Inspire" (Acts)
2123   "Loving Spirit" (Acts)
2247   "Wonder of Wonders" (Acts, Baptism)
2282   "I'll Fly Away" (Acts, Ascension)
3039   "Jesus, the Saving Name" (Acts)
302   "Christ the Lord Is Risen Today" (Acts, Luke)
305   "Camina, Pueblo de Dios" ("Walk on, O People of
          God") (Acts, Luke)
315   "Come, Ye Faithful, Raise the Strain" (Acts, Luke)
319   "Christ Jesus Lay in Death's Strong Bands" (Acts,
          Luke)
324   "Hail Thee, Festival Day" (Acts, Luke)
2114   "At the Font We Start Our Journey" (Acts, Luke,
          Baptism)
2115   "Christ Has Risen" (Acts, Luke)
2116   "Christ the Lord Is Risen" (Acts, Luke, Ascension)
2117   "Spirit of God" (Acts, Luke, Ascension)
308   "Thine Be the Glory" (Acts, Luke, Ps.)
2279   "The Trees of the Field" (Ps.)
178   "Hope of the World" (Eph.)
368   "My Hope Is Built" (Eph.)
711   "For All the Saints" (Eph.)
2147   "There Are Some Things I May Not Know" (Eph.)
2220   "We Are God's People" (Eph.)
2261   "Life-Giving Bread" (Eph., Communion)
2269   "Come, Share the Lord" (Eph., Communion)
3032   "Across the Lands" (Eph.)
3035   "Bless Christ through Whom All Things Are Made"
          (Eph.)
3105   "In Christ Alone" (Eph.)
326   "The Head That Once Was Crowned" (Eph., Luke)
302   "Christ the Lord Is Risen Today" (Luke Ascension)
307   "Christ Is Risen" (Luke, Ascension)
2077   "You Alone Are Holy" (Luke, Ascension)
2184   "Sent Out in Jesus' Name" (Luke)
2241   "The Spirit Sends Us Forth to Serve" (Luke)

Additional Contemporary Suggestions

S2118   "Holy Spirit, Come to Us" (Acts)
S2125   "Come, Holy Spirit" (Acts)
S2273   "Jesus, We Are Here" ("Yesu Tawa Pano") (Acts)
M88   "Holy Spirit, Rain Down" (Acts, Eph)
S2028   "Clap Your Hands" (Ps.)
S2074   "Shout to the Lord" (Ps.)
          M16
S2276   "Glory to God in the Highest" (Ps.)
WS3023 "Forever" (Ps.)
          M68

M120   "Lord Most High" (Ps.)
S2088   "Lord, I Lift Your Name on High" (Ps., Ascension)
          M2
M77   "Above All" (Eph., Ascension)
S2006   "Lord God Almighty" (Luke)
S2078   "Alleluia" (Ascension, Easter)
M78   "Once Again" (Ascension)
WS3105 "In Christ Alone" (Ascension)
          M138

Vocal Solos

"Jesus Christ Is Risen Today" (Ascension, Easter)
     V-1   p. 50
"Rejoice Now, My Spirit" (Ascension, Easter)
     V-9   p. 30

Anthems

"Come, You People, Rise and Sing" (Ascension, Easter)
Kenneth Dake; MorningStar MSM-50-2526
SATB, organ

"Jesus Came, Adored by Angels" (Ascension)
Robert Lehman; Paraclete Press PPM01219
SATB, *a cappella*

Other Suggestions

These ideas may be used on June 1 as Ascension Sunday.
Visuals:
     O   Risen Christ, baptism, 7 flames, ascension, angels
     P   Clapping, singing, shouting, crown/throne, shields
     E   Open Bible, Christ, right hand, feet, Church
     G   Open Bible, crucifix, Christ, lifted hands
Introit: UM494. "Kumbayah" (Acts, Luke)
Greeting: BOW402 (Ascension)
Call to Worship: WSL35. Let us gather (Acts)
Affirmation of Faith: WSL76. We believe (Eph.)
Prayer: UM323 or BOW403 (Ascension, Acts, Luke, Eph.)
Prayer: WSL34. Enlighten our hearts (Acts)
Blessing: WSL163. From where we are (Luke)

JUNE 1, 2014

Acts 1:6-14

[6]So when they had come together, they asked him, "Lord, is this the time when you will restore the kingdom to Israel?" [7]He replied, "It is not for you to know the times or periods that the Father has set by his own authority. [8]But you will receive power when the Holy Spirit has come upon you; and you will be my witnesses in Jerusalem, in all Judea and Samaria, and to the ends of the earth." [9]When he had said this, as they were watching, he was lifted up, and a cloud took him out of their sight. [10]While he was going and they were gazing up toward heaven, suddenly two men in white robes stood by them. [11]They said, "Men of Galilee, why do you stand looking up toward heaven? This Jesus, who has been taken up from you into heaven, will come in the same way as you saw him go into heaven."

[12]Then they returned to Jerusalem from the mount called Olivet, which is near Jerusalem, a sabbath day's journey away. [13]When they had entered the city, they went to the room upstairs where they were staying, Peter, and John, and James, and Andrew, Philip and Thomas, Bartholomew and Matthew, James son of Alphaeus, and Simon the Zealot, and Judas son of James. [14]All these were constantly devoting themselves to prayer, together with certain women, including Mary the mother of Jesus, as well as his brothers.

Psalm 68:1-10

1 Let God rise up, let his enemies be scattered;
   let those who hate him flee before him.
2 As smoke is driven away, so drive them away;
   as wax melts before the fire, let the wicked perish
      before God.
3 But let the righteous be joyful;
   let them exult before God;
   let them be jubilant with joy.
4 Sing to God, sing praises to his name;
   lift up a song to him who rides upon the clouds—
   his name is the LORD— be exultant before him.
5 Father of orphans and protector of widows
   is God in his holy habitation.
6 God gives the desolate a home to live in;
   he leads out the prisoners to prosperity,
      but the rebellious live in a parched land.
7 O God, when you went out before your people,
   when you marched through the wilderness, Selah
8 the earth quaked, the heavens poured down rain
   at the presence of God, the God of Sinai,
   at the presence of God, the God of Israel.
9 Rain in abundance, O God, you showered abroad;
   you restored your heritage when it languished;
10 your flock found a dwelling in it;
   in your goodness, O God, you provided for the needy.

1 Peter 4:12-14; 5:6-11

[12] Beloved, do not be surprised at the fiery ordeal that is taking place among you to test you, as though something strange were happening to you. [13]But rejoice in so far as you are sharing Christ's sufferings, so that you may also be glad and shout for joy when his glory is revealed. [14]If you are reviled for the name of Christ, you are blessed, because the spirit of glory, which is the Spirit of God, is resting on you. . . .

[6] Humble yourselves therefore under the mighty hand of God, so that he may exalt you in due time. [7]Cast all your anxiety on him, because he cares for you. [8]Discipline yourselves; keep alert. Like a roaring lion your adversary the devil prowls around, looking for someone to devour. [9]Resist him, steadfast in your faith, for you know that your brothers and sisters throughout the world are undergoing the same kinds of suffering. [10]And after you have suffered for a little while, the God of all grace, who has called you to his eternal glory in Christ, will himself restore, support, strengthen, and establish you. [11]To him be the power for ever and ever. Amen.

John 17:1-11

After Jesus had spoken these words, he looked up to heaven and said, 'Father, the hour has come; glorify your Son so that the Son may glorify you, [2]since you have given him authority over all people, to give eternal life to all whom you have given him. [3]And this is eternal life, that they may know you, the only true God, and Jesus Christ whom you have sent. [4]I glorified you on earth by finishing the work that you gave me to do. [5]So now, Father, glorify me in your own presence with the glory that I had in your presence before the world existed.

[6] 'I have made your name known to those whom you gave me from the world. They were yours, and you gave them to me, and they have kept your word. [7]Now they know that everything you have given me is from you; [8]for the words that you gave to me I have given to them, and they have received them and know in truth that I came from you; and they have believed that you sent me. [9]I am asking on their behalf; I am not asking on behalf of the world, but on behalf of those whom you gave me, because they are yours. [10]All mine are yours, and yours are mine; and I have been glorified in them. [11]And now I am no longer in the world, but they are in the world, and I am coming to you. Holy Father, protect them in your name that you have given me, so that they may be one, as we are one.

COLOR: WHITE

7th SUNDAY OF EASTER

Primary Hymns and Songs for the Day

312   "Hail the Day That Sees Him Rise" (Acts) (O)
          H-3   Hbl-72; Chr-50; Desc-69; Org-78
          S-1   #213-214. Transposition with descant
          S-1   #213. Descant

3087   "O Christ, When You Ascended" (Acts)

529   "How Firm a Foundation" (Ps., 1 Pet.) (C)
          H-3   Hbl-27, 69; Chr-102; Desc-41; Org-41
          S-1   #133. Harmonization
                #134. Performance note

2070   "He Is Exalted" (Acts) (C)
          SP66

Additional Hymn Suggestions

541   "See How Great a Flame Aspires" (Acts)
603   "Come, Holy Ghost, Our Hearts Inspire" (Acts)
718   "Lo, He Comes With Clouds Descending" (Acts)
2123   "Loving Spirit" (Acts)
2247   "Wonder of Wonders" (Acts, Baptism)
2282   "I'll Fly Away" (Acts)
3039   "Jesus, the Saving Name" (Acts)
302   "Christ the Lord Is Risen Today" (Acts)
315   "Come, Ye Faithful, Raise the Strain" (Acts)
324   "Hail Thee, Festival Day" (Acts)
2115   "Christ Has Risen" (Acts)
2116   "Christ the Lord Is Risen" (Acts)
2117   "Spirit of God" (Acts)
60   "I'll Praise My Maker While I've Breath" (Ps.)
66   "Praise, My Soul, the King of Heaven" (Ps.)
519   "Lift Every Voice and Sing" (Ps., 1 Pet.)
2216   "When We Are Called to Sing Your Praise"
          (Ps., 1 Pet.)
502   "Thy Holy Wings, O Savior" (Ps., 1 Pet., John)
354   "I Surrender All" (1 Pet.)
369   "Blessed Assurance" (1 Pet.)
512   "Stand By Me" (1 Pet.)
2131   "Humble Thyself in the Sight of the Lord" (1 Pet.)
          SP223
2279   "The Trees of the Field" (1 Pet.)
3139   "We Cannot Measure How You Heal" (1 Pet.)
517   "By Gracious Powers" (1 Pet., John)
396   "O Jesus, I Have Promised" (John)
547   "O Church of God, United" (John)
2150   "Lord, Be Glorified" (John)
          SP196
3075   "Glory in the Cross" (John)
325   "Hail, Thou Once Despised Jesus" (Acts) (C)
413   "A Charge to Keep I Have" (John) (C)

Additional Contemporary Suggestions

S2118   "Holy Spirit, Come to Us" (Acts)
M88   "Holy Spirit, Rain Down" (Acts, Ps.)
M2   "Lord, I Lift Your Name on High" (Ps.)
S2074   "Shout to the Lord" (Ps.)
          M16
WS3026 "God Is Good All the Time" (1 Pet.)
          M45
S2056   "God Is So Good" (1 Pet.)
S2265   "Time Now to Gather" (1 Pet., Communion)
M223   "Today Is the Day" (1 Pet.)
M227   "I Will Boast" (1 Pet.)

S2003   "Praise You" (John)
          M84
S2150   "Lord, Be Glorified" (John)
          SP196
M13   "Be Glorified" (John)
S2215   "Cares Chorus" (John)
          SP221

Vocal Solos

"Above All" (Acts, Easter, Ascension)
    V-3   p. 17
"My Heart Is Steadfast" (1 Pet.)
    V-5(2)   p. 40

Anthems

"I'm Going up a Yonder" (Acts)
Hawkins / Read; Boosey & Hawkes 48004366
SATB, piano

"Hail the Day" (Acts, John)
Lani Smith, Lorenz 10/2263S
SATB, keyboard

Other Suggestions

This Sunday may also be celebrated as Ascension Sunday
using the ideas for May 29.
Visuals:
    Acts: Cloud, ascension, Jesus ascending, angels, prayer
    P   Melting candle, music notes, clouds, broken chains, abundant rain
    E   Fire, trials, testing, suffering, relief from suffering
    G   Jesus ascending, sun, lifted hands
Introit: S2273. "Jesus, We Are Here" ("Yesu Tawa Pano")
    (Acts)
Call to Worship: WSL35. Let us gather (Acts)
Prayer: WSL34. Enlighten our hearts (Acts)
Prayer: WSL42. God, whose fingers sculpt (Acts)
Prayer: WSL67. Jesus Christ, Lord of the Church (Acts)
Offertory: S2262. "Let Us Offer to the Father" ("Te
    Ofrecemos Padre Nuestro") (1 Pet.)
Introit and Sung Benediction: WS3017, verses 1 and 3.
    "Come, Join the Dance of Trinity" (Luke)

JUNE 8, 2014

Acts 2:1-21

[1]When the day of Pentecost had come, they were all together in one place. [2]And suddenly from heaven there came a sound like the rush of a violent wind, and it filled the entire house where they were sitting. [3]Divided tongues, as of fire, appeared among them, and a tongue rested on each of them. [4]All of them were filled with the Holy Spirit and began to speak in other languages, as the Spirit gave them ability.

[5]Now there were devout Jews from every nation under heaven living in Jerusalem. [6]And at this sound the crowd gathered and was bewildered, because each one heard them speaking in the native language of each. [7]Amazed and astonished, they asked, "Are not all these who are speaking Galileans? [8]And how is it that we hear, each of us, in our own native language? [9]Parthians, Medes, Elamites, and residents of Mesopotamia, Judea and Cappadocia, Pontus and Asia, [10]Phrygia and Pamphylia, Egypt and the parts of Libya belonging to Cyrene, and visitors from Rome, both Jews and proselytes, [11]Cretans and Arabs—in our own languages we hear them speaking about God's deeds of power." [12]All were amazed and perplexed, saying to one another, "What does this mean?" [13]But others sneered and said, "They are filled with new wine."

[14]But Peter, standing with the eleven, raised his voice and addressed them, "Men of Judea and all who live in Jerusalem, let this be known to you, and listen to what I say. [15]Indeed, these are not drunk, as you suppose, for it is only nine o"clock in the morning. [16]No, this is what was spoken through the prophet Joel:

[17] 'In the last days it will be, God declares,
     that I will pour out my Spirit upon all flesh,
        and your sons and your daughters shall prophesy,
     and your young men shall see visions,
        and your old men shall dream dreams.
[18] Even upon my slaves, both men and women,
        in those days I will pour out my Spirit; and they
           shall prophesy.
[19] And I will show portents in the heaven above
        and signs on the earth below,
           blood, and fire, and smoky mist.
[20] The sun shall be turned to darkness
        and the moon to blood,
           before the coming of the Lord's great and glorious
              day.
[21] Then everyone who calls on the name of the Lord shall
        be saved.'

Psalm 104:24-34, 35b

[24] O Lord, how manifold are your works!
     In wisdom you have made them all;
        the earth is full of your creatures.
[25] Yonder is the sea, great and wide,
        creeping things innumerable are there,
           living things both small and great.
[26] There go the ships,
        and Leviathan that you formed to sport in it.
[27] These all look to you
        to give them their food in due season;
[28] when you give to them, they gather it up;
        when you open your hand, they are filled with
           good things.
[29] When you hide your face, they are dismayed;

when you take away their breath, they die
     and return to their dust.
[30] When you send forth your spirit, they are created;
        and you renew the face of the ground.
[31] May the glory of the Lord endure forever;
        may the Lord rejoice in his works—
[32] who looks on the earth and it trembles,
        who touches the mountains and they smoke.
[33] I will sing to the Lord as long as I live;
        I will sing praise to my God while I have being.
[34] May my meditation be pleasing to him,
        for I rejoice in the Lord.
[35b] Bless the Lord,
        O my soul.

1 Corinthians 12:3b-13

[3]Therefore I want you to understand that no one speaking by the Spirit of God ever says "Let Jesus be cursed!" and no one can say "Jesus is Lord" except by the Holy Spirit.

[4]Now there are varieties of gifts, but the same Spirit; [5]and there are varieties of services, but the same Lord; [6]and there are varieties of activities, but it is the same God who activates all of them in everyone. [7]To each is given the manifestation of the Spirit for the common good. [8]To one is given through the Spirit the utterance of wisdom, and to another the utterance of knowledge according to the same Spirit, [9]to another faith by the same Spirit, to another gifts of healing by the one Spirit, [10]to another the working of miracles, to another prophecy, to another the discernment of spirits, to another various kinds of tongues, to another the interpretation of tongues. [11]All these are activated by one and the same Spirit, who allots to each one individually just as the Spirit chooses.

[12]For just as the body is one and has many members, and all the members of the body, though many, are one body, so it is with Christ. [13]For in the one Spirit we were all baptized into one body—Jews or Greeks, slaves or free—and we were all made to drink of one Spirit.

John 7:37-39

[37]On the last day of the festival, the great day, while Jesus was standing there, he cried out, "Let anyone who is thirsty come to me, [38]and let the one who believes in me drink. As the scripture has said, 'Out of the believer's heart shall flow rivers of living water.' " [39]Now he said this about the Spirit, which believers in him were to receive; for as yet there was no Spirit, because Jesus was not yet glorified.

COLOR: RED   **PENTECOST SUNDAY**

Primary Hymns and Songs for the Day
539   "O Spirit of the Living God" (Acts) (O)
         H-3 Hbl-44; Chr-21; Desc-40; Org-40
         S-1 #131-132. Introduction and descant
393   "Spirit of the Living God" (Acts, Pentecost)
         SP131
         S-1 #212 Vocal descant idea
555   "Forward Through the Ages" (1 Cor.) (C)
         H-3 Hbl-59; Chr-156; Org-140

Additional Hymn Suggestions
324   "Hail Thee, Festival Day" (Acts)
332   "Spirit of Faith, Come Down" (Acts)
336   "Of All the Spirit's Gifts to Me" (Acts)
422   "Jesus, Thine All-Victorious Love" (Acts)
465   "Holy Spirit, Truth Divine" (Acts)
475   "Come Down, O Love Divine" (Acts)
537   "Filled With the Spirit's Power" (Acts)
538   "Wind Who Makes All Winds That Blow" (Acts)
540   "I Love Thy Kingdom, Lord" (Acts)
541   "See How Great a Flame Aspires" (Acts)
2027   "Now Praise the Hidden God of Love" (Acts)
2077   "You Alone Are Holy" (Acts, Pentecost)
2117   "Spirit of God" (Acts, Pentecost)
2120   "Spirit, Spirit of Gentleness" (Acts, Pentecost)
2122   "She Comes Sailing on the Wind" (Acts, Pentecost)
2123   "Loving Spirit" (Acts, Pentecost)
2125   "Come, Holy Spirit" (Acts)
2236   "Gather Us In" (Acts)
2237   "As a Fire Is Meant for Burning" (Acts)
2238   "In the Midst of New Dimensions" (Acts, Pentecost)
2241   "The Spirit Sends Us Forth to Serve" (Acts,
         Pentecost)
2246   "Deep in the Shadows of the Past" (Acts, Pentecost)
2269   "Come, Share the Lord" (Acts, Communion)
3017   "Come, Join the Dance of Trinity" (Acts, Pentecost)
543   "O Breath of Life" (Acts, Communion)
552   "Here, O Lord, Your Servants Gather" (Acts)
3185   "Send Us Your Spirit" (Ps., Pentecost)
114   "Many Gifts, One Spirit" (1 Cor.)
547   "O Church of God, United" (Acts, 1 Cor.)
550   "Christ, from Whom All Blessings Flow" (1 Cor.)
554   "All Praise to Our Redeeming Lord" (1 Cor.)
620   "One Bread, One Body" (1 Cor., Communion)
2181   "We Need a Faith" (1 Cor.)
2245   "Within the Day-to-Day" (1 Cor.)
113   "Source and Sovereign, Rock and Cloud" (John)
328   "Eat This Bread" (John, Communion)
350   "Come, All of You" (John)

Additional Contemporary Suggestions
UM328   "Surely the Presence of the Lord" (Acts, Pentecost)
         SP243; S-2, #200 Stanzas for soloist
UM334   "Sweet, Sweet Spirit" (Acts, Pentecost)
         SP136
UM347   "Spirit Song" (Acts, Pentecost)
         SP134
S2039   "Holy, Holy" (Acts, Pentecost)
         SP141
S2119   "Where the Spirit of the Lord Is" (Acts, Pentecost)
S2272   "Holy Ground" (Acts)
         SP86

S2086   "Open Our Eyes, Lord" (Acts)
         SP199
WS3092   "Come, Holy Spirit" (Acts)
WS3008   "Open the Eyes of My Heart" (Acts)
         M57
M88   "Holy Spirit, Rain Down" (Acts)
M4   "Let it Rise" (Acts)
UM333   "I'm Goin'a Sing When the Spirit Says Sing"
         (1 Cor., Pentecost)
S2227   "We Are the Body of Christ" (1 Cor.)
S2132   "You Who Are Thirsty" (John)
         SP219
WS3093   "Fill My Cup, Lord" (John, Communion)
         UM641 refrain; S-2 stanzas for soloist
M5   "The River Is Here" (John, Pentecost)
M28   "Who Can Satisfy My Soul Like You?" (John)
M32   "Holy and Anointed One" (John)
M154   "Dwell" (Pentecost)
M155   "Be My Centre" (Pentecost)

Vocal Solos
"Spirit of Faith Come Down" (Acts, Pentecost)
         V-1   p. 43
"Spirit of God" (Acts)
         V-8   p. 170
"Creation Sings" (Acts)
         WS3018
"Maybe the Rain" (John)
         V-5(2)   p. 27

Anthems
"Ev'ry Time I Feel The Spirit" (Acts)
Moses Hogan; Hal Leonard 08740285
SATB *a cappella*

"By the Grace of the Spirit" (Pentecost)
Andrew Gant: Oxford A-447
SATB, organ

Other Suggestions
Visuals:
   Acts   Wind, tongues of fire, praise, all races
   P   Sea/ships, whales, dove, volcano, quake,
              Ps. 104:35*b*
   E   Pile of gifts, 7 flames, clasped hands, circle,
              baptism, drinking glasses
   G   Water/pitcher/glasses, river fountain
Introit: S2124, S2125 or WS3091. "Come, Holy Spirit" (Acts)
Call to Worship: WSL39. Spirit of the living God (Acts,
   Pentecost)
Call to Prayer: S2118. "Holy Spirit, Come to Us" (Acts, 1 Cor.)
Greeting or Scripture Litany: BOW406 (Acts, Pentecost)
Offertory Prayer: WSL132. Loving Father (Acts, John)
Blessing: WSL41. Wisdom, knowledge, faith (1 Cor., Acts)
Sung Benediction: WS3161, verse 3. "Gracious Creator of Sea
   and of Land" (Acts, Pentecost)

JUNE 15 2014

FATHER'S DAY/PEACE WITH JUSTICE SUNDAY

Genesis 1:1–2:4a

[1]In the beginning when God created the heavens and the earth, [2]the earth was a formless void and darkness covered the face of the deep, while a wind from God swept over the face of the waters.

[3]Then God said, "Let there be light"; and there was light. [4]And God saw that the light was good; and God separated the light from the darkness. [5]God called the light Day, and the darkness he called Night. And there was evening and there was morning, the first day.

[6]And God said, "Let there be a dome in the midst of the waters, and let it separate the waters from the waters." [7]So God made the dome and separated the waters that were under the dome from the waters that were above the dome. And it was so. [8]God called the dome Sky. And there was evening and there was morning, the second day.

[9]And God said, "Let the waters under the sky be gathered together into one place, and let the dry land appear." And it was so. [10]God called the dry land Earth, and the waters that were gathered together he called Seas. And God saw that it was good. [11]Then God said, "Let the earth put forth vegetation: plants yielding seed, and fruit trees of every kind on earth that bear fruit with the seed in it." And it was so. [12]The earth brought forth vegetation: plants yielding seed of every kind, and trees of every kind bearing fruit with the seed in it. And God saw that it was good. [13]And there was evening and there was morning, the third day.

[14]And God said, "Let there be lights in the dome of the sky to separate the day from the night; and let them be for signs and for seasons and for days and years, [15]and let them be lights in the dome of the sky to give light upon the earth." And it was so. [16]God made the two great lights—the greater light to rule the day and the lesser light to rule the night—and the stars. [17]God set them in the dome of the sky to give light upon the earth, [18]to rule over the day and over the night, and to separate the light from the darkness. And God saw that it was good. [19]And there was evening and there was morning, the fourth day.

[20]And God said, "Let the waters bring forth swarms of living creatures, and let birds fly above the earth across the dome of the sky." [21]So God created the great sea monsters and every living creature that moves, of every kind, with which the waters swarm, and every winged bird of every kind. And God saw that it was good. [22]God blessed them, saying, "Be fruitful and multiply and fill the waters in the seas, and let birds multiply on the earth." [23]And there was evening and there was morning, the fifth day.

[24]And God said, "Let the earth bring forth living creatures of every kind: cattle and creeping things and wild animals of the earth of every kind." And it was so. [25]God made the wild animals of the earth of every kind, and the cattle of every kind, and everything that creeps upon the ground of every kind. And God saw that it was good.

[26]Then God said, "Let us make humankind in our image, according to our likeness; and let them have dominion over the fish of the sea, and over the birds of the air, and over the cattle, and over all the wild animals of the earth, and over every creeping thing that creeps upon the earth." [27]So God created humankind in his image, in the image of God he created them; male and female he created them. [28]God blessed them, and God said to them, "Be fruitful and multiply, and fill the earth and subdue it; and have dominion over the fish of the sea and over the birds of the air and over every living thing that moves upon the earth."

[29]God said, "See, I have given you every plant yielding seed that is upon the face of all the earth, and every tree with seed in its fruit; you shall have them for food. [30]And to every beast of the earth, and to every bird of the air, and to everything that creeps on the earth, everything that has the breath of life, I have given every green plant for food." And it was so. [31]God saw everything that he had made, and indeed, it was very good. And there was evening and there was morning, the sixth day.

2Thus the heavens and the earth were finished, and all their multitude. [2]And on the seventh day God finished the work that he had done, and he rested on the seventh day from all the work that he had done. [3]So God blessed the seventh day and hallowed it, because on it God rested from all the work that he had done in creation.

[4]These are the generations of the heavens and the earth when they were created.

Psalm 8

[1] O LORD, our Sovereign,
        how majestic is your name in all the earth!
    You have set your glory above the heavens.
        [2]Out of the mouths of babes and infants
    you have founded a bulwark because of your foes,
        to silence the enemy and the avenger.
[3] When I look at your heavens, the work of your fingers,
        the moon and the stars that you have established;
[4] what are human beings that you are mindful of them,
        mortals that you care for them?
[5] Yet you have made them a little lower than God,
        and crowned them with glory and honor.
[6] You have given them dominion over the works of
            your hands;
        you have put all things under their feet,
[7] all sheep and oxen,
        and also the beasts of the field,
[8] the birds of the air, and the fish of the sea,
        whatever passes along the paths of the seas.
[9] O LORD, our Sovereign,
        how majestic is your name in all the earth!

2 Corinthians 13:11-13

[11]Finally, brothers and sisters, farewell. Put things in order, listen to my appeal, agree with one another, live in peace; and the God of love and peace will be with you. [12]Greet one another with a holy kiss. All the saints greet you.

[13]The grace of the Lord Jesus Christ, the love of God, and the communion of the Holy Spirit be with all of you.

Matthew 28:16-20

[16]Now the eleven disciples went to Galilee, to the mountain to which Jesus had directed them. [17]When they saw him, they worshiped him; but some doubted. [18]And Jesus came and said to them, "All authority in heaven and on earth has been given to me. [19]Go therefore and make disciples of all nations, baptizing them in the name of the Father and of the Son and of the Holy Spirit, [20]and teaching them to obey everything that I have commanded you. And remember, I am with you always, to the end of the age."

COLOR: WHITE　　　　　　　　　　　　　　　　　**TRINITY SUNDAY**

Primary Hymns and Songs for the Day

2023　"How Majestic Is Your Name" (Ps.) (O)
　　　　　SP14
62　　"All Creatures of Our God and King" (Gen., Ps., Trinity) (O)
　　　　　H-3　Hbl-44; Chr-21; Desc-66; Org-73
　　　　　S-1　#198-204. Various treatments
3017　"Come, Join the Dance of Trinity" (Matt., Trinity)
389　　"Freely, Freely" (Matt.) (C)
　　　　　S-1　#135. Vocal descant idea
571　　"Go, Make of All Disciples" (Matt.) (C)
　　　　　H-3　Hbl-74; Chr-123; Desc-64; Org-71
　　　　　S-1　#9-197. Various treatments

Additional Hymn Suggestions

145　　"Morning Has Broken" (Gen.)
147　　"All Things Bright and Beautiful" (Gen.)
151　　"God Created Heaven and Earth" (Gen.)
443　　"O God Who Shaped Creation" (Gen.)
538　　"Wind Who Makes All Winds That Blow" (Gen.)
539　　"O Spirit of the Living God" (Gen.)
688　　"God, That Madest Earth and Heaven" (Gen.)
331　　"Holy Spirit, Come, Confirm Us" (Gen., Trinity)
3129　"Touch the Earth Lightly" (Gen.)
3159　"Let Our Earth Be Peaceful" (Gen.)
2046　"Womb of Life" (Gen., Trinity, Communion)
2047　"Bring Many Names" (Gen., Father's Day)
2050　"Mothering God, You Gave Me Birth" (Gen., Trinity)
2059　"I Am Your Mother" ("Earth Prayer") (Gen.)
2060　"God the Sculptor of the Mountains" (Gen.)
2120　"Spirit, Spirit of Gentleness" (Gen.)
2122　"She Comes Sailing on the Wind" (Gen.)
2123　"Loving Spirit" (Gen.)
2117　"Spirit of God" (Gen., Matt.)
2170　"God Made from One Blood" (Gen., Father's Day)
3129　"Touch the Earth Lightly" (Gen.)
152　　"I Sing the Almighty Power of God" (Gen., Ps.)
61　　"Come, Thou Almighty King" (Ps., Trinity)
77　　"How Great Thou Art" (Ps.)
2185　"For One Great Peace" (2 Cor.)
3148　"There's a Spirit of Love in This Place" (2 Cor.)
584　　"Lord, You Give the Great Commission" (2 Cor., Matt.)
312　　"Hail the Day That Sees Him Rise" (Matt.)
583　　"Sois la Semilla" ("You Are the Seed") (Matt.)
632　　"Draw Us in the Spirit's Tether" (Matt., Communion)
2239　"Go Ye, Go Ye into the World" (Matt.)
2241　"The Spirit Sends Us Forth to Serve" (Matt.)
2243　"We All Are One in Mission" (Matt.)
2184　"Sent Out in Jesus' Name" (Matt.)
2208　"Guide My Feet" (Matt.)
3158　"Go to the World" (Matt.)
85　　"We Believe in One True God" (Trinity)

Additional Contemporary Suggestions

S2041　"Thou Art Worthy" (Gen.)
　　　　　SP5
S2118　"Holy Spirit, Come to Us" (Gen.)
S2125　"Come, Holy Spirit" (Gen.)
SP2　　"Ah, Lord God" (Gen., Trinity)
WS3032　"Across the Lands" (Gen., Ps.)

WS3034　"God of Wonders" (Gen., Ps.)
　　　　　M80
M178　"Majestic" (Ps.)
WS3015　"How Great You Are" (Ps.)
WS3027　"Hallelujah" ("You're Love is Amazing") (Ps.)
S2141　"There's a Song" (2 Cor.)
S2223　"They'll Know We Are Christians" (2 Cor., Trinity)
S2171　"Make Me a Channel of Your Peace" (2 Cor.)
S2186　"Song of Hope" (2 Cor.)
S2006　"Lord God Almighty" (Matt., Trinity)
WS3105　"In Christ Alone" (Matt.)
　　　　　M138
SP121　"Celebrate Jesus" (Matt.)
M6　　"Because We Believe" (Trinity)
S2039　"Holy, Holy" (Trinity)
　　　　　SP141
S2251　"We Were Baptized in Christ Jesus" (Trinity, Baptism)
S2188　"The Family Prayer Song" (Father's Day)
　　　　　M54

Vocal Solos

"This Is My Father's World" (Gen.)
　　V-6　　　p. 42
"A Song of Joy" (Ps.)
　　V-11　　p. 2
"Alleluia" (Trinity)
　　V-8　　　p. 358

Anthems

"Look All Around Us, Then Join the Glad Song" (Gen.)
Hal Hopson; Choristers Guild CGA-1240
Unison/two-part, piano, opt. handbells

"Breath of Life" (Gen., Ps.)
Mark Hayes; Hinshaw HMC1889
SATB, piano

"O God, Creator" (Ps.)
Marcello; arr. Grotenhuis; MorningStar 50-9420
Two-part, keyboard

Other Suggestions

Visuals:
　O　Wind, light/dark, sky (evening/morning)
　P　Majesty, earth, infants, sky/stars, people, sheep/ox
　E　Waving, circle (unity), dove/branch, kiss/parting
　G　Jesus, 11 men, Christ candle, worship, globe, baptism
　Trinity Sunday: Symbols of the Trinity, 3-wick candle
Introit: UM552. "Here, O Lord, Your Servants Gather" (2 Cor.)
Opening Prayer: WSL64. God of all creation (Gen.)
Canticle: UM80. "Canticle of the Holy Trinity" (Trinity)
Litany: WSL48. O Lord, our God, creator (Gen.)
Prayer of Confession: BOW494 (Gen.)
Prayer: WSL69. Creator God, how great (Ps.)
Prayer: WSL201. God our Creator (Father's Day)
Offertory Prayer: WSL109. O great and holy God (Ps.)
Prayers of Thanksgiving: BOW556-558 (Gen.)
Blessing: WSL178. May the God who made (Gen.)
Sung Benediction: WS3183. "As We Go" (Matt.)

113

JUNE 22, 2014

Genesis 21:8-21

[8]The child grew, and was weaned; and Abraham made a great feast on the day that Isaac was weaned.

[9]But Sarah saw the son of Hagar the Egyptian, whom she had borne to Abraham, playing with her son Isaac. [10]So she said to Abraham, "Cast out this slave woman with her son; for the son of this slave woman shall not inherit along with my son Isaac." [11]The matter was very distressing to Abraham on account of his son. [12]But God said to Abraham, "Do not be distressed because of the boy and because of your slave woman; whatever Sarah says to you, do as she tells you, for it is through Isaac that offspring shall be named for you. [13]As for the son of the slave woman, I will make a nation of him also, because he is your offspring."

[14]So Abraham rose early in the morning, and took bread and a skin of water, and gave it to Hagar, putting it on her shoulder, along with the child, and sent her away. And she departed, and wandered about in the wilderness of Beer-sheba. [15]When the water in the skin was gone, she cast the child under one of the bushes. [16]Then she went and sat down opposite him a good way off, about the distance of a bow-shot; for she said, "Do not let me look on the death of the child." And as she sat opposite him, she lifted up her voice and wept. [17]And God heard the voice of the boy; and the angel of God called to Hagar from heaven, and said to her, "What troubles you, Hagar? Do not be afraid; for God has heard the voice of the boy where he is. [18]Come, lift up the boy and hold him fast with your hand, for I will make a great nation of him." [19]Then God opened her eyes and she saw a well of water. She went, and filled the skin with water, and gave the boy a drink. [20]God was with the boy, and he grew up; he lived in the wilderness, and became an expert with the bow. [21]He lived in the wilderness of Paran; and his mother got a wife for him from the land of Egypt.

Psalm 86:1-10, 16-17

1 Incline your ear, O LORD, and answer me,
      for I am poor and needy.
2 Preserve my life, for I am devoted to you;
      save your servant who trusts in you.
   You are my God; [3] be gracious to me, O Lord,
      for to you do I cry all day long.
4 Gladden the soul of your servant,
      for to you, O Lord, I lift up my soul.
5 For you, O Lord, are good and forgiving,
      abounding in steadfast love to all who call on you.
6 Give ear, O LORD, to my prayer;
      listen to my cry of supplication.
7 In the day of my trouble I call on you,
      for you will answer me.
8 There is none like you among the gods, O Lord,
      nor are there any works like yours.
9 All the nations you have made shall come
      and bow down before you, O Lord,
         and shall glorify your name.
10 For you are great and do wondrous things;
      you alone are God.
. . . .
16 Turn to me and be gracious to me;
      give your strength to your servant;
      save the child of your serving girl.
17 Show me a sign of your favor,

so that those who hate me may see it
   and be put to shame,
because you, LORD, have helped
   me and comforted me.

Romans 6:1b-11

[1b] Should we continue in sin in order that grace may abound? [2]By no means! How can we who died to sin go on living in it? [3]Do you not know that all of us who have been baptized into Christ Jesus were baptized into his death? [4]Therefore we have been buried with him by baptism into death, so that, just as Christ was raised from the dead by the glory of the Father, so we too might walk in newness of life.

[5] For if we have been united with him in a death like his, we will certainly be united with him in a resurrection like his. [6]We know that our old self was crucified with him so that the body of sin might be destroyed, and we might no longer be enslaved to sin. [7]For whoever has died is freed from sin. [8]But if we have died with Christ, we believe that we will also live with him. [9]We know that Christ, being raised from the dead, will never die again; death no longer has dominion over him. [10]The death he died, he died to sin, once for all; but the life he lives, he lives to God. [11]So you also must consider yourselves dead to sin and alive to God in Christ Jesus.

Matthew 10:24-39

[24] 'A disciple is not above the teacher, nor a slave above the master; [25]it is enough for the disciple to be like the teacher, and the slave like the master. If they have called the master of the house Beelzebul, how much more will they malign those of his household!

[26] 'So have no fear of them; for nothing is covered up that will not be uncovered, and nothing secret that will not become known. [27]What I say to you in the dark, tell in the light; and what you hear whispered, proclaim from the housetops. [28]Do not fear those who kill the body but cannot kill the soul; rather fear him who can destroy both soul and body in hell. [29]Are not two sparrows sold for a penny? Yet not one of them will fall to the ground unperceived by your Father. [30]And even the hairs of your head are all counted. [31]So do not be afraid; you are of more value than many sparrows.

[32] 'Everyone therefore who acknowledges me before others, I also will acknowledge before my Father in heaven; [33]but whoever denies me before others, I also will deny before my Father in heaven.

[34] 'Do not think that I have come to bring peace to the earth; I have not come to bring peace, but a sword.
[35] For I have come to set a man against his father,
      and a daughter against her mother,
      and a daughter-in-law against her mother-in-law;
[36] and one's foes will be members of one's own household.

[37]Whoever loves father or mother more than me is not worthy of me; and whoever loves son or daughter more than me is not worthy of me; [38]and whoever does not take up the cross and follow me is not worthy of me. [39]Those who find their life will lose it, and those who lose their life for my sake will find it.

COLOR: GREEN

2nd SUNDAY AFTER PENTECOST

Primary Hymns and Songs for the Day

702   "Sing with All the Saints in Glory" (Rom.) (O)
129   "Give to the Winds Thy Fears" (Gen., Matt.)
       H-3 Chr-71; Desc-39; Org-39
       S-1 #129. Descant
141   "Children of the Heavenly Father" (Gen., Matt.)
       H-3 Chr-46; Desc-102
       S-2 #180-185. Various treatments
610   "We Know That Christ is Raised" (Rom., Baptism)
       H-3 Hbl-100; Chr-214; Desc- ; Org-37
       S-1 #118-127. Various treatments
2129   "I Have Decided to Follow Jesus" (Matt.) (C)

Additional Hymn Suggestions

100   "God, Whose Love is Reigning O'er Us" (Gen.)
116   "The God of Abraham Praise" (Gen.)
506   "Wellspring of Wisdom" (Gen.)
523   "Saranam, Saranam" (Gen.)
2246   "Deep in the Shadows of the Past" (Gen.)
397   "I Need Thee Every Hour" (Gen., Ps.)
430   "O Master, Let Me Walk With Thee" (Gen., Ps.)
3131   "Hear My Prayer, O God" (Gen., Ps.)
2044   "My Gratitude Now Accept, O God ("Gracias, Señor") (Ps.)
2146   "His Eye Is on the Sparrow" (Gen., Matt.)
162   "Alleluia, Alleluia" (Rom.)
363   "And Can It Be That I Should Gain" (Rom.)
365   "Grace Greater Than Our Sin" (Rom.)
378   "Amazing Grace" (Rom.)
528   "Nearer, My God, to Thee" (Rom.)
608   "This Is the Spirit's Entry Now" (Rom., Baptism)
2158   "Just a Closer Walk with Thee" (Rom.)
2248   "Baptized in Water" (Rom., Baptism)
2251   "We Were Baptized in Christ Jesus" (Rom., Baptism)
3110   "By Grace We Have Been Saved" (Rom.)
3147   "Built on a Rock" (Rom.)
3118   "Take This Moment, Sign, and Space" (Rom., Matt.)
377   "It is Well with My Soul" (Rom., Matt.)
2142   "Blessed Quietness" (Rom., Matt.)
2149   "Living for Jesus" (Rom., Matt.)
130   "God Will Take Care of You" (Matt.)
141   "Children of the Heavenly Father" (Matt.)
522   "Leave It There" (Matt.)
338   "Where He Leads Me" (Matt.) (C)
415   "Take Up Thy Cross" (Matt.)
424   "Must Jesus Bear the Cross Alone" (Matt.)
553   "And Are We Yet Alive" (Matt.)
2102   "Swiftly Pass the Clouds of Glory" (Matt.)
2137   "Would I Have Answered When You Called" (Matt.)
3128   "Whatever You Do" (Matt.)

Additional Contemporary Suggestions

WS3099   "Falling on My Knees" (Gen.)
       M155
S2002   "I Will Call Upon the Lord" (Ps.)
       SP224
S2087   "We Will Glorify" (Ps.)
       SP68
S2016   "Glorify Thy Name" (Ps.)
       SP19

S2207   "Lord, Listen to Your Children" (Ps.)
SP18   "I Exalt You" (Ps.)
M257   "Came to My Rescue" (Ps.)
S2162   "Grace Alone" (Rom.)
       M100
WS3026   "God Is Good All the Time" (Rom.)
       M45
WS3104   "Amazing Grace" ("My Chains Are Gone") (Rom.)
       M205
WS3187   "We Fall Down" (Rom.)
       M66
M228   "Stronger" (Rom.)
M242   "Salvation Is Here" (Rom.)
S2145   "I've Got Peace Like a River" (Rom., Matt.)
M53   "Let It Be Said of Us" (Matt.)
M122   "Every Move I Make" (Matt.)
M150   "Everyday" (Matt.)
M248   "One Way" (Matt.)
WS3160   "We Will Follow" ("Somlandela") (Matt.)

Vocal Solos

"Lost in the Night" (Gen., Ps.)
       V-5(1)   p. 18
"His Eye Is on the Sparrow" (Gen., Matt.)
       V-8   p. 166
"And Can It Be That I Should Gain" (Rom.)
       V-1   p. 29
"Lead Me to Calvary" (Matt.)
       V-8   p. 226

Anthems

"Bow down Thine Ear" (Ps.)
Franck / Sowerby; Fred Bock Music F2058
SATB, organ

"You Must Be Ready" (Matt.)
John Horman; Chorister Guild CGA-334
Unison/Two-part, keyboard (opt. flute)

Other Suggestions

Visuals:
     O   Toddler/woman, bread/waterbag, wilderness, well, bow
     P   Praying hands, people bowing, Ps. 86:9
     E   Baptism, crucifix, open manacles
     G   Cross for each, light, housetop, 2 sparrows/penny/hair, sword
Opening Prayer: BOW464 (Gen.)
Litany: WSL49. For rebirth and resilience (Gen., Ps., Matt.)
Prayer of Confession: BOW486 (Ps., Matt.)
Affirmation of Faith: WSL82. We are children of God (Rom.)
Response: WS3119. Take, O Take Me As I Am (Rom.)
Prayer: UM531 or BOW545 (Gen.)
Prayer: BOW524. For Strength (Gen., Matt.)
Prayer: BOW527. For the World and Its Peoples (Gen., Rom.)
Response: S2200. "O Lord, Hear My Prayer" (Ps.)
Blessing: BOW564 (Gen.)

JUNE 29, 2014

Genesis 22:1-14

[1]After these things God tested Abraham. He said to him, "Abraham!" And he said, "Here I am." [2]He said, "Take your son, your only son Isaac, whom you love, and go to the land of Moriah, and offer him there as a burnt offering on one of the mountains that I shall show you." [3]So Abraham rose early in the morning, saddled his donkey, and took two of his young men with him, and his son Isaac; he cut the wood for the burnt offering, and set out and went to the place in the distance that God had shown him. [4]On the third day Abraham looked up and saw the place far away. [5]Then Abraham said to his young men, "Stay here with the donkey; the boy and I will go over there; we will worship, and then we will come back to you." [6]Abraham took the wood of the burnt offering and laid it on his son Isaac, and he himself carried the fire and the knife. So the two of them walked on together. [7]Isaac said to his father Abraham, "Father!" And he said, "Here I am, my son." He said, "The fire and the wood are here, but where is the lamb for a burnt offering?" [8]Abraham said, "God himself will provide the lamb for a burnt offering, my son." So the two of them walked on together.

[9]When they came to the place that God had shown him, Abraham built an altar there and laid the wood in order. He bound his son Isaac, and laid him on the altar, on top of the wood. [10]Then Abraham reached out his hand and took the knife to kill his son. [11]But the angel of the LORD called to him from heaven, and said, "Abraham, Abraham!" And he said, "Here I am." [12]He said, "Do not lay your hand on the boy or do anything to him; for now I know that you fear God, since you have not withheld your son, your only son, from me." [13]And Abraham looked up and saw a ram, caught in a thicket by its horns. Abraham went and took the ram and offered it up as a burnt offering instead of his son. [14]So Abraham called that place "The LORD will provide"; as it is said to this day, "On the mount of the LORD it shall be provided."

Psalm 13

[1] How long, O LORD? Will you forget me forever?
       How long will you hide your face from me?
[2] How long must I bear pain in my soul,
       and have sorrow in my heart all day long?
     How long shall my enemy be exalted over me?
[3] Consider and answer me, O LORD my God!
       Give light to my eyes, or I will sleep the sleep of death,
[4] and my enemy will say, "I have prevailed";
       my foes will rejoice because I am shaken.
[5] But I trusted in your steadfast love;
       my heart shall rejoice in your salvation.
[6] I will sing to the LORD,
       because he has dealt bountifully with me.

Romans 6:12-23

[12]Therefore, do not let sin exercise dominion in your mortal bodies, to make you obey their passions. [13]No longer present your members to sin as instruments of wickedness, but present yourselves to God as those who have been brought from death to life, and present your members to God as instruments of righteousness. [14]For sin will have no dominion over you, since you are not under law but under grace.

[15]What then? Should we sin because we are not under law but under grace? By no means! [16]Do you not know that if you present yourselves to anyone as obedient slaves, you are slaves of the one whom you obey, either of sin, which leads to death, or of obedience, which leads to righteousness? [17]But thanks be to God that you, having once been slaves of sin, have become obedient from the heart to the form of teaching to which you were entrusted, [18]and that you, having been set free from sin, have become slaves of righteousness. [19]I am speaking in human terms because of your natural limitations. For just as you once presented your members as slaves to impurity and to greater and greater iniquity, so now present your members as slaves to righteousness for sanctification.

[20]When you were slaves of sin, you were free in regard to righteousness. [21]So what advantage did you then get from the things of which you now are ashamed? The end of those things is death. [22]But now that you have been freed from sin and enslaved to God, the advantage you get is sanctification. The end is eternal life. [23]For the wages of sin is death, but the free gift of God is eternal life in Christ Jesus our Lord.

Matthew 10:40-42

[40]"Whoever welcomes you welcomes me, and whoever welcomes me welcomes the one who sent me. [41]Whoever welcomes a prophet in the name of a prophet will receive a prophet's reward; and whoever welcomes a righteous person in the name of a righteous person will receive the reward of the righteous; [42]and whoever gives even a cup of cold water to one of these little ones in the name of a disciple—truly I tell you, none of these will lose their reward."

COLOR: GREEN   **3rd SUNDAY AFTER PENTECOST**

Primary Hymns and Songs for the Day
116	"The God of Abraham Praise" (Gen.) (O)
123	"El Shaddai" (Gen.)
	S-2 #54 Vocal solo
420	"Breathe on Me, Breath of God" (Rom.)
	H-3 Hbl-49; Chr-45; Desc-101; Org-166
2149	"Living for Jesus" (Rom., Matt.)
2241	"The Spirit Sends Us Forth to Serve" (Matt.) (C)
	H-3 Hbl-129; Chr-106; Desc-65; Org-72
	S-2 #105. Flute/violin descant
	#106. Harmonization

Additional Hymn Suggestions
100	"God, Whose Love Is Reigning O'er Us" (Gen.)
508	"Faith, While Trees Are Still in Blossom" (Gen.)
593	"Here I Am, Lord" (Gen.)
710	"Faith of Our Fathers" (Gen.)
2196	"We Walk by Faith" (Gen.)
2209	"How Long, O Lord" (Ps.)
2211	"Faith Is Patience in the Night" (Gen.)
2180	"Why Stand So Far Away, My God?" (Gen., Ps.)
517	"By Gracious Powers" (Gen., Ps.)
142	"If Thou But Suffer God to Guide Thee" (Ps.)
515	"Out of the Depths I Cry to You" (Ps.)
534	"Be Still, My Soul" (Ps.)
650	"Give Me the Faith Which Can Remove" (Gen., Matt.)
361	"Rock of Ages" (Gen., Rom.) (C)
181	"Ye Servants of God" (Rom.)
363	"And Can It Be That I Should Gain" (Rom.)
378	"Amazing Grace" (Rom.)
396	"O Jesus, I Have Promised" (Rom.)
399	"Take My Life, and Let It Be" (Rom.)
417	"O For a Heart to Praise My God" (Rom.)
419	"I Am Thine, O Lord" (Rom.)
421	"Make Me a Captive, Lord" (Rom.)
467	"Trust and Obey"
579	"Lord God, Your Love Has Called Us Here" (Rom.)
427	"Where Cross the Crowded Ways of Life" (Rom., Matt.)
3110	"By Grace We Have Been Saved" (Rom.)
432	"Jesu, Jesu" (Rom., Matt.)
192	"There's a Spirit in the Air" (Matt.)
430	"O Master, Let Me Walk with Thee" (Matt.)
434	"Cuando El Pobre" ("When the Poor Ones") (Matt.)
2170	"God Made from One Blood" (Matt.)
2175	"Together We Serve" (Matt.)
2254	"In Remembrance of Me" (Matt., Communion)
2268	"As We Gather at Your Table" (Matt., Communion)
3152	"Welcome" (Matt.)
437	"This Is My Song" (Independence Day)

Additional Contemporary Suggestions
WS3099	"Falling on My Knees" (Gen., Ps.)
	M155
M189	"Your Love, Oh Lord" (Gen., Ps.)
S2002	"I Will Call Upon the Lord" (Ps.)
	SP224
S2144	"Someone Asked the Question" (Ps.)
SP185	"The Steadfast Love of the Lord" (Ps.)

WS3023	"Forever" (Ps.)
	M68
M103	"How Great Are You, Lord" (Ps., Rom.)
S2141	"There's a Song" (Rom.)
S2162	"Grace Alone" (Rom.)
	M100
S2195	"In the Lord I'll Be Ever Thankful" (Rom.)
SP208	"I Am Crucified with Christ" (Rom.)
WS3104	"Amazing Grace" ("My Chains Are Gone") (Rom.)
	M205
WS3187	"We Fall Down" (Rom.)
	M66
S2176	"Make Me a Servant" (Matt.)
	SP193
S2244	"People Need the Lord" (Matt.)

Vocal Solos
"Here I Am" (Gen., Rom.)
    V-11   p. 19
"And Can It Be That I Should Gain" (Rom.)
    V-1   p. 29
"Grace Greater Than Our Sin" (Rom.)
    V-8   p. 180
"Take My Life" ("Consecration") (Rom.)
    V-8   p. 262
"Reach Out to Your Neighbor" (Matt.)
    V-8   p. 372

Anthems
"Little Lamb" (Gen.)
David M. Cherwien; MorningStar 50-6511
SATB divisi, *a cappella*

"This Is My Song" (Independence Day)
arr. Carl/Neuen; Choristers Guild CGA-1249
SATB, organ, opt. orchestra

Other Suggestions
Visuals:
O	Gen. 22:1*c*, mountain, dawn, donkey, man/boy, wood/knife, altar, angel. ram
P	Praying hands, eyes/sleep, joy, singing
E	Baptism, manacles, Rom. 6:23
G	Welcome, cup of water offered

Introit: S2271. "Come! Come! Everybody Worship" (Rom.)
Greeting: BOW457 (Ps., Rom.)
Prayer of Confession: BOW478 (Gen., Rom.)
Prayer of Confession: BOW480 (Rom.)
Prayer: BOW530. A Prayer of Saint Thomas Aquinas (Gen.)
Response: S2200. "O Lord, Hear My Prayer" (Ps.)
Prayer of Thanksgiving: BOW552 (Gen., Rom.)
Prayer: BOW442, 492, 513, 515, 516, 520, 524, or 544 (Independence Day)
Prayer: WSL203. God of all nations (Independence Day)
See more suggestions in *The Abingdon Worship Annual 2014.*

JULY 6, 2014

Genesis 24:34-38, 42-49, 58-67

[34]So he said, "I am Abraham's servant. [35]The LORD has greatly blessed my master, and he has become wealthy; he has given him flocks and herds, silver and gold, male and female slaves, camels and donkeys. [36]And Sarah my master's wife bore a son to my master when she was old; and he has given him all that he has. [37]My master made me swear, saying, 'You shall not take a wife for my son from the daughters of the Canaanites, in whose land I live; [38]but you shall go to my father's house, to my kindred, and get a wife for my son.' . . .

[42]"I came today to the spring, and said, 'O LORD, the God of my master Abraham, if now you will only make successful the way I am going! [43]I am standing here by the spring of water; let the young woman who comes out to draw, to whom I shall say, "Please give me a little water from your jar to drink,"

[44]and who will say to me, "Drink, and I will draw for your camels also" —let her be the woman whom the LORD has appointed for my master's son.' [45]"Before I had finished speaking in my heart, there was Rebekah coming out with her water jar on her shoulder; and she went down to the spring, and drew. I said to her, 'Please let me drink.' [46]She quickly let down her jar from her shoulder, and said, 'Drink, and I will also water your camels.' So I drank, and she also watered the camels. [47]Then I asked her, 'Whose daughter are you?' She said, 'The daughter of Bethuel, Nahor's son, whom Milcah bore to him.' So I put the ring on her nose, and the bracelets on her arms. [48]Then I bowed my head and worshiped the LORD, and blessed the LORD, the God of my master Abraham, who had led me by the right way to obtain the daughter of my master's kinsman for his son. [49]Now then, if you will deal loyally and truly with my master, tell me; and if not, tell me, so that I may turn either to the right hand or to the left." . . .

[58]And they called Rebekah, and said to her, "Will you go with this man?" She said, "I will." [59]So they sent away their sister Rebekah and her nurse along with Abraham's servant and his men. [60]And they blessed Rebekah and said to her,

"May you, our sister, become
   thousands of myriads;
may your offspring gain possession
   of the gates of their foes."

[61]Then Rebekah and her maids rose up, mounted the camels, and followed the man; thus the servant took Rebekah, and went his way.

[62]Now Isaac had come from Beer-lahai-roi, and was settled in the Negeb. [63]Isaac went out in the evening to walk in the field; and looking up, he saw camels coming. [64]And Rebekah looked up, and when she saw Isaac, she slipped quickly from the camel, [65]and said to the servant, "Who is the man over there, walking in the field to meet us?" The servant said, "It is my master." So she took her veil and covered herself. [66]And the servant told Isaac all the things that he had done. [67]Then Isaac brought her into his mother Sarah's tent. He took Rebekah, and she became his wife; and he loved her. So Isaac was comforted after his mother's death.

Psalm 45:10-17

[10] Hear, O daughter, consider and incline your ear;
   forget your people and your father's house,
      [11]and the king will desire your beauty.
   Since he is your lord, bow to him;

[12]the people of Tyre will seek your favor with gifts,
   the richest of the people [13]with all kinds of wealth.

   The princess is decked in her chamber with
         gold-woven robes;
[14]   in many-colored robes she is led to the king;
      behind her the virgins, her companions, follow.
[15] With joy and gladness they are led along
      as they enter the palace of the king.

[16] In the place of ancestors you, O king, shall have sons;
      you will make them princes in all the earth.
[17] I will cause your name to be celebrated in all generations;
      therefore the peoples will praise you forever and ever.

Romans 7:15-25a

[15]I do not understand my own actions. For I do not do what I want, but I do the very thing I hate. [16]Now if I do what I do not want, I agree that the law is good. [17]But in fact it is no longer I that do it, but sin that dwells within me. [18]For I know that nothing good dwells within me, that is, in my flesh. I can will what is right, but I cannot do it. [19]For I do not do the good I want, but the evil I do not want is what I do. [20]Now if I do what I do not want, it is no longer I that do it, but sin that dwells within me.

[21]So I find it to be a law that when I want to do what is good, evil lies close at hand. [22]For I delight in the law of God in my inmost self, [23]but I see in my members another law at war with the law of my mind, making me captive to the law of sin that dwells in my members. [24]Wretched man that I am! Who will rescue me from this body of death? [25]Thanks be to God through Jesus Christ our Lord!

Matthew 11:16-19, 25-30

[16] "But to what will I compare this generation? It is like children sitting in the marketplaces and calling to one another,
[17] 'We played the flute for you, and
         you did not dance;
      we wailed, and you did not mourn.'
[18]For John came neither eating nor drinking, and they say, 'He has a demon'; [19]the Son of Man came eating and drinking, and they say, 'Look, a glutton and a drunkard, a friend of tax collectors and sinners!' Yet wisdom is vindicated by her deeds." . . .

[25]At that time Jesus said, "I thank you, Father, Lord of heaven and earth, because you have hidden these things from the wise and the intelligent and have revealed them to infants; [26]yes, Father, for such was your gracious will. [27]All things have been handed over to me by my Father; and no one knows the Son except the Father, and no one knows the Father except the Son and anyone to whom the Son chooses to reveal him.

[28]"Come to me, all you that are weary and are carrying heavy burdens, and I will give you rest. [29]Take my yoke upon you, and learn from me; for I am gentle and humble in heart, and you will find rest for your souls. [30]For my yoke is easy, and my burden is light."

COLOR: GREEN　　　　　　　　　　　　　　　　　**4th SUNDAY AFTER PENTECOST**

Primary Hymns and Songs for the Day

384　"Love Divine, All Loves Excelling" (Rom.) (O)
　　　　　H-3 Chr-134; Desc-18; Org-13
　　　　　S-1 #41-42. Descant and harmonization
402　"Lord, I Want to Be a Christian" (Rom.)
　　　　　H-3 Chr-130
400　"Come, Thou Fount of Every Blessing" (Rom.,
　　　Matt., Communion)
　　　　　H-3 Chr-57; Desc-79; Org-96
　　　　　S-1 #244. Descant
2158　"Just a Closer Walk with Thee" (Rom., Matt.)
529　"How Firm a Foundation" (Rom., Matt.) (C)
　　　　　H-3 Hbl-27, 69; Chr-102; Desc-41; Org-41
　　　　　S-1 #133. Harmonization
　　　　　　　#134. Performance note

Additional Hymn Suggestions

108　"God Hath Spoken by the Prophets" (Gen., Matt.)
643　"When Love Is Found" (Gen., Ps., Communion)
647　"Your Love, O God, Has Called Us Here" (Gen.,
　　　Ps.)
247　"O Morning Star, How Fair and Bright" (Ps.)
2267　"Taste and See" (Ps., Communion)
98　"To God Be the Glory" (Rom.)
305　"Camina, Pueblo de Dios" ("Walk On, O People of
　　　God") (Rom.)
421　"Make Me a Captive, Lord" (Rom.)
500　"Spirit of God, Descend Upon My Heart" (Rom.)
579　"Lord God, Your Love Has Called Us Here" (Rom.)
596　"Blessed Jesus, At Thy Word" (Rom.)
142　"If Thou But Suffer God to Guide Thee" (Rom.,
　　　Matt.)
182　"Word of God, Come Down on Earth" (Rom.,
　　　Matt.)
267　"O Love, How Deep" (Rom., Matt.)
340　"Come, Ye Sinners, Poor and Needy" (Rom., Matt.)
513　"Soldiers of Christ, Arise" (Rom., Matt.)
191　"Jesus Loves Me" (Matt.)
350　"Come, All of You" (Matt., Communion)
451　"Be Thou My Vision" (Matt.)
526　"What a Friend We Have in Jesus" (Matt.)
616　"Come, Sinners, to the Gospel Feast" (Matt.,
　　　Communion) (O)
650　"Give Me the Faith Which Can Remove" (Matt.)
2052　"The Lone, Wild Bird" (Matt.)
2142　"Blessed Quietness" (Matt.)
2149　"Living for Jesus" (Matt.)
2202　"Come Away with Me" (Matt.)
2218　"You Are Mine" (Matt.)
2262　"Let Us Offer to the Father" (Matt., Communion)
2265　"Time Now to Gather" (Matt., Communion)
3017　"Come, Join the Dance of Trinity" (Matt.)

Additional Contemporary Suggestions

M63　"I Could Sing of Your Love Forever" (Ps., Matt.)
M46　"I Will Celebrate" (Ps.)
　　　　　SP147
S2068　"I Love You, Lord" (Ps.)
　　　　　SP72
S2081　"Thank You, Jesus" ("Tino tenda, Jesu") (Rom.)
S2195　"In the Lord I'll Be Ever Thankful" (Rom.)
S2271　"Come! Come! Everybody Worship" (Rom.)

UM84　"Thank You, Lord" (Rom.)
UM99　"My Tribute" (Rom.)
　　　　　SP118; V-8 p. 5 Vocal Solo
UM601　"Thy Word Is a Lamp" (Rom.)
　　　　　SP183
S2036　"Give Thanks" (Rom., Matt.)
　　　　　SP170
S2132　"You Who Are Thirsty" (Matt.)
　　　　　SP219
S2199　"Stay with Us" (Matt.)
S2215　"Cares Chorus" (Matt.)
　　　　　SP221
WS3094　"Come to Me" (Matt.)
M32　"Holy and Anointed One" (Matt.)
M73　"My Redeemer Lives" (Matt.)

Vocal Solos

"Bridal Prayer" (Gen., Ps.)
　　　V-8　　　p. 104
"A Song of Joy" (Ps., Matt.)
　　　V-11　　p. 2
"Just a Closer Walk With Thee" (Rom., Matt.)
　　　V-5(2)　p. 31
　　　V-8　　　p. 323
"He Shall Feed His Flock" from *Messiah* (Matt.)
　　　V-2
　　　V-8　　　p. 334
"A Song of Trust" (Matt.)
　　　V-4　　　p. 20
"I Will Sing of Thy Great Mercies" (Matt.)
　　　V-4　　　p. 43

Anthems

"I Will Arise and Go to Jesus" (Rom., Matt.)
arr. Robert W. Lehman; Paraclete Press PPM01220
SATB, *a cappella*

"Jesus Loves Me" (Matt.)
arr. Margaret R. Tucker; Choristers Guild CGA1065
Unison/two-part organ, opt. congregation and flute

"Come to Me" (Matt.)
Bradley Ellingboe; Choristers Guild CGA1050
SAT(B), piano

Other Suggestions

See July 2 for Independence Day ideas.
Visuals:
　O　　Spring, water jar, nose ring, bracelets, ring
　P　　Many-colored/gold robes, joy, bride/maids
　E　　Open Bible, manacles (closed/open), Christ
　G　　Children playing, marketplace, flute, John, Jesus,
　　　　eating/drinking, infants, burdens, yoke
Call to Worship: WSL65. Jesus said Come unto me (Matt.)
Canticle: UM646. "Canticle of Love" (Gen., Ps.)
Call to Prayer: WS3094. Come to Me (Matt.)
Prayer of Confession: BOW476 (Matt.)
Response: WS3110, verses 4-5 "By Grace We Have Been
　　　Saved" (Rom.)
Prayer: UM423. Finding Rest in God (Matt.)

JULY 13, 2014

Genesis 25:19-34

¹⁹ These are the descendants of Isaac, Abraham's son: Abraham was the father of Isaac, ²⁰and Isaac was forty years old when he married Rebekah, daughter of Bethuel the Aramean of Paddan-aram, sister of Laban the Aramean. ²¹Isaac prayed to the LORD for his wife, because she was barren; and the LORD granted his prayer, and his wife Rebekah conceived. ²²The children struggled together within her; and she said, 'If it is to be this way, why do I live?' So she went to inquire of the LORD. ²³And the LORD said to her,

"Two nations are in your womb,
    and two peoples born of you shall be divided;
the one shall be stronger than the other,
    the elder shall serve the younger."

²⁴When her time to give birth was at hand, there were twins in her womb. ²⁵The first came out red, all his body like a hairy mantle; so they named him Esau. ²⁶Afterwards his brother came out, with his hand gripping Esau's heel; so he was named Jacob. Isaac was sixty years old when she bore them.

²⁷ When the boys grew up, Esau was a skilful hunter, a man of the field, while Jacob was a quiet man, living in tents. ²⁸Isaac loved Esau, because he was fond of game; but Rebekah loved Jacob.

²⁹ Once when Jacob was cooking a stew, Esau came in from the field, and he was famished. ³⁰Esau said to Jacob, 'Let me eat some of that red stuff, for I am famished!' (Therefore he was called Edom.) ³¹Jacob said, 'First sell me your birthright.' ³²Esau said, 'I am about to die; of what use is a birthright to me?' ³³Jacob said, 'Swear to me first.' So he swore to him, and sold his birthright to Jacob. ³⁴Then Jacob gave Esau bread and lentil stew, and he ate and drank, and rose and went his way. Thus Esau despised his birthright. sold his birthright to Jacob. ³⁴Then Jacob gave Esau bread and lentil stew, and he ate and drank, and rose and went his way. Thus Esau despised his birthright.

¹⁹ These are the descendants of Isaac, Abraham's son: Abraham was the father of Isaac, ²⁰and Isaac was forty years old when he married Rebekah, daughter of Bethuel the Aramean of Paddan-aram, sister of Laban the Aramean. ²¹Isaac prayed to the LORD for his wife, because she was barren; and the LORD granted his prayer, and his wife Rebekah conceived. ²²The children struggled together within her; and she said, 'If it is to be this way, why do I live?' So she went to inquire of the LORD. ²³And the LORD said to her,

"Two nations are in your womb,
    and two peoples born of you shall be divided;
the one shall be stronger than the other,
    the elder shall serve the younger."

²⁴When her time to give birth was at hand, there were twins in her womb. ²⁵The first came out red, all his body like a hairy mantle; so they named him Esau. ²⁶Afterwards his brother came out, with his hand gripping Esau's heel; so he was named Jacob. Isaac was sixty years old when she bore them.

²⁷ When the boys grew up, Esau was a skilful hunter, a man of the field, while Jacob was a quiet man, living in tents. ²⁸Isaac loved Esau, because he was fond of game; but Rebekah loved Jacob.

²⁹ Once when Jacob was cooking a stew, Esau came in from the field, and he was famished. ³⁰Esau said to Jacob, 'Let me eat some of that red stuff, for I am famished!' (Therefore he was called Edom.) ³¹Jacob said, 'First sell me your birthright.' ³²Esau said, 'I am about to die; of what use is a birthright to me?' ³³Jacob said, 'Swear to me first.' So he swore to him, and sold his birthright to Jacob. ³⁴Then Jacob gave Esau bread and lentil stew, and he ate and drank, and rose and went his way. Thus Esau despised his birthright. sold his birthright to Jacob. ³⁴Then Jacob gave Esau bread and lentil stew, and he ate and drank, and rose and went his way. Thus Esau despised his birthright.

Psalm 119:105-112

¹⁰⁵   Your word is a lamp to my feet
        and a light to my path.
¹⁰⁶   I have sworn an oath and confirmed it,
            to observe your righteous ordinances.
¹⁰⁷   I am severely afflicted;
            give me life, O LORD, according to your word.
¹⁰⁸   Accept my offerings of praise, O LORD,
            and teach me your ordinances.
¹⁰⁹   I hold my life in my hand continually,
            but I do not forget your law.
¹¹⁰   The wicked have laid a snare for me,
            but I do not stray from your precepts.
¹¹¹   Your decrees are my heritage forever;
            they are the joy of my heart.
¹¹²   I incline my heart to perform your statutes
            forever, to the end.

Romans 8:1-11

¹There is therefore now no condemnation for those who are in Christ Jesus. ²For the law of the Spirit of life in Christ Jesus has set you free from the law of sin and of death. ³For God has done what the law, weakened by the flesh, could not do: by sending his own Son in the likeness of sinful flesh, and to deal with sin, he condemned sin in the flesh, ⁴so that the just requirement of the law might be fulfilled in us, who walk not according to the flesh but according to the Spirit. ⁵For those who live according to the flesh set their minds on the things of the flesh, but those who live according to the Spirit set their minds on the things of the Spirit. ⁶To set the mind on the flesh is death, but to set the mind on the Spirit is life and peace. ⁷For this reason the mind that is set on the flesh is hostile to God; it does not submit to God's law—indeed it cannot, ⁸and those who are in the flesh cannot please God.

⁹But you are not in the flesh; you are in the Spirit, since the Spirit of God dwells in you. Anyone who does not have the Spirit of Christ does not belong to him. ¹⁰But if Christ is in you, though the body is dead because of sin, the Spirit is life because of righteousness. ¹¹If the Spirit of him who raised Jesus from the dead dwells in you, he who raised Christ from the dead will give life to your mortal bodies also through his Spirit that dwells in you.

Matthew 13:1-9, 18-23

¹That same day Jesus went out of the house and sat beside the sea. ²Such great crowds gathered around him that he got into a boat and sat there, while the whole crowd stood on the beach. ³And he told them many things in parables, saying: "Listen! A sower went out to sow. ⁴And as he sowed, some seeds fell on the path, and the birds came and ate them up. ⁵Other seeds fell on rocky ground, where they did not have much soil, and they sprang up quickly, since they had no depth of soil. ⁶But when the sun rose, they were scorched; and since they had no root, they withered away. ⁷Other seeds fell among thorns, and the thorns grew up and choked them. ⁸Other seeds fell on good soil and brought forth grain, some a hundredfold, some sixty, some thirty. ⁹Let anyone with ears listen!" . . .

¹⁸ "Hear then the parable of the sower. ¹⁹When anyone hears the word of the kingdom and does not understand it, the evil one comes and snatches away what is sown in the heart; this is what was sown on the path. ²⁰As for what was sown on rocky ground, this is the one who hears the word and immediately receives it with joy; ²¹yet such a person has no root, but endures only for a while, and when trouble or persecution arises on account of the word, that person immediately falls away. ²²As for what was sown among thorns, this is the one who hears the word, but the cares of the world and the lure of wealth choke the word, and it yields nothing. ²³But as for what was sown on good soil, this is the one who hears the word and understands it, who indeed bears fruit and yields, in one case a hundredfold, in another sixty, and in another thirty."

COLOR: GREEN

5th SUNDAY AFTER PENTECOST

Primary Hymns and Songs for the Day

539   "O Spirit of the Living God" (Rom.) (O)
       H-3 Hbl-44; Chr-21; Desc-40; Org-40
       S-1 #131-132. Introduction and descant
393   "Spirit of the Living God" (Rom.)
       SP131; S-1#212 Vocal descant idea
601   "Thy Word Is a Lamp" (Ps., Matt.)
       SP183
583   "Sois la Semilla" ("You Are the Seed") (Matt.)
2076   "O Blessed Spring" (Matt.)
       H-3 Chr-200; Org-45
707   "Hymn of Promise" (Matt.) (C)
       H-3 Chr-112; Org-117
       S-1 #270. Descant

Additional Hymn Suggestions

100   "God, Whose Love Is Reigning O'er Us" (Gen.)
116   "The God of Abraham Praise" (Gen.)
427   "Where Cross the Crowded Ways of Life" (Gen.)
428   "For the Healing of the Nations" (Gen.) (C)
431   "Let There Be Peace on Earth" (Gen.)
443   "O God Who Shaped Creation" (Gen.)
475   "Come Down, O Love Divine" (Gen., Rom.)
2135   "When Cain Killed Abel" (Gen.)
2136   "Out of the Depths" (Gen.)
2170   "God Made From One Blood" (Gen.)
411   "Dear Lord, Lead Me Day by Day" (Ps.)
473   "Lead Me, Lord" (Ps.)
596   "Blessed Jesus, at Thy Word" (Ps., Matt.)
598   "O Word of God Incarnate" (Ps., Matt.) (O)
600   "Wonderful Words of Life" (Ps., Matt.) (O)
695   "O Lord, May Church and Home Combine" (Ps., Matt.)
2158   "Just a Closer Walk with Thee" (Ps., Rom., Matt.)
451   "Be Thou My Vision" (Ps., Rom.)
2214   "Lead Me, Guide Me" (Ps., Rom.)
2084   "Come, Let Us with Our Lord Arise" (Rom.)
3110   "By Grace We Have Been Saved" (Rom.)
57   "O For a Thousand Tongues to Sing" (Rom.)
98   "To God Be the Glory" (Rom.)
332   "Spirit of Faith, Come Down" (Rom.)
294   "Alas! and Did My Savior Bleed" (Rom.)
359   "Alas! and Did My Savior Bleed" (Rom.)
363   "And Can It Be that I Should Gain" (Rom.)
404   "Every Time I Feel the Spirit" (Rom.)
420   "Breathe on Me, Breath of God" (Rom., Matt.)
465   "Holy Spirit, Truth Divine" (Rom., Matt.)
109   "Creating God, Your Fingers Trace" (Matt.)
182   "Word of God, Come Down on Earth" (Matt.)
565   "Father, We Thank You" (Matt.)
650   "Give Me the Faith Which Can Remove" (Matt.) (C)
671   "Lord, Dismiss Us with Thy Blessing" (Matt.)
694   "Come, Ye Thankful People, Come" (Matt.)
732   "Come, We That Love the Lord" (Matt.) (O)
733   "Marching to Zion" (Matt.) (O)
2050   "Mothering God, You Gave Me Birth" (Matt., Communion)
2182   "When God Restored Our Common Life" (Matt.)
2190   "Bring Forth the Kingdom" (Matt.)

Additional Contemporary Suggestions

S2188   "The Family Prayer Song" (Gen.)
       M54
S2032   "My Life Is in You, Lord" (Ps.)
       SP204
S2165   "Cry of My Heart" (Ps.)
       M39
SP181   "God Is the Strength of My Heart" (Ps.)
M38   "In the Secret" ("I Want to Know You") (Ps.)
M30   "Knowing You" ("All I Once Held Dear") (Ps.)
M32   "Holy and Anointed One" (Ps.)
M107   "Show Me Your Ways" (Ps.)
WS3056   "Jesus, the Light of the World" (Ps.)
WS3112   "Breathe" (Ps., Rom.)
       M61
S2065   "More Precious than Silver" (Ps., Rom.)
       SP99
S2161   "To Know You More" (Ps., Rom.)
WS3001   "O For a Thousand Tongues to Sing" (Rom.)
WS3111   "Redemption" (Rom.)
UM99   "My Tribute" (Rom.)
       SP118; V-8 p. 5 Vocal solo
UM347   "Spirit Song" (Rom.)
       SP134
WS3001   "O For a Thousand Tongues to Sing (Rom.)
WS3004   "Step By Step" (Matt.)
       M51

Vocal Solos

"Just a Closer Walk With Thee" (Ps., Rom., Matt.)
     V-5(2)   p. 31
     V-8   p. 323
"Spirit of Faith Come Down" (Rom.)
     V-1   p. 43

Anthems

"Just a Closer Walk with Thee (Ps., Rom., Matt.)
arr. Graham Farrell; Hinshaw HPC7099
SATB, organ and trumpet solo

"The Best of Rooms" (Matt.)
Wood / arr. Wagner; H.W. Gray GCMRM05002
SATB, organ

Other Suggestions

Visuals:
   O   Wedding, prayer, newborn twins, birth certificate
   P   Open Bible, lamp, path, open hand, snare, Ps. 119:11
   E   Open manacles, Spirit symbols, open/closed Bibles
   G   Boat/sea, sower/sea, birds/sun/thorns, soil/grain
Matthew as drama can be enacted by one sower or a dozen persons, acting as sower, seeds, birds, and thorns.
Introit: M18. "Come and Behold Him" (Ps.)
Prayers: BOW461 and UM493 (Ps.)
Prayers: BOW508, BOW510 (Matt.)
Prayer of Thanksgiving: , BOW558 (Matt.)
Prayer: BOW514. For the Mind of Christ (Rom.)
Prayer: BOW522. For Purity (Ps., Rom.)

JULY 20, 2014

Genesis 28:10-19 a

[10]Jacob left Beer-sheba and went toward Haran. [11]He came to a certain place and stayed there for the night, because the sun had set. Taking one of the stones of the place, he put it under his head and lay down in that place. [12]And he dreamed that there was a ladder set up on the earth, the top of it reaching to heaven; and the angels of God were ascending and descending on it. [13]And the LORD stood beside him and said, "I am the LORD, the God of Abraham your father and the God of Isaac; the land on which you lie I will give to you and to your offspring; [14]and your offspring shall be like the dust of the earth, and you shall spread abroad to the west and to the east and to the north and to the south; and all the families of the earth shall be blessed in you and in your offspring. [15]Know that I am with you and will keep you wherever you go, and will bring you back to this land; for I will not leave you until I have done what I have promised you." [16]Then Jacob woke from his sleep and said, "Surely the LORD is in this place—and I did not know it!" [17]And he was afraid, and said, "How awesome is this place! This is none other than the house of God, and this is the gate of heaven."

[18]So Jacob rose early in the morning, and he took the stone that he had put under his head and set it up for a pillar and poured oil on the top of it. [19]He called that place Bethel;

Psalm 139:1-12, 23-24

1 O LORD, you have searched me and known me.
2 You know when I sit down and when I rise up;
    you discern my thoughts from far away.
3 You search out my path and my lying down,
    and are acquainted with all my ways.
4 Even before a word is on my tongue,
    O LORD, you know it completely.
5 You hem me in, behind and before,
    and lay your hand upon me.
6 Such knowledge is too wonderful for me;
    it is so high that I cannot attain it.
7 Where can I go from your spirit?
    Or where can I flee from your presence?
8 If I ascend to heaven, you are there;
    if I make my bed in Sheol, you are there.
9 If I take the wings of the morning
    and settle at the farthest limits of the sea,
10 even there your hand shall lead me,
    and your right hand shall hold me fast.
11 If I say, "Surely the darkness shall cover me,
    and the light around me become night,"
12 even the darkness is not dark to you;
    the night is as bright as the day,
    for darkness is as light to you.
. . . .
23 Search me, O God, and know my heart;
    test me and know my thoughts.
24 See if there is any wicked way in me,
    and lead me in the way everlasting.

Romans 8:12-25

[12]So then, brothers and sisters, we are debtors, not to the flesh, to live according to the flesh— [13]for if you live according to the flesh, you will die; but if by the Spirit you put to death the deeds of the body, you will live. [14]For all who are led by the Spirit of God are children of God. [15]For you did

not receive a spirit of slavery to fall back into fear, but you have received a spirit of adoption. When we cry, "Abba! Father!" [16]it is that very Spirit bearing witness with our spirit that we are children of God,

[17]and if children, then heirs, heirs of God and joint heirs with Christ—if, in fact, we suffer with him so that we may also be glorified with him.

[18]I consider that the sufferings of this present time are not worth comparing with the glory about to be revealed to us. [19]For the creation waits with eager longing for the revealing of the children of God; [20]for the creation was subjected to futility, not of its own will but by the will of the one who subjected it, in hope [21]that the creation itself will be set free from its bondage to decay and will obtain the freedom of the glory of the children of God. [22]We know that the whole creation has been groaning in labor pains until now; [23]and not only the creation, but we ourselves, who have the first fruits of the Spirit, groan inwardly while we wait for adoption, the redemption of our bodies. [24]For in hope we were saved. Now hope that is seen is not hope. For who hopes for what is seen? [25]But if we hope for what we do not see, we wait for it with patience.

Matthew 13:24-30, 36-43

[24]He put before them another parable: "The kingdom of heaven may be compared to someone who sowed good seed in his field; [25]but while everybody was asleep, an enemy came and sowed weeds among the wheat, and then went away. [26]So when the plants came up and bore grain, then the weeds appeared as well. [27]And the slaves of the householder came and said to him, 'Master, did you not sow good seed in your field? Where, then, did these weeds come from?' [28]He answered, 'An enemy has done this.' The slaves said to him, 'Then do you want us to go and gather them?' [29]But he replied, 'No; for in gathering the weeds you would uproot the wheat along with them. [30]Let both of them grow together until the harvest; and at harvest time I will tell the reapers, Collect the weeds first and bind them in bundles to be burned, but gather the wheat into my barn.' " . . .

[36]Then he left the crowds and went into the house. And his disciples approached him, saying, "Explain to us the parable of the weeds of the field." [37]He answered, "The one who sows the good seed is the Son of Man; [38]the field is the world, and the good seed are the children of the kingdom; the weeds are the children of the evil one, [39]and the enemy who sowed them is the devil; the harvest is the end of the age, and the reapers are angels. [40]Just as the weeds are collected and burned up with fire, so will it be at the end of the age. [41]The Son of Man will send his angels, and they will collect out of his kingdom all causes of sin and all evildoers, [42]and they will throw them into the furnace of fire, where there will be weeping and gnashing of teeth. [43]Then the righteous will shine like the sun in the kingdom of their Father. Let anyone with ears listen!"

COLOR: GREEN　　　　　　　　　　　　　　　　　**6th SUNDAY AFTER PENTECOST**

Primary Hymns and Songs for the Day

694　"Come, Ye Thankful People, Come" (Matt.) (O)
　　　　　H-3　Hbl-54; Chr-58; Desc-94; Org-137
　　　　　S-1　#302-303. Harm. with descant
418　"We Are Climbing Jacob's Ladder" (Gen.)
　　　　　H-3　Chr-205
　　　　　S-1　#187. Choral arr.
528　"Nearer, My God, to Thee" (Gen.)
2190　"Bring Forth the Kingdom" (Matt.)
384　"Love Divine, All Loves Excelling" (Rom.) (C)

Additional Hymn Suggestions

3009　"Praise God for This Holy Ground" (Gen.)
3129　"Touch the Earth Lightly" (Gen.)
3011　"All My Days" (Ps.)
109　"Creating God, Your Fingers Trace" (Ps.)
139　"Praise to the Lord, the Almighty" (Ps.)
206　"I Want to Walk as a Child of the Light" (Ps.)
411　"Dear Lord, Lead Me Day by Day" (Ps.)
663　"Savior, Again to Thy Dear Name" (Ps.)
2052　"The Lone, Wild Bird" (Ps.)
2172　"We Are Called" (Ps.)
2208　"Guide My Feet" (Ps.)
2214　"Lead Me, Guide Me" (Ps.)
2051　"I Was There to Hear Your Borning Cry" (Ps.,
　　　　　Baptism)
414　"Thou Hidden Love of God" (Ps., Rom.)
2046　"Womb of Life" (Ps., Rom., Communion)
2050　"Mothering God, You Gave Me Birth" (Ps., Rom.,
　　　　　Communion)
2117　"Spirit of God" (Ps., Rom.)
2123　"Loving Spirit" (Ps., Rom.)
2236　"Gather Us In" (Ps., Matt.) (O)
332　"Spirit of Faith, Come Down" (Rom.)
372　"How Can We Sinners Know" (Rom.)
388　"O Come and Dwell in Me" (Rom.)
404　"Every Time I Feel the Spirit" (Rom.)
533　"We Shall Overcome" (Rom.)
546　"The Church's One Foundation" (Rom.)
2019　"Holy" ("Santo") (Rom.)
2121　"O Holy Spirit, Root of Life" (Rom.)
2248　"Baptized in Water" (Rom., Baptism)
3018　"Creation Sings" (Rom.)
3020　"God of the Bible" (Rom.)
3127　"I Have a Dream" (Rom.)
275　"The Kingdom of God" (Matt.)
563　"Father, We Thank You" (Matt.)
583　"Sois la Semilla" ("You Are the Seed") (Matt.)
2060　"God the Sculptor of the Mountains" (Matt.)
2241　"The Spirit Sends Us Forth to Serve" (Matt.)
2243　"We All Are One in Mission" (Matt.)
2262　"Let Us Offer to the Father" (Matt.)

Additional Contemporary Suggestions

UM328　"Surely the Presence of the Lord" (Gen.)
　　　　　SP243; S-2, #200 Stanzas for soloist
S2272　"Holy Ground" (Gen.)
　　　　　SP86
S2163　"He Who Began a Good Work in You" (Gen.)
　　　　　SP180
WS3042　"Shout to the North" (Gen.)
　　　　　M99

WS3132　"House of God" (Gen.)
WS3019　"Bidden, Unbidden" (Ps.)
WS3034　"God of Wonders" (Ps.)
　　　　　M80
S2139　"Oh, I Know the Lord's Laid His Hands on Me"
　　　　　(Ps.)
SP2　"Ah, Lord God" (Ps.)
SP40　"God Will Make a Way" (Ps.)
M38　"In the Secret" ("I Want to Know You") (Ps.)
M85　"The Potter's Hand" (Ps.)
M101　"These Hands" (Ps.)
M109　"He Knows My Name" (Ps.)
M108　"Lead Me, Lord" (Ps.)
UM393　"Spirit of the Living God" (Rom.)
　　　　　SP131; S-1#212 Vocal descant idea
S2019　"Holy" ("Santo") (Rom.)
S2039　"Holy, Holy" (Rom.)
　　　　　SP141
WS3092　"Come, Holy Spirit" (Rom.)
UM143　"On Eagle's Wings" (Matt.)
　　　　　S-2　#143 Stanzas for soloist
WS3186　"Days of Elijah" (Matt.)
　　　　　M139

Vocal Solos

"When I Lay My Burden Down" (Gen.)
　　V-7　　　p. 76
"Borning Cry" (Matt.)
　　V-5(1)　　p. 10
"Wings Like Eagles" (Matt.)
　　V-11　　p. 9
"Religion Is a Fortune" (Matt.)
　　V-7　　　p. 72

Anthems

"All My Days" (Ps.)
Mark A. Miller; Abingdon Press 0687493013
SATB, piano

"Even So Lord Jesus Quickly Come" (Matt.)
Paul Manz; Morningstar 50-0900
TTBB, *a cappella* (SATB also available)

Other Suggestions

Visuals:
　O　Night, stone, ladder, angels, dust, gate, oil
　P　Sit/stand, path, bed, hand, wings, sea, light/dark
　E　Children, fear, adoption papers, will, fruit, labor
　G　Seed, bundle of weeds/wheat, scythe, harvest/field,
　　　　angels, fire, Matt. 13:43, sun
Greeting: BOW450 (Gen.)
Call to Prayer: WS3092. "Come, Holy Spirit" (Rom.)
Prayer of Confession: BOW480 (Ps.)
Prayer of Confession: BOW484 or BOW494 (Rom.)
Litany: WSL58. Worriers of the world, unite (Gen., Rom.)
Canticle: UM205. "Canticle of Light and Darkness" (Ps.)
Sung Prayer: WS3115. "Covenant Prayer" (Rom.)
Blessing: BOW562 (Gen.)

JULY 27, 2014

Genesis 29:15-28

¹⁵Then Laban said to Jacob, "Because you are my kinsman, should you therefore serve me for nothing? Tell me, what shall your wages be?" ¹⁶Now Laban had two daughters; the name of the elder was Leah, and the name of the younger was Rachel. ¹⁷Leah's eyes were lovely, and Rachel was graceful and beautiful. ¹⁸Jacob loved Rachel; so he said, "I will serve you seven years for your younger daughter Rachel." ¹⁹Laban said, "It is better that I give her to you than that I should give her to any other man; stay with me." ²⁰So Jacob served seven years for Rachel, and they seemed to him but a few days because of the love he had for her. ²¹Then Jacob said to Laban, "Give me my wife that I may go in to her, for my time is completed." ²²So Laban gathered together all the people of the place, and made a feast. ²³But in the evening he took his daughter Leah and brought her to Jacob; and he went in to her. ²⁴(Laban gave his maid Zilpah to his daughter Leah to be her maid.) ²⁵When morning came, it was Leah! And Jacob said to Laban, "What is this you have done to me? Did I not serve with you for Rachel? Why then have you deceived me?" ²⁶Laban said, "This is not done in our country—giving the younger before the firstborn. ²⁷Complete the week of this one, and we will give you the other also in return for serving me another seven years." ²⁸Jacob did so, and completed her week; then Laban gave him his daughter Rachel as a wife.

Psalm 105:1-11, 45b

¹ O give thanks to the LORD, call on his name,
      make known his deeds among the peoples.
² Sing to him, sing praises to him;
      tell of all his wonderful works.
³ Glory in his holy name;
      let the hearts of those who seek the LORD rejoice.
⁴ Seek the LORD and his strength;
      seek his presence continually.
⁵ Remember the wonderful works he has done,
      his miracles, and the judgments he uttered,
⁶ O offspring of his servant Abraham,
      children of Jacob, his chosen ones.
⁷ He is the LORD our God;
      his judgments are in all the earth.
⁸ He is mindful of his covenant forever,
      of the word that he commanded, for a thousand
         generations,
⁹ the covenant that he made with Abraham,
      his sworn promise to Isaac,
¹⁰ which he confirmed to Jacob as a statute,
      to Israel as an everlasting covenant,
¹¹ saying, "To you I will give the land of Canaan
      as your portion for an inheritance."
. . . .
⁴⁵ Praise the LORD!

Romans 8:26-39

²⁶Likewise the Spirit helps us in our weakness; for we do not know how to pray as we ought, but that very Spirit intercedes with sighs too deep for words. ²⁷And God, who searches the heart, knows what is the mind of the Spirit, because the Spirit intercedes for the saints according to the will of God.

²⁸We know that all things work together for good for those who love God, who are called according to his purpose.

²⁹For those whom he foreknew he also predestined to be conformed to the image of his Son, in order that he might be the firstborn within a large family. ³⁰And those whom he predestined he also called; and those whom he called he also justified; and those whom he justified he also glorified.

³¹What then are we to say about these things? If God is for us, who is against us? ³²He who did not withhold his own Son, but gave him up for all of us, will he not with him also give us everything else? ³³Who will bring any charge against God's elect? It is God who justifies. ³⁴Who is to condemn? It is Christ Jesus, who died, yes, who was raised, who is at the right hand of God, who indeed intercedes for us. ³⁵Who will separate us from the love of Christ? Will hardship, or distress, or persecution, or famine, or nakedness, or peril, or sword? ³⁶As it is written,

"For your sake we are being killed all day long;
   we are accounted as sheep to be slaughtered."

³⁷No, in all these things we are more than conquerors through him who loved us. ³⁸For I am convinced that neither death, nor life, nor angels, nor rulers, nor things present, nor things to come, nor powers, ³⁹nor height, nor depth, nor anything else in all creation, will be able to separate us from the love of God in Christ Jesus our Lord.

Matthew 13:31-33, 44-52

³¹He put before them another parable: "The kingdom of heaven is like a mustard seed that someone took and sowed in his field; ³²it is the smallest of all the seeds, but when it has grown it is the greatest of shrubs and becomes a tree, so that the birds of the air come and make nests in its branches." ³³He told them another parable: "The kingdom of heaven is like yeast that a woman took and mixed in with three measures of flour until all of it was leavened." . . .

⁴⁴"The kingdom of heaven is like treasure hidden in a field, which someone found and hid; then in his joy he goes and sells all that he has and buys that field.

⁴⁵"Again, the kingdom of heaven is like a merchant in search of fine pearls; ⁴⁶on finding one pearl of great value, he went and sold all that he had and bought it.

⁴⁷"Again, the kingdom of heaven is like a net that was thrown into the sea and caught fish of every kind; ⁴⁸when it was full, they drew it ashore, sat down, and put the good into baskets but threw out the bad. ⁴⁹So it will be at the end of the age. The angels will come out and separate the evil from the righteous ⁵⁰and throw them into the furnace of fire, where there will be weeping and gnashing of teeth.

⁵¹"Have you understood all this?" They answered, "Yes." ⁵²And he said to them, "Therefore every scribe who has been trained for the kingdom of heaven is like the master of a household who brings out of his treasure what is new and what is old."

COLOR: GREEN   **7th SUNDAY AFTER PENTECOST**

Primary Hymns and Songs for the Day
540   "I Love Thy Kingdom, Lord" (Matt.) (O)
           H-3 Hbl-53; Chr-167; Desc-97; Org-147
           S-1 #311. Descant and harmonization
2190   "Bring Forth the Kingdom" (Matt.)
405   "Seek Ye First" (Matt.)
           SP182
730   "O Day of God, Draw Nigh" (Matt., Ps.) (C)
           H-3 Hbl-79; Chr-141; Desc-95; Org-143
           S-1 #306-308. Various treatments

Additional Hymn Suggestions
643   "When Love Is Found" (Gen.)
124   "Seek the Lord" (Ps.)
2001   "We Sing to You, O God" (Ps.)
2216   "When We Are Called to Sing Your Praise" (Ps.)
3012   "When Words Alone Cannot Express" (Ps.)
2061   "Praise Our God Above" (Ps., Matt.)
79   "Holy God, We Praise Thy Name" (Rom.)
141   "Children of the Heavenly Father" (Rom.)
169   "In Thee Is Gladness" (Rom.)
178   "Hope of the World" (Rom.) (C)
363   "And Can It Be that I Should Gain" (Rom.)
419   "I Am Thine, O Lord" (Rom.)
480   "O Love That Wilt Not Let Me Go" (Rom.)
492   "Prayer Is the Soul's Sincere Desire" (Rom.)
517   "By Gracious Powers" (Rom.)
544   "Like the Murmur of the Dove's Song" (Rom.)
551   "Awake, O Sleeper" (Rom.)
566   "Blest Be the Dear Uniting Love" (Rom.)
627   "O the Depth of Love Divine" (Rom., Communion)
2121   "O Holy Spirit, Root of Life" (Rom.)
2140   "Since Jesus Came Into My Heart" (Rom.)
2160   "Into My Heart" (Rom.)
2205   "The Fragrance of Christ" (Rom.)
2262   "Let Us Offer to the Father" (Rom., Matt.)
3039   "Jesus, the Saving Name" (Rom.)
3107   "Just a Little Talk with Jesus" (Rom.)
3115   "Covenant Prayer" (Rom.)
275   "The Kingdom of God" (Matt.)
532   "Jesus, Priceless Treasure" (Matt.)
583   "Sois la Semilla" ("You Are the Seed") (Matt.)
694   "Come, Ye Thankful People, Come" (Matt.)
2241   "The Spirit Sends Us Forth to Serve" (Matt.)
2243   "We All Are One in Mission" (Matt.)

Additional Contemporary Suggestions
WS3003   "How Great Is Our God" (Ps.)
S2195   "In the Lord I'll Be Ever Thankful" (Ps.)
S2144   "Someone Asked the Question" (Ps., Rom.)
UM333   "I'm Goin'a Sing When the Spirit Says Sing" (Rom.)
S2165   "Cry of My Heart" (Rom.)
          M39
S2203   "In His Time" (Rom.)
S2152   "Change My Heart, O God" (Rom.)
          SP195
S2073   "Celebrate Love" (Rom.)
S2141   "There's a Song" (Rom.)
WS3027   "Hallelujah" ("Your Love Is Amazing") (Rom.)
          M118
WS3042   "Shout to the North" (Rom.)
          M99

WS3092   "Come, Holy Spirit" (Rom.)
WS3106   "Your Grace Is Enough (Rom.)
          M191
SP50   "Think about His Love" (Rom.)
M25   "No Greater Love" (Rom.)
M26   "The Power of Your Love" (Rom.)
M63   "I Could Sing of Your Love Forever" (Rom.)
M107   "Show Me Your Ways" (Rom.)
M164   "Good to Me" (Rom.)
M167   "The Happy Song" (Rom.)
WS3040   "You Are My All in All" (Rom., Matt.)
          SP220
S2065   "More Precious than Silver" (Matt.)
          SP99
M33   "Jesus, You Are My Life" (Matt.)
M115   "When It's All Been Said and Done" (Matt.)
WS3186   "Days of Elijah" (Matt.)
          M139

Vocal Solos
"A Song of Joy" (Ps.)
    V-11   p. 2
"If God Be For Us" (Rom.)
    V-2
"I Am His, and He Is Mine" (Rom.)
    V-8   p. 348

Anthems
"By Gracious Powers" (Rom.)
William B. Roberts; Augsburg Fortress 9780800678210
SATB, organ

"The Kingdom" (Matt.)
Andre Thomas; Hinshaw HMC-1307
SATB, keyboard

Other Suggestions
Visuals:
    O   Young lovers, no. 7, feast, engagement
    P   Singing, hearts, covenant, praise
    E   Prayer, Spirit, heart, Rom. 8:28, 31, 38, Jesus, newborn, cross, disaster, love
    G   Mustard seed/shrub, birds/nest, yeast/flour, treasure, pearl, net/fish/baskets, fire, new/old
Greeting: BOW452 (Ps.)
Opening Prayer: BOW463 (Rom.)
Canticle: UM406. "Canticle of Prayer" (Rom.)
Call to Prayer: WS3091. "Come, Holy Spirit" (Rom.)
Call to Prayer: S2273, BOW187. "Jesus, We Are Here" (Rom.)
Prayer of Confession: BOW480 or BOW488 (Rom.)
Prayer: S2201. "Prayers of the People" (Rom., Matt.)
Affirmation of Faith: UM887 (Rom.)
Affirmation of Faith: WSL76 or WSL77 (Rom.)

AUGUST 3, 2014

Genesis 32:22-31

[22]The same night he got up and took his two wives, his two maids, and his eleven children, and crossed the ford of the Jabbok. [23]He took them and sent them across the stream, and likewise everything that he had. [24]Jacob was left alone; and a man wrestled with him until daybreak. [25]When the man saw that he did not prevail against Jacob, he struck him on the hip socket; and Jacob's hip was put out of joint as he wrestled with him. [26]Then he said, "Let me go, for the day is breaking." But Jacob said, "I will not let you go, unless you bless me." [27]So he said to him, "What is your name?" And he said, "Jacob." [28]Then the man said, "You shall no longer be called Jacob, but Israel, for you have striven with God and with humans, and have prevailed." [29]Then Jacob asked him, "Please tell me your name." But he said, "Why is it that you ask my name?" And there he blessed him. [30]So Jacob called the place Peniel, saying, "For I have seen God face to face, and yet my life is preserved." [31]The sun rose upon him as he passed Penuel, limping because of his hip.

Psalm 17:1-7, 15

[1] Hear a just cause, O Lord; attend to my cry;
    give ear to my prayer from lips free of deceit.
[2] From you let my vindication come;
    let your eyes see the right.
[3] If you try my heart, if you visit me by night,
    if you test me, you will find no wickedness in me;
    my mouth does not transgress.
[4] As for what others do, by the word of your lips
    I have avoided the ways of the violent.
[5] My steps have held fast to your paths;
    my feet have not slipped.
[6] I call upon you, for you will answer me, O God;
    incline your ear to me, hear my words.
[7] Wondrously show your steadfast love,
    O savior of those who seek refuge
    from their adversaries at your right hand.
. . . .
[15] As for me, I shall behold your face in righteousness;
    when I awake I shall be satisfied, beholding
        your likeness.

Romans 9:1-5

[1]I am speaking the truth in Christ—I am not lying; my conscience confirms it by the Holy Spirit— [2]I have great sorrow and unceasing anguish in my heart. [3]For I could wish that I myself were accursed and cut off from Christ for the sake of my own people, my kindred according to the flesh. [4]They are Israelites, and to them belong the adoption, the glory, the covenants, the giving of the law, the worship, and the promises; [5]to them belong the patriarchs, and from them, according to the flesh, comes the Messiah, who is over all, God blessed forever. Amen.

Matthew 14:13-21

[13]Now when Jesus heard this, he withdrew from there in a boat to a deserted place by himself. But when the crowds heard it, they followed him on foot from the towns. [14]When he went ashore, he saw a great crowd; and he had compassion for them and cured their sick. [15]When it was evening, the disciples came to him and said, "This is a deserted place, and the hour is now late; send the crowds away so that they may go into the villages and buy food for themselves." [16]Jesus said to them, "They need not go away; you give them something to eat." [17]They replied, "We have nothing here but five loaves and two fish." [18]And he said, "Bring them here to me." [19]Then he ordered the crowds to sit down on the grass. Taking the five loaves and the two fish, he looked up to heaven, and blessed and broke the loaves, and gave them to the disciples, and the disciples gave them to the crowds. [20]And all ate and were filled; and they took up what was left over of the broken pieces, twelve baskets full. [21]And those who ate were about five thousand men, besides women and children.

COLOR: GREEN　　　　　　　　　　　　　　　　　　　**8th SUNDAY AFTER PENTECOST**

Primary Hymns and Songs for the Day

386	"Come, O Thou Traveler Unknown" (Gen.) (O)
	S-2 #33-37. Various treatments
480	"O Love That Wilt Not Let Me Go" (Gen.)
	H-3 Chr-146; Org-142
599	"Break Thou the Bread of Life (Matt., Communion)
	H-3 Chr-44; Org-15
2260	"Let Us Be Bread" (Matt., Communion) (C)

Additional Hymn Suggestions

111	"How Can We Name a Love" (Gen.)
105	"God of Many Names" (Gen.)
113	"Source and Sovereign, Rock and Cloud" (Gen.)
116	"The God of Abraham Praise" (Gen.)
185	"When Morning Gilds the Skies" (Gen.)
341	"I Sought the Lord" (Gen.)
451	"Be Thou My Vision" (Gen.) (O)
623	"Here, O My Lord, I See Thee" (Gen., Communion)
2196	"We Walk By Faith" (Gen.)
479	"Jesus, Lover of My Soul" (Gen., Ps.)
672	"God Be With You Till We Meet Again" (Gen., Matt.) (C)
496	"Sweet Hour of Prayer" (Gen., Matt.)
498	"My Prayer Rises to Heaven" (Ps.)
351	"Pass Me Not, O Gentle Savior" (Ps.)
2001	"We Sing to You, O God" (Ps.)
2117	"Spirit of God" (Ps.)
132	"All My Hope Is Firmly Grounded" (Ps., Rom.)
142	"If Thou But Suffer God to Guide Thee" (Rom.)
374	"Standing on the Promises" (Rom.)
465	"Holy Spirit, Truth Divine" (Rom.)
589	"The Church of Christ in Every Age" (Rom.)
344	"Lord, You Have Come to the Lakeshore" (Matt.)
348	"Softly and Tenderly, Jesus Is Calling" (Matt.)
358	"Dear Lord and Father of Mankind" (Matt.)
614	"For the Bread Which You Have Broken" (Matt., Communion)
616	"Come, Sinners, to the Gospel Feast" (Matt., Communion)
618	"Let Us Break Bread Together" (Matt., Communion)
624	"Bread of the World" (Matt., Communion)
631	"O Food to Pilgrims Given" (Matt., Communion)
634	"Now Let Us from This Table Rise" (Matt., Communion)
2126	"All Who Hunger" (Matt.)
2202	"Come Away with Me" (Matt.)
2269	"Come, Share the Lord" (Matt., Communion)
3149	"A Place at the Table" (Matt., Communion)

Additional Contemporary Suggestions

UM405	"Seek Ye First" (Gen.)
	SP182
M70	"No Higher Calling" (Gen.)
M83	"Just Let Me Say" (Gen.)
SP185	"The Steadfast Love of the Lord" (Gen., Ps.)
M189	"Your Love, Oh Lord" (Gen., Ps.)
WS3027	"Hallelujah" ("Your Love Is Amazing") (Ps.)
	M118
S2002	"I Will Call Upon the Lord" (Ps.)
	SP224

S2200	"O Lord, Hear My Prayer" (Ps.)
S2071	"Jesus, Name Above All Names" (Rom.)
	SP76
WS3023	"Forever" (Ps., Rom.)
	M68
M77	"Above All" (Rom.)
UM347	"Spirit Song" (Matt., Communion)
	SP134
S2273	"Jesus, We Are Here" (Matt.)
S2132	"You Who Are Thirsty" (Matt., Communion)
	SP219

Vocal Solos

"Come, O Thou Traveler Unknown" (Gen.)
V-1	p. 21
V-9	p. 44

"A Contrite Heart" (Ps.)
V-4	p. 10

"Softly and Tenderly" (Matt.)
V-5(3)	p. 52

"Let Us Break Bread Together" (Matt., Communion)
V-6	p. 38

Anthems

"Come O Thou Traveler Unknown" (Gen.)
Robert H. Young; Alliance Music AMP 0498
SATB, *a cappella*

"God Bestows on Each One a Name" (Gen.)
Fred Gramann; E.C. Schirmer #7330
SATB, *a cappella*

Other Suggestions

Visuals:

O	River ford, wrestling, hip, cane, Gen. 32:26b, name
P	Prayer, heart, night, feet/path, listening
E	Broken heart, salvation history, Christ
G	Boat, healing, loaves/ 2 fish, 12 baskets, 5,000

Greeting: BOW455 (Matt.)
Opening Prayer: BOW462 (Gen.)
Prayer of Confession: BOW485 (Matt.)
Response: S2207. "Lord, Listen to Your Children" (Ps.)
Prayer: UM477. For Illumination (Gen.)
Prayer: BOW510. For Discernment (Gen.)
Poem: UM387. Come, O Thou Traveler Unknown (Gen.)
Prayer: WSL55. Almighty God, you sustained (Matt.)
Offertory Prayer: WSL134. Loving Father, you powerfully fill (Matt.)
Response: UM614 or 615. "For the Bread Which You Have Broken" (Matt., Communion)
Benediction: WSL167. Go! Never stop going out (Matt.)

127

AUGUST 10, 2014

Genesis 37:1-4, 12-28

¹Jacob settled in the land where his father had lived as an alien, the land of Canaan. ²This is the story of the family of Jacob. Joseph, being seventeen years old, was shepherding the flock with his brothers; he was a helper to the sons of Bilhah and Zilpah, his father's wives; and Joseph brought a bad report of them to their father.

³Now Israel loved Joseph more than any other of his children, because he was the son of his old age; and he had made him a long robe with sleeves. ⁴But when his brothers saw that their father loved him more than all his brothers, they hated him, and could not speak peaceably to him. . . .

¹²Now his brothers went to pasture their father's flock near Shechem. ¹³And Israel said to Joseph, "Are not your brothers pasturing the flock at Shechem? Come, I will send you to them." He answered, "Here I am." ¹⁴So he said to him, "Go now, see if it is well with your brothers and with the flock; and bring word back to me." So he sent him from the valley of Hebron.

He came to Shechem, ¹⁵and a man found him wandering in the fields; the man asked him, "What are you seeking?" ¹⁶"I am seeking my brothers," he said; "tell me, please, where they are pasturing the flock." ¹⁷The man said, "They have gone away, for I heard them say, 'Let us go to Dothan.'" So Joseph went after his brothers, and found them at Dothan. ¹⁸They saw him from a distance, and before he came near to them, they conspired to kill him. ¹⁹They said to one another, "Here comes this dreamer. ²⁰Come now, let us kill him and throw him into one of the pits; then we shall say that a wild animal has devoured him, and we shall see what will become of his dreams." ²¹But when Reuben heard it, he delivered him out of their hands, saying, "Let us not take his life." ²²Reuben said to them, "Shed no blood; throw him into this pit here in the wilderness, but lay no hand on him" — that he might rescue him out of their hand and restore him to his father. ²³So when Joseph came to his brothers, they stripped him of his robe, the long robe with sleeves that he wore; ²⁴and they took him and threw him into a pit. The pit was empty; there was no water in it.

²⁵Then they sat down to eat; and looking up they saw a caravan of Ishmaelites coming from Gilead, with their camels carrying gum, balm, and resin, on their way to carry it down to Egypt. ²⁶Then Judah said to his brothers, "What profit is it if we kill our brother and conceal his blood? ²⁷Come, let us sell him to the Ishmaelites, and not lay our hands on him, for he is our brother, our own flesh." And his brothers agreed. ²⁸When some Midianite traders passed by, they drew Joseph up, lifting him out of the pit, and sold him to the Ishmaelites for twenty pieces of silver. And they took Joseph to Egypt.

Psalm 105:1-6, 16-22, 45b

¹ O give thanks to the LORD, call on his name,
      make known his deeds among the peoples.
² Sing to him, sing praises to him;
      tell of all his wonderful works.
³ Glory in his holy name;
      let the hearts of those who seek the LORD rejoice.
⁴ Seek the LORD and his strength;
      seek his presence continually.
⁵ Remember the wonderful works he has done,
      his miracles, and the judgments he uttered,
⁶ O offspring of his servant Abraham,
      children of Jacob, his chosen ones.
. . . .
¹⁶ When he summoned famine against the land,
      and broke every staff of bread,
¹⁷ he had sent a man ahead of them,

Joseph, who was sold as a slave.
¹⁸ His feet were hurt with fetters,
      his neck was put in a collar of iron;
¹⁹ until what he had said came to pass,
      the word of the LORD kept testing him.
²⁰ The king sent and released him;
      the ruler of the peoples set him free.
²¹ He made him lord of his house,
      and ruler of all his possessions,
²² to instruct his officials at his pleasure,
      and to teach his elders wisdom.
. . . .
⁴⁵ Praise the LORD!

Romans 10:5-15

⁵Moses writes concerning the righteousness that comes from the law, that "the person who does these things will live by them." ⁶But the righteousness that comes from faith says, "Do not say in your heart, 'Who will ascend into heaven?'" (that is, to bring Christ down) ⁷or 'Who will descend into the abyss?'" (that is, to bring Christ up from the dead). ⁸But what does it say?
      "The word is near you,
         on your lips and in your heart"
(that is, the word of faith that we proclaim); ⁹because if you confess with your lips that Jesus is Lord and believe in your heart that God raised him from the dead, you will be saved. ¹⁰For one believes with the heart and so is justified, and one confesses with the mouth and so is saved. ¹¹The scripture says, "No one who believes in him will be put to shame." ¹²For there is no distinction between Jew and Greek; the same Lord is Lord of all and is generous to all who call on him. ¹³For, "Everyone who calls on the name of the Lord shall be saved."

¹⁴But how are they to call on one in whom they have not believed? And how are they to believe in one of whom they have never heard? And how are they to hear without someone to proclaim him? ¹⁵And how are they to proclaim him unless they are sent? As it is written, "How beautiful are the feet of those who bring good news!"

Matthew 14:22-33

²²Immediately he made the disciples get into the boat and go on ahead to the other side, while he dismissed the crowds. ²³And after he had dismissed the crowds, he went up the mountain by himself to pray. When evening came, he was there alone, ²⁴but by this time the boat, battered by the waves, was far from the land, for the wind was against them. ²⁵And early in the morning he came walking toward them on the sea. ²⁶But when the disciples saw him walking on the sea, they were terrified, saying, "It is a ghost!" And they cried out in fear. ²⁷But immediately Jesus spoke to them and said, "Take heart, it is I; do not be afraid."

²⁸Peter answered him, "Lord, if it is you, command me to come to you on the water." ²⁹He said, "Come." So Peter got out of the boat, started walking on the water, and came toward Jesus. ³⁰But when he noticed the strong wind, he became frightened, and beginning to sink, he cried out, "Lord, save me!" ³¹Jesus immediately reached out his hand and caught him, saying to him, "You of little faith, why did you doubt?" ³²When they got into the boat, the wind ceased. ³³And those in the boat worshiped him, saying, "Truly you are the Son of God."

COLOR: GREEN

9th SUNDAY AFTER PENTECOST

Primary Hymns and Songs for the Day

512	"Stand By Me" (Matt.) (O)
	H-3 Chr-177
141	"Children of the Heavenly Father" (Gen., Ps.)
	H-3 Chr-46; Desc-102
	S-2 #180-185. Various treatments
2019	"Holy" ("Santo)" (Rom.)
593	"Here I Am, Lord" (Gen., Matt., Rom.) (C)
	H-3 Chr-97; Org-54

Additional Hymn Suggestions

127	"Guide Me, O Thou Great Jehovah" (Gen.) (O)
533	"We Shall Overcome" (Gen.)
2135	"When Cain Killed Abel" (Gen.)
139	"Praise to the Lord, the Almighty" (Gen., Ps.)
505	"When Our Confidence Is Shaken" (Gen., Matt., Rom.)
3012	"When Words Alone Cannot Express" (Ps.)
114	"Many Gifts, One Spirit" (Rom.)
156	"I Love to Tell the Story" (Rom.)
168	"At the Name of Jesus" (Rom.)
552	"Here, O Lord, Your Servants Gather" (Rom., Communion)
649	"How Shall They Hear the Word of God" (Rom.)
337	"Only Trust Him" (see especially stanza 1) (Rom.)
357	"Just As I Am" (Rom.)
417	"O For a Heart to Praise My God" (Rom.)
569	"We've a Story to Tell to the Nations" (Rom.) (C)
714	"I Know Whom I Have Believed" (Rom.)
2140	"Since Jesus Came Into My Heart" (Rom.)
2160	"Into My Heart" (Rom.)
2196	"We Walk by Faith" (Rom., Matt.)
2211	"Faith Is Patience in the Night" (Rom., Matt.)
188	"Christ Is the World's Light" (Rom., Matt.)
529	"How Firm a Foundation" (Rom., Matt.)
129	"Give to the Winds Thy Fears" (Matt.)
152	"I Sing the Almighty Power of God" (Matt.)
179	"O Sing a Song of Bethlehem" (Matt.)
277	"Tell Me the Stories of Jesus" (Matt.)
341	"I Sought the Lord" (Matt.)
358	"Dear Lord and Father of Mankind" (Matt.)
380	"There's Within My Heart a Melody" (Matt.)
476	"Lonely the Boat" (Matt.)
479	"Jesus, Lover of My Soul" (Matt.)
509	"Jesus, Savior, Pilot Me" (Matt.)
2107	"Wade in the Water" (Matt.)
2151	"I'm So Glad Jesus Lifted Me" (Matt.)
2202	"Come Away with Me" (Matt.)
2218	"You Are Mine" (Matt.)
3101	"Love Lifted Me" (Matt.)

Additional Contemporary Suggestions

S2036	"Give Thanks" (Ps.)
	SP170
S2144	"Someone Asked the Question" (Ps.)
S2195	"In the Lord I'll Be Ever Thankful" (Ps.)
WS3003	"How Great Is Our God" (Ps.)
WS3004	"Step By Step" (Ps., Matt.)
	M51
WS3023	"Forever" (Ps., Matt.)
	M68
S2154	"Please Enter My Heart, Hosanna" (Rom.)

UM177	"He Is Lord" (Rom.)
	SP122
UM620	"One Bread, One Body" (Rom., Communion)
S2056	"God Is So Good" (Rom.)
WS3026	"God Is Good All the Time" (Rom.)
	M45
WS3176	"Come, Now Is the Time to Worship" (Rom.)
	M56
M111	"The Heavens Shall Declare" (Rom.)
M140	"We Will Dance" (Rom.)
SP64	"Our God Reigns" (Rom.)
M7	"I Believe In Jesus" (Rom., Matt.)
S2215	"Cares Chorus" (Matt.)
	SP221
WS3105	"In Christ Alone" (Matt.)
	M138

Vocal Solos

"Here I Am" (Gen.)
  V-11   p. 19
"Jesus, Lover of My Soul" (Matt.)
  V-1   p. 37
"Wade in the Water" (Matt., Baptism)
  V-5(2)   p. 46

Anthems

"O Lord Increase My Faith" (Matt.)
Orlando Gibbons; E.C. Schirmer #375SATB
a cappella

"Lonely the Boat" (Matt.)
arr. William Rose; Abingdon Press 0687495199
SATB, piano

Other Suggestions

Visuals:
  O   Staff, colorful robe, pit, caravan, 20 coins, Egypt
  P   Singing, hearts, famine, open manacles, iron collar
  E   Christ, heart, speaking, Rom. 10:8*b*, 13, 15*b*, feet
  G   Boat, mountain, prayer, storm/sea, Jesus/Peter/water, Matt. 14:30*b*, 31*b*, 33*b*

Greeting: BOW457 (Matt.)
Opening Prayer: BOW460 (Rom., Matt.) or BOW464 (Gen.)
Prayer of Confession: BOW492 or BOW493 (Gen., Rom.)
Call to Prayer: UM499. "Serenity" (Matt.)
Prayer: BOW500 or BOW524 (Gen., Matt.)
For more prayers and litanies, see *The Abingdon Worship Annual 2014.*

AUGUST 17, 2014

Genesis 45:1-15

[1]Then Joseph could no longer control himself before all those who stood by him, and he cried out, "Send everyone away from me." So no one stayed with him when Joseph made himself known to his brothers. [2]And he wept so loudly that the Egyptians heard it, and the household of Pharaoh heard it. [3]Joseph said to his brothers, "I am Joseph. Is my father still alive?" But his brothers could not answer him, so dismayed were they at his presence.

[4]Then Joseph said to his brothers, "Come closer to me." And they came closer. He said, "I am your brother, Joseph, whom you sold into Egypt. [5]And now do not be distressed, or angry with yourselves, because you sold me here; for God sent me before you to preserve life. [6]For the famine has been in the land these two years; and there are five more years in which there will be neither plowing nor harvest. [7]God sent me before you to preserve for you a remnant on earth, and to keep alive for you many survivors. [8]So it was not you who sent me here, but God; he has made me a father to Pharaoh, and lord of all his house and ruler over all the land of Egypt. [9]Hurry and go up to my father and say to him, 'Thus says your son Joseph, God has made me lord of all Egypt; come down to me, do not delay. [10]You shall settle in the land of Goshen, and you shall be near me, you and your children and your children's children, as well as your flocks, your herds, and all that you have. [11]I will provide for you there— since there are five more years of famine to come—so that you and your household, and all that you have, will not come to poverty.' [12]And now your eyes and the eyes of my brother Benjamin see that it is my own mouth that speaks to you. [13]You must tell my father how greatly I am honored in Egypt, and all that you have seen. Hurry and bring my father down here." [14]Then he fell upon his brother Benjamin's neck and wept, while Benjamin wept upon his neck. [15]And he kissed all his brothers and wept upon them; and after that his brothers talked with him.

Psalm 133

[1] How very good and pleasant it is
    when kindred live together in unity!
[2] It is like the precious oil on the head,
    running down upon the beard,
  on the beard of Aaron,
    running down over the collar of his robes.
[3] It is like the dew of Hermon,
    which falls on the mountains of Zion.
  For there the LORD ordained his blessing,
    life forevermore.

Romans 11:1-2a, 29-32

[1]I ask, then, has God rejected his people? By no means! I myself am an Israelite, a descendant of Abraham, a member of the tribe of Benjamin. [2]God has not rejected his people whom he foreknew. . . .

[29]for the gifts and the calling of God are irrevocable. [30]Just as you were once disobedient to God but have now received mercy because of their disobedience, [31]so they have now been disobedient in order that, by the mercy shown to you, they too may now receive mercy. [32]For God has imprisoned all in disobedience so that he may be merciful to all.

Matthew 15:(10-20), 21-28

[10]Then he called the crowd to him and said to them, "Listen and understand: [11]it is not what goes into the mouth that defiles a person, but it is what comes out of the mouth that defiles." [12]Then the disciples approached and said to him, "Do you know that the Pharisees took offense when they heard what you said?" [13]He answered, "Every plant that my heavenly Father has not planted will be uprooted. [14]Let them alone; they are blind guides of the blind. And if one blind person guides another, both will fall into a pit." [15]But Peter said to him, "Explain this parable to us." [16]Then he said, "Are you also still without understanding? [17]Do you not see that whatever goes into the mouth enters the stomach, and goes out into the sewer? [18]But what comes out of the mouth proceeds from the heart, and this is what defiles. [19]For out of the heart come evil intentions, murder, adultery, fornication, theft, false witness, slander. [20]These are what defile a person, but to eat with unwashed hands does not defile."

[21]Jesus left that place and went away to the district of Tyre and Sidon. [22]Just then a Canaanite woman from that region came out and started shouting, "Have mercy on me, Lord, Son of David; my daughter is tormented by a demon." [23]But he did not answer her at all. And his disciples came and urged him, saying, "Send her away, for she keeps shouting after us." [24]He answered, "I was sent only to the lost sheep of the house of Israel." [25]But she came and knelt before him, saying, "Lord, help me." [26]He answered, "It is not fair to take the children's food and throw it to the dogs." [27]She said, "Yes, Lord, yet even the dogs eat the crumbs that fall from their masters' table." [28]Then Jesus answered her, "Woman, great is your faith! Let it be done for you as you wish." And her daughter was healed instantly.

COLOR: GREEN   **10th SUNDAY AFTER PENTECOST**

Primary Hymns and Songs for the Day

553	"And Are We Yet Alive" (Gen., Ps.) (O)
549	"Where Charity and Love Prevail" (Gen., Ps.)
	S-2 #162. Harmonization
2226	"Bind Us Together" (Gen., Ps.)
	SP140
383	"This Is a Day of New Beginnings (Gen., Rom., Matt.)
	H-3 Chr-196
452	"My Faith Looks Up to Thee" (Matt.) (C)
	H-3 Hbl-77; Chr-138; Org-108
	S-2 #142. Flute/violin descant

Additional Hymn Suggestions

140	"Great Is Thy Faithfulness" (Gen.) (O)
390	"Forgive Our Sins as We Forgive" (Gen.)
2134	"Forgive Us, Lord" ("Perdon, Señor") (Gen.)
2138	"Sunday's Palms Are Wednesday's Ashes" (Gen.)
2169	"God, How Can We Forgive" (Gen.)
2135	"When Cain Killed Abel" (Gen., Ps.)
2170	"God Made from One Blood" (Gen., Ps.)
551	"Awake, O Sleeper" (Gen., Ps.)
554	"All Praise to Our Redeeming Lord" (Gen., Ps.)
560	"Help Us Accept Each Other" (Gen., Ps.)
361	"Rock of Ages, Cleft for Me" (Gen., Matt.) (C)
2182	"When God Restored Our Common Life" (Gen., Matt.)
2237	"As a Fire Is Meant for Burning" (Gen., Matt.)
632	"Draw Us in the Spirit's Tether" (Gen., Communion)
2269	"Come, Share the Lord" (Gen., Communion)
562	"Jesus, Lord, We Look to Thee" (Ps.)
557	"Blest Be the Tie That Binds" (Ps.)
548	"In Christ There Is No East or West" (Ps., Rom.)
566	"Blest Be the Dear Uniting Love" (Ps., Rom.)
121	"There's a Wideness in God's Mercy" (Rom., Matt.)
265	"O Christ, the Healer" (Rom., Matt.)
355	"Depth of Mercy" (Rom., Matt.)
3097	"Depth of Mercy" (Rom., Matt.)
363	"And Can It Be that I Should Gain" (Rom., Matt.)
374	"Standing on the Promises" (Rom., Matt.)
539	"O Spirit of the Living God" (Rom., Matt.)
568	"Christ for the World We Sing" (Rom., Matt.)
57	"O For a Thousand Tongues to Sing" (Matt.)
154	"All Hail the Power of Jesus' Name" (Matt.)
155	"All Hail the Power of Jesus' Name" (Matt.)
157	"Jesus Shall Reign" (Matt.)
263	"When Jesus the Healer Passed Through Galilee" (Matt.)
264	"Silence, Frenzied, Unclean Spirit" (Matt.)
368	"My Hope Is Built" (Matt.)
370	"Victory in Jesus" (Matt.)
389	"Freely, Freely" (Matt.)
402	"Lord, I Want to Be a Christian" (Matt.)
410	"I Want a Principle Within" (Matt.)
2104	"An Outcast among Outcasts" (Matt.)
2177	"Wounded World that Cries for Healing" (Matt.)
2196	"We Walk by Faith" (Matt.)
2211	"Faith Is Patience in the Night" (Matt.)
2213	"Healer of Our Every Ill" (Matt.)
2275	"Kyrie" (Matt.)
2277	"Lord, Have Mercy" (Matt.)

Additional Contemporary Suggestions

UM394	"Something Beautiful" (Gen.)
S2171	"Make Me a Channel of Your Peace" (Gen.)
S2224	"Make Us One" (Gen., Ps.)
	SP137
M53	"Let It Be Said of Us" (Gen., Ps.)
S2244	"People Need the Lord" (Gen., Matt.)
S2179	"Ubi Caritas" ("Live in Charity") (Ps.)
S2231	"O Look and Wonder" ("Miren Que Bueno!") (Ps., Rom.)
S2139	"Oh, I Know the Lord's Laid His Hands on Me" (Matt.)
S2151	"I'm So Glad Jesus Lifted Me" (Matt.)
WS3001	"O For a Thousand Tongues to Sing (Matt.)
M90	"Purify My Heart" (Matt.)
M104	"There Is None Like You" (Matt.)

Vocal Solos

"Help Us Accept Each Other" (Gen., Ps.)
    V-8   p. 343
"A Song of Joy" (Gen., Ps.)
    V-11   p. 2
"I Heard About a Man" (Matt.)
    V-8   p. 72

Anthems

"Hine Mah Tov" (Ps.)
Simon Sargon; Transcontinental Music 991250
SATB, flute and keyboard

"Ubi Caritas" (Ps.)
James Biery; MorningStar MSM-50-3055
SATB, *a cappella*

"All Hail the Power of Jesus' Name" (Matt.)
Michael McCabe; Paraclete Press PPM01222
SATB, organ, opt. trumpet and/or congregation

Other Suggestions

Visuals:

O	Weeping, remnant, famine, Gen. 45:5c, 8, men hugging
P	Unity, Ps. 133:1, oil, robe, dew, mountain
E	No/yes, Rom. 11:29, 32, gifts, calling, prison/manacles
G	Woman shouting, Jesus, dogs/crumbs, girl healed,

Greeting: BOW455 (Gen.)
Opening Prayer: BOW464 (Gen.)
Call to Prayer: UM371, stanza 1. "I Stand Amazed" (Matt.)
Prayer of Confession: BOW479 or BOW489 (Gen., Ps.)
Prayer: BOW518 or BOW519. For Others (Gen., Matt.)
For more prayers and litanies, see *The Abingdon Worship Annual 2014.*

AUGUST 24, 2014

Exodus 1:8–2:10

8Now a new king arose over Egypt, who did not know Joseph. 9He said to his people, "Look, the Israelite people are more numerous and more powerful than we. 10Come, let us deal shrewdly with them, or they will increase and, in the event of war, join our enemies and fight against us and escape from the land." 11Therefore they set taskmasters over them to oppress them with forced labor. They built supply cities, Pithom and Rameses, for Pharaoh. 12But the more they were oppressed, the more they multiplied and spread, so that the Egyptians came to dread the Israelites. 13The Egyptians became ruthless in imposing tasks on the Israelites, 14and made their lives bitter with hard service in mortar and brick and in every kind of field labor. They were ruthless in all the tasks that they imposed on them.

15The king of Egypt said to the Hebrew midwives, one of whom was named Shiphrah and the other Puah, 16"When you act as midwives to the Hebrew women, and see them on the birthstool, if it is a boy, kill him; but if it is a girl, she shall live." 17But the midwives feared God; they did not do as the king of Egypt commanded them, but they let the boys live. 18So the king of Egypt summoned the midwives and said to them, "Why have you done this, and allowed the boys to live?" 19The midwives said to Pharaoh, "Because the Hebrew women are not like the Egyptian women; for they are vigorous and give birth before the midwife comes to them." 20So God dealt well with the midwives; and the people multiplied and became very strong. 21And because the midwives feared God, he gave them families. 22Then Pharaoh commanded all his people, "Every boy that is born to the Hebrews you shall throw into the Nile, but you shall let every girl live."

2 Now a man from the house of Levi went and married a Levite woman. 2The woman conceived and bore a son; and when she saw that he was a fine baby, she hid him three months. 3When she could hide him no longer she got a papyrus basket for him, and plastered it with bitumen and pitch; she put the child in it and placed it among the reeds on the bank of the river. 4His sister stood at a distance, to see what would happen to him.

5The daughter of Pharaoh came down to bathe at the river, while her attendants walked beside the river. She saw the basket among the reeds and sent her maid to bring it. 6When she opened it, she saw the child. He was crying, and she took pity on him, "This must be one of the Hebrews' children," she said. 7Then his sister said to Pharaoh's daughter, "Shall I go and get you a nurse from the Hebrew women to nurse the child for you?" 8Pharaoh's daughter said to her, "Yes." So the girl went and called the child's mother. 9Pharaoh's daughter said to her, "Take this child and nurse it for me, and I will give you your wages." So the woman took the child and nursed it. 10When the child grew up, she brought him to Pharaoh's daughter, and she took him as her son. She named him Moses, "because," she said, "I drew him out of the water."

Psalm 124

1 If it had not been the LORD who was on our side
—let Israel now say—
2 if it had not been the LORD who was on our side,
when our enemies attacked us,
3 then they would have swallowed us up alive,
when their anger was kindled against us;
4 then the flood would have swept us away,
the torrent would have gone over us;
5 then over us would have gone
the raging waters.
6 Blessed be the LORD,
who has not given us
as prey to their teeth.
7 We have escaped like a bird
from the snare of the fowlers;
the snare is broken,
and we have escaped.
8 Our help is in the name of the LORD,
who made heaven and earth.

Romans 12:1-8

1I appeal to you therefore, brothers and sisters, by the mercies of God, to present your bodies as a living sacrifice, holy and acceptable to God, which is your spiritual worship. 2Do not be conformed to this world, but be transformed by the renewing of your minds, so that you may discern what is the will of God—what is good and acceptable and perfect.

3For by the grace given to me I say to everyone among you not to think of yourself more highly than you ought to think, but to think with sober judgment, each according to the measure of faith that God has assigned. 4For as in one body we have many members, and not all the members have the same function, 5so we, who are many, are one body in Christ, and individually we are members one of another. 6We have gifts that differ according to the grace given to us: prophecy, in proportion to faith; 7ministry, in ministering; the teacher, in teaching; 8the exhorter, in exhortation; the giver, in generosity; the leader, in diligence; the compassionate, in cheerfulness.

Matthew 16:13-20

13Now when Jesus came into the district of Caesarea Philippi, he asked his disciples, "Who do people say that the Son of Man is?" 14And they said, "Some say John the Baptist, but others Elijah, and still others Jeremiah or one of the prophets." 15He said to them, "But who do you say that I am?" 16Simon Peter answered, "You are the Messiah, the Son of the living God." 17And Jesus answered him, "Blessed are you, Simon son of Jonah! For flesh and blood has not revealed this to you, but my Father in heaven. 18And I tell you, you are Peter, and on this rock I will build my church, and the gates of Hades will not prevail against it. 19I will give you the keys of the kingdom of heaven, and whatever you bind on earth will be bound in heaven, and whatever you loose on earth will be loosed in heaven." 20Then he sternly ordered the disciples not to tell anyone that he was the Messiah.

COLOR: GREEN   **11th SUNDAY AFTER PENTECOST**

Primary Hymns and Songs for the Day

555	"Forward Through the Ages" (Matt.) (O)	
	H-3 Hbl-59; Chr-156; Org-140	
114	"Many Gifts, One Spirit" (Rom.)	
399	"Take My Life, and Let It Be" (Rom.) (C)	
	H-3 Chr-34, 177; Desc-51; Org-53	
	S-2 #78-80. Various treatments	

Additional Hymn Suggestions

127	"Guide Me, O Thou Great Jehovah" (Exod.) (O)
	H-3 Hbl-25, 51, 58; Chr-89; Desc-26; Org-23
	S-1 #76-77. Descant and harmonization
105	"God of Many Names" (Exod.)
117	"O God Our Help in Ages Past" (Exod.)
130	"God Will Take Care of You" (Exod.)
378	"Amazing Grace" (Exod.)
479	"Jesus, Lover of My Soul" (Exod.)
2120	"Spirit, Spirit of Gentleness" (Exod.)
2180	"Why Stand So Far Away, My God?" (Exod.)
2189	"A Mother Lined a Basket" (Exod.)
400	"Come, Thou Fount of Every Blessing" (Exod., Rom.)
2246	"Deep in the Shadows of the Past" (Exod., Ps.)
731	"Glorious Things of Thee Are Spoken" (Exod., Ps., Matt.)
132	"All My Hope Is Firmly Grounded" (Ps.)
140	"Great Is Thy Faithfulness" (Ps.)
670	"Go Forth for God" (Ps.) (C)
361	"Rock of Ages" (Ps., Matt.)
419	"I Am Thine, O Lord" (Rom.)
438	"Forth in Thy Name, O Lord" (Rom.) (C)
544	"Like the Murmur of the Dove's Song" (Rom.)
575	"Onward, Christian Soldiers" (Rom.)
2149	"Living for Jesus" (Rom.)
2153	"I'm Gonna Live So God Can Use Me" (Rom.)
2260	"Let Us Be Bread" (Rom., Communion)
2261	"Life-Giving Bread" (Rom., Communion)
3132	"House of God" (Rom.)
617	"I Come with Joy" (Rom., Communion)
632	"Draw Us in the Spirit's Tether" (Rom., Communion)
637	"Una Espiga" ("Sheaves of Summer") (Rom., Communion)
565	"Father, We Thank You" (Rom., Matt., Communion)
413	"A Charge to Keep I Have" (Rom., Matt.)
546	"The Church's One Foundation" (Rom., Matt.)
550	"Christ, From Whom All Blessings Flow" (Rom., Matt.)
559	"Christ Is Made the Sure Foundation" (Rom., Matt.)
563	"Father, We Thank You" (Rom., Matt., Communion)
593	"Here I Am, Lord" (Rom., Matt.)
175	"Jesus, the Very Thought of Thee" (Matt.)
188	"Christ Is the World's Light" (Matt.)
368	"My Hope Is Built" (Matt.)
568	"Christ for the World We Sing" (Matt.)
589	"The Church of Christ, in Every Age" (Matt.)
2151	"I'm So Glad Jesus Lifted Me" (Matt.)
2237	"As a Fire Is Meant for Burning" (Matt.)
2242	"Walk with Me" (Matt.)
3147	"Built on a Rock" (Matt.)

Additional Contemporary Suggestions

S2192	"Freedom Is Coming" (Exod.)
S2053	"If It Had Not Been for the Lord" (Ps.)
S2034	"Blessed Be the Name of the Lord" (Ps.)
	M12
UM620	"One Bread, One Body" (Rom., Communion)
UM640	"Take Our Bread" (Rom., Communion)
S2031	"We Bring the Sacrifice of Praise" (Rom.)
	SP1
S2162	"Grace Alone" (Rom.)
	M100
S2164	"Sanctuary" (Rom.)
	M52
S2226	"Bind Us Together" (Rom.)
	SP140
M33	"Jesus, You Are My Life" (Rom.)
M71	"The Heart of Worship"
M79	"I Stand Amazed" (Rom.)
M98	"Take This Life" (Rom.)
M101	"These Hands" (Rom.)
M211	"I Will Not Forget You" (Rom.)
WS3111	"Redemption" (Rom.)
S2151	"I'm So Glad Jesus Lifted Me" (Matt.)

Vocal Solos

"Oh, Freedom" (Exod.)
　　V-7　　　　p. 10
"I Will Lift Up Mine Eyes" (Ps.)
　　V-11　　　p. 27
"Take My Life" ("Consecration") (Rom.)
　　V-8　　　　p. 262
"A Covenant Prayer" (Rom.)
　　V-11　　　p. 6

Anthems

"Search Me, O God" (Rom.)
arr. Ken Berg; Choristers Guild CGA-1245
Unison, piano

"Tu es Petrus" (Matt.)
David M. Cherwien; MorningStar 50-6512
SATB, organ

"In Christ Alone" (Matt.)
arr. Angerman; Harold Flammer A-8019
SATB, piano

Other Suggestions

Visuals:

O	Bricks/mortar, birthstool, newborn, basket/reeds/river
P	Enemies, flood/torrent/water, bird/broken snare, Ps. 124:8
E	Transformer, dance, offering plate, 7 gifts
G	Jesus teaching, Peter, large rock/keys, Rom. 16:15, 16

Greeting: WSL192. All your gifts are welcome (Rom.)
Greeting: BOW456 (Matt.)
Prayer of Confession: BOW482 (Rom.)
Prayer: UM607. A Covenant Prayer (Rom.)
Prayers: BOW502–506. For the Church (Rom., Matt.)
Prayer of Thanksgiving: BOW555 (Rom.)

AUGUST 31, 2014

Exodus 3:1-15

[1]Moses was keeping the flock of his father-in-law Jethro, the priest of Midian; he led his flock beyond the wilderness, and came to Horeb, the mountain of God. [2]There the angel of the LORD appeared to him in a flame of fire out of a bush; he looked, and the bush was blazing, yet it was not consumed. [3]Then Moses said, "I must turn aside and look at this great sight, and see why the bush is not burned up." [4]When the LORD saw that he had turned aside to see, God called to him out of the bush, "Moses, Moses!" And he said, "Here I am." [5]Then he said, "Come no closer! Remove the sandals from your feet, for the place on which you are standing is holy ground." [6]He said further, "I am the God of your father, the God of Abraham, the God of Isaac, and the God of Jacob." And Moses hid his face, for he was afraid to look at God.

[7]Then the LORD said, "I have observed the misery of my people who are in Egypt; I have heard their cry on account of their taskmasters. Indeed, I know their sufferings, [8]and I have come down to deliver them from the Egyptians, and to bring them up out of that land to a good and broad land, a land flowing with milk and honey, to the country of the Canaanites, the Hittites, the Amorites, the Perizzites, the Hivites, and the Jebusites. [9]The cry of the Israelites has now come to me; I have also seen how the Egyptians oppress them. [10]So come, I will send you to Pharaoh to bring my people, the Israelites, out of Egypt." [11]But Moses said to God, "Who am I that I should go to Pharaoh, and bring the Israelites out of Egypt?" [12]He said, "I will be with you; and this shall be the sign for you that it is I who sent you: when you have brought the people out of Egypt, you shall worship God on this mountain."

[13]But Moses said to God, "If I come to the Israelites and say to them, 'The God of your ancestors has sent me to you,' and they ask me, 'What is his name?' what shall I say to them?" [14]God said to Moses, "I AM WHO I AM." He said further, "Thus you shall say to the Israelites, 'I AM has sent me to you.'" [15]God also said to Moses, "Thus you shall say to the Israelites, 'The LORD, the God of your ancestors, the God of Abraham, the God of Isaac, and the God of Jacob, has sent me to you':

This is my name forever,
and this my title for all generations

Psalm 105:1-6, 23-26, 45c

[1] O give thanks to the LORD, call on his name,
   make known his deeds among the peoples.
[2] Sing to him, sing praises to him;
   tell of all his wonderful works.
[3] Glory in his holy name;
   let the hearts of those who seek the LORD rejoice.
[4] Seek the LORD and his strength;
   seek his presence continually.
[5] Remember the wonderful works he has done,
   his miracles, and the judgments he uttered,
[6] O offspring of his servant Abraham,
   children of Jacob, his chosen ones.
. . . .
[23] Then Israel came to Egypt;
   Jacob lived as an alien in the land of Ham.
[24] And the LORD made his people very fruitful,
   and made them stronger than their foes,

[25] whose hearts he then turned to hate his people,
   to deal craftily with his servants.
[26] He sent his servant Moses,
   and Aaron whom he had chosen.
. . . .
[45] Praise the LORD!

Romans 12:9-21

[9]Let love be genuine; hate what is evil, hold fast to what is good; [10]love one another with mutual affection; outdo one another in showing honor. [11]Do not lag in zeal, be ardent in spirit, serve the Lord. [12]Rejoice in hope, be patient in suffering, persevere in prayer. [13]Contribute to the needs of the saints; extend hospitality to strangers.

[14]Bless those who persecute you; bless and do not curse them. [15]Rejoice with those who rejoice, weep with those who weep. [16]Live in harmony with one another; do not be haughty, but associate with the lowly; do not claim to be wiser than you are. [17]Do not repay anyone evil for evil, but take thought for what is noble in the sight of all. [18]If it is possible, so far as it depends on you, live peaceably with all. [19]Beloved, never avenge yourselves, but leave room for the wrath of God; for it is written, "Vengeance is mine, I will repay, says the Lord." [20]No, "if your enemies are hungry, feed them; if they are thirsty, give them something to drink; for by doing this you will heap burning coals on their heads." [21]Do not be overcome by evil, but overcome evil with good.

Matthew 16:21-28

[21]From that time on, Jesus began to show his disciples that he must go to Jerusalem and undergo great suffering at the hands of the elders and chief priests and scribes, and be killed, and on the third day be raised. [22]And Peter took him aside and began to rebuke him, saying, "God forbid it, Lord! This must never happen to you." [23]But he turned and said to Peter, "Get behind me, Satan! You are a stumbling block to me; for you are setting your mind not on divine things but on human things."

[24]Then Jesus told his disciples, "If any want to become my followers, let them deny themselves and take up their cross and follow me. [25]For those who want to save their life will lose it, and those who lose their life for my sake will find it. [26]For what will it profit them if they gain the whole world but forfeit their life? Or what will they give in return for their life?

[27]"For the Son of Man is to come with his angels in the glory of his Father, and then he will repay everyone for what has been done. [28]Truly I tell you, there are some standing here who will not taste death before they see the Son of Man coming in his kingdom."

COLOR: GREEN   **12th SUNDAY AFTER PENTECOST**

Primary Hymns and Songs for the Day

116   "The God of Abraham Praise" (Exod.) (O)
        H-3 Hbl-62, 95; Chr-59; Org-77
        S-1 #211. Harmonization
448   "Go Down, Moses" (Exod.)
        H-3 Chr-215; Org-46
3029   "In the Desert, on God's Mountain" (Exod.)
2129   "I Have Decided to Follow Jesus" (Matt.)
242   "Walk with Me" (Exod., Matt.)
415   "Take Up Thy Cross" (Matt.) (C)
        H-3 Chr-178, 180; Org-44
        S-1 #141-143 Various treatments

Additional Hymn Suggestions

2230   "Lord, We Come to Ask Your Blessing" (Exod.) (O)
111   "How Can We Name a Love" (Exod.)
116   "The God of Abraham Praise" (Exod.)
315   "Come, Ye Faithful, Raise the Strain" (Exod.)
436   "The Voice of God Is Calling" (Exod.)
577   "God of Grace and God of Glory" (Exod.)
2060   "God the Sculptor of the Mountains" (Exod.)
2180   "Why Stand So Far Away, My God" (Exod.)
2246   "Deep in the Shadows of the Past" (Exod.)
3009   "Praise God for This Holy Ground" (Exod.)
3012   "When Words Alone Cannot Express" (Exod., Ps.)
87   "What Gift Can We Bring" (Exod., Ps.)
100   "God, Whose Love Is Reigning o'er Us" (Exod., Ps.)
336   "Of All the Spirit's Gifts to Me" (Rom.)
431   "Let There Be Peace on Earth" (Rom.)
670   "Go Forth for God" (Rom.) (C)
2169   "God, How Can We Forgive" (Rom.)
2202   "Come Away with Me" (Rom.)
2205   "The Fragrance of Christ" (Rom.)
2213   "Healer of Our Every Ill" (Rom.)
2254   "In Remembrance of Me" (Rom., Communion)
3117   "Rule of Life" (Rom.)
465   "Holy Spirit, Truth Divine" (Rom., Matt.)
534   "Be Still, My Soul" (Rom., Matt.)
581   "Lord, Whose Love Through Humble Service"
        (Rom., Matt.)
608   "This Is the Spirit's Entry Now" (Matt., Baptism)
297   "Beneath the Cross of Jesus" (Matt.)
338   "Where He Leads Me" (Matt.)
399   "Take My Life, and Let It Be" (Matt.)
419   "I Am Thine, O Lord" (Matt.)
424   "Must Jesus Bear the Cross Alone" (Matt.)
442   "Weary of All Trumpeting" (Matt.)
453   "More Love to Thee, O Christ" (Matt.)
528   "Nearer, My God, to Thee" (Matt.)
553   "And Are We Yet Alive" (Matt.) (O)
2102   "Swiftly Pass the Clouds of Glory" (Matt.)
2137   "Would I Have Answered When You Called" (Matt.)
2149   "Living for Jesus" (Matt.)

Additional Contemporary Suggestions

S2087 "We Will Glorify" (Exod.)
        SP68
S2272 "Holy Ground" (Exod.)
        SP86
M36   "Awesome in this Place" (Exod.)
M55   "Jehovah Reigns" (Exod.)

WS3003 "How Great Is Our God" (Ps.)
        M117
S2195 "In the Lord I'll Be Ever Thankful" (Ps.)
S2219 "Goodness Is Stronger than Evil" (Rom.)
S2171 "Make Me a Channel of Your Peace" (Rom.)
S2224 "Make Us One" (Rom.)
        SP137
S2222 "The Servant Song" (Rom.)
        SP193
S2223 "They'll Know We Are Christians" (Rom.)
S2226 "Bind Us Together" (Rom.)
        SP140
S2179 "Live in Charity" ("Ubi Caritas") (Rom.)
WS3148 "There's a Spirit of Love in This Place" (Rom.)
WS3153 "O God in whom We Live" (Rom.)
WS3154 "Draw the Circle Wide" (Rom.)
WS3160 "We Will Follow" ("Somlandela") (Matt.)
M53   "Let It Be Said of Us" (Matt.)
M122   "Every Move I Make" (Matt.)
M150   "Everyday" (Matt.)
M76   "The Wonderful Cross" (Matt.)

Vocal Solos

"In Remembrance" (Rom., Communion)
    V-5(2)   p. 7
"May the Mind of Christ" (Rom.)
    V-8   p. 114
"Nothing...Everything" (Matt.)
    V-8   p. 162
"Here I Am" (Matt.)
    V-11   p. 19

Anthems

"Take Up Your Cross" (Matt.)
arr. Anthony Giamanco; Augsburg 9780800678968
Two-part mixed, piano

"Lord of the Dance" (Matt.)
arr. Larry Fleming; Augsburg 9780800655358
SATB, *a cappella*

Other Suggestions

Visuals
    O   Sandals, burning bush, mountain, milk/honey,
          Exod. 3:14
    P   Musical notes, singing
    E   Images of love overcoming hate, service to others,
    G   Wooden cross on its side, self-denial, sandals
          (follow me), (stumbling) block
Introit: WS3047, stanza 1. "God Almighty, We Are Waiting"
    (Exod.)
Canticle: UM646. "Canticle of Love" (Rom.)
Prayer: WSL57. Days pass and the years vanish (Exod.)
Prayer: UM392 or BOW510 (Exod., Matt.)
Prayer: UM401 or BOW522 (Rom.)
Offertory Prayer: WSL103. Blessed God (Rom.)
Blessing: WSL165. Go out into the world (Rom.)
Sung Benediction: WS3159. "Let Our Earth Be Peaceful"
    (Rom.)

SCRIPTURE INDEX

Genesis 1:1–2:4a 6/15/14

Genesis 2:15-17; 3:1-7 . . . . 3/9/14

Genesis 12:1-4a 3/16/14

Genesis 21:8 21 . . . . 6/22/14

Genesis 22:1-14 . . . . 6/29/14

Genesis 24:34-38, 42-49, 58-67 . . . . 7/6/14

Genesis 25:19-34 . . . . 7/13/14

Genesis 28:10-19 a 7/20/14

Genesis 29:15-28 . . . . 7/27/14

Genesis 32:22-31 . . . . 8/3/14

Genesis 37:1-4, 12-28 . . . . 8/10/14

Genesis 45:1-15 . . . . 8/17/14

Exodus 1:8–2:10 . . . . 8/24/14

Exodus 3:1-15 . . . . 8/31/14

Exodus 12:1-4 (5-10) 11-14 . . . . 4/17/14

Exodus 17:1-7 . . . . 3/23/14

Exodus 24:12-18 . . . . 3/2/14

Leviticus 19:1-2, 9-18 . . . . 2/23/14

Deuteronomy 26:1-11 . . . . 11/28/13

Deuteronomy 30:15-20 . . . . 2/16/14

1 Samuel 16:1-13 . . . . 3/30/14

Psalm 8 . . . . 1/1/14, 6/15/14

Psalm 13 . . . . 6/29/14

Psalm 14:1-7 . . . . 9/15/13

Psalm 15 . . . . 2/2/14

Psalm 16 . . . . 4/27/14

Psalm 17:1-7, 15 . . . . 8/3/14

Psalm 22 . . . . 4/18/14

Psalm 23 . . . . 3/30/14, 5/11/14

Psalm 27:1, 4-9 . . . . 1/26/14

Psalm 29 . . . . 1/12/14

Psalm 31:1-5, 15-16 . . . . 5/18/14

Psalm 31:9-16 . . . . 4/13/14

Psalm 32 . . . . 3/9/14

Psalm 40:1-11 . . . . 1/19/14

Psalm 45:10-17 . . . . 7/6/14

Psalm 47 . . . . 5/29/14

Psalm 51:1-17 . . . . 3/5/14

Psalm 65 . . . . 10/27/13

Psalm 66:1-12 . . . . 10/13/13

Psalm 66:8-20 . . . . 5/25/14

Psalm 72:1-7, 10-14 . . . . 1/6/14

Psalm 72:1-7, 18-19 . . . . 12/8/13

Psalm 79:1-9 . . . . 9/22/13

Psalm 80:1-7, 17-19 . . . . 12/22/13

Psalm 81:1, 10-16 . . . . 9/1/13

Psalm 86:1-10, 16-17 . . . . 6/22/14

Psalm 91:1-6, 14-16 . . . . 9/29/13

Psalm 95 . . . . 3/23/14

Psalm 96 . . . . 12/24-25/13

Psalm 99 . . . . 3/2/14

Psalm 68:1-10 . . . . 6/1/14

Psalm 100 . . . . 11/28/13

Psalm 104:24-34, 35b 6/8/14

Psalm 105:1-11, 45b 7/27/14

Psalm 105:1-6, 16-22, 45b 8/10/14

Psalm 105:1-6, 23-26, 45c 8/31/14

Psalm 112:1-10 . . . . 2/9/14

Psalm 116:1-4, 12-19 . . . . 4/17/14, 5/4/14

Psalm 118:1-2, 14-24 . . . . 4/20/14

Psalm 118:1-2, 19-29 . . . . 4/13/14

Psalm 119:1-8 . . . . 2/16/14

Psalm 119:33-40 . . . . 2/23/14

Psalm 119:97-104 . . . . 10/20/13

Psalm 119:105-112 . . . . 7/13/14

Psalm 119:137-144 . . . . 11/3/13

Psalm 121 . . . . 3/16/14	Jeremiah 32:1-3a, 6-15 . . . . 9/29/13
Psalm 122 . . . . 12/1/13	Lamentations 1:1-6 . . . . 10/6/13
Psalm 124 . . . . 8/24/14	Ezekiel 37:1-14 . . . . 4/6/14
Psalm 130 . . . . 4/6/14	Daniel 7:1-3, 15-18 . . . . 11/1/13
Psalm 133 . . . . 8/17/14	Joel 2:1-2, 12-17 . . . . 3/5/14
Psalm 137 . . . . 10/6/13	Joel 2:23-32 . . . . 10/27/13
Psalm 139:1-12, 23-24. . . . . 7/20/14	Micah 6:1-8 . . . . 2/2/14
Psalm 139:1-6, 13-18. . . . . 9/8/13	Habakkuk 1:1-4; 2:1-4 . . . . 11/3/13
Psalm 145:1-5, 17-21 . . . . 11/10/13	Haggai 1:15b–2:9 . . . . 11/10/13
Psalm 147:12-20 . . . . 1/5/14	Matthew 1:18-25 . . . . 12/22/13
Psalm 148 . . . . 12/29/13	Matthew 2:1-12 . . . . 1/6/14
Psalm 149 . . . . 11/1/13	Matthew 2:13-23 . . . . 12/29/13
Ecclesiastes 3:1-13 . . . . 1/1/14	Matthew 3:1-12 . . . . 12/8/13
Isaiah 2:1-5 . . . . 12/1/13	Matthew 3:13-17 . . . . 1/12/14
Isaiah 7:10-16 . . . . 12/22/13	Matthew 4:1-11 . . . . 3/9/14
Isaiah 9:1-4 . . . . 1/26/14	Matthew 4:12-23 . . . . 1/26/14
Isaiah 9:2-7 . . . . 12/24-25/13	Matthew 5:1-12 . . . . 2/2/14
Isaiah 11:1-10 . . . . 12/8/13	Matthew 5:13-20 . . . . 2/9/14
Isaiah 12 . . . . 11/17/13	Matthew 5:21-37 . . . . 2/16/14
Isaiah 35:1-10 . . . . 12/15/13	Matthew 5:38-48 . . . . 2/23/14
Isaiah 42:1-9 . . . . 1/12/14	Matthew 6:1-6, 16-21 . . . . 3/5/14
Isaiah 49:1-7 . . . . 1/19/14	Matthew 10:24-39. . . . . 6/22/14
Isaiah 50:4-9 a. 4/13/14	Matthew 10:40-42 . . . . 6/29/14
Isaiah 52:13–53:12 . . . . 4/18/14	Matthew 11:2-11 . . . . 12/15/13
Isaiah 58:1-9a (9b -12) 2/9/14	Matthew 11:16-19, 25-30 . . . . 7/6/14
Isaiah 60:1-6 . . . . 1/6/14	Matthew 13:1-9, 18-23 . . . . 7/13/14
Isaiah 63:7-9 . . . . 12/29/13	Matthew 13:24-30, 36-43 . . . . 7/20/14
Isaiah 65:17-25 . . . . 11/17/13	Matthew 13:31-33, 44-52 . . . . 7/27/14
Jeremiah 2:4-13 . . . . 9/1/13	Matthew 14:13-21. . . . . 8/3/14
Jeremiah 4:11-12, 22-28 . . . . 9/15/13	Matthew 14:22-33 . . . . 8/10/14
Jeremiah 8:18–9:1 . . . . 9/22/13	Matthew 15:(10-20), 21-28. . . . . 8/17/14
Jeremiah 18:1-11 . . . . 9/8/13	Matthew 16:13-20 . . . . 8/24/14
Jeremiah 23:1-6 . . . . 11/24/13	Matthew 16:21-28 . . . . 8/31/14
Jeremiah 29:1, 4-7 . . . . 10/13/13	Matthew 17:1-9 . . . . 3/2/14
Jeremiah 31:27-34 . . . . 10/20/13	Matthew 21:1-11 . . . . 4/13/14
Jeremiah 31:7-14 . . . . 1/5/14	Matthew 24:36-44 . . . . 12/1/13

Matthew 25:31-46	1/1/14	John 20:1-18	4/20/14
Matthew 26:14-27:66 (27:11-54)	4/13/14	John 20:19-31	4/27/14
Matthew 28:16-20	6/15/14	Acts 1:1-11	5/29/14
Luke 1:47-55	12/15/13	Acts 1:6-14	6/1/14
Luke 1:68-79	11/24/13	Acts 2:1-21	6/8/14
Luke 2:1-20	12/24-25/13	Acts 2:14a, 22-32	4/27/14
Luke 6:20-31	11/1/13	Acts 2:14a, 36-41	5/4/14
Luke 14:1, 7-14	9/1/13	Acts 2:42-47	5/11/14
Luke 14:25-33	9/8/13	Acts 7:55-60	5/18/14
Luke 15:1-10	9/15/13	Acts 10:34-43	1/12/14, 4/20/14
Luke 16:1-13	9/22/13	Acts 17:22-31	5/25/14
Luke 16:19-31	9/29/13	Romans 1:1-7	12/22/13
Luke 17:5-10	10/6/13	Romans 4:1-5, 13-17	3/16/14
Luke 17:11-19	10/13/13	Romans 5:1-11	3/23/14
Luke 18:1-8	10/20/13	Romans 5:12-19	3/9/14
Luke 18:9-14	10/27/13	Romans 6:1b-11	6/22/14
Luke 19:1-10	11/3/13	Romans 6:12-23	6/29/14
Luke 20:27-38	11/10/13	Romans 7:15-25a	7/6/14
Luke 21:5-19	11/17/13	Romans 8:1-11	7/13/14
Luke 23:33-43	11/24/13	Romans 8:6-11	4/6/14
Luke 24:44-53	5/29/14	Romans 8:12-25	7/20/14
Luke 24:13-35	5/4/14	Romans 8:26-39	7/27/14
John 1: (1-9), 10-18	1/5/14	Romans 9:1-5	8/3/14
John 1:29-42	1/19/14	Romans 10:5-15	8/10/14
John 3:1-17	3/16/14	Romans 11:1-2a, 29-32	8/17/14
John 4:5-42	3/23/14	Romans 12:1-8	8/24/14
John 6:25-35	11/28/13	Romans 12:9-21	8/31/14
John 7:37-39	6/8/14	Romans 13:11-14	12/1/13
John 9:1-41	3/30/14	Romans 15:4-13	12/8/13
John 10:1-10	5/11/14	1 Corinthians 1:1-9	1/19/14
John 11:1-45	4/6/14	1 Corinthians 1:10-18	1/26/14
John 13:1-17, 31b -35	4/17/14	1 Corinthians 1:18-31	2/2/14
John 14:1-14	5/18/14	1 Corinthians 2:1-12 (13-16)	2/9/14
John 14:15-21	5/25/14	1 Corinthians 3:1-9	2/16/14
John 17:1-11	6/1/14	1 Corinthians 3:10-11, 16-23	2/23/14
John 18:1–19:42	4/18/14	1 Corinthians 11:23-26	4/17/14

1 Corinthians 12:3b-13	6/8/14	2 Timothy 1:1-14	10/6/13
2 Corinthians 5:20 b–6:10	3/5/14	2 Timothy 2:8-15	10/13/13
2 Corinthians 13:11-13	6/15/14	2 Timothy 3:14–4:5	10/20/13
Ephesians 1:3-14	1/5/14	2 Timothy 4:6-8, 16-18	10/27/13
Ephesians 1:11-23	11/1/13	Titus 2:11-14	12/24-25/13
Ephesians 1:15-23	5/29/14	Philemon 1-21	9/8/13
Ephesians 3:1-12	1/6/14	Hebrews 2:10-18	12/29/13
Ephesians 5:8-14	3/30/14	Hebrews 10:16-25	4/18/14
Philippians 2:5-11	4/13/14	Hebrews 13:1-8, 15-16	9/1/13
Philippians 4:4-9	11/28/13	James 5:7-10	12/15/13
Colossians 1:11-20	11/24/13	1 Peter 1:3-9	4/27/14
Colossians 3:1-4	4/20/14	1 Peter 1:17-23	5/4/14
2 Thessalonians 1:1-4, 11-12	11/3/13	1 Peter 2:2-10	5/18/14
2 Thessalonians 2:1-5, 13-17	11/10/13	1 Peter 2:19-25	5/11/14
2 Thessalonians 3:6-13	11/17/13	1 Peter 3:13-22	5/25/14
1 Timothy 1:12-17	9/15/13	1 Peter 4:12-14; 5:6-11	6/1/14
1 Timothy 2:1-7	9/22/13	2 Peter 1:16-21	3/2/14
1 Timothy 6:6-19	9/29/13	Revelation 21:1-6a	1/1/14

REPRODUCIBLE

WORSHIP PLANNING SHEET 1

Date: _____ Color: _____

Preacher: _____

Liturgist: _____

Selected Scripture: _____

Selected Hymns   No.   Placement

_____

_____

_____

_____

Psalter #_____

Keyboard Selections

Title   Composer   Placement

_____

_____

_____

Anthems

Title   Choir   Composer   Placement

_____

_____

Vocal Solos

Title   Singer   Composer   Placement

_____

_____

Other Ideas:

Acolytes: _____

Head Usher: _____

Altar Guild Contact: _____

Other Participants: _____

WORSHIP PLANNING SHEET 2

REPRODUCIBLE

Date: _____ Sunday: _____ Color: _____

Preacher: _____

Liturgist: _____

Opening Voluntary   Composer

_____

_____

Hymn   Tune Name   No.

_____

Opening Prayer: _____

Prayer for Illumination: _____

First Lesson: _____

Psalter: _____

Second Lesson: _____

Gospel Lesson: _____

Hymn   Tune Name   No.

_____

Response to the Word: _____

Prayers of the People: _____

Offertory   Composer

_____

Communion Setting: _____

Communion Hymns   Tune Name   No.

_____

_____

_____

Closing Hymn   Tune Name   No.

_____

Benediction: _____

Closing Voluntary   Composer

_____

REPRODUCIBLE

CONTEMPORARY WORSHIP PLANNING SHEET

Because of the diversity in orders of worship, you will want to adjust this planning sheet to meet the needs of your worship planning team. A common order used would consist of three to four opening praise choruses and lively hymns, a time of informal prayers of the congregation along with songs of prayer, reading of the primary scripture for the day, a drama or video to illustrate the day's theme, a message from the preacher, a testimony on the theme for the day (if a drama or video was not presented earlier), followed by closing songs appropriate to the mood of the service and the message. Any offering would usually be taken early in the service, and Holy Communion would normally take place following the message. Special music (solos, duets, instrumental music) can be used wherever it best expresses the theme of the service.

Date: _____ Sunday: _____

Thematic Emphasis or Topic: _____

Color: _____ Visual Focus: _____

Opening Songs:

_____

_____

Prayer Songs:

_____

Scripture Selection(s):

_____

Drama or Video:

_____

Message Title:

_____

Testimony: _____

Special Music:

_____

Closing Songs:

_____

Preacher: _____ Music Leader: _____

Worship Facilitator: _____ Prayer Leader: _____

2013–2014 LECTIONARY CALENDAR

Lectionary verses and worship suggestions in this edition of *The United Methodist Planner*
relate to the unshaded dates in the calendar below.
Lectionary Year C: September 1, 2013–November 28, 2013
Lectionary Year A: December 1, 2013–August 31, 2014

2013

JANUARY 2013								FEBRUARY 2013								MARCH 2013								APRIL 2013						
S	M	T	W	T	F	S		S	M	T	W	T	F	S		S	M	T	W	T	F	S		S	M	T	W	T	F	S
		1	2	3	4	5							1	2							1	2			1	2	3	4	5	6
6	7	8	9	10	11	12		3	4	5	6	7	8	9		3	4	5	6	7	8	9		7	8	9	10	11	12	13
13	14	15	16	17	18	19		10	11	12	13	14	15	16		10	11	12	13	14	15	16		14	15	16	17	18	19	20
20	21	22	23	24	25	26		17	18	19	20	21	22	23		17	18	19	20	21	22	23		21	22	23	24	25	26	27
27	28	29	30	31				24	25	26	27	28				24	25	26	27	28	29	30		28	29	30				
																31														

MAY 2013								JUNE 2013								JULY 2013								AUGUST 2013						
S	M	T	W	T	F	S		S	M	T	W	T	F	S		S	M	T	W	T	F	S		S	M	T	W	T	F	S
			1	2	3	4								1			1	2	3	4	5	6						1	2	3
5	6	7	8	9	10	11		2	3	4	5	6	7	8		7	8	9	10	11	12	13		4	5	6	7	8	9	10
12	13	14	15	16	17	18		9	10	11	12	13	14	15		14	15	16	17	18	19	20		11	12	13	14	15	16	17
19	20	21	22	23	24	25		16	17	18	19	20	21	22		21	22	23	24	25	26	27		18	19	20	21	22	23	24
26	27	28	29	30	31			23	24	25	26	27	28	29		28	29	30	31					25	26	27	28	29	30	31
								30																						

SEPTEMBER 2013								OCTOBER 2013								NOVEMBER 2013								DECEMBER 2013						
S	M	T	W	T	F	S		S	M	T	W	T	F	S		S	M	T	W	T	F	S		S	M	T	W	T	F	S
1	2	3	4	5	6	7				1	2	3	4	5							1	2		**1**	2	3	4	5	6	7
8	9	10	11	12	13	14		**6**	7	8	9	10	11	12		**3**	4	5	6	7	8	9		**8**	9	10	11	12	13	14
15	16	17	18	19	20	21		**13**	14	15	16	17	18	19		**10**	11	12	13	14	15	16		**15**	16	17	18	19	20	21
22	23	24	25	26	27	28		**20**	21	22	23	24	25	26		**17**	18	19	20	21	22	23		**22**	23	**24**	**25**	26	27	28
29	30							**27**	28	29	30	31				**24**	25	26	27	**28**	29	30		**29**	30	**31**				

2014

JANUARY 2014								FEBRUARY 2014								MARCH 2014								APRIL 2014						
S	M	T	W	T	F	S		S	M	T	W	T	F	S		S	M	T	W	T	F	S		S	M	T	W	T	F	S
			1	2	3	4								1								1				1	2	3	4	5
5	**6**	7	8	9	10	11		**2**	3	4	5	6	7	8		**2**	3	4	**5**	6	7	8		**6**	7	8	9	10	11	12
12	13	14	15	16	17	18		**9**	10	11	12	13	14	15		**9**	10	11	12	13	14	15		**13**	14	15	16	**17**	**18**	19
19	20	21	22	23	24	25		**16**	17	18	19	20	21	22		**16**	17	18	19	20	21	22		**20**	21	22	23	24	25	26
26	27	28	29	30	31			**23**	24	25	26	27	28			**23**	24	25	26	27	28	29		**27**	28	29	30			
																30	31													

MAY 2014								JUNE 2014								JULY 2014								AUGUST 2014						
S	M	T	W	T	F	S		S	M	T	W	T	F	S		S	M	T	W	T	F	S		S	M	T	W	T	F	S
				1	2	3		**1**	2	3	4	5	6	7				1	2	3	4	5							1	2
4	5	6	7	8	9	10		**8**	9	10	11	12	13	14		**6**	7	8	9	10	11	12		**3**	4	5	6	7	8	9
11	12	13	14	15	16	17		**15**	16	17	18	19	20	21		**13**	14	15	16	17	18	19		**10**	11	12	13	14	15	16
18	19	20	21	22	23	24		**22**	23	24	25	26	27	28		**20**	21	22	23	24	25	26		**17**	18	19	20	21	22	23
25	26	27	28	29	30	31		**29**	30							**27**	28	29	30	31				**24**	25	26	27	28	29	30
																								31						

SEPTEMBER 2014								OCTOBER 2014								NOVEMBER 2014								DECEMBER 2014						
S	M	T	W	T	F	S		S	M	T	W	T	F	S		S	M	T	W	T	F	S		S	M	T	W	T	F	S
	1	2	3	4	5	6					1	2	3	4								1			1	2	3	4	5	6
7	8	9	10	11	12	13		5	6	7	8	9	10	11		2	3	4	5	6	7	8		7	8	9	10	11	12	13
14	15	16	17	18	19	20		12	13	14	15	16	17	18		9	10	11	12	13	14	15		14	15	16	17	18	19	20
21	22	23	24	25	26	27		19	20	21	22	23	24	25		16	17	18	19	20	21	22		21	22	23	24	25	26	27
28	29	30						26	27	28	29	30	31			23	24	25	26	27	28	29		28	29	30	31			
																30														

NOTES